BEST LITTLE STORIES

VOICES *of the* CIVIL ★ WAR ★

NEARLY 100 TRUE STORIES

★ BY ★

C. BRIAN KELLY

WITH

INGRID SMYER

CUMBERLAND HOUSE™

Published by Cumberland House, an imprint of Sourcebooks, Inc.
P.O. Box 4410, Naperville, Illinois 60567-4410
(630) 961-3900
Fax: (630) 961-2168
www.sourcebooks.com

The Library of Congress has cataloged the earlier edition published as *Best Little Stories of the Blue and the Gray* as follows

Kelly, C. Brian.
    Best little stories of the Blue and the Gray / C. Brian Kelly ; with "Generals' Wives" by Ingrid Smyer.
        p.   cm.
    Includes bibliographical references.
    (pbk. : alk. paper)
    (pbk. : alk. paper)
    1. United States—History—Civil War, 1861–1865—Anecdotes. 2. United States—History—Civil War, 1861–1865—Biography—Anecdotes. 3. United States. Army—History—Civil War, 1861–1865—Anecdotes. 4. United States. Army—Biography—Anecdotes. 5. Confederate States of America. Army—Anecdotes. 6. Confederate States of America. Army—Biography—Anecdotes. 7. Soldiers—United States—Biography—Anecdotes. 8. Soldiers—Confederate States of America—Biography—Anecdotes. I. Smyer-Kelly, Ingrid, 1927– Generals' wives. II. Title. III. Title: Generals' wives.
E655.K26 2006
973.7092'2—dc22   2006016585

Printed and bound in the United States of America.
VP 10 9 8 7 6 5 4 3 2 1

Other Books by C. Brian Kelly

Best Little Stories from the American Revolution
with "Select Founding Mothers" by Ingrid Smyer

Best Little Stories from the Civil War
with "Variana: Forgotten First Lady" by Ingrid Smyer

Best Little Ironies, Oddities, and Mysteries of the Civil War
with "Mary Todd Lincoln: Troubled First Lady" by Ingrid Smyer

Best Little Stories from the White House
with "First Ladies in Review" by Ingrid Smyer

Best Little Stories of the Wild West
with "Fascinating Women of the West" by Ingrid Smyer

Best Little Stories from World War II

Best Little Stories from Virginia
with "The Women Who Counted" by Ingrid Smyer

Best Little Stories from World War I

To
Ingrid Frances
and
Carleigh Anne,
in order of appearance

Contents

Introduction

EVEN AFTER TWO PREVIOUS BOOKS on the Civil War, we keep finding so many appealing stories. But no wonder, with so many stories still out there, still little known, still moving in some way. After all, everybody taking part in—or affected by—the Civil War had his or her own story to tell. And that literally means millions of personal tales.

Many of them were harrowing to be sure—but then, it was a war and a calamity all wrapped in one. So, often harrowing tales, yes, but also frequently edifying, even inspiring in some way as well.

The broad outlines of the American Civil War of course are well known and available in the multitude of histories that have been pouring off the presses ever since the cataclysm itself. So many histories, so many biographies, diaries, and memoirs and studies of all kinds! It's been a deluge. Absolutely.

But none of that is exactly what we do here, although those are the places where we hunt down our stories, since they are true, they are taken from history itself. We just try to ferret out from any number of sources and retell, in our own factual fashion, the *little* stories about the people, places, and events of the Civil War. Thus, we've done *Best Little Stories from the Civil War* and *Best Little Ironies, Oddities, and Mysteries of the Civil War*…and now may we proudly present our latest: *Best Little Stories: Voices of the Civil War*.

As some readers know, our Best Little Stories series extends to five other historical books: *Best Little Stories from World War II…from the White House… of the Wild West…from Virginia…from the American Revolution*. As some readers also may have noted, a very special hallmark of these past volumes has been the section researched and written by my wife, Ingrid Smyer-Kelly, on the women in the historical period covered. Thus, in our two previous Civil War books, she wrote first about the "Forgotten First Lady," Varina Howell Davis, wife of Confederate president Jefferson Davis, and then about the "Troubled First Lady," Mary Todd Lincoln.

In this, our latest Civil War offering, however, my wife and collaborator has outdone herself with a quartet of biographies on four fascinating female personalities who were right there, in the thick of things from start to finish, as the wives of four leading Civil War generals. And so, in the section titled

"Generals' Wives," please find the in-depth life stories of Mary Custis Lee, Julia Dent Grant, Anna Morrison Jackson, and Ellen Ewing Sherman.

As for the rest of the book, it's all personal glimpses, all true *little stories* taken from before, during, and after the great conflict between the Blue and the Gray. Thus, the stories of an obscure Confederate general still memorialized by a major statue in Washington, D.C., once the Union capital; or of the former Union drummer boy who went down with the *Titanic*; of the VMI cadet (and future Confederate general) who dared to argue with Professor Thomas (later, "Stonewall") Jackson; or of the Confederate soldier who later would write close to a thousand novels and novellas. Also to be found here is the tale of the teenage witness to the three days of battle in his hometown of Gettysburg; the account given by the young actress who was pushed aside by John Wilkes Booth in his haste to flee Ford's Theatre; and the stories of Ulysses S. Grant's secret ally inside Richmond (a woman) and of the Confederacy's youngest soldier.

Here, too, is the story behind a prototype combat submarine…and no, it's not the Confederacy's *Hunley* this time, but rather the Union's *Alligator*.

Here, too, is the story of a witness to a last, seemingly stiff meeting between Robert E. Lee and his old mentor and commanding general, Winfield Scott.

Here, as well, are the stories of Jefferson Davis's last home and of his last trip up and down the Mississippi; of Ulysses S. Grant's last battle in life; and of Abraham Lincoln's long, long train ride home to Springfield, Illinois. Then, too, a look at the last great reunion at Gettysburg, and finally (how can one ignore it?), the story of the private cemetery where forty-one Union generals lie buried. Yes, *forty-one*.

—*C. Brian Kelly*
Charlottesville, Virginia
March 2006

Acknowledgments

As MENTIONED, OUR MATERIAL COMES from the work of so many others, whether participants who wrote of their experiences or their historians and biographers. Traditionally, these and related sources were available in print—in books, monographs, local and regional histories, and the like. To them we owe so many thanks! But now comes an entirely new crop of sources to whom we must bow in gratitude as well—the plethora of Internet sources, some in the form of reproduced primary documents, some as histories (long and short), others in all kinds of written form. Thus, as an example, for our discovery of the forty-one Union generals interred in a single cemetery, we owe thanks to a Civil War round-table paper available on the Internet (see page 236 for the citation).

To all these sources, the traditional and the electronic, dead or living, we acknowledge our ongoing debt.

Then, too, to Primedia, Inc., publisher of *Military History* magazine, we owe specific thanks for permission to reprint the stories herein called "Song Is Born"; "Sibley's Ubiquitous Tent"; "Name Would Live On"; "Patton's Gritty Forebears"; "Honors for an Englishman"; "California's Crucial Role"; "Brother William's War"; "A Most Prolific Author"; "Amazing Postwar Résumé"; and "His Last Trip," all of which appeared in the same or similar form in my Best Little Stories column in recent issues of *Military History* magazine.

In addition, I owe personal thanks to Joan Biddle, Eugene Meyung, Charley Mott, historians John S. Watterson and Gary Gallagher, all of Charlottesville, Virginia, and historical reenactor and interpreter Bill Young of Richmond, Virginia, for providing badly needed advice, helpful proofreading, and/or materials that led in one way or another to information and/or stories appearing herein.

Last but far from least, we owe many thanks to our publisher, Ron Pitkin, president of Cumberland House Publishing in Nashville, Tennessee, and his highly capable staff of editors, marketing experts, and publicists for their faith in the potential of our books and their help in producing and placing them before the reading public.

Jefferson Davis's inauguration in Montgomery, Alabama, on February 18, 1861

PART 1

★ **BEGINNINGS...** ★

CONFEDERATE
First a Military Man

TRAVELING NORTH TO ATTEND THE U.S. Military Academy at West Point, New York, in the 1820s was one Jefferson Davis, very young and recently schooled in the Greek and Latin classics at Transylvania University in Lexington, Kentucky. He would have attended the University of Virginia next, but older brother Joseph, a prominent Mississippi planter and attorney, had secured Jefferson's West Point appointment by President James Monroe, and that settled that.

At West Point, Davis first shared a South Barracks room of eleven square feet with two fellow cadets. For furniture they had three chairs, one table, and a few bookshelves. At night they slept on mattresses spread on the floor. Water came from a nearby outdoors spring. In good weather, they took their baths in the neighboring Hudson River; in the winter, they made do with a small tub by a log fire.

After two years, the young man from Mississippi—born in Kentucky, actually—was able to share a larger North Barracks room of eighteen square feet…but now with four roommates instead of just two. All were subject to the same Spartan regimen that saw the day's activities begin at 4:30 a.m. and continue until bed check at 10 p.m., with room inspections, meals, classes, drill, roll calls, a form of study hall, and morning prayer coming in between.

His best friends were Albert Sidney Johnston, a fellow Kentuckian destined to bleed to death from a mortal wound at Shiloh, and Leonidas Polk, the future Episcopal bishop who doubled as a Confederate general and also died of wounds suffered in Civil War combat. Just behind Davis at West Point were future Confederate generals Robert E. Lee and Joseph E. Johnston, but he wasn't particularly close to either one. He and Johnston allegedly had a fight over a local tavern keeper's daughter in which the taller Johnston prevailed. Another time Davis was court-martialed but pardoned for drinking at a "public house" two miles from the military school, and still another time, he fell down a cliff fleeing possible arrest at the same drinking establishment.

Clearly, Jefferson Davis wasn't exactly a goody-goody, but he wasn't incorrigible either. He and his fellow cadets were allowed 200 demerits a year before dismissal, and the most he ever earned in any one year was 137 in his third and final year. He graduated, class of 1828, ranked twenty-third in his class of thirty-three.

UNION
First Love Remembered

POOR ABE LINCOLN, THAT GANGLY and homely fellow from New Salem, Illinois, where he was both a surveyor and the local postmaster in the early 1830s, single and always at arm's length from the unmarried women in town...always at some distance from them all, excepting Ann Rutledge, the tavern keeper's daughter. He had known Ann since her schoolgirl days, and with her he had an easygoing, bantering relationship. After all, she was safely engaged to another man.

A New Yorker boarding at the Rutledge Tavern (all-log construction, two rooms downstairs, two rooms upstairs) and first name John, Ann's betrothed had come to town first saying his last name was McNeil but then telling Ann his real name was McNamar. A mysterious business about his real name, certainly...something to do with avoiding responsibility for family debts back east while he built up a financial stake in partnership with New Salem storekeeper Samuel Hill.

Some time after it became known that he and Ann were to be married, McNeil-McNamar announced he had saved up enough money from the store and a farm to go back home and retrieve his family. He and Ann could be married after his return to New Salem.

As Lincoln biographer David Herbert Donald has noted, postmaster Abe Lincoln "was necessarily aware of the letters the engaged couple exchanged—fairly frequently at first, and then more and more rarely, until correspondence from McNamar ceased." Even so...she still was engaged, wasn't she? With any other unmarried woman, Lincoln remained "distant and formal," but not so with comely Ann Rutledge. Since she "was committed to another," he felt comfortable keeping up "a joking, affectionate relationship with her."

The long and short of it is, McNeil-McNamar stayed away and the "joking" relationship blossomed into a good deal more. Just when or how much more is not certain, but "sometime" in 1835, "Lincoln and Ann came to an understanding," wrote Donald in his biography *Lincoln*. The gangly surveyor-postmaster, "who had no [real] profession and little money, doubted his ability to support a wife," and Ann felt she needed personal "release" from McNamar before committing herself to marriage or even a formal engagement. Additionally, Lincoln, also a neophyte state legislator, already was studying to enter the legal profession. As one result, reported Ann's cousin James McCrady Rutledge later, the two young people had agreed "to wait a year for their marriage after their engagement until Abraham Lincoln was Admitted to the bar."

The fateful and unexpected factor undoing all their best-laid plans that summer would be the weather—the unusually hot summer days combined with unremitting rain. "When Lincoln was not slogging through the water that covered the whole country, completing his surveys, he worked so unceasingly on his law books that friends feared for his health."

But it was Ann who fell ill in August, with "brain fever," which could have been typhoid, "caused when the flood contaminated the Rutledge well."

The long and short of it now was that she died.

And Lincoln was "devastated." It was a blow that "must have brought to mind memories of earlier losses: his brother Thomas, his sister Sarah, and, above all, his mother." Even as president many years later, an old friend from New Salem (Isaac Cogdal) once said, Lincoln expressed his love for Ann, saying he still thought of her "often."

In his campaigning for reelection to the Illinois House the very next year, not so incidentally, he frequently would find himself in the company of Ninian W. Edwards, the socially prominent son of a former governor of the state, a fellow legislative contender (one of sixteen)…and one day destined to be Lincoln's brother-in-law, through marriage to Mary Todd Lincoln's older sister Elizabeth.

UNION & CONFEDERATE
Portents of Drama

JUST THREE YEARS BEFORE ANN Rutledge's unfortunate death, fate played one of its wry historical tricks by placing four principals from the pending national drama in one place at one time. Gathered in Illinois at the time of the Black Hawk War, they were U.S. Army Col. Zachary Taylor, future U.S. president and future, if adamantly unwilling, father-in-law to Jefferson Davis; plus young Lt. Jefferson Davis himself; along with raw-boned state militia Capt. Abe Lincoln in his denim suit; plus, just for good measure, a young Lt. Robert Anderson, who would be the federal officer in command of Fort Sumter when it came under Confederate fire in Charleston Harbor in April 1861…with the same Jefferson Davis then the sitting Confederate president and the same Abraham Lincoln then the sitting U.S. president.

But wait, there also was on hand a fifth principal from future events, Colonel Taylor's attractive daughter, Knox, who becomes a central figure in another, more personal drama.

In 1832, Jefferson Davis was stationed at Fort Crawford, near the corner formed by the confluence of the Wisconsin River with the Mississippi, a frontier setting in the "Indian Country" of the day, and here he came into contact with the outpost's commander, Colonel Taylor, and his daughter, Sarah Knox Taylor.

While Davis was soon smitten, Colonel Taylor did not welcome the young Southerner's attentions. Just why is not entirely clear today, although he did say he didn't wish to see her married to any army officer. Then, too, by one account, Davis once was overexuberant dancing with a young Indian woman at an Indian wedding to the point that her brother objected and pulled Davis's nose. When Davis pushed him away and pulled out a pistol, the incensed Indian brave yanked out his scalping knife and approached again, but Colonel Taylor at this point pushed his way between them and stopped the potentially ugly fight before it could begin. Later, recalled historian Joseph McElroy in his biography *Jefferson Davis*, Taylor told the young man's intermediaries "he had no desire to acquire Davis as a son-in-law." The friction between them only worsened when the West Point–educated Davis "ventured to vote against the Colonel's wishes" in a frontier court-martial proceeding. "In the end, Taylor forbade Davis [access to] the [Taylor] house and swore 'by the Eternal,' that he should never become a member of his family."

Young Davis after this had to be dissuaded by a fellow officer from issuing a challenge to his potential father-in-law to a duel. The fellow officer's wife told him she would arrange visits allowing him to continue his courtship of the more-than-willing Sarah Knox Taylor.

But now the Sacs chief Black Hawk interrupted by recrossing the Mississippi in an apparent effort to reclaim lands—fifty million acres—he previously had agreed to sell to the U.S. government for "not much more than $1,000." Unfamiliar with the white man's concept of property ownership, Black Hawk complained he didn't understand his agreement meant that "I gave away my village." Reason, he declared, teaches that land cannot be sold. "The Great Spirit gave it to his children to live upon…. Nothing can be sold but such things as can be carried away."

It was the resulting brief "war" that placed Taylor, Davis, Lincoln, and Anderson in close proximity one to another, as the white man sent his armed forces into motion against the Indian braves led by the aggrieved Black Hawk. By some accounts also, the spic-and-span young lieutenant, Davis, was the federal officer who swore the uncouthly dressed militia captain Lincoln into federal service for the occasion. In her biography of Davis, his future wife Varina (yes, true, *not* Sarah) described the Lincoln of 1832 as "a tall, gawky, slab-sided, homely man, dressed in a suit of blue jeans." The poet William Cullen Bryant, also on the scene at the time, tuned in with a description of Lincoln's militia group as "hard-looking…unkempt, and unshaven, wearing shirts of dark calico, and sometimes calico capotes." Lincoln he found to be a "raw youth" of "quaint and pleasant talk," but quite interesting.

The future Mrs. Davis, meanwhile, described her future husband as "a very fascinating young man, of easy manners and affable disposition." His fellow lieutenant, Robert Anderson, "was equally pleasant and extremely modest," even "bashful."

In the end, Black Hawk of course lost his small war. Lincoln returned to civilian life after days of storytelling 'round the campfire, occasional alarms and marches, and, by his own self-deprecating account, "a good many bloody struggles with the mosquitoes." Added historian McElroy's Jefferson Davis biography: "In defiance of the dignity of the service, which meant so much to Davis, Lincoln raced, boxed, and wrestled with all comers. By the end of his thirty days' enlistment, Lincoln was 'the most popular man in the army,' to quote a member of his company."

CONFEDERATE
Takes a Wife

AFTER ESCORTING THE CAPTURED BLACK Hawk to Jefferson Barracks in St. Louis, Lt. Jefferson Davis next served postings at Fort Monroe, Virginia (where one future day he himself would be held as a prisoner), St. Louis again, and finally

Fort Gibson in Cherokee Country, a part of future Oklahoma. Two years passed, during which he maintained his courtship of the forbidden Miss Taylor by mail. Her father still opposed any notion of allowing her to marry an army officer…but the would-be couple had an answer to *that*. Jefferson Davis would resign from the army; she would *not* be married to an army officer.

To which the stubborn colonel finally assented, but only if they married at the Kentucky home of her aunt, Gibson Taylor, who had joined in the campaign to win his approval. Wasting no time, they did just that on June 17, 1835, and just days later Davis resigned, as promised.

Meanwhile, on the day of her wedding, Knox wrote to her mother that "the part of the country to which I am going is quite healthy."

The "part of the country" that now took in the young couple was a little-worked plantation, dubbed Brierfield, on a Mississippi River island just off a bend—Palmyra Bend—twenty miles below Vicksburg. Jefferson's land here, seventy feet off the mainland, once had been a part of older brother Joseph's plantation known as Hurricane. Joseph had swapped the 890 acres for ownership of the family slaves their father had bequeathed to Jefferson. As a result, the new bride came to a home that, in the words of biographer McElroy, "was hardly a home, as it consisted of a mass of tangled undergrowth, trees and briers."

Worse, "It was by no means so healthy as it had been reported."

Also worth noting is the fact that, until this moment, Jefferson Davis "had had no long or close relationship to any one section of the country." Both Kentucky, his birthplace, and Mississippi "had been hardly more than incidents in his roaming life." But from now on, Mississippi would be his home and "sovereign state," even in his old age.

At this point in time, the still-developing state had grown in population from a mere 5,000 souls in 1800 to nearly 375,000 inhabitants, with few real natives among its political leaders. It definitely was a Southern state, however, and slavery was the norm on its plantations, including the two Davis plantations. According to a slave's post–Civil War deposition, the slaves that Jefferson Davis now acquired included Old Uncle Robert, Aunt Rhina, Rhina No. 2, William and Jack, Frances, Charley, Old Charley, Solomon, Betsy, Fanny, Moses, Jeffrey, Young Hagar, Kizziarch, and Old Hagar. "With the help of these and other slaves, especially that of the superior, one might also say the super-slave, James Pemberton, Davis took up the task of converting 'Brierfield' into a home," wrote McElroy.

The slavery issue was hardly news to Davis's bride Knox, whose own father was born in Virginia and raised in Louisiana, both slave states…and as president would be the last occupant of the White House to include his own slaves among its staff of servants.

At first, however, it would seem that neither of these young people was paying much attention to another issue of life in early Mississippi: fever season. So severe was the danger, according to contemporary accounts, most plantation owners spent their summers elsewhere, with their slaves staying behind to do the necessary work, under supervision of an overseer. "Rarely," said one writer, "is there more than one white man upon a plantation at a time during the summer."

Warned by her mother, the new bride at Brierfield again sought to reassure. "Do not make yourself uneasy about me," she wrote, "the country is quite healthy."

Her husband apparently did know better and "started with his bride" for a visit to his sister's Locust Grove plantation in neighboring Louisiana. "But," added McElroy in his biography of the future Confederate leader, "the dreaded fever already was in their systems, and developed as they journeyed southward. Soon after their arrival, both were at death's door."

Davis rallied one day to hear his wife singing a favorite song "associated with the days of their courtship." Unaware that she was delirious from her own raging fever, he hurried to her bedside in another room, only to find she was unconscious. She died later the same day, September 15, 1835.

UNION
True Soldier's Son

NOT ONLY A KENTUCKIAN BY birth, federal officer Robert Anderson was proslavery and married to a Georgia woman. He also was the son of a Revolutionary War officer who had fought for establishment of the Union in the first place and a West Point graduate (class of 1825). After his brief service in the Black Hawk affair, artillery officer Anderson spent two years in the U.S. Army's long campaign against the Seminoles in Florida. He translated French artillery manuals into English, and he served gallantly in the Mexican War of the late 1840s. Come the Civil War, he would be the federal officer in command of beleaguered Fort Sumter.

At Fort Sumter in April 1861 he would be gallant again, surrendering his command only after Southern guns had pounded the island fort for thirty-four hours. He then marched out his small garrison with colors flying—and with a fifty-gun salute to the flag. That striking scenario would be well remembered in both the North and the South.

And again it would be remembered when he would return to Fort Sumter in another April exactly four years later...*with the same American flag.*

Widely forgotten in the meantime and since was his comment after Sumter's fall: "Our Southern brethren have done grievously wrong, they have rebelled and have attacked their father's house and their loyal brothers. They must be punished and brought back, but this necessity breaks my heart."

CONFEDERATE
First a Bishop

AFTER GRADUATION FROM WEST POINT in 1827, it didn't take long, just six months, for Jefferson Davis's good friend Leonidas Polk to resign his commission as an artillery officer...to attend Virginia Theological Seminary and then to become an Episcopal priest. A native of Raleigh, North Carolina, and a cousin of future president James K. Polk, the newly ordained clergyman first served a church in Richmond, Virginia, as assistant rector, but he then left for travels in Europe because of ill health.

He took on a huge task in 1838, however, when he accepted a post as missionary bishop of the Southwest, a region encompassing the states of Arkansas, Alabama, Louisiana, and Mississippi, along with the Indian Territory (future Oklahoma). He then, in 1841, became the first bishop of Louisiana. Both bishoprics involved extensive travel by primitive means, but Polk also found his attentions were needed at home—spreading the gospel among his wealthy wife's many slaves by establishing a Sunday school for them, among other pastoral activities.

All this led to his dream of founding an Episcopal institution of higher learning that would inculcate white slave owners with the idea of eventually freeing their slaves. Also setting himself the task of finding the funds for such a school, he managed to raise $500,000 in time to lay the cornerstone for the University of the South at Sewanee, Tennessee, on October 9, 1860.

Because the Civil War interrupted construction, the school wouldn't open for the business of education until 1868. In the meantime, Bishop Polk was off to war as a Confederate general.

UNION
Duel Canceled, Wedding On

AFTER LEADING THE LEGISLATIVE BATTLE that moved the Illinois state capital from Vandalia to Springfield, Abraham Lincoln himself moved from New Salem to Springfield in 1837, armed with his new credentials as a licensed attorney...but little else.

To the sophisticated easterner William Cullen Bryant, the new state capital was a town of "dirt and discomfort." And, true, most of its homes were built of logs, the horse manure piled up outside the stables, and hogs roamed the unpaved streets. To Lincoln, however, the frontier town "was the most cosmopolitan and sophisticated place" he had ever lived, noted David Herbert Donald in his biography *Lincoln*.

Here, the still-poor Lincoln shared a bed with another young man, a frequent custom of the time, in this case a storekeeper named Joshua Speed. But newcomer Lincoln had the good fortune to begin a law practice as junior partner to a prominent local attorney who was planning to run for Congress (and did so successfully). In certain circles, too, Lincoln already was known as an up-and-coming state legislator, with the capital's move to Springfield as one bright feather in his cap.

A year or so after the death of Ann Rutledge, Lincoln had weathered a brief relationship with a comely but distinctly overweight (the estimates are 150 to 180 pounds) young woman, Mary Owens. Now taking over most of his campaigning partner's everyday law cases, Lincoln kept busy and did well as an attorney. When the courts in Springfield were not in session, he joined the lawyers and judges riding the circuit of outlying towns to try cases. Ambitious politically, determined to make his mark in the world, he emerged in the Illinois House as leader of its Whig members.

Now, too, as the decade of the 1830s neared its close, there came to town another newcomer, a young woman from a prominent family in Lexington, Kentucky, Mary Todd. She came to visit her older sister Elizabeth, Mrs. Ninian

Edwards. And it wasn't long before the unattached Lincoln, still rough around the edges and lacking in finances, was her consistent squire around town…and at the frequent social gatherings staged by the prominent Edwards couple. At or near Christmas in 1840, they became engaged.

Oddly, it was Lincoln who suddenly developed cold feet, broke off their engagement…and then suffered highly visible pain over their breakup.

Mary responded with a generous letter releasing him but also saying that her feelings for him were still the same. "Instead of feeling relieved, Lincoln was devastated," wrote biographer David Herbert Donald. "Mary's letter made him realize what he had lost. He became deeply depressed. During the first week in January he was able to go about his business, in a more or less perfunctory way, and to answer roll calls in the house of representatives. But then the burden of guilt and unhappiness became too great, and he took to his bed for about a week, unwilling to see anybody except [his bedmate] Speed and Dr. [Anson] Henry [another good friend]."

So obvious was Lincoln's unhappiness that many of his acquaintances in Springfield assumed Mary had dropped *him*. Before the breakup, the snobbish Edwards couple only slowly had come around to feeling he might be an acceptable prospect for Mary, and now they "said flatly that he was crazy." No surprise, then, that Lincoln disappeared from their social circle, avoided many mutual friends, and plunged into his work as distraction. With his original law partner's time now taken up with congressional duties, Lincoln entered into a new partnership that kept him busy, but far from rich…or happy.

That August, he took time for a refreshing visit with his friend Speed and family at their spacious home near Louisville in Lincoln's native state of Kentucky. Here, interestingly enough, he was "assigned" a house slave as "his personal servant," biographer Donald noted. Then, too, on the steamboat carrying him back home to Illinois, he ran across twelve slaves all chained together. He was "so charmed by his Kentucky experiences [with Speed and his family] that he did not even wince," but later in life, "he would remember the brutality of the scene."

For the moment, Lincoln still was in emotional turmoil over his relationship with Mary Todd, a focus only strengthened now by the fact that his good friend Speed was planning to marry…and yet, himself, was struggling with second thoughts. Once Speed had married, Lincoln anxiously awaited word on how it was working out. He expressed delight when Speed reported all was well…but months later, Lincoln wanted to know all over again—and quickly, please—if Speed had any regrets. (He didn't.)

By now, it turns out, Lincoln "once more was approaching marriage with Mary Todd." Thanks to the good offices of a mutual friend who arranged for them to visit at her own home, they had been seeing each other in secret. They especially didn't want the Edwards couple to know, since they surely would be opposed to Mary's spending any more time with young Mr. Lincoln, much less marrying him.

Before any such wedding could take place, however, both the nation and Mary came *fairly* close to losing the future president and bridegroom to a duel of honor. During their renewed courtship, it seems, they and a mutual friend had collaborated in writing anonymous letters to a local newspaper ridiculing state auditor James Shields, a Democrat.

When Shields demanded to know who wrote the letters, Lincoln took full responsibility for all of them, followed by a demand from Shields for "full, positive and absolute retraction of all offensive allusions used by you in these communications." But now Lincoln, egged on by a "hot-blooded" young doctor friend, stubbornly refused to apologize.

Next came Shields's challenge to a duel and Lincoln's acceptance, with his choice of broadswords as the weapons to be employed. Since dueling was illegal in Illinois, the two would-be combatants and their seconds crossed the Mississippi River into Missouri on September 22, 1841, to engage in the head-to-head fray. Fortunately, a last-minute intervention by friends headed off the duel.

Even though the two principals were able to shake hands and part company unharmed, wrote Donald in his biography, "The episode remained one of Lincoln's most painful memories." He was "so ashamed," that he and Mary agreed it never was to be discussed in the future. Not only did Lincoln realize "he had acted foolishly," but "he was embarrassed that as a lawyer and officer of the court, he had deliberately violated the law." Galling, too, "he had allowed himself to be ruled by his turbulent emotions."

Ironically, during the Civil War, Shields would wind up a Union general acting under orders from President Lincoln...and the two men would become close friends.

As another positive outcome of the contretemps back in 1841, Mary was deeply touched by Lincoln's chivalry in taking the blame for her own role in writing the anonymous letters. And Lincoln about that time was emboldened by Speed's assurances that marriage could be a happy state of affairs after all. A combination of events and feelings...Lincoln proposed, Mary accepted.

So secretive—and last minute—were their plans, that Mary's sister, Elizabeth

Edwards, had only a few hours to prepare for the wedding in her own house on November 4, 1841, Donald noted. And Lincoln did not ask his good friend James H. Matheny, a circuit court worker, to be best man until the afternoon of the wedding. Even then, Matheny later said, the prospective groom "looked and acted as if he were going to the slaughter."

Then, too, asked by his landlord's son where he was going, Lincoln allegedly said, "To hell, I suppose."

CONFEDERATE
Helpmate for Life

WIDOWED IN 1835, JEFFERSON DAVIS virtually disappeared from public view for several years, nursing his grief almost alone at his brother Joseph's Mississippi River plantation Hurricane while supervising his own nearby island property, Brierfield, with "super-slave" Jim Pemberton acting as overseer over his fellow slaves.

Davis and Pemberton worked closely and amicably together. "Together they studied the slaves, seeking the occupation best suited to each," wrote Davis biographer Joseph McElroy. Thus, one slave would keep a store, with the Davises themselves as customers. "Others looked after the plantation nursery for black children. Some made themselves useful in connection with the store-rooms which carried the plantation's implements, medicines, saddles and harnesses, household goods, and even sweetmeats. Moreover, they were allowed the privilege, common on the best Southern plantations, of cultivating patches of land, products of which, vegetables, fruits, pigs, chickens, etc., they were free to sell to the master or to any other market that offered."

Births, weddings, and deaths among the slaves would result in donated clothing, foodstuffs, or other presents for the families concerned. "A dentist came regularly to both plantations, and every care was taken to keep the slaves not only fit for work, but happy."

Grieving or not, Davis could boast a plantation that "ran smoothly and brought in an ample income." He had, on one hand, "a body of slaves who proved that self-discipline is not incompatible with slavery," but on the other, his feelings about blacks "had not the remotest resemblance" to the Declaration of Independence, "which had assured the world that 'all men are created equal.'"

In time, Davis began to stir from his preoccupation with plantation affairs to show some interest in Mississippi and national politics—and in a young woman from Natchez his brother Joseph had invited to visit during the Christmas season of 1843: Varina Howell. Although she subsequently wrote that she liked Joseph best of the two, in a short time she changed that opinion sufficiently to agree to marriage with Jefferson Davis, who at age thirty-seven was nearly twenty years her senior.

James K. Polk, elected in the fall of 1844, was about to take office as president when Jefferson Davis stepped aboard the Mississippi steamboat that would carry him downriver to Natchez in February 1845 for his wedding to the fair Varina. Of all times, he now encountered on the boat Gen. Zachary Taylor, his former father-in-law, on *his* way to the disputed Texas-Mexican border zone. Considering earlier events, it could have been an uncomfortable meeting, but McElroy assured: "Time had softened Taylor's resentment for the defiance of old days, and they met as friends and traveled as comrades."

As Taylor continued southward, "towards the scenes [the pending Mexican War] which were to make him President," the wedding took place on February 26, and this time Jefferson Davis would be married for the rest of his life...to an intelligent, strong-willed woman who would be the mother of his children, his solicitous confidant and closest political adviser, chief biographer, and his most dedicated apostle.

★★★

Additional note: This was also the year (1845) when Jefferson Davis took a seat in Congress for the first time, as a House member from Mississippi. But he resigned to serve in the Mexican War, during which he once again would serve under Zachary Taylor, notably at the battle of Buena Vista, where Taylor beat back Mexican strongman Antonio Lopez de Santa Anna's fourteen thousand attacking men with only forty-eight hundred of his own.

Here, Colonel Davis's Mississippi Rifles, wrote Taylor in his official report, "were highly conspicuous for their gallantry and steadiness."

Faced by "an immensely superior force," Taylor also wrote, "they maintained themselves for a long time unsupported...and held an important part of the field until reinforced." Not only that, Colonel Davis, "though severely wounded, remained in the saddle until the close of the action. His distinguished coolness and gallantry, and the heavy loss of his regiment on this day, entitle him to the particular notice of the government."

What soldier could want better praise? Except that Taylor did provide an even more meaningful accolade when he personally told the wounded Jefferson Davis, "My daughter was a better judge of men than I."

UNION
"Uncle Sam" Grant

"THEN, IN MY PARTICULAR CASE," wrote Ulysses S. Grant in his post–Civil War *Personal Memoirs*, "I had been at West Point at about the right time to meet most of the graduates who were of suitable age at the breaking out of the rebellion [the Civil War] to be trusted with large commands. Graduating in 1843, I was at the military academy from one to four years with all cadets who graduated between 1840 and 1846—seven years. These classes embraced more than fifty officers who afterwards became generals on one side or the other in the rebellion, many of them holding high commands."

Just as important to Grant's military career, he also rubbed elbows with some of the same West Point graduates—and many others, such as his chief antagonist of the Civil War, Robert E. Lee—in the Mexican War of the late 1840s. He allegedly once was dressed down by the same prim-and-proper Lee for failing to wear full uniform when reporting to headquarters.

Be that as it may, Grant later would write that, thanks to his Mexican War service, he had known the older, more experienced Lee personally, "and knew that he was mortal; and it was just as well that I felt this."

Among others of Civil War fame mentioned by Grant in his recollections of the Mexican War were George Gordon Meade, the Union general in command at the battle of Gettysburg; the future Confederate general Pierre G. T. Beauregard; and the future Union general George B. McClellan. Grant served in the successful campaigns conducted by both Zachary Taylor and Winfield Scott against numerically superior Mexican forces. As one highlight, at Monterrey, he volunteered to carry word of the advancing Americans' dire need for more ammunition to the rear and then rode his galloping horse past one exposed street crossing after another crouched out of sight from potential shooters on one side of his mount, Indian-style. Not for nothing was Grant regarded in his days at West Point as a superb horseman.

Then, too, when the Americans stormed Mexico City as the culmination to a highly successful campaign begun with Scott's landing at Veracruz, Grant noticed an enticing church belfry that would allow an artillery piece a commanding field of fire on the Mexican defenders just behind a fortified city gate. Taking a small party of men and a dismantled mountain howitzer, Second Lieutenant Grant led the way through "several ditches breast deep in water and grown up with water plants," past a remonstrating priest at the door of the church, and up the steps to the belfry, where they quickly assembled the small gun and unleashed an effective fire.

"The shots from our little gun dropped in upon the enemy and created great confusion," Grant wrote. "Why they did not send out a small party and capture us, I do not know. We had no infantry or other defences besides our one gun."

American Gen. William J. Worth, on the other hand, saw the effectiveness of Grant's small gun and sent another young lieutenant "to bring me to him." Worth then ordered a second howitzer to be set up in the belfry, but Grant didn't make use of it because "there was not room enough in the steeple for another gun." Perhaps more interesting historically, that other lieutenant who fetched Grant to Worth's side that day at the gates to Mexico City was John C. Pemberton, later to be the Confederate general in command of Vicksburg when it was besieged and fell to Union forces commanded by Ulysses S. Grant.

★★★

Additional note: While serving in Mexico, Grant briefly ran into Maj. Thomas L. Hamer, who, as an Ohio congressman, had appointed Grant to West Point a few years before...and inadvertently created the misnomer "U. S. Grant" by assuming Grant's middle name was his mother's maiden name, Simpson. The young man's real full name at the time was Hiram Ulysses Grant, but Grant himself did not want to use his name in that form, for fear of being nicknamed "Hug." When he registered at West Point, he tried to have his name "corrected" to Ulysses Hiram Grant, but so far as the military academy was concerned, he already was Ulysses Simpson Grant, and so U. S. Grant he would remain...often at West Point to be called "Uncle Sam Grant" or plain "Sam."

CONFEDERATE
Ascending the
Career Ladder

BORN THE SON OF A distinguished Revolutionary War hero and a Virginia Carter (and later marrying a great-granddaughter of Martha Washington), this uncommon soldier not only finished his four years at West Point in 1829 without incurring a single demerit against him (and ranking second in his class), he later, in 1852, wound up as superintendent of the U.S. Military Academy. Well…not exactly "wound up," since he of course accomplished a good deal more both before and after his stint as superintendent.

From his cadet years at West Point, the young second lieutenant of engineers moved to duty posts at Forts Pulaski, Monroe, and Hamilton and then to assignment as superintending engineer for St. Louis harbor. His marriage in 1831 to Mary Anna Randolph Custis, daughter and only child of George Washington Parke Custis, Martha Washington's grandson by her first marriage (as a young widow, she later married George Washington), set the stage for Mary's inheritance of her father's historic Arlington estate across the Potomac River from Washington, D.C. (and today's Lincoln Memorial) upon his death in 1857.

Mary's husband, in the meantime, had reached the rank of captain of engineers by 1846, and at that point, he was serving as assistant engineer to Gen. John E. Wool at San Antonio, Texas. With the Mexican War breaking out that same year, the rising military careerist found himself at Veracruz under Gen. Winfield Scott, who then led his American forces all the way into Mexico City after the amphibious assault that took Veracruz. Surviving a slight wound en route to the Mexican capital, the West Point engineer serving under Scott was brevetted three times to the rank of full colonel for bravery and distinguished conduct in the field.

Much closer to home and family, he oversaw the construction of Fort Carroll in Baltimore Harbor. Then came three years as superintendent at West Point.

For his next assignment, he returned to Texas as lieutenant colonel of the Second Cavalry, a move approved by Jefferson Davis, secretary of war under President Franklin Pierce. By now, too, this uncommon Virginia-born soldier and his wife had produced a family of three sons and four daughters. Like Illinois state legislator Abraham Lincoln, he politically was a Whig: *Robert E. Lee*.

UNION
Cows and Sheep Grazing

THE WASHINGTON, D.C., THAT ABRAHAM Lincoln first came to know—as a one-term U.S. House member from 1847 to 1849—was an incomplete capital city of thirty-eight thousand souls. At this time, wrote William Seale in his history of the White House, *The President's House*, Washington "was like many American cities in its combination of town and pasture." Thus, Pennsylvania Avenue, the main avenue of commerce, was "lined on both sides with buildings from the Capitol to the White House." Beyond that, "Washington was a town of monotonous red-brick row houses, usually mounted on raised, or 'English,' basements, with high stairs leading to the front doors." Many lots were still vacant, and the great, stately circles of today were "barren, with snaggled rows of houses surrounding them."

While some streets were paved with stone, many others were gravel and dirt lanes. "The Mall was a prodigious grassy field. Cows and sheep grazed there, making bare dirt paths from one side to the other. It seemed a vast waste; at the east end the Capitol [not yet domed] stood taller than any building around, but even so, it was not sufficiently imposing for its site."

With so much still to be done to fulfill Pierre L'Enfant's plans for a magnificent capital city, a sore spot about to be addressed in vigorous fashion was the soggy miasma just south of the White House itself. This area, noted Seale's history, was "believed to give off unhealthful vapors, especially in summer." The fear was cholera, a concern that drove many residents out of town for the summer months.

President James K. Polk, who had presided over the Mexican War, had insisted on staying at home base, "and when he died a few months after leaving office it was generally believed he could have preserved himself had he spent his presidential summers in more salubrious climates." Who's to say that really was the case, yet it *is* true that Polk suddenly died, albeit after leaving Washington...and it *is* true one of Abe Lincoln's young children, twelve-year-old Willie, would die in the White House of a fever later diagnosed as typhoid.

Lincoln, the congressman of 1847–49, certainly had no inkling, nor was his boardinghouse abode on Capitol Hill the slightest harbinger of his years to be spent in the President's House itself. But no matter for the moment, since Lincoln, earnest political student and political philosopher, could hardly have arrived in Washington at a more interesting time. With the Mexican War just ending (victoriously of course), with the presidency soon to change hands (in March 1849), with gold just discovered in California, and with the national argument over slavery fast heating up, it was a riveting and profound moment in American history.

Naturally Lincoln hated it when the voters saw fit to send him back home after just one term in office as a Whig. First, though, he and Mary Todd Lincoln did join in the campaigning for the Whig Party's presidential candidate of 1848, Mexican War hero Zachary Taylor, the former father-in-law of Mississippi's new *senator* Jefferson Davis. If slave owner Taylor were aware of the Lincolns' labors on his behalf, however, he didn't offer Lincoln any ambassadorships or cabinet posts.

In Washington, meanwhile, Charles Douglas, commissioner of public buildings, was concerned about the well-being of the president. Thus, he "decided in 1848 to improve the lowlands south of the White House," reported Seale. "He proposed to grade the southward sloping fields into 'terraces handsomely turfed, and their tops ornamented with suitable trees and shrubbery.'"

While beautification appeared to be his goal, the real purpose "was actually drainage and sanitation, to eliminate the bad air that hung ominously around the house." Given a small congressional appropriation of $3,628 for the landscaping work, Douglas quickly began, and "the project was well under way when President Taylor moved into the White House."

★★★

Additional note: Approaching his few months as a House member, Lincoln was *not* noted for taking strong stands against slavery. In the House, though, he voted for the Wilmot Proviso, which forbade slavery in territory acquired as a result of the Mexican War. He also proposed a ban on slavery in Washington itself. That would have been embarrassing for newly installed president Taylor, who moved into the White House in March 1849 with about fifteen slaves.

Upon his return to Springfield, Illinois, meanwhile, Lincoln plunged back into his law practice—for a time. The political Lincoln reemerged in 1858, however, as the newly formed Republican Party's U.S. Senate contender from

Illinois. As such, and engaging his opponent, Democrat Stephen Douglas, in a series of debates that became famous, Lincoln lost the Senate race but developed the national reputation that led to his nomination two years later as the party's presidential nominee. In his 1858 acceptance speech of his party's nomination for the Senate seat held by Douglas, Lincoln uttered that well-known line, "A house divided against itself cannot stand," coupled with the warning that "this Government cannot endure permanently, half Slave half free."

CONFEDERATE
"Damned Traitors!"

ALSO TAKING A SEAT IN Congress in 1847, but as a U.S. senator from Mississippi rather than a member of the House, was Abraham Lincoln's fellow Kentucky native and fellow Black Hawk War veteran, Jefferson Davis…at this point far better known as a recently emerged hero of the Mexican War.

And now, historical irony would pile upon irony after irony.

As Lincoln departed from the Washington scene in 1849 for a period of years, Davis and his second wife, Varina, became central figures—socially and politically—in the federal capital. This was due in large part to their ever-closer relationship with newly installed president Zachary and Margaret Taylor, once the estranged in-laws of the same Jefferson Davis. Then, too, with slavery ever the burning issue as new western territories moved toward statehood, Davis increasingly became a Southern spokesman in the Senate.

In an odd reflection of the times, when the Southern-born-and-raised Taylor moved into the White House with a retinue of about fifteen slaves (including children), he kept them out of public view, apparently in deference to the growing debate over the morality of slavery. "It seems clear that these slaves were restricted to the family's private rooms upstairs," wrote White House historian William Seale in his two-volume *President's House*. "They must have slept in the eight attic rooms."

Although Washington in those days was a town reflecting Southern culture and attitudes in many ways, it was also home to many Northerners "increasingly uncomfortable about the presence of slaves," Seale noted. Allowing slaves "to move about in public view in the White House might have invited incident," he wrote, "for hundreds of people poured through the state rooms every week."

They still do, not so incidentally, but under much tighter security restrictions than ever imagined in the 1840s and 1850s. On Saturday evenings, historian Seale also noted, the president was wont to stroll on the south lawn "and mingle with people there to hear the Marine Band." No Secret Service escort, rather only the guards at the gates who had been instructed to keep out "pickpockets, gamblers, and prostitutes." Allowed inside was "a fairly genteel group," a non-threatening crowd of "Senators and their ladies, public officials great and small, shopkeepers, nurses with children—a cross section of Washington."

Another attraction for the public was Taylor's wartime steed, Old Whitey, put out to comfortable pasture on the White House grounds. Grown fat and even shaggy, "He forged along the paths and in the flower beds, tolerantly allowing people to pluck hairs from his tail as souvenirs."

Himself reportedly uncomfortable with the idea of owning slaves, troubled also by Southern objections to the proposed Compromise of 1850, Taylor one day simply blew up when a trio of visiting House members from the South raised the specter of secession and military intervention if California were admitted to the Union as a nonslave state. They threatened that the Southern states "would band together and send their militias to take New Mexico and declare it a slave territory," Seale wrote.

The old army campaigner reacted so angrily, the three visitors fled his second-floor office, with Taylor yelling down the stairs in their wake that he would hang anyone found "in rebellion against the Union." Just then, Maine's senator Hannibal Hamlin arrived to find Taylor "rushing around like a caged lion" and calling his departed visitors "those damned traitors."

Ironically enough, the same legislator would later become Abraham Lincoln's first vice president, while Davis, Taylor's former son-in-law and now good friend, would become president of the Confederacy.

Oddly enough, too, other than family, the president and his wife appeared closer these days to the Davis couple than to anyone else in Washington, even while Davis was emerging in the Senate debates on the historic compromise "as successor to [South Carolina's late John C.] Calhoun, champion of the South." In part, the friendship dated back to the Davis-Taylor rapprochement on the battlefields of the Mexican War; in part, too, it stemmed from Varina Davis's solicitous friendship with First Lady Margaret Taylor, who fell ill soon after moving into the White House. "The doctors blamed the vapors rising from the south grounds," wrote historian Seale. "Gases seemed to be rising as the workmen graded the soil, although this was never proved."

Whatever the case, Margaret Taylor usually wasn't up to going out, and as one friendly favor, Varina Davis often brought the more interesting, socially prominent ladies about town to visit the first lady in her own White House quarters. "To the ailing Mrs. Taylor these visits were the greatest joy, which naturally pleased the President," noted Seale. As one result, his friendship with his former son-in-law only "deepened," a happy development that "did no damage to Davis."

Indeed, as a "fixture at family meals in the small dining room," Seale noted, "the Mississippi Democrat was believed to be party to every secret of the mansion and aware of the President's feelings on every subject before anyone else." Helpfully also, the Taylors had warmed to the vivacious Varina right from the start. Often stiff, even wooden as a personality, Jefferson Davis himself was "very nervous and suffered severely from facial neuralgia," but his pretty young wife "could be depended upon to sparkle."

So close to the seat of power were the Davises that, along with Taylor's immediate family members, they were at the president's bedside when he died on July 9, 1850, after suddenly being taken ill on July 4.

In the aftermath of this stunning development, Davis did not remain in the U.S. Senate for very long. Just months later, he indeed was reelected to a six-year term—not by popular vote, but by the Mississippi legislature, as such was the practice in the mid-nineteenth century—and he even took his new oath of office on March 4, 1851, but then other events intervened. Davis was persuaded to become a last-minute candidate for governor of Mississippi when the incumbent, John A. Quitman, resigned under pressure...first as governor and then as the Democratic Party's nominee to regain his post. Pressed into sudden service for his party, Davis resigned his Senate seat, then lost the election.

He retired to his Brierfield plantation, but only briefly. With the presidential race of 1852 looming, Davis himself was touted by some as a possible prospect for president or vice president, but the Democrats that year turned to the fairly obscure Franklin Pierce as their chief standard-bearer. Significantly for Davis, Pierce not only was a fellow veteran of the Mexican War but also, despite his New England background, an old friend. In short order, Davis once more was back in Washington, once more was remarkably close to the seat of federal power—this time as President Pierce's secretary of war. In short order, too, both the new president and first lady were frequent guests of Jefferson and Varina Davis in the latest of their Washington quarters.

Next, with the departure of one-term president Pierce in 1857 and the arrival of James Buchanan in the White House, Davis again was "sent" to the

U.S. Senate by the Mississippi legislature, this time for a stay ended only by his state's secession in early 1861.

★★★

Additional note: At this time in his life, Jefferson Davis, born in 1808, was barely in his fifties and, to many, an impressive but somewhat unbending figure. German-born Carl Schurz, a future Union general, observed that the Southern leader was "slender, tall and erect." His bearing reflected a dignity "which seemed entirely natural and unaffected," but which also "does not invite familiar approach."

On the other hand, Pierce's postmaster general, James Campbell, observed, "I know that Jefferson Davis is not popularly known as a socially genial man, but he was, as I came to know him." Campbell added: "He was very quiet and domestic in his habits, correct in his private life, and exceedingly temperate in both eating and drinking." He also was "the best educated man I ever came in contact with" and "famous for his retentive memory and the extent and range of his knowledge that was encyclopedic."

UNION & CONFEDERATE
Cast of Thousands

TRAVELING SOUTH SOME YEARS BEFORE the Civil War was young Wesley Culp from Gettysburg, Pennsylvania, in search of the right place to live and work. As events turned out, a job making wagons and carriages in Shepherdstown, then in Virginia, later a West Virginia address, would do nicely enough. Also traveling south before the war was vagabond teacher-poet Albert Pike, by some accounts in flight from rumored scandal back home in New England.

- In Richmond, Virginia, Jennings Wise, editor of the *Enquirer* and son of Governor Henry Alexander Wise, attended a play and commented that a certain cast member could turn out to be quite an actor.
  John Wilkes Booth.
- Born May 1, 1851, in Ellijay, Georgia, was David Bailey Freeman, son of a lawyer, grandson and great-grandson of sea captains, himself to

become a newspaper editor. But first, just ten years hence, he would be the youngest Confederate soldier.

- Traveling to the North in those same years before the Civil War, from France, came novelist Jules Verne's onetime mathematics teacher, Brutus De Villeroi, with visions of submarine designs dancing in his head.
- In future West Virginia, young attorney George S. Patton, a recent graduate of the Virginia Military Institute (VMI), sensed that war was coming and organized a militia company in the Charleston area (called the Kanawha Riflemen). Miles away, another young Virginian—cashiered from VMI for talking back to stodgy Professor Thomas J. Jackson—labored away near Pulaski as a dairy farmer. With more general impact came the notice posted at the front door of a Richmond newspaper on October 18, 1859: "The men at Harpers Ferry are not workmen. They are Kansas border ruffians, who have attacked and captured the place, fired upon and killed several unarmed citizens, and captured Colonel Washington and other prominent citizens of the neighborhood…. We cannot understand their plans or ascertain their numbers."

Soon after, it was Col. Robert E. Lee, Capt. J. E. B. Stuart, and a contingent of marines who recaptured the engine house at the federal arsenal at Harpers Ferry and subdued the fanatic abolitionist John Brown, who was hanged six weeks later.

- New state law in Georgia: no deceased slave owner's will or deed may grant that owner's slaves their freedom.
- Meeting in Chicago, the still-new Republican Party chose its second candidate ever for president on the third ballot of a national convention. The first ever, defeated in 1856, was "Pathfinder" John C. Frémont, a western explorer. Now, in 1860, the contender would be the Illinois state legislator Abraham Lincoln. Later in 1860, the Democratic Party nominated his old U.S. Senate rival Stephen Douglas for the presidency, but the party split over the slavery issue, and the Southern Democrats met separately to name the sitting vice president, John C. Breckinridge of Kentucky, as their nominee…on a platform that would assure the right to own slaves. Lincoln, of course, won in the general election of November 6, with a clear majority of the electoral vote but only a plurality of the popular vote. Throughout the South, secession was in the air.
- A Virginian destined for service in the Confederate army, an attorney and

a state legislator, Jubal Early by name, would be taking part in the Virginia Secession Convention of April 1861…and voting against secession.

- Meanwhile, it's not known at exactly what moment George S. Patton's good friend, fellow VMI graduate and future Confederate compatriot, George Smith, fell in love with Patton's wife.

- To the north, German-born Godfrey Weitzel, recent West Point graduate, married Louisa Moor, daughter of a fellow German who owned and operated a beer garden in Cincinnati, Ohio.

Young Weitzel graduated as second in the class of 1855, the very year that Robert E. Lee would be leaving his post as superintendent of the same U.S. Military Academy. Weitzel soon would be designing the defenses of New Orleans for Pierre G. T. Beauregard, who just weeks before the Civil War erupted also would serve as superintendent at West Point…but very briefly indeed, since the war did come along and he would be needed at Charleston—to oversee the shelling of Fort Sumter, Maj. Robert Anderson's federal outpost in the harbor.

Four years later, it would be Weitzel at the head of Union troops marching into the Confederate capital of Richmond, and Anderson would be raising the Stars and Stripes over Fort Sumter once more.

★★★

Quotes for thought: "Secession is nothing but revolution," and "The framers of our Constitution never exhausted so much labour, wisdom, and forbearance in its formation, and surrounded it with so many guards, and securities, if it was intended to be broken by every member of the Confederacy at will. It was intended for 'perpetual union,' so expressed in the preamble, and for the establishment of a government, not a compact, which can only be dissolved by revolution."—Robert E. Lee.

CONFEDERATE
A Virginia Whoop

ON THIS MONDAY, RICHMOND, VIRGINIA, was decked out in its finest to celebrate America's Independence Day a day late because the Fourth of July had fallen on Sunday…decked out also to welcome home the remains of President James Monroe twenty-seven years after his death in New York City—like both Thomas Jefferson and John Adams, on another Fourth of July.

July 5, 1858, it was…and just four years later, to the very day, the same state capital would become the capital of the Confederacy. In the meantime, thanks to Virginia-born-and-raised president Monroe, on this day Richmond would be marking "such a celebration of the day as that city, long accustomed to patriotic celebrations though it was, had never seen before and was never to see again," wrote historian Alfred Hoyt Bill in his 1946 book *The Beleaguered City*.

Founding Father Monroe had died in New York City on July 4, 1831, while visiting his daughter; he was buried in the Second Street Cemetery. "And now New York was uniting with Virginia to give him honorable interment in his native state."

Thus, a stream of Richmond-area military units, a salute by cannon, and the national colors dipping to half-mast greeted the steamer *Jamestown* as it nosed into the city's wharves to deliver Monroe's remains for reburial in Hollywood Cemetery. Just behind was the steamer *Ericcson* carrying the famous Seventh Regiment of New York, Bill noted. "The splendid regimental band wailed a dirge from the forward deck; and as the vessel rounded to at the wharf, the men and boys in the waiting crowd welcomed her with what the special correspondent of *Harper's Weekly* described as 'a Virginia whoop.'"

Next in this city of thirty-eight thousand, a hearse drawn by six white horses led by six black groomsmen "in white frock coats and trousers" came forward to receive the casket at a gangplank. "The Henrico Light Dragoons, resplendent in Frenchified Greek helmets and pantaloons strapped under the insteps [of] their polished boots, presented sabers."

In the future capital of the Confederacy, the Seventh New York was given the lead position in the marching column that now somberly stepped off in the direction of the waiting cemetery. "Behind them followed the First Virginia. Richmond Grays in gray, Blues in blue, Montgomery Guard in green, Rifles in blue and green, Young Guard in blue and red, the Virginians made so variously gorgeous a contrast to the uniform column of the New Yorkers that the brass-bound shakos, gray coatees, and white crossbelts of the latter looked plain and workmanlike and were much admired therefor."

As the procession moved up Main Street, then to Second and then to Cary, and finally to the burial ground, "the bells tolled; the minute guns thudded," while homes and stores along the way were "hung with black." At the cemetery, Virginia governor Henry Alexander Wise "emphasized the idea of union."

"Who knows, this day, here around this grave," he commented, "that New York is of the North and Virginia is of the South?"

Such is the circling of history that on another day in the future, with far less ceremony, another president would be buried at Hollywood as well.

Jefferson Davis.

UNION
Self-Appointed Bodyguard

ON ELECTION DAY IN 1860, Republican presidential candidate Abraham Lincoln had gone to his polling place in Springfield, Illinois, with three faithful companions—his current law partner, William H. Herndon; the nationally famous Zouave drillmaster Col. Elmer E. Ellsworth; and Lincoln's sometime courtroom associate and fellow "circuit rider" among the courts of Illinois's Eighth Judicial Circuit, the burly, sometimes hard-drinking, frequently song-singing Ward Hill Lamon.

Lincoln performed his civic duty by casting his ballot in the state elections but cut off the top, where the presidential electors were listed…to avoid voting for himself.

By two o'clock the next morning, the returns, while still unofficial, made it clear that he had won the presidency.

This turn of events meant that Lincoln would be leaving his law practice with Herndon, never to return; that Ellsworth would die an early death in the now-likely civil war; that Lamon would appoint himself Lincoln's dogged personal bodyguard, so often worried and so on guard against assassination attempts… except for that one night after the Union victory over the Confederacy nearly five years later when the Lincolns, against Lamon's fervent advice, attended a play at Ford's Theatre in Washington.

But first, Ellsworth and Lamon would be traveling to Washington by train with the Lincolns in February 1861 for their good friend's installation as president. Of the two, militia officer Ellsworth would be the one "entrusted with the responsibility of passing the President-elect through the crowds at his stopping places on the route," noted Margaret Leech in her book *Reveille in Washington, 1860–1865.* But it would be a heavily armed Lamon who then secretly rode a night train into the nation's capital with the disguised president–elect to avoid possible trouble from gangs of Southern sympathizers in Baltimore.

On the way east, Lamon had brought out his banjo and entertained the travelers with his playing and singing of various songs. "Of these," added Leech, "*The Blue-tailed Fly*, a buzzing ballad, was a favorite of Mr. Lincoln; and he loved to listen to many other simple tunes, both sad and comical, that Lamon sang." More seriously, Leech noted, "In addition to the banjo, Lamon carried an assortment of pistols and knives, a slingshot and brass knuckles. He was powerfully built and fearless, and he considered himself especially charged with Mr. Lincoln's safe-conduct to Washington."

In addition to safeguarding Lincoln both before and after his inauguration in March, Lamon took on the job of marshal of the District of Columbia, thanks to an appointment by Lincoln himself, and as a result, he ran the local jail. While that responsibility sometimes embroiled him in controversies with members of Congress and other occasional critics, he remained a zealous guardian of the president's safety and well-being. For a time in 1861, however, he was away, raising a brigade of fellow Virginians to fight for the Union. In 1863, noted Mark E. Neely Jr. in his *Abraham Lincoln Encyclopedia*, "he was marshal-in-chief of the procession at Gettysburg before Lincoln's famous address and introduced the President on the platform."

Even as the Civil War then tilted more and more in favor of the Union, Lamon worried more and more about possible assassination attempts against Lincoln…so much so that on election night of 1864, when Lincoln was reelected, Lamon slept at the foot of his bedroom door in the White House armed with a pistol and two Bowie knives.

He almost desperately warned Lincoln never to go to the theater unattended. When Lincoln did attend a play in December 1864, alone except for Massachusetts senator Charles Sumner and a foreign diplomat, the overwrought Lamon told Lincoln that neither of his two companions "could defend themselves against an assault from any able-bodied woman in this City."

Ironically, when Lincoln later dreamed of his own body lying in state in the East Room of the White House in early 1865, the two persons he shakily informed were his wife, Mary Todd, and Lamon. Worse, the night that Lincoln was fatally shot at Ford's Theatre, Good Friday, April 14, 1865, Lamon was absent, out of town…sent to Richmond three days before by Lincoln himself to look into ideas for a reconstruction policy for Virginia.

"He returned to be marshal of the civil part of the state funeral," added Neely. Lamon later failed to win appointment as governor in the Idaho and

Colorado territories. He entered a law practice in Washington and still later joined one of his law partners in producing a surprisingly unflattering biography of Lincoln that was not well received and sold less than two thousand copies.

★★★

Additional note: Ellsworth, in the meantime, had been killed soon after Lincoln's first inauguration in an ugly encounter with a hotheaded hotel proprietor in Alexandria, across the Potomac from Washington. Apparently the first Union officer to be killed in the Civil War, the part-time Zouave drillmaster had become a favorite of the Lincolns while "reading the law" in Lincoln's own law office in Springfield. After traveling to Washington on the Lincoln inaugural train, he first was appointed (by Lincoln) as adjutant and inspector general of militia, but after hostilities broke out with the firing on Fort Sumter in April, Ellsworth organized and led the Fire Zouaves of New York City (Eleventh New York Volunteer Infantry) as the unit's colonel.

Leading his firemen-soldiers on May 24 in an attempt to remove a Rebel flag flying above the Marshal House hostelry in Alexandria, Ellsworth ran into hotel proprietor James W. Jackson. Shots were exchanged and both were killed, Ellsworth by Jackson and Jackson by a soldier with Ellsworth, Cpl. Francis E. Brownell. Thus two martyrs were born of the early bloodletting, one for the North and one for the South…but only Ellsworth could lie in state in the East Room of the White House. His death, as Neely also pointed out in his Lincoln compendium, meant that the saddened Lincoln would compose "the first of the famous letters of condolence he would write in the tragic years to come." Many more deaths were yet to come, but for a short time, "Ellsworth and his avenger Brownell were early sensations in the war."

CONFEDERATE

Song Is Born

WAY DOWN IN THE LAND of cotton (*Look away, look away, look away, Dixieland*) they did *not* come up with the rousing, still-beloved song called "Dixie."

Nor was it first heard and sung during the Civil War, much less in the South itself. And yet, even today, what other song is more closely associated with the Confederacy, its fighting spirit, or its mingled romance of magnolia blossoms and the Lost Cause?

Few could have imagined any such possibility on that Saturday night in New York City—in 1859, mind you—when the impresario of Bryant's Minstrels approached the troupe's songwriter, Dan Emmett, and said they needed a lively new "walk-around" for the following Monday night. He picked on the Ohio-born Emmett because he was the composer of all the troupe's show-closing walk-arounds.

Emmett at first struggled at finding something fresh and lively, but then, according to an apparently knowledgeable acquaintance, "at last hit upon the first two bars." Any composer of music can tell you, added Dr. G. A. Kane of Baltimore in a letter to the *Richmond Dispatch* in 1893, "how good a start that is in the manufacture of a tune."

Even better, Emmett by Sunday afternoon had his lyrics, beginning with the words, "I wish I was in Dixie."

Those were not the lament of a Southerner pining for his own Southland, however, but rather a common expression among circus or theater people engaged in their annual Northern circuit and beginning to yearn by fall for their warm winter quarters in the South. At that point, wrote Kane, the common expression would be, 'Well, I wish I was down in Dixie.'"

By his account also: "This gave the catch line; the rest of the song was original. On Monday morning the song was rehearsed and highly commended, and at night a crowded house caught up the refrain and half the audience went home whistling 'Dixie.'"

And the rest, as they say, is history…except for one or two footnotes worth reporting here as well. Among them, Emmett's boss paid him five dollars for the song, and a few other minstrel shows also paid five dollars each for the privilege of using Emmett's lively tune.

But then, watch out! It hit New Orleans. And what a bounce from there. A New Orleans impresario paid Emmett a princely $600 to use the song, but printed "thousands of copies without giving Dan a [additional] nickel."

Then, in the spring of 1861, with *Pocahontas* playing at the Big Easy's Varieties Theatre, the orchestra leader was looking for a good song to accompany a Zouaves march in the last scene. "Trying several, he finally hit upon 'Dixie.'" It still wasn't all that well known, but it did seem to strike just the right note.

Did it ever. "Night came, the Zouaves marched on, led by Miss Susan Denin, singing 'I wish I was in Dixie.' The audience became wild with delight and seven encores were demanded. Soon after, the war broke out. The Washington Artillery [of New Orleans] had the tune arranged for a quickstep.... The saloons, the parlors, the streets rang with the 'Dixie' air, and 'Dixie' became to the South what the 'Marseillaise' is to France."

The highly respected *Cambridge History of English and American Literature* fully agrees "Dixie" was composed in 1859 by Dan Emmett "on forty-eight hours notice" as a "rollicking measure" that "scored a natural success with every audience." Indeed, the air really did make "an especially sensational 'hit'" at New Orleans late in 1860 and early 1861, "and soon all the Confederate states rang with it." It even was played at the inauguration of Jefferson Davis as president of the Confederate States of America in Montgomery, Alabama.

So popular was the ditty that others claimed its authorship or wrote their own lyrics for the tune. Probably the best-known alternate version came from Albert Pike, New England–born but a Confederate brigadier general and leader of an Indian brigade at the battle of Pea Ridge (Elkhorn Tavern) in 1862. The University of Texas's *Handbook of Texas Online* opines that Pike's "Dixie" offered "a lusty vigor that makes it perhaps the best of the many versions of the famous Southern anthem." As noted by the *Cambridge History*, however, Pike's "stirring lyric" is "now a literary memory."

Even less remembered today, and a failure utterly, was Fanny J. Crosby's attempt to recapture the "Dixie" tune for the North with a set of pro-Union lyrics.

As for original composer, Dan Emmett, he of course never recovered the full compensation he deserved for use of his song. Even worse, he "got into trouble" with his fellow Northerners, noted letter-writer Kane, because his "Dixie" was such a hit down South. "It was considered a rebel song, and a sapient Maine editor declared Dan to be a 'Secesh' (or secessionist), and that he should be treated as one," noted Kane.

UNION & CONFEDERATE
Double Leave-Takings

THE DAY FINALLY CAME...THE DAY when Jefferson Davis and Abraham Lincoln, born in Kentucky sixty miles and a year apart, each would leave home to assume the presidency in an awaiting capital.

Theirs were separate and rival presidencies of now-separate nations, of course…and sadly, tragically so, for now, very soon, more than six hundred thousand would die untimely deaths as a direct result of the same *separatedness*. Among these would be one of the two rival presidents, while the other, for a time, would be held as a prisoner in irons at Fort Monroe, Virginia.

But first, they had to be on their way.

For Davis, the slightly older of the two, that meant starting out by steamboat— Capt. Thomas Leathers's *Natchez*—from his Mississippi River plantation. But there was an early complication that very morning. He didn't get to the landing three miles downstream in time.

No real problem, according to his slave Isaiah Montgomery. With a rowboat as their conveyance, he said later, they made for an island in the middle of the river, "so as to meet the steamer when she came out from behind the island." Captain Leather, not finding Davis at the official landing as expected, now "was looking out for our boat." When each saw the other, "He stopped the steamer, we rowed up, and Mr. Davis was taken on board," added the slave. "That was the last time I ever saw him."

His master's destination was Montgomery, Alabama, the temporary capital of the newly formed Confederacy (which did not yet include Virginia and the future Confederate capital Richmond), but first there would be a detour to the Mississippi governor's office in Jackson on February 12 (Lincoln's birthday, it so happened), allowing Davis a moment to resign in writing as major general of the "Army of Mississippi."

Next, on his way from there to Montgomery, he would be making at least twenty-five speeches at various stops along the way. His wife, Varina, in the meantime, had stayed behind to wind up affairs at their Brierfield plantation before joining him in Alabama.

Lincoln that same morning of February 11 delivered a sometimes emotional farewell speech to a throng of well-wishers gathered at the local railroad station in Springfield, Illinois. Traveling a distance of 1,904 miles by train on a zigzag course that would take him to points as far north as Buffalo, New York, or on detours such as going from New York City to Harrisburg, Pennsylvania, then back to Philadelphia and Baltimore, Maryland, Lincoln of course was on his way to Washington, D.C., capital of the now-divided United States. His trip, with many speech-making stops along the way, would take twelve days in all.

Unlike alter ego Jefferson Davis, president-elect Lincoln traveled with his whole family. Also riding the chartered train, in addition to a retinue of

Abraham Lincoln's inauguration on March 4, 1861

aides, friends, political associates, and military men, were his wife, Mary Todd Lincoln, and their three surviving sons—Robert, Tad, and Willie. All were thriving and in good health for the moment, whereas young Eddie Lincoln had died in childhood. As noted before, the entourage included Zouaves drillmaster Elmer Ellsworth and Virginia-born Ward Hill Lamon, Lincoln's self-appointed off-and-on bodyguard over the next four years.

For the record, Lincoln's train was hauled eastward by a Hinckley engine called the *L. M. Wiley*. Noted biographer David Herbert Donald: "For most of the journey the presidential train consisted of three cars—a fourth was sometimes added—with the first assigned to journalists, who covered the journey in great detail, the second to local dignitaries who gained prestige from traveling part of the way with the President-elect, and the third for the Lincoln family."

The point of such an extended and "roundabout" trip east, Donald added, "was to give the people an opportunity to become acquainted with their new Chief Executive, the first American president to be born west of the Appalachian Mountains." Thus, Lincoln, no doubt mindful that he was only a plurality winner in a four-way race for president, wished "to satisfy this natural curiosity" by making frequent appearances at the rear of his train...and the people did respond. At small towns in Ohio, "large crowds assembled, often with bands playing and artillery booming." At Columbus, Ohio, "perhaps 60,000 citizens joined in the celebration," but in the larger cities yet to come, "the throngs were immense and police could not keep them from pressing close around the incoming President."

Similarly, it would appear, Davis's journey from Jackson to Montgomery was described by a contemporary as "one continuous ovation," noted Joseph McElroy in his biography *Jefferson Davis*. Eight miles out, he was met by a committee of the Confederate Congress and another from the city government. At Montgomery proper, "salvos of artillery greeted his approach and a large crowd...hailed his appearance with tremendous cheering."

By sharp contrast, thanks to assassination warnings, Lincoln reluctantly changed trains and slipped through Baltimore, a hotbed of Southern sympathizers, incognito by night before disembarking in Washington the next morning unannounced...no bands, no greeting crowds, absolutely no fanfare. Mary and the children arrived later in the day on the official Lincoln train, as previously scheduled.

On their separate journeys to their respective capitals, neither Civil War leader sounded a notably bellicose note. To the contrary, both talked of resolving the national crisis *peacefully*. Neither one wanted war, it *almost* seemed.

Davis, said his wife years later, "approached the task of creating a nation with a longing beyond expression to have his extended hand of fellowship grasped by that of the North before blood had been spilt, and with many humble petitions to Almighty God for guidance and support." Indeed, many of the more fiery secessionists considered him to be a bit too peaceable-sounding. But then came his firm statement upon arrival in Montgomery that the "separation" from the Union was "complete," and "no compromise; no reconstruction can now be entertained."

Lincoln, for his part, frequently called the national crisis a creation of "designing politicians" and declared the "crisis, the panic, the anxiety of the country" all to be "artificial." He told the New Jersey legislature "that he would seek a peaceful settlement of the crisis," noted biographer Donald.

Like Davis, however, Lincoln also had a stubbornly held bottom line. Whereas the Southern leader's was separation from the Union, Lincoln's was preservation of the Union

And in Trenton, New Jersey, he clearly warned, "It may be necessary to put the foot down firmly."

★★★

Additional note: Jefferson Davis was formally inaugurated as president of the newly created Confederate States of America on February 18, 1861, and Lincoln as president of the United States on March 4, 1861. And at the time, we know today by their own words, each certainly had some sense of the enormity of the task before him. The very day he left Springfield, Lincoln had said he was leaving (perhaps never to come back, he warned as well) "to assume a task more difficult than that which devolved upon [George] Washington.

"Unless the great God who assisted him shall be with me and aid me, I must fail," Lincoln added. With God's guidance, on the other hand, he would succeed.

In similar vein, Davis wrote to Varina after his inauguration to say: "Upon my weary heart were showered smiles, plaudits, and flowers; but beyond them I saw troubles and thorns innumerable. We are without machinery, without means, and threatened by a powerful opposition; but I do not despond, and will not shrink from the task imposed upon me."

Related aside: A comparison of their two inaugural addresses, said Davis biographer Joseph McElroy, "leaves one wondering that, while in education and culture, superiority was with the Southern Chief, eloquence and deep insight were with the unschooled leader of the Black-Republicans." That same eloquent Republican, according to Donald, personally had tied and secured his family trunks back in Springfield. He tagged them: "A. Lincoln, the White House, Washington, D.C."

On April 12, 1861, Confederate batteries opened fire on Fort Sumter

PART 2
★ WAR UNDER WAY ★

CONFEDERATE
"Pawnee Sunday"

EXCEPT FOR THE BOMBARDMENT AND surrender of Fort Sumter in Charleston Harbor, the real fighting had not yet started. Richmond was not yet the Confederate capital. Neither Jefferson Davis nor Robert E. Lee was yet in town. But Richmond was poised and even eager for battle. Poised, fevered…and ripe for rumor.

The pleasant April Sunday morning after Virginia's state convention secretly voted for secession, alarm bells suddenly startled men, women, and children at their church services. "The people poured into the streets," wrote historian Alfred Hoyt Bill in his book *The Beleaguered City*.

To arms, to arms…against a federal warship making its way up the James River pathway to the city's very gates was the message—a fast-spreading rumor actually. "Already the city militia were forming. Prominent citizens in the uniforms of field officers and aides-de-camp were galloping hither and thither."

Already, too, the city was in a fever over the secession movement that had overtaken the Deep South months earlier. First had come South Carolina's decision to cast loose from the Union the previous December, with formation of the nuclear Confederacy soon following at the newly declared capital of Montgomery, Alabama. In more recent days, Jefferson Davis had been declared president by invitation, Lincoln had been installed as the Union's president, by election (but only by a plurality in the popular vote). Fort Sumter had surrendered. Lincoln then issued his call for seventy-five thousand volunteers, including men from Border State Virginia, to flesh out the shaken federal army. With that, the staid Old Dominion finally had fallen from the vine as well, its secession vote of April 17, 1861, at first a badly kept secret but definite and final.

The days leading up to Sunday, April 21, had been frenzied days for the Virginia capital. "Lincoln declares war on the South, and his Secretary demands from Virginia a quota of cut-throats to desolate Southern firesides," declared the *Richmond Examiner*.

On news of the Sumter surrender, noted Bill's book: "In Capitol Square the Fayette Artillery fired a hundred-gun salute. Secession flags flew from a thousand housetops. Tar barrels blazed and rockets soared that evening. The joy bells rang all night, and the streets resounded with, 'Down with the old flag!' and cheers for [P. G. T.] Beauregard, the commander of the victorious troops at Charleston."

One escalation in the mood of jubilation followed another. The night of April 19 "saw the greatest torchlight procession in Richmond history…. [With] bands blaring the new national airs, hoarse voices shouting them, roman candles popping and rockets bursting overhead." And of course, the speeches flowed one after another.

Thus, by the quiet Sunday morning that immediately followed, news of a warlike threat from the James River came as a shock that somehow fit the overall feelings of bellicosity. Both the Richmond Howitzers and the Fayette Artillery wasted no time in rushing to the Wilton Bluffs overlooking the river from a height eight miles below the town. More of the local soldiery hurried to the city's wharves. "Civilians armed with ancestral muskets, half-grown boys with shotguns, men with nothing but pistols followed the troops." Other would-be defenders among the citizenry abandoned a Revolutionary-era French cannon after its wagon broke down in front of the post office on Main Street, there to stay unheeded for the moment.

Many others, this time mere spectators, "thronged" the city's Chimborazo Heights in hopes of seeing the threatening ship, which by all the rumored accounts would be the steam-driven sloop-of-war *Pawnee*.

Just out from an overhaul at the Washington Navy Yard, she could be a real menace despite her relatively small size. "If she reached Rocketts [Landing] even her four guns would be enough to knock Richmond into kindling wood and smoking rubble," added Bill's account.

A rather large *if*, as events turned out. Less breathless with excitement as the day wore on, and no warship in sight, Richmond gradually calmed down…but then, "toward sunset," came the unmistakable "thud" of cannon firing downstream.

Thrills once again, but only for the moment, since "it soon became known that this was from the Howitzers improving the shining hour down at Wilton with a little target practice at trees on the opposite bank." The artillerymen did get to spend the night under blankets and the stars before marching back to town the next morning. Meanwhile, the term "Pawnee Sunday" permanently entered the city's lexicon, even though it was soon overtaken by much greater and far more grim events.

★★★

Additional note: In actual fact, the 1,533-ton *Pawnee*, commissioned in 1860, had been in Charleston Harbor earlier that April, sent there to help relieve Fort Sumter…but too late to prevent its surrender. The federal warship then headed north, soon to be employed on another rescue mission. As of April 20, *Pawnee* was in the Hampton Roads area, not all that far from the upper James and tremulous Richmond, but busy towing the wooden frigate USS *Cumberland* away from the Norfolk Navy Yard as that important facility fell into Confederate hands. On April 21, Pawnee Sunday, no one on board had the slightest notion of bombarding Richmond. Later in the war, the fighting now on in earnest, the *Pawnee* served in the upper Potomac River by Washington, D.C.; Alexandria and Aquia Creek, Virginia; off Cape Hatteras, North Carolina; at Port Royal, South Carolina; and off the Georgia and north Florida coasts.

UNION
Ringed by Rebellion

AS THE FIRST TROOP TRAIN from the North pulled into town, great was the relief in the recently truncated Union's capital city…until the greeters saw the wounded being carried off on stretchers. Four dead and thirty-one wounded was the official report.

Just days after Fort Sumter and Abraham Lincoln's call for seventy-five thousand volunteers from the various states still remaining in the Union, a grim truth suddenly dawned: Lincoln in the White House and all of Washington were precariously alone, potentially cut off as if on a small island ringed all around by threatening seas.

After all, Virginia to the immediate south had just voted to secede and likely would join the Confederacy. And Maryland…well, that was the real rub. Maryland, that Maryland to the immediate north, that very same Maryland that Lincoln himself had passed through incognito, was dangerous territory these days, was rife with Southern sympathizers, was itself a slave state, and worst of all, was the only pathway by rail to Washington from the North. And it was in that very state's largest city, Baltimore, that the men of the Massachusetts Sixth Infantry Regiment had run into trouble on Friday, April 19, as they marched from one rail station to another.

While historically better known for its dead and injured, the Bay State's contingent actually was not the first to suffer a stoning while passing through Baltimore to reinforce the few militiamen and regulars guarding Washington. No, that unwelcome honor actually went to 460 volunteers from Pennsylvania and a single company of regulars from Minnesota who all arrived in town by rail the evening before the April 19 entry of the Massachusetts infantrymen. Thus, the very first Civil War casualty to grace the streets of Washington was an old black man who wasn't even a soldier but a sort of mascot for the Washington Artillery of Pottsville, Pennsylvania. As explained in Margaret Leech's book, *Reveille in Washington, 1860–1865*, he was Nick Biddle, and "he had put on a uniform for this grand excursion, and blood still oozed from the rags around his head, where the stones of the rowdies [in Baltimore] had found a mark."

Biddle's reaction: "He told people he was not afraid to fight, but he never wanted to go through Baltimore again."

That night, the new arrivals were given quarters alongside the local District of Columbia militiamen already housed in the Capitol itself, while various citizen volunteers bivouacked in the East Room of the White House as the Lincolns slept in their second-floor accommodations above, at the west end of the executive mansion.

That afternoon, not so incidentally, Col. Robert E. Lee had ridden for the last time across Washington's Long Bridge to his Arlington House mansion (his wife's, Mary Anna Custis Lee's, home actually) overlooking the federal city from across the Potomac. In Washington that day, he had been offered overall command of the Union armies. That night, Washington received word that Virginia at last had succumbed to the secession movement, which meant that Lee, after earnest prayer and pondering, would cast his lot with his native state rather than the Union.

The next day, Friday, April 19, loyalists in Washington anxiously awaited their promised reinforcements from Massachusetts while Southern sympathizers and proslavery adherents looked on with considerably less enthusiasm. When the reinforcements finally did arrive late in the day, "they were soldierly figures in their dark-gray overcoats, with neat knapsacks and new rifles," wrote Leech, "but their young faces were dirty and haggard. They had fought their way through a mob...[that was] hurling stones and firing guns, in the streets of Baltimore."

As the wounded were carried from their train on stretchers, a corps of women "sprang forward to dress the wounds with handkerchiefs." Among them was a U.S. Patent Office clerk originally from Massachusetts, Clara Barton—future founder of the American Red Cross. While the wounded were taken to an infirmary, the remainder of the Sixth Massachusetts, like the Pennsylvanians of the night before, also were quartered in the Capitol— specifically in the Senate chamber.

And now, noted Leech, the capital, Washington, D.C., itself, "was ringed by rebellion." That night, "All Washington looked for an attack before morning." Instead, a committee from Baltimore appeared, "urging that no more soldiers be sent through their city," because feelings there now "had been whipped into a frenzy by the casualties among the citizens, on whom the Massachusetts troops had fired, and armed secessionists were in control." By morning, Washington also heard that the bridges for the rail links to Philadelphia and Harrisburg could be burned. In sum: "Washington awoke on Saturday, to find itself without railway communication with the loyal states, without mail or newspapers from the North. Until Sunday night, the telegraph faltered on. Then rioters seized the Baltimore office, and the capital was left in silence, isolation and fear."

All this time, too, "secession sympathizers" were crossing the Potomac from the city to Maryland and Virginia "in droves, carrying the story of Washington's helplessness and alarm." At the same time, "Army and Navy officers were leaving for the Confederacy by scores, and civil servants by hundreds."

Among those resigning and/or departing on Monday, April 22, were the army's quartermaster, Gen. Joseph E. Johnston, a classmate of Robert E. Lee at West Point and soon to be a ranking Confederate general, as well as the notoriously high-living "Prince John" Magruder, who previously "had made repeated protestations of fidelity to the President," and Com. Franklin Buchanan, a forty-seven-year navy veteran who served as commander of the Washington Navy Yard.

Lincoln in the meantime had agreed with the Maryland authorities to have any further reinforcements bypass Baltimore instead of passing through the turbulent town. He had a feeling, though, that he next would be told that even going around the city would not suffice. And sure enough, wavering Unionist governor Thomas Hicks "asked him to stop sending any troops through Maryland and suggested asking Lord Lyons, the British minister, to mediate the sectional conflict," reported David Herbert Donald in his biography, *Lincoln*.

Wrote Donald: "That was too much for Lincoln. When a Baltimore committee descended on his office on April 22 and demanded that he bring no more troops across Maryland and make peace with the Confederacy on any terms, he had had enough. 'You would have me break my oath and surrender the Government without a blow,' he exploded. 'There is no Washington in that—no Jackson in that—no manhood nor honor in that.' He had to have troops to defend the capital, and they could only come across Maryland. 'Our men are not moles, and can't dig under the earth; they are not birds, and can't fly through the air,' he reminded the committee. 'Go home and tell your people that if they will not attack us, we will not attack them; but if they do attack us, we will return it, and that severely.'"

For the time being, however, the half-empty federal capital's siege-like isolation continued…although the solution already was close at hand.

In Maryland, meanwhile, the railroad bridges indeed were destroyed and the telegraph lines were cut. "A Confederate assault from Virginia was expected daily," wrote Donald, "and everyone predicted that it would be aided by the thousands of secessionist sympathizers in the city. In the lonely hours, Lincoln paced the floor of the White House, gazing wistfully down the Potomac for the sight of ships bringing reinforcements and breaking out eventually in anguish: 'Why don't they come! Why don't they come!'"

Visiting with some of the injured soldiers from the Sixth Massachusetts on Wednesday, April 24, he half-jokingly remarked: "I don't believe there is any North. The [New York] Seventh Regiment [supposedly on its way to Washington] is a myth. R. Island [also sending troops] is not known in our geography any longer. You are the only Northern realities."

Not quite so, of course. The surprising fact was, ever since midnight Saturday, salvation—in the form of Northern troops—had been just forty miles away.

But it wasn't until Thursday, April 25, wrote Leech in her book on Civil War Washington, that "the spell was broken." Washington's six days of isolation—dangerously vulnerable days, to be sure—were over. "The sight of a train, filled and covered with soldiers, set the militia at the [rail]depot cheering. At the Capitol, the Sixth Massachusetts raised a shout. Crowds came running, and housetops, windows and balconies swarmed with people."

Ironically enough, the newly arriving troops had been waiting at nearby Annapolis, Maryland, just forty miles away, since the weekend. Skipping much of Maryland and bypassing Baltimore altogether, they had traveled down the Chesapeake Bay by ship, debarked at Annapolis, but then had been stymied from riding the short rail line to Washington by torn-up tracks.

Finally, however, they were here—and so, crisis over. In short order, thousands more troops would be arriving by the same route.

Among the first to arrive were the men of the Seventh New York, who had spent time helping the men of the Eighth Massachusetts repair the torn-up tracks outside Annapolis. (Among the Pennsylvania Railroad's civilian personnel also working hard to make the rail repairs, incidentally, was the private secretary and personal telegrapher for the "Pennsy's" vice president Thomas A. Scott—one Andrew Carnegie by name. The future industrialist and steel mogul also "was the engineer of the first train which carried solders to Washington over the reconstructed line from Annapolis." Stopping the train to personally repair a downed telegraph line on the way, he accidentally lashed and cut his face and "was bleeding profusely when he arrived at the capital.")

Meanwhile, the Seventh New York was quartered in the House chambers at the Capitol and the Eighth Massachusetts in the rotunda. Noted Leech: "In both wings [the Senate and House chambers] mock sessions of Congress were the favorite diversion. The uproar started every morning with the rattle of reveille. A self-appointed presiding officer rapped for order, the galleries shouted to the floor, and the floor bawled back. There were pompous speeches and burlesque debates, greeted by howls of applause and hoots of derision. In the midst of the racket, some men were always writing letters. The militia thought it comical to sit at the legislators' desks and use the stationery of the House and Senate; and their prolific correspondence did not even entail the expense of three cents' postage, for the letters all were franked."

For the moment, the war, real war, seemed far away.

★★★

Additional note: Among those defections of Union officers in Washington on Monday, April 22, it seems that the Washington Navy Yard's commander, Commo. Franklin Buchanan, resigned with the expectation that his native Maryland would join the secession parade. When it didn't, the old salt tried to withdraw his resignation, but the Lincoln administration's navy secretary, Gideon Welles, refused to allow such a change of mind. Buchanan then joined the Confederate navy, and as the first captain of the ironclad CSS *Virginia*, fought a history-making maritime duel, ironclad-versus-wooden sailing ships, with the federal *Cumberland* and *Congress* in Hampton Roads, Virginia, on March 8, 1862, the day before the unprecedented battle of the *Virginia* and the Union's ironclad *Monitor*. As master of the *Virginia*, Buchanan sank both Union warships but suffered a sniper's wound in the leg that kept him from commanding the Southern ironclad the next day. His older brother McKean was serving aboard the *Congress* when it came under Franklin's fire, but McKean survived the subsequent destruction of his ship.

The U.S. Army's departing quartermaster general, Brig. Gen. Joseph E. Johnston, was destined to play major roles as a Confederate general in the Civil

War battles lying ahead…albeit not always with desirable outcomes. In one instance with far-reaching consequences, he was severely wounded at Seven Pines (Fair Oaks) east of Richmond in May 1862.

Taking over his command and soon to become absolute star of the Confederate firmament was Johnston's old West Point classmate, Robert E. Lee. Two years later, the same Johnston, by now recuperated from his wounds and leading the Army of Tennessee (in place of Braxton Bragg), was ousted from his command by Jefferson Davis while preparing to defend Atlanta, Georgia, against William T. Sherman. Ironically, Johnston would surrender the last sizable Confederate force to the same Sherman in North Carolina in April 1865—after Lee's more celebrated surrender at Appomattox on April 9. Johnston, briefly a postwar U.S. House member from Virginia, died in Washington in 1891—supposedly after catching cold at Sherman's funeral.

CONFEDERATE
Lectures Suspended

As THE SOUTHERN STATES SECEDED one by one, great was the excitement among the young men at the University of Virginia in Charlottesville, many of them scions of what might be called the First Families of the South. By early 1861, the students had formed two military companies—the Sons of Liberty and the Southern Guard—even though Virginia had not yet joined the "Secesh Seven" making up the Confederate States of America.

For these incipient young Rebels, a favorite place for practice drilling was the famous Lawn of Thomas Jefferson's university. "The spectacle of so many young men conspicuously uniformed and handling muskets, and marching backwards and forwards, at the spirited word of command, could not fail to kindle a martial flame even among those who were simply looking on," wrote Professor Philip Alexander Bruce in a centennial history of the university (1819–1919).

For the more ardent UVA students, however, this simply wouldn't be enough.

The newly organized Confederate States of America already had a flag, didn't it? That being the case, shouldn't its admirers at the university also have the flag…have it and find a way to display it *prominently*?

A pair of students took it upon themselves to rectify the omission. Hurrying into town, "they bought the requisite quantity of inexpensive colored cambric, and took it to a seamstress on Main Street, the owner of a sewing machine, who soon manufactured out of it the flag so eagerly desired," Bruce wrote.

But that was only a beginning. Since a bit more equipage would be needed for what they had in mind, they stopped on the way back to the university campus to pick up a saw and a hole-boring gimlet…just the items needed for their grand scheme.

They also arranged with a black carpenter in town to fashion a flagstaff and deliver it at the odd hour of eleven o'clock that night.

At or about this point, original conspirators R. C. M. Page and Randolph H. McKim decided their "proposed adventure" would be "too complicated for two men only to carry it through successfully." Thus they enlisted five accomplices and waited for the surreptitious delivery of the flagstaff "by a backway."

That done, they attached the "virgin ensign of the new republic" to its pole and waited for the midnight hour before moving out for the curious round building at the top of the sacrosanct Lawn—Jefferson's heralded Rotunda, home of the university's library. They carried both the new flag and the tools obtained that afternoon.

The Rotunda library, they knew, would be locked.

No problem…quite yet.

With the gimlet and saw they cut a hole in the back door large enough for each of the conspirators to squeeze through.

But now, unexpectedly, the door providing access to the roof would not be giving way as easily. Not quite. "It was too solid and too full of nails to be pierced by the saw." Deciding the only way past the barrier would be to "butt it down," the would-be flag raisers took turns smashing into the door until it, at last, gave way.

Even now, though, they were not exactly home free. Ahead was the tall cupola atop the Rotunda, and the only decent, respectable place to raise the Rebel flag had to be the top of the cupola overlooking the entire university grounds.

How to scale it? "They accomplished this feat by holding onto the lightning rod as they climbed up in Indian file—a course now doubly dangerous as the wind was sharp and blowing fiercely."

At the very top, the lightning rod offered a second service: "To this upstanding rod, the staff, with the flag wrapped around it, was firmly tied; and then the folds were unwound and allowed to flow with the wind."

Mission accomplished! But with dawn approaching, it was time to vacate the premises unseen. For some, however, descent could be more perilous than ascent. In fact, one of the conspirators cut himself in the cheek with the saw while climbing down.

Any such cuts and bruises notwithstanding, the stunned reaction of the academic community that same day made all the effort worthwhile. "It is recorded that the excitement caused by the discovery of the flag on the Rotunda, when day fairly broke," wrote Bruce, "was so great that lectures and recitations were suspended."

What about reprisals from the university administration? After all, "Virginia had not [yet] withdrawn from the Union, and the sentiment in favor of secession at the University was not aggressive enough to suffer the flag to continue to float where it was."

Down from on high came an order that was quite benign: "If it [the flag] was lowered by those who had raised it, no further notice would be taken of the act," wrote Bruce. As events turned out, another group of students took down the flag, which then "found its way" to at least one other, more "modest" campus structure. From this time on, it also seems, "the Confederate flag began to be descried here and there in town."

A student diary mentioned sightings at several places on the streets of Charlottesville toward the end of March. In addition, he attended "an assembly" at a professor's house "at which a Confederate flag was unfolded, toasts to the new Republic drunk, and speeches of a warlike character delivered." And all before Virginia seceded from the Union.

On April 19, the traditional parade in honor of university founder Jefferson's birthday took place on the Lawn. Marching in the parade were about four hundred young members of military units from both the university community and the local area. A dispatch from Richmond interrupted the proceedings.

"Fort Sumter has surrendered, and the Palmetto flag [of South Carolina] now floats over its walls," it announced.

"It is recorded that this sensational announcement was received with many evidences of satisfaction by all who were present," wrote Bruce with old-fashioned understatement. Even so, Virginia would *not* secede until hearing of Lincoln's call for seventy-five thousand volunteers to take up arms for the Union. Now, she *would* secede.

At Jefferson's "academical village" in Charlottesville, one morning not long before that, several students were heatedly discussing the national quandary over slavery, the possibility of secession, and the likelihood of war. As W. Gordon McCabe later wrote, "It is needless to say our voice was all for war."

All except for a good friend, a leading student, and later in life a professor at a theological seminary. He alone, it seems, "remonstrated against our abandonment of our studies, and spoke so sensibly and temperately as to cast a very decided damper on our martial aspirations." Later that same day, however, shortly after Lincoln's call for volunteers became known, McCabe and another friend encountered the future theology professor near the rotunda.

Instead of the cautious soul seen and heard earlier, McCabe now found "a familiar figure clad in a uniform known to no service in Christendom; a revolver as large as a small howitzer was buckled about his waist; and a cavalry sabre of huge dimensions clanked furiously as he came towards us." And what was the meaning of all this?

"Have not got time to talk to you boys," was the reply. "Lincoln has called for 75,000 troops. I enlisted five minutes ago in the Albemarle [County] troop." Clearly, too, he did *not* mean as a Lincoln volunteer.

Drily added the McCabe account: "So sped away our peaceful counsellor of the morning!"

In the war that now lay ahead, the same school's Sons of Liberty and Southern Guards briefly took part in the Confederate occupation of Harpers Ferry, then returned to Charlottesville, with most of the students then scattering for service with their home units. A third student company, just "fifty strong," briefly took part in Robert E. Lee's ill-fated 1861 campaign in western Virginia, then disbanded in early 1862, also in favor of their home-based units. Still another two companies "were formed for drill," but their members soon left the Virginia school as well.

By the end of 1861, wrote historian Bruce, an estimated 515 of roughly 630 students registered for the 1860–61 academic year had "joined the armies in the field." Of those who left the university in 1861 "to enter the war," sadly, an estimated 86 "perished in the field or hospital."

★★★

Additional note: Among other Virginia schools, the Virginia Military Institute (VMI) rather famously contributed to the armies in the field as well—not only by sending forth its cadets for the battle of New Market, Virginia, but also in the form of faculty member Thomas J. Jackson, that is *Stonewall* Jackson, and a number of distinguished alumni, such as World War II Gen. George S. Patton Jr.'s grandfather. Another school, however, small and far better known for its academics than any military laurels, could lay claim to no less than six Confederate generals and one Union general among its alumni and former students, a contingent led by the flamboyant cavalry star James Ewell Brown "Jeb" Stuart.

Both Stuart and his subordinate William E. "Grumble" Jones attended tiny Emory and Henry College near Abingdon, Virginia, before moving on to West Point and finishing their studies there. Both were killed in the Civil War, as was Emory and Henry's Brig. Gen. James B. Gordon—mortally wounded near Meadow Bridge, Virginia, on the day after Stuart's mortal wounding at nearby Yellow Springs in May 1864. Like Stuart, Gordon died in Richmond, but some days later.

Also rising to the rank of general but surviving the war were Emory and Henry graduates Henry DeLamar Clayton, a lawyer and Alabama legislator before the war; William F. Tucker, also a lawyer; and John Creed Moore, who moved on to West Point from Emory and Henry and then became a college professor before the Civil War. Rising to the rank of major general, Clayton served well at Chickamauga and in the Atlanta and Nashville campaigns after being severely wounded at Murfreesboro. After the war, he first was a circuit court judge and then president of the University of Alabama. Tucker—a regimental commander at Perryville, Chickamauga, Murfreesboro, and Chattanooga who rose to brigadier general—temporarily was sidelined by a severe wound at Resaca. He returned home to Mississippi after the war, resumed his legal practice, and served in the state legislature. In 1881 he was murdered in connection with a disputed legal case. Brigadier General Moore, for *his* part, was cited for gallantry as head of a Texas regiment at Shiloh, then served and was captured during the Vicksburg campaign. After his exchange, he assisted in the defense of Mobile. He later taught in Texas and wrote articles for periodicals.

The single Union general who passed through the portals of Emory and Henry was Virginia-born James Stewart Martin, whose home by 1846 was in Illinois. A lawyer just before the war, he also rose to brigadier general and led a regiment during the war. Later a judge, he briefly served as a U.S. House member from Illinois.

UNION & CONFEDERATE
Painful Interview

ROBERT E. LEE MAY HAVE been General-in-Chief Winfield Scott's "pet" among the officers of the U.S. Army in the days before the Civil War, he may indeed have been offered the job of leading the Northern armies in the war about to come, but he still had a somewhat testy last interview with his old mentor.

So it sounds, at any rate, from the recapitulation offered by the only apparent witness to that confrontation, Bvt. Maj. Gen. Edward Davis Townsend, former adjutant general of the army…also, former chief of staff to Scott.

The "painful" confrontation is spelled out in Townsend's intriguing postwar (1883) book, *Anecdotes of the Civil War in the United States.*

Setting up his Lee anecdote, Townsend noted that the Virginia-born officer was at home in early April 1861, on leave from his post as colonel of the Second (later the Fifth) U.S. Cavalry, which was then stationed in Texas. Thus, he was staying at his wife's famous mansion, Arlington House, on a high ridge over-looking Washington City from the Virginia shores of the Potomac River. It was a stressful, highly charged time when army and navy officers were resigning right and left to join the recently seceded states of the Confederacy.

The day came, apparently right after the surrender of Fort Sumter in Charleston Harbor on April 14, when Scott asked Townsend if he had seen or heard of Colonel Lee lately.

When Townsend said no, Scott said, "It is time he should show his hand, and, if he remains loyal, should take an important command." Townsend wrote that he then sent Lee a note asking him to come see Scott. The very next day, Lee appeared at the general's office.

"When Lee came in I was alone in the room with the general, and the door to the aides' office was closed," wrote Townsend. "I quietly arose, keeping my eye on the general, for it seemed probable he might wish to be alone with Lee."

Scott, however, "secretly motioned me to keep my seat, and I sat down with-out Lee having a chance to notice that I had arisen." In a footnote, Townsend acknowledged that Scott's aide George Washington Cullum, also later a general, "thinks" he was present for the Lee interview. Not so, Townsend maintained: "I am quite confident no one but myself witnessed the conversation between General Scott and Colonel Lee."

Meanwhile, after Scott asked Lee to have a seat, "the following conversation, as nearly as I can remember, took place":

General Scott. You are at present on leave of absence, Colonel Lee?
Colonel Lee. Yes, general, I am staying with my family at Arlington.
General Scott. These are times when every officer in the United States service should fully determine what course he will pursue, and frankly

declare it. No one should continue in government employ without being actively engaged. (*No response from Lee.*)

General Scott (after a pause). Some of the Southern officers are resigning, possibly with the intention of taking part with their states. They make a fatal mistake. The contest may be long and severe, but eventually the issue must be in favor of the Union. (*Another pause, and no reply from Lee.*)

General Scott (seeing evidently that Lee showed no disposition to declare himself loyal, or even in doubt). I suppose you will go with the rest. If you propose to resign, it is proper that you should do so at once; your present attitude is an equivocal one.

Colonel Lee. General, the property belonging to my children, all they possess, lies in Virginia. They will be ruined if they do not go with their state. I can not raise my hand against my children.

That, allegedly, was it. Interview over. "The general signified that he had nothing further to say, and Colonel Lee withdrew. The next day, April 20, 1861, he tendered his resignation, and it was accepted the 25th. General Scott made no remark upon the subject, but he was evidently much grieved at thus parting with a man of whom he had been justly proud, and for whom he had cherished the highest personal regard. He had no more devoted or efficient staff officer than Lee was in the Mexican War."

As Townsend might also have mentioned, when home on an earlier leave, Lee was the very officer Scott asked to take charge of the troops suppressing the crazed abolitionist John Brown affair in nearby Harpers Ferry.

UNION
"Little Mac" in Town

FOR BELEAGUERED WASHINGTON IN THE doleful first months of the Civil War, the highly visible comings and goings of the dashing George B. McClellan were a thrill and a tonic. Arriving fresh from victory all his own in western Virginia and on the heels of the Union's disaster in the July heat at Bull Run, he galloped back and forth from one Washington camp to the next, he organized parades, he looked and sounded young, vigorous, and strong.

His very appearance, wrote Margaret Leech in her book *Reveille in Washington, 1860–1865*, was "stalwart." Although a bit short, "he had a sturdy, muscular figure, with broad shoulders and a massive throat." Further: "There was a dramatic quality about him. He had imagination. With that audacity of conception which subdues or inspires timid minds, he began at once to discuss his command in terms of three hundred thousand men."

For a few weeks, "Little Mac," as he fondly was called, could do nothing wrong. Instilling order and discipline, reported Leech, "he spent twelve and fourteen hours a day on horseback, and worked at his desk until early morning." To which, David Herbert Donald added in his biography *Lincoln*, "He began rigorously training his men and he kept a close eye on them as they performed close-order drills, did target practice and engaged in practice maneuvers." Just as important, he drew upon his engineering expertise to develop Washington's ring of defensive fortifications.

Only thirty-four, the "young Napoleon," as he also was also dubbed, came to town with a background as a West Point graduate and an exemplary record of service in the Mexican War under the now-aging, grossly overweight general-in-chief Winfield Scott. He also had instructed at West Point, visited the Crimean War as an official observer, and developed the army's now-standard "McClellan saddle," based on a Hungarian model. He spent the four years before the Civil War as a railroad executive. After McClellan's appointment in April 1861 as a major general of volunteers commanding all of Ohio's forces, President Lincoln made him a major general in the regular army, which meant that only Scott outranked him.

Acting quickly, McClellan led the Rich Mountain campaign in western Virginia that secured much of future West Virginia—and vital segments of the Baltimore and Ohio Railroad—for the Union.

Then called to Washington just five days after the disastrous battle at Bull Run in Northern Virginia, noted Ezra Warner in his *Generals in Blue*, McClellan "brought order out of chaos, reduced the several dissident commands to a state of discipline and won for himself a regard by his men which would not soon be equaled." He leaped to command of the Army of the Potomac that August 1861 and then vaulted "into the office of General-in-Chief of the Armies of the United States on November 1, 1861, upon the retirement of General Scott."

All this for a man who had resigned his captain's commission in the army just four years before meant that "in two bounds" he "took charge of the greatest military establishment ever assembled by the nation up to that time."

He was accorded near-adulation by official Washington from the moment of his arrival. "The shaken little world of Washington received him with flattering respect," wrote Leech in her study of wartime Washington. "The President and the Cabinet—General Scott himself—deferred to him. When he visited the Senate Chamber, gray-haired men gathered around this general who was not quite thirty-five years old."

It was all so very flattering. He, himself, obviously was impressed. With even a small military victory, he told his wife by letter, he almost could think he "could become Dictator or anything else that might please me." But he immediately added (in case she took him seriously?), "Nothing of that kind would please me,—*therefore* I *won't* be dictator. Admirable self denial!"

Rightfully, though, he saw his new responsibility as twofold: fortify the city and hone the Army of the Potomac into fighting trim. And, as all Washington could see, he certainly was a busy man. "McClellan was the man in the saddle—and even the saddle bore his name," noted Leech, adding:

> No one looked at the President, walking through the streets or driving in his carriage in his gray suit and slouched hat. All eyes were on the young commander.... Every street lounger knew his stocky, high-booted figure. His passing, in clouds of dust or fountains of mud, was an event, a clatter, a cavalcade. Round the corner, hell for leather, he posted on his favorite horse, Dan Webster, with his staff and escort of dragoons hard put to follow him. He delighted in wearing them out, and thought nothing of a dash from the Chain Bridge all the way to Alexandria, through the Virginia encampments which made a continuous military city, more populous than the capital. McClellan wanted his troops to know and trust him. The latest raw recruits were familiar with their general's face, called him "Our George" and "Little Mac," and joined lustily in the shouts which greeted him.

McClellan stayed in a house on H Street, hard by Lafayette Square, and "was always galloping to and from the camps." Busy with his reorganizations and training, his fortification plans as well, he also found time for parades, lots of them. "In the crisp, cool days of autumn, McClellan began to stage the grand reviews of the Army of the Potomac.... Week after week whole divisions paraded at McClellan's command. Hundreds of sightseers were drawn to the capital by the fame of these military spectacles."

Most of them were held "on the commons east of the Capitol," but one "monster" parade of fifty thousand men was held out at Bailey's Cross Roads in Virginia on a "raw November day of mud and wind."

But there were cracks developing in the grand McClellan facade, mere fissures, but still, portents of shattering events to come.

One was the delay...nothing on the war front was happening. There the enemy was, it seemed, just beyond the Potomac and few swales of green Virginia countryside, posted there, ominously, ever since his victory at First Manassas (Bull Run). That turned out to be not quite so...Johnny Reb had withdrawn some distance back to the south.

And what about the river itself? A fine supply route...except that downriver it was blockaded.

A pinch or two of hubris did not improve McClellan's long-range prospects. When members of Congress asked in October why such a long delay without any significant action, McClellan "assured them" that the aging General Scott "was the principal barrier to action."

Not only that, from the first, "McClellan had treated Scott with contemptuous neglect," a factor hastening the old hero's retirement in November and allowing McClellan himself to vault into the post of general-in-chief.

Worse, McClellan treated Lincoln with arrogant disrespect as well.

The president from time to time would pop into the general's quarters with no advance word, and he sometimes had to wait to see the young military commander. "Lincoln deferred to McClellan, with a civilian's respect for a military specialist," wrote Leech, and McClellan addressed Lincoln with "ceremonious deference" as "your Excellency," but in private he mocked Lincoln's "homely phrases and manners." The final and unbelievable straw came the night in November that Lincoln, Secretary of State William H. Seward, and Lincoln's private secretary John M. Hay dropped in at McClellan's H Street home near the White House, only to be told the general was at a wedding and would return soon. They took seats in the parlor and waited.

Almost an hour later, McClellan returned and, although told the president was waiting upon him, went upstairs. When Lincoln sent a servant to find out what happened, the answer was that McClellan had gone to bed. "Mr. Lincoln quietly passed it over; but he let McClellan come to him thereafter."

Meanwhile, word of a small battle upstream on the Potomac was a shock to all Washington. Late in October, English-born Col. Edward D. Baker—senator from Oregon and an old lawyer friend of Lincoln's from shared days in Springfield, Illinois—was ambushed and killed while leading his men in an

Col. Edward Baker's death at Ball's Bluff, October 21, 1861

attack from the Maryland shoreline across the Potomac at Ball's Bluff, where the Confederates held the Virginia high ground. Many of his men simply drowned in the river, some of their bodies floating all the way down to Washington itself days later. Lincoln was in tears when he heard the news.

These bad tidings were presage to a dreary, rain-swept winter season ahead, during which McClellan and an ever-growing force of some two hundred thousand men camped in Washington and nearby Virginia still remained right there. For a time, too, Little Mac himself was down with fever, possibly typhoid.

Under pressure to take action, Lincoln was denied access to the sickroom…but McClellan managed to regain his feet after Lincoln began conferring with other army officers on the long-standing goal of taking the battle to the Southerners at Manassas. But the Union strategists discovered in March 1862 that the Confederates under Joseph E. Johnston had retired to Fredericksburg. The new strategy then, usually attributed to McClellan himself, was to transport the bulk of the great army to the lower Chesapeake Bay and land between the James and York rivers for an advance up the Virginia Peninsula to Richmond…the slowly executed strategy that, in the end, would lead to McClellan's downfall.

Forever overestimating the size of the forces opposing him and slow to move in any case, McClellan gave up his goal of Richmond after the Seven Days' battles against Lee outside the Confederate capital and retired to Harrison's Landing on the James River. "Insisting that his failure lay in the lack of support from Washington and, as usual, greatly overestimating the enemy's forces, McClellan refused to resume the offensive until given reinforcements[,] which the administration and Henry W. Halleck, now general-in-chief, were unwilling to provide," noted Ezra Warner in his *Generals in Blue*.

Recalled to Washington, McClellan was replaced at the head of the Army of the Potomac by John Pope, who then lost the battle of Second Bull Run in late August 1862. To protect Washington and its flanks, the administration once more turned to McClellan for his organizational and morale-building skills. Despite a significant edge in manpower, however, the best he could do in battle against Lee at Antietam, the bloodiest single day of the war in total casualties, was hardly better than a standoff. McClellan again was replaced, this time by Ambrose E. Burnside, and sent home to Trenton, New Jersey, to await further orders that never came.

He briefly reappeared on the national scene as Lincoln's Democratic opponent in the presidential election of 1864 and was soundly defeated. Later he served as governor of New Jersey. He died, still relatively young, in 1885 at the age of sixty.

CONFEDERATE
Sibley's Ubiquitous Tent

A WEST POINT GRADUATE, THIS Louisiana-born, plantation-raised Confederate general would serve in battle before and during the Civil War, but it would be his conical tent that lent his name to posterity.

For Henry Hopkins Sibley, the future once looked bright indeed. Graduating from the U.S. Military Academy in the same class of 1838 that produced the illustrious Pierre G. T. Beauregard, a fellow Louisianan, Sibley soon was off to the Seminole wars in Florida and then on to Mexico, where he was commended for his bravery in battle. Along the way he married a young lady with Northern ties, Charlotte Kendall by name.

After the Mexican War came duty at several frontier forts in the Southwest. He also served in the forces sent to suppress antebellum violence in Kansas and in expeditions against the Mormons in Utah and the Navaho in the Southwest.

All this, and yet there still was time for his tent. "On April 22, 1856," reported history professor Carrol H. Quenzel in the April 1956 issue of *The Virginia Magazine of History and Biography*, "he was granted United States Patent 14,740 for an improved conical tent which he described as easily pitched by a single pole."

No pup tent for his own, strictly personal use, this was to be a tent that could accommodate a fire at center and a number of soldiers sleeping "comfortably with their feet to the fire," as explained by Quenzel, a history professor at Mary Washington College (now the University of Mary Washington) in 1956. If that sounds somewhat like an Indian tepee, *absolutely*. Only Sibley went a step further than the Native Americans he had fought and observed close at hand—instead of a smoke hole at the top of his tepee, he provided a portable camp stove and stovepipe to vent the smoke through the top of his tent.

By far, this in fact was a tent that would be useful for many years ahead to thousands of soldiers. A fixture at many a Union—and *Confederate*—encampment during the Civil War, his Sibley tent was destined to be manufactured for use by the U.S. Army until 1888, with a total of nearly fifty thousand sold. Since Sibley also was the man behind the Sibley tent stove, wrote Quenzel, "one of his inventions provided shelter for United States soldiers for almost forty years and another heated their tents for eighty years."

That is not to say, however, that inventor Henry Sibley still was receiving his five-dollar royalty for every tent purchased. Far from it. The most Sibley and his heirs ever received for the Sibley tent was a paltry $8,500, according to Professor Quenzel's figures.

One reason Sibley profited so little from his tent was that, soon after receiving the patent, he assigned a half interest to William W. Burns, a younger army officer. As partners, both conceivably might have retired with considerable tent money in the bank, but along came the Civil War with all its well-known encumbrances and disruptions.

Most notably among the latter, Henry Sibley wound up very much on the wrong side, so far as the U.S. Army—now the Union army—was concerned. And Burns, a fellow West Point graduate, remained loyal to the Union.

No surprise, then, that Sibley's royalties were stopped in 1861, the year the war began. Union officer Burns and his estate, by contrast, would be receiving a total of $110,000 in royalties for the Sibley tent, even though his payments briefly were frozen as well.

While choosing opposite sides for the war period, both Burns and Sibley reached the rank of brigadier general in their respective armies. Stationed in

Texas, Sibley led the Rebel forces fighting the battles of Valverde and Glorieta Pass, but as commander of the Confederate Department of New Mexico, he also was held responsible for losing that campaign. After Sibley allowed the Union forces arrayed against him to intercept his supply line, all hopes for Confederate control of New Mexico were written off as a lost cause.

There were unfortunate reports of drinking that marred Sibley's performance in this and other matters.

Burns, on the other hand, after being wounded in the Peninsula campaign of 1862 outside Richmond, was officially commended for his conduct there. He also took part in other engagements of note, in roles up to division command, before retiring to the war's backwaters in an administrative role. As events turned out also, the Ohio-born brigadier could look forward to a handsome return from his investment in the Sibley tent venture of the 1850s.

But not Sibley himself. And he could only blame his own decision of that fateful May 13, 1861, the very day, apparently, that he had won promotion to major of the First U.S. Dragoons in the regular army but chose to resign his commission in order to join the Confederacy as a colonel three days later. In Brooklyn, New York, his wife was distressed to hear the news. She tried to persuade her husband to come home and stay out of the war altogether if he could not bring himself to fight on behalf of the Union…to no avail.

After the war, Sibley faced another battle—regaining his share of the royalties earned by his tent.

Unfortunately for any such hopes, he repeatedly found himself flailing at legal windmills and fighting red tape. When Sibley eventually saw Burns receive more than $100,000 in owed tent royalties, the spurned inventor redoubled his efforts in court, but too late—"by that time he was barred from instituting a suit by the statute of limitations."

That left Congress as his only possible remedy, but there he would encounter various delays, disinterest—or fierce opposition, since, after all, he had gone to war against the very same federal government that he now expected to provide payment for his tents. Still, bills to do just that were introduced on his (or his estate's) behalf in twenty different sessions of Congress, some extending into the early twentieth century.

By that time, Henry Sibley, U.S. Army officer, Confederate general, and even (after the Civil War) Egyptian army general, long since had passed from this earth…but with a legacy of additional inventions. Among them were modifications of his original tent for special uses such as field hospitals, camp meetings, even circuses, but he also had created a mobile bake oven for field kitchens; an airtight, watertight, unsinkable metallic boat to preserve treasure or mail "in the most violent storm"; and even his own version of the old-fashioned rocking chair.

For all that, though, he was in a state of near poverty and broken in health when he died in Fredericksburg, Virginia, on August 23, 1886, at the age of seventy.

★★★

Additional note: In Minnesota, they still remember the Civil War–era general Henry Sibley. Not Henry *Hopkins* Sibley, but his distant cousin Henry *Hastings* Sibley, early Minnesota settler, early territorial delegate to Congress, first governor of the new state of Minnesota. Initially a *Union* brigadier general and then a major general during the Civil War, this Henry Sibley spent his war years either fighting hostile Sioux Indians or negotiating peace terms with restive tribes. According to Ezra J. Warner's definitive *Generals in Blue*, "It is probable that General Sibley never saw an armed Confederate."

UNION
Air "Thick" with Balls

RIGHT AND LEFT OF JOSHUA Kite, Second Virginia Infantry, men went down. "It was a hail of musket balls and why it didn't sweep every man down is a mystery," he would say later.

"But it did kill scores." Further, "The balls were millions." And moreover, "The balls plowed up the ground all around."

All different, but fast-moving moments from Second Bull Run, August 1862. And still to come, the moment he saw, coming right at him, "one big shell."

But first, he had joined up in Ohio after Lincoln's call for seventy-five thousand volunteers back in the spring of 1861. Because Ohio filled its quota before he could sign up, he later told the *Ironton (Ohio) Register*, he joined a company of the Second Virginia (U.S.) Regulars forming up just then at Ironton.

Next heard from, Kite was at Second Bull Run, late August 1862. "Our regiment was in [Robert H.] Milroy's Brigade of [Franz] Sigel's division, and made a charge on the rebel line, which was behind a graded fill of the railroad, which made a splendid breastworks. At first we were not aware that there were any troops there. When we drove in the rebel skirmishers they went over the breastworks and kept going, so we did not think there were any troops hid behind the railroad, until we got 30 to 40 steps, when they rose and let fly."

That's when the air became thick with deadly musket balls, a hailstorm of them. "I was so paralyzed I didn't know what to do. I didn't ever think of running, though the whole line retreated with great confusion. I did jump behind a clump of oak bushes and fired up my old musket at the railroad fill."

At this time and place, "I was the only fellow there and the balls were millions, I thought."

Why not fall to the ground and play dead, he also thought...he briefly thought. "But then I thought that a stray ball of the few thousand would hit me and end the make-believe." Or the Rebels would come forward and capture him. In that event, "I believe I would rather be killed."

As all such thoughts whirled 'round and 'round in his head, he finally decided his best course "was to strike for the rear, as fast as my legs would carry me."

He "bounded forth" from his oak bush sanctuary "like a streak of greased lightning." Kite was himself amazed at how fast he could run. "My, how I flew! The earth seemed to skip beneath my feet like a flash of powder."

But now it seemed as if an entire Confederate corps opened fire on him.

Union troops engaged at the August 29–30, 1862, Battle of Second Manassas (Bull Run)

"The balls plowed up the ground all around. I wondered if I wasn't full of ball, and I was going so fast I couldn't stop. They zipped all around me."

As for that one big shell coming right at him, "I looked back and saw it coming. I thought sure it would burst as it struck my head, but it went on."

So did he…until he came across a wounded man who called out to him. Kite stopped to help. "He was shot in the calf of the leg. I took him and carried him behind a sycamore tree for protection, and set him up in as comfortable a place as I could."

Here too was a chance for Kite to catch his breath, but not for long. "[A] ball struck the tree, and I began to think the sharpshooters were now after me. I moved back further and soon got where our line was re-forming."

As to the long and short of his tale, Kite survived the day. He then survived the next day of fighting at Second Bull Run as well…even though "that too was terrible"; even though he, himself, was "struck by a grape[shot] ball, with a thump that nearly knocked me over." Amazingly, it didn't break the skin and only lodged in his blouse. His final thought? Simply, "excuse me from a closer call than I got at Bull Run."

★★★

Additional note: Based on one of a series of combat memories published in the 1880s in the *Ironton (Ohio) Register*, which can be seen on the Sons of Union Veterans of the Civil War website (http://suvcw.org/pr/notes.htm), as transcribed by Donald E. Darby, SUVCW national patriotic instructor. Meanwhile, the outcome of Second Bull Run (Second Manassas) by far was *not* to the Union's advantage. After five days of fighting, the Union forces under John Pope withdrew to the safety of Washington, D.C., having lost 16,054 men to the Confederacy's 9,197 under Robert E. Lee, or a 21 percent Union loss versus 19 percent for the South.

CONFEDERATE
One of the "Immortal 600"

For 1st Lt. George W. Finley, Company K, Fifty-Sixth Virginia Infantry, the errant shell first appeared as a mere speck in the sky above. Growing ever larger by the instant, it was a mortar round, and it certainly was *not* going to miss Finley and the men gathered before him, all POWs held in confinement at the Union prison camp on Morris Island at Charleston, South Carolina.

"As the shell came down, it grew larger and larger," wrote William "Bill" A. Young Jr. in the *Confederate Veteran* (vol. 2, 2002). "It shrieked, screeched, and hissed like a frightened bird."

It was one of those riveting moments when scenes from your whole life flash through your mind. For the young Virginia officer that meant "the old oak tree with the rope swing; the one-room schoolhouse with his slate of sums on the desk top; the frown on the face of the manager when young Finley reported for work his first day at the bank; and the sweet smile of his wife, Margaret, as she started down the aisle toward him on their wedding day."

Surely he also would have remembered that dramatic and searing moment when, with a few surviving comrades of the Fifty-Sixth Virginia, he reached and actually crossed the Union's ridgetop lines at the very apex of Pickett's Charge at Gettysburg on July 3, 1863, that third and last day of the great battle. Really, how to forget those very last seconds of the famous charge?

"Two gunners of [Union] Lieutenant Alonzo H. Cushing's battery, Fourth U.S. Artillery Regiment, jerked their lanyards and fired two double loads of canister full into the faces of the men in butternut and gray," the same Bill Young wrote in *America's Civil War* magazine (March 1993). Finley himself "felt a cannon muzzle flame against his cheek."

Somehow, however, he survived what was a terrible day for the Fifty-Sixth Virginia and so many other Confederate regiments that utterly spent themselves charging the Yankee entrenchments on Cemetery Ridge. As noted by Young: "The 56th Virginia, like many of the regiments of Pickett's division, was almost annihilated at Gettysburg. Company H, the largest company in the regiment, took 37 officers and men into the charge. Fourteen were killed, 16 were wounded, six were captured, and one escaped. Company D had 23 officers and men—every one of them was killed or wounded. The color guard marched to the [Union stone] wall with six men. Four were killed, one was badly wounded and captured, and one escaped."

By some miracle, Finley "was one of the handful of men who got over the stone wall [atop the ridge] and lived to tell about it," added Young in his *Confederate Veteran* article. But the young officer still paid a price—he was taken prisoner and held as a POW in six different confines for the next two years.

As part of the price, he was among the prisoners sent south in June 1864 aboard the paddle wheeler *Crescent City* to the Union prison camp on Morris

Island. There he became one of the "Immortal 600," the Rebel prisoners held in a stockade more or less in the middle of Union and Confederate artillery batteries quite busy firing back and forth. As explained by Young in *Confederate Veteran*, the Yankee stockade was built between heavy-gun Batteries Gregg and Wagner. "All day and all night the Union guns fired on Fort Sumter, Sullivan's Island, and other points along Charleston Harbor," Young noted. "The Confederate guns across the water always returned the fire. Luckily for the prisoners, the Southern artillerymen had the exact range. Their shells arced over the stockade and dropped on the Yankees behind it." Usually.

Meanwhile, with Presbyterian minister N. B. Handy the only clergyman among all the Confederate prisoners being held on Morris Island, the day came when he and a few others approached Lieutenant Finley and asked him to "read the Scripture, preach the sermon, teach Sunday school, hold Wednesday night prayer meetings, and say the words over us when we die."

Finley was stunned at the request. "But I'm not a minister," he pointed out. "I've never set foot in divinity school."

But they were persuasive…or perhaps deep in his heart and soul he didn't really need much persuading. In any case, added Young, Finley became "acting chaplain to his fellow prisoners." In fact, "he swore a secret vow that if he survived the war he would go to a seminary and become a real Presbyterian parson."

Then came the Sunday morning he was leading a group in worship inside the stockade at Morris Island. They had just recited the last two lines of Psalm 23:

> Surely goodness and mercy shall follow me all the days of my life:
> And I will dwell in the house of the Lord for ever.

And they heard an especially loud BOOM, "like a terrible clap of thunder." It came from the Charleston side of the harbor. With a "bright flash of orange flame and a rolling cloud of black powder smoke," the Confederates had fired a mortar round in the direction of the prison camp…but, as usual, not aimed for it.

Finley and his small congregation of POWs watched, mesmerized, as the shell first vaulted upward, seemingly "into the heavens." But then, a mere speck at its zenith, "it turned, rolled, and headed down."

As the mortar shell then grew in size, it dawned on the captives that this was no optical illusion. Aimed or not, the errant shell would fall short of the usual Union targets beyond their stockade. It would fall right among the small congregation of POWs.

That's when those scenes from his life flashed before his mind's eye…but also when he closed his eyes and began reciting a familiar prayer: "Our Father, who art in heaven, hallowed be thy…"

Before he could finish, the mortar shell "slammed" into the ground just a few feet away.

He waited for the explosion. "He waited…and waited…and waited."

No explosion.

Buried nose down in the sand, the shell was a dud.

Related Finley later, "We all then continued our little worship service with renewed enthusiasm."

When he finally was released after another year as a POW, he wasted no time in fulfilling his secret vow to serve God and man as a man of the cloth. Enrolling at Union Theological Seminary at Hampden-Sydney, Virginia, he was ordained two years later as a Presbyterian minister. He then "served the Lord in the pulpit of the Tinkling Spring Presbyterian Church in Fishersville, Virginia, until the end of his days."

As noted by Young, the Reverend Finley "never forgot his years in prison [camp]." Late in life, he wrote, "And God sent us back to our wasted land and stricken people to take up the work for which He had been preparing us."

UNION
A Name to Live On

WHEN U.S. NAVY CMDR. JAMES Harmon Ward was buried, his hometown *Hartford (Connecticut) Courant* reported that the city streets were filled with a "saddened concourse of people." The city council complained to heaven itself with a resolution saying, "We deeply deplore the Divine dispensation which has bereaved our National Union of one of its most efficient defenders."

James Harmon Ward…let's see now, where in American history has that name come up again…and again? The Ward part at least?

It's both a fact and a statistic that Commander Ward briefly came to public attention during the Civil War as the first Union naval officer to be killed in action in that conflict. But that was early in the war, in June 1861. He only briefly was in the news, his outstanding career and life story then largely forgotten in the deluge of more than six hundred thousand war dead that would traumatize the divided nation.

Still, in certain circles, his name clung on…and on.

As one commemorative acknowledgment of his sacrifice, there would be the now-restored and much-visited Fort Ward at Alexandria, Virginia. Preserved as an example of the Civil War defenses the Union threw up in a ring around Washington, D.C., the Fort Ward Museum and Historic Site today is open to the public on a daily basis.

Then, too, anyone familiar with the campus at the U.S. Naval Academy at Annapolis, Maryland, probably knows the size, shape, and location of venerable Ward Hall, its name not only honoring Ward's Civil War service but also recognizing his role in the 1840s in the formation of the academy itself…for he was one of the naval school's first seven faculty members and, more exclusively, its first executive officer (a post later called the commandant of midshipmen). He also was president of the academy's academic board. "Ward's forceful, energetic character, his devotion to the Service [the Navy], as well as his high professional attainments, made a lasting impression on the school," notes *The First Academic Staff*, published by the U.S. Naval Institute Proceedings.

Both a scholar and a veteran sailor, Ward wrote books on naval gunnery, naval tactics, and the future of steam propulsion. As his first sea duty, he served as a midshipman aboard the imposing USS *Constitution* for four years, followed by a year's scientific study ashore, and then fifteen more years of steady sea

Alfred Waud sketched James H. War shortly before the commander's death.

duty. During the Mexican War, he served as captain of the wooden frigate USS *Cumberland*, Commo. Matthew Perry's flagship. Next, while commanding the sailing sloop USS *Jamestown* off Africa, Ward wrote *Manual of Naval Tactics*, soon to become a required text at the naval academy.

With the advent of the Civil War, there was no doubting the fifty-four-year-old officer's loyal choice of the Union. Indeed, he reportedly would have led a navy expedition dispatched to the relief of isolated Fort Sumter in Charleston Harbor, but his superiors decided it would be a futile effort. Instead, Commander Ward took command of the Potomac Flotilla, an assemblage of gunboats and schooners operating on the Potomac River.

With the USS *Thomas Freeborn* as its flagship, the flotilla shelled Confederate batteries at Aquia Creek in May and June 1861, then, on June 27, attempted a landing at Mathias Point, also on the Virginia shoreline. It was here that Ward was mortally wounded, struck by a sharpshooter's musket ball while aiming the *Freeborn*'s bow gun.

Thus, it was only natural that both a small fort and a building at the naval academy would be named for the navy's early Civil War hero…but wait, that's not all. The name Ward was destined to live on in yet another venue, to recall another war—indeed, to ring in another devastating (albeit victorious) war for the United States. *Remember Pearl Harbor!* Not so long ago, that was the familiar battle cry, the informal-yet-national slogan for the early days of World War II. Remember? The early morning sneak attack of December 7, 1941, on the naval base at Pearl Harbor in the Hawaiian Islands by the Japanese Empire? And President Roosevelt's ringing condemnation before a joint session of Congress, before the American people and the world: *A date which will live in infamy!*

More than twenty-four hundred American military personnel died in the raid by carrier-based Japanese aircraft. Seven of the eight battleships in port were destroyed or significantly damaged. Scores more naval vessels, along with U.S. Army and Marine Corps airplanes, barracks, and other facilities, fell victim to the same surprise attack.

And yet, as close examination of the facts revealed, it was actually an American ship that struck the first blow of the Pacific war with Japan—a mere destroyer that came across a Japanese midget submarine attempting to slip into Pearl Harbor just hours before the air raid. The destroyer was the USS *Ward*, commanded by William W. Outerbridge, who had responded in his pajamas to the dawn sighting of the submersible. At his orders, the *Ward* engaged and sank the midget sub, then fired off a radio report to the naval district headquarters in Hawaii, home of the Pacific Fleet, but the warning went unheeded until too late.

As the war progressed, the *Ward*, originally commissioned in 1918 for duty in World War I, served valiantly and well in the Pacific…until, three years later, another December 7 rolled around. That was the day a kamikaze found her in Ormoc Bay during the invasion of Leyte in the Philippines…found her and crashed into her. As uncontrollable fires erupted aboard the destroyer, the crew was ordered to abandon ship.

The nearby USS *O'Brien* then opened fire to sink the burning hulk of James Harmon Ward's World War II namesake. And talk about circles within circles, it was William Outerbridge who was in command of the *O'Brien*, instead of the *Ward*, on *this* December 7.

All of which is how the name Ward persisted long after Commander Ward's sacrifice early in the Civil War.

CONFEDERATE
Patton's Gritty Forebears

ALREADY BADLY WOUNDED IN 1861, the young Confederate officer went down again at the relatively minor battle of Giles Court House in May 1862. As his son later told the story, "Being struck in the belly with a minié ball he thought the wound was fatal and so dismissed the surgeon, telling him to spend his time on those he could save."

No surprise there…not with this officer. After all, back in 1861, he had refused to allow the proposed amputation of his arm when wounded and captured in the battle of Scary Creek (at the creek's juncture with the Kanawha River near today's St. Albans, West Virginia). In that case, it would have been Yankee surgeons taking off his right arm, its upper portion shattered by a minié ball.

But the young prisoner absolutely refused…and he had the means to enforce his point. Explains biographer Carlo D'Este: "He had somehow been permitted to retain his pistol and made it uncompromisingly clear that he would shoot anyone who attempted to try."

As a result, the arm stayed, but it "did not heal properly, and Patton never regained full use of it."

Nonetheless, Lt. Col. George S. Patton, grandfather and namesake to America's famous World War II Gen. George S. Patton Jr., would fight on. "Patton was eventually paroled and permitted to return to his family," added D'Este in his biography of the twentieth-century general titled *Patton: A Genius for War*. "When he recovered sufficiently from his wound he returned to the 22nd Virginia [Infantry] as its commander, with the rank of lieutenant colonel."

The light colonel thus continued in his service to the Confederacy, often in southwestern and western Virginia, but also, in time, at New Market and Cold Harbor; often also under Stonewall Jackson, his own former professor at the Virginia Military Institute (VMI).

The fact is, six Patton brothers served the Confederacy, two of whom—George and his brother Tazewell ("Taz")—were VMI graduates who each briefly taught there before becoming lawyers. Younger brother William was a cadet at VMI who fought at New Market with the Cadet Corps in 1864.

Taking up residence some years before in the area of future Charleston, West Virginia, George (second in his VMI Class of 1852) soon sensed the war clouds gathering over his beloved Virginia. He organized and led the Kanawha Riflemen, a militia outfit later to become Company H of the Twenty-Second Virginia. His brother Waller Tazewell Patton during the same prewar days had taken command of the Culpeper (VA) Minutemen, founded in 1776 by a Patton family forebear.

When secession came and war loomed close, the Patton clan—men, women, and children—gathered at their ancestral homestead in Culpeper and battened down for the storm ahead. They of course would remain loyal to Virginia in the choice she made to side with the Confederate states. "The Patton homestead became a beehive of activity as the family prepared for war en masse," biographer D'Este wrote. "While the women made ponchos and uniforms, the Patton men went about the grim business of preparing themselves for war." Their mother, Margaret French Williams Patton, gave each of them a thoroughbred horse and a black "body servant" before they went off to war.

The subsequent dispersal of the fighting Patton brothers would find James serving as brigade inspector in brother George's brigade, and John (still another VMI graduate and attorney) as colonel of the Twenty-First Virginia Infantry until ill health forced him to resign. Also, Isaac, who had moved earlier to New Orleans, would be colonel of the Twenty-Second Louisiana Infantry (and later mayor of New Orleans), and Hugh would serve as a staff officer for Brig. Gen. John R. Cooke.

The two brothers with the most notable combat service, however, were

George and Taz. And of the two, it was Taz who would survive only until the third day at Gettysburg (July 3, 1863). There, his Seventh Virginia Infantry would be among the thirteen regiments taking part in Pickett's Charge… with all thirteen regimental commanders to become casualties, either killed or wounded, D'Este noted. "One of those commanders, lying mortally wounded near a stone wall that afternoon, was twenty-nine-year-old Col. Waller Tazewell Patton, whose 7th Virginia had advanced the farthest before it was repulsed."

A Union artillery officer—named Lee, ironically, Lt. Henry T. Lee—saw it happen. As mere eddies of the gray tide reached the stone wall atop Cemetery Ridge, in front of Lee's own battery, he saw two Confederate officers mount the wall holding hands, then they fell back. With the action abating, Lee went forward to see what had become of them. One, apparently a Patton cousin and the regimental adjutant, already was dead. The other, his jaw shattered, was Taz Patton. Gravely wounded, he still could write with pencil and paper.

"Send this to my mother," he painfully scribbled, "so that she may know that her son has lived up to and died according to her ideals." (His mother's views were so strong, incidentally, that one time after the war, she struck a former Confederate colonel with a whip after he acknowledged saying amen to a minister's prayer for the president of the United States and "all others in authority.") Writing on a slate board, the dying Tazewell added: "Tell my mother that I am about to die in a foreign land; but I cherish the same intense affection for her as ever." And he did die of his wound, in caring Northern hands, twenty days later.

Unfortunately for the Patton clan, Tazewell was only the first to succumb to the ravages of civil war. Return now to the first George Smith Patton, commander of the Twenty-Second Virginia, and the day he was laid low at Giles Court House (in West Virginia today) on May 10, 1862, when struck in the stomach by a minié ball. After sending away the surgeon, this Colonel Patton, certain he was dying, began a farewell letter to his wife, Susan…but was interrupted by a general-grade officer who asked to see the wound, stuck a finger in it, and withdrew a battered gold coin.

The minié ball had struck the coin and merely created a flesh wound, which would soon heal but first send him home—for the moment in Richmond—to recuperate from a case of blood poisoning.

With that narrow escape behind him, Confederate Col. George S. Patton carried on his war, still largely in western Virginia. He, in fact, moved his family to Lewisburg. Close by, as the war continued unabated, he and his men shortly experienced defeat at Droop Mountain, thanks largely to Union cavalry commanded by his old friend Brig. Gen. William W. Averell. Retreating through Lewisburg, George Patton gave his wife a letter asking Averell to ensure the safety of his dependents during the coming Union occupation of the area.

But, D'Este pointed out, this was not to be George Patton's last encounter with Averell's troopers. "One morning he was breakfasting at a house when an orderly suddenly yelled: 'The Yankees are coming!' Patton and his staff barely had time to escape Averell's cavalry by jumping out the back window while the lady of the house rushed to hide his saber under a mattress."

Still ahead for Patton, meanwhile, for a flock of Pattons, actually, was the battle of New Market in May 1864. As the "greatest triumph of the Patton family during the Civil War," D'Este wrote, four Pattons "and their kin" participated in the famous victory for the Confederacy—and for the VMI corps of cadets. At one point, George Patton's Twenty-Second Virginia "came to the rescue of his close friend and first cousin Col. George Hugh Smith, whose 62d Virginia was in dire straits after being trapped in a ravine and badly decimated by canister [artillery fire]."

Not only that, he at another point proved himself "an outstanding and innovative commander" by his hastily improvised—and successful—defense against a Union cavalry attack on his left flank. With his brigade commander often absent, D'Este reported, George Patton just as often was the officer in charge… by a fateful day in September 1864, in fact, it was "Patton's Brigade" sharing the brunt of Union Gen. Phil Sheridan's attack on Jubal A. Early in the "lower" (read *upper*, geographically speaking) Shenandoah Valley.

In the interim, though, George Patton had moved his family again—this time to brother John Mercer Patton Jr.'s home in Albemarle County, called "the Meadows." Assigned to Early's Army of the Valley, George would see his wife, Susan, and their four children one last time before Early's attempted raid on Washington, D.C., in July 1864 that was stopped at Monocracy, Maryland, by a hastily gathered Union force.

As his young son and namesake George Patton II later recalled that final glimpse of his father, he had stepped off a troop train passing through Albemarle on a rail line located at the bottom of the garden at the Meadows. After several hours, a train consisting of flat cars carrying cannon came by and stopped for the visiting colonel. "I remember seeing a soldier on a car give him a hand to get aboard and as the train moved out he was leaning against a gun and waved us goodbye. I never saw him again."

The sad denouement came September 19 in the battle of Third Winchester, pitting Sheridan against Early, two fierce bulldogs, in the wake of Early's foray into Maryland that carried him within a few miles of the Lincoln White House itself. "Outnumbered by twelve thousand, Early's army could not withstand a whirlwind Union attack on the Confederate left flank. Patton was then in command of his own 'Patton's Brigade,' and although he had survived three earlier wounds, this time his luck ran out."

Exactly how it happened is not fully known, except that "Patton's brigade was attempting to defend the left flank that was eventually crushed by Sheridan's cavalry, which captured two thousand Confederate soldiers, among them the mortally wounded George Smith Patton." He lived until September 25—apparently in the home of another cousin, Mary Williams—before succumbing, probably to fever and gangrene, at the age of thirty-one.

★★★

Additional note: The first George S. Patton, slain as a war hero, grandfather of the twentieth-century George S. Patton, is buried in Winchester's Stonewall Cemetery together with his brother Taz, also a slain war hero. Biographer D'Este provides the dramatic and somewhat bizarre story behind their joint reburial in the 1870s.

First, both bodies were removed from their original graves. George's casket was taken to meet his brother's remains as they arrived in Winchester by train. Risking arrest, a number of Confederate veterans were on hand *in uniform* to accompany the two bodies to the cemetery. Young George Patton II, now a VMI cadet, also was in attendance. It was nighttime, and they all moved in silence to the double grave site. There, the old veterans "formed an honor guard," D'Este noted.

But then the unthinkable happened. As the caskets were being lowered into their common grave, they bumped, and Waller Tazewell Patton's body broke free. It was a shock to those attending, but the result was only a temporary halt to the somber proceedings.

As those present for the nocturnal honors given the two slain warriors might have realized, and as D'Este reported, "In all, some sixteen members of the Patton family and their kin fought for the Confederacy, and three of them died in its service."

Such was the family tradition, such were the memories, imbuing the childhood—and the developing personality—of the twentieth century's Gen.

George S. Patton Jr. as he grew up in Southern California just a generation later. Even more lore and legend of the South generously was provided by real-life visits to the family of John Singleton Mosby, "Gray Ghost of the Confederacy." By this time, the widow Susan, no longer a Patton, had married George Hugh Smith, not only a good friend, former VMI classmate, and Confederate compatriot of her first husband, but the very same Colonel Smith whose Sixty-Second Virginia had been in such dire straits at New Market until rescued by the original George Patton. Susan's son George Patton II of course retained his father's name; his own child, "Georgie," would grow up with the Patton name as well…to become the most famous Patton of them all.

One reason, quite naturally, was the often-romanticized steeping he received as a child in the stories of family heroics—"tales," wrote D'Este, "in which exemplars of the Civil War like Stonewall Jackson and the Patton colonels of VMI, who died a warrior-hero's death became symbols to cherish and emulate." The family legends, he added, "were dispensed with almost evangelical fervor." Thus, "It is hardly surprising that by the age of perhaps seven he was hopelessly seduced into the conviction that his life and destiny lay in perpetuating the Patton family name and its even more valorous achievements. Old Virginia and the glory of its cause; great battles such as Bull Run and Gettysburg; the beauty and majesty of cavalrymen clothed in Confederate gray, who charged courageously into a hail of enemy fire, sabers flashing; the belief that dying for such a cause was honorable—all these images and more were indelibly carved into the psyche of the young man nightly in the living room of the Patton home."

Thus, too, did the Civil War have major impact on a major figure of the Second World War, a figure whose "veneration of his forefathers verged on obsession" and who "saw himself as the modern embodiment of his heroic Confederate antecedents."

UNION & CONFEDERATE
"Brave Fellow"

AT MALVERN HILL, EAST OF Richmond, on July 1, 1862, a young Confederate officer and his men were firing from a clump of trees and making things hot for their Union counterparts. They "kept up a fierce fire on us and actually charged out on our advance," wrote the Irish Brigade's Capt. D. P. Conyngham after the Civil War. The chief culprit was their officer, who "seemed to be a daring, reckless boy."

Conyngham said to his sergeant, a man named Driscoll, who was one of the best shots in the entire Irish Brigade, "If that officer is not taken down, many of us will fall before we pass that clump."

As so often was the case in this as well as any other war, the rule was kill or be killed.

Said Driscoll, "Leave that to me."

Up went musket to shoulder. A moment's time only to sight and aim.

The daring young officer showed himself.

"Bang went Driscoll, and over went the officer, his company at once breaking away."

As the Union men then approached and prepared to pass on by, Conyngham had an added thought. "Driscoll," he said, "see if that officer is dead—he was a brave fellow."

While the narrator of the story looked on, Driscoll approached and rolled the inert body over onto his back.

"He opened his eyes for a moment, and faintly murmured, 'Father,' and closed them forever."

Conyngham of course would never forget "the frantic grief of Driscoll," whose son "had gone south before the war."

The man's grief was "harrowing to witness"…but it would not last for long.

Minutes later their unit was ordered to charge the Rebels, and momentarily Conyngham's men left Driscoll alone to his grief. But then, "as we were closing in on the enemy, he rushed up, with his coat off, and, clutching his musket, charged right up at the enemy, calling on the men to follow. He soon fell, but jumped up again. We knew he was wounded. On he dashed, but he soon rolled over like a top. When we came up he was dead, riddled with bullets."

★★★

Additional note: This story is based on an account that apparently was first reported in *The Irish Brigade and Its Campaigns, With Some Accounts of the Corcoran Legion, and Sketches of the Principal Officers* (1867) by D. P. Conyngham, later repeated in B. A. Botkin's *A Civil War Treasury of Tales, Legends and Folklore* (1960) and James P. McPherson's *Battle Cry of Freedom: The Civil War Era* (1988).

CONFEDERATE
"Prince" John's Fall

ALREADY A SOLDIER BUT NOT yet a prominent Civil War figure, the bon vivant known to friends and enemies alike as "Prince John" succumbed to drink one night in Baltimore and woke up in Washington, D.C., the next morning... with no idea how he got there.

The same "Prince" John Magruder would perform well in the first stages of the Civil War, receiving plaudits in the Southern press for his exploits, but he then fell into a tailspin outside Richmond during the Seven Days' campaign of 1862. Fair or not, whether alcohol really was the specific problem at the Seven Days', he never quite would recover in reputation, despite subsequent success in distant Galveston, Texas.

Long before the Civil War erupted, Magruder did some serious soldiering, acquitting himself quite well. As Ezra Warner noted in his valuable compendium *Generals in Gray*, Magruder "was three times brevetted for gallant and meritorious conduct in Mexico as an artillery officer." While in Mexico, he endeared himself to Gen. Winfield Scott, his commander in chief and later head of the U.S. Army. Prior to that, the Port Royal, Virginia, native had spent two years at the University of Virginia, then switched to West Point, from which he was graduated in 1830.

Clearly he was not exactly a dewy-eyed youngster when he resigned from the U.S. Army to join the Confederate cause in 1861, thirty years–plus after leaving West Point. By this time, he had picked up the sobriquet "Prince" for his well-known love of the good life and his "princely" ways. As historian Gary W. Gallagher explained in his book *Lee and His Generals in War and Memory*, "A dark-haired, handsome, six footer of erect bearing and flawless manners, he had a profound attachment to elegant uniforms and a flair for the dramatic.... He loved the pomp of military reviews, conducting them with great panache even while on distant western duty where only a handful of people might be watching."

In like vein, Magruder's own good friend John N. Edwards observed: "Magruder was a born soldier.... He would fight all day and dance all night. He wrote love songs and sang them, and won an heiress rich beyond comparison."

Even the usually dry reference tome *Webster's American Military Biographies* devoted valuable space to mention that, after the Mexican War, Magruder spent an otherwise unremarkable tour of duty at Newport, Rhode Island, as "a great social success."

That "heiress rich beyond comparison" he married was a wealthy Baltimore merchant's daughter, but Gallagher pointed out that the high-living Magruder "relied on her to pay his debts and asked that she serve as hostess at gatherings when he returned to Baltimore on infrequent furloughs"; that after she removed to Europe with their three children, his "spendthrift habits" and his drinking "probably" were the reasons she stayed there.

As for the alleged drinking problem, there hardly can be any doubt. For example, take that morning he awoke in Washington instead of Baltimore. As Gallagher recounted the story, Magruder one night in Baltimore drank heavily, stumbled home to his hotel, and found it locked. Going to a next-door stage office, he "passed out" on top of the mail sacks.

The following morning, a stagecoach arrived to pick up the mail and a passenger going to Washington. "Thinking Magruder to be his passenger, and unable to wake him, the driver put him aboard and proceeded to Washington, where he deposited his unconscious rider on a bench outside a hotel."

When Magruder awoke, he didn't know where he was and was embarrassed to ask.

After a while, however, he came across a West Point classmate and asked him. This may have been an unfortunate choice because the officer corps of the prewar army was a small and intimate circle. "Thus," noted Gallagher, "there was sufficient knowledge of Magruder's past to give credence to rumors during and after the Seven Days that he abused the bottle."

And in that crucial campaign at the doorstep of Richmond, he clearly wasn't the steady, self-possessed tactician seen just a few weeks earlier and playing a decisive role in the Confederate victory at Big Bethel, the first fair-sized battle of the war. He also wasn't the happy warrior next seen mounting a campaign of deception and bluff with just twelve thousand men that held Union Gen. George B. McClellan's massive army at bay in Yorktown for four vital weeks.

In the Seven Days' campaign that followed, now serving under newly appointed commander Robert E. Lee, Magruder's first assignment was to hold a defensive line south of the Chickahominy River against federal pressure in the direction of Richmond and, next, to press forward…go on the offensive. But now the cocky Prince Magruder, so recently lauded in the press for his exploits in the lower Virginia Peninsula, for some reason had become shaky and uncertain in his moves.

As part explanation, Gallagher pointed out that Magruder had "slept very little for several days"; that he was suffering from a stomach ailment "made worse by the tension of holding Lee's right flank against great odds"; and that the medication he was taking for his indigestion "probably contained some form of morphine, to which he was allergic."

In sum, "This combination of fatigue, nerves, and pain, together with Magruder's inherent difficulty in functioning as a subordinate [he tended to perform more effectively when in largely independent command], contributed to a sub-par performance during the next three days."

For that matter, the widely heralded but also sleep-deprived Stonewall Jackson was another Lee subordinate who failed to follow orders and generally performed in lackluster fashion during the same Seven Days' campaign. Consider, too, the fact that none of the Confederate generals opposing McClellan's ponderous march on Richmond were accustomed to having Lee as a field commander—for the simple reason that Lee had just taken the place of the wounded Joseph E. Johnston.

Whatever the reason or combination of reasons, Magruder two or three days into the Seven Days' absolutely was not his old "princely" self. By June 30, five days after the start of the Seven Days' campaign, noted Gallagher, Magruder "displayed great nervous energy, galloping back and forth to no apparent purpose, reversing orders, and bogging down in details better handled by junior officers." When a staff officer asked if he didn't feel well, Magruder acknowledged, "I am feeling horribly." He cited his lack of sleep, two days of indigestion, and the possible allergic reaction to his medicine.

To make matters worse, Magruder would get no more sleep until three o'clock the next morning, at which time he would enjoy "his second hour's sleep in three days."

His breakfast that morning, July 1, was his first meal "in nearly twenty-four hours." Ordered to join in a coordinated attack against the Federals that day, Magruder took the wrong one of two "Quaker Roads" in the area, and thus arrived at his assigned spot far behind schedule. But Lee himself had made a major mistake. "Unbelievably," added Gallagher's account, "Lee issued no orders to William Nelson Pendleton's reserve artillery, which contained the heavy guns needed to implement the plan. Division field batteries went into action, achieved no concentration of fire, and were quickly disabled by superior Union artillery."

It was after this, late in the afternoon, that a freshly agitated Magruder finally arrived in place. "Want of sleep and the reaction to his medicine continued to take a toll. 'The wild expression of his eyes and his excited manner,' remembered one Confederate officer, 'impressed me at once with the belief that he was under the influence of some powerful stimulant, spirits or perhaps opium.'"

Meanwhile, Magruder was told that Gen. Lewis A. Armistead's troops were in pursuit of the Union's Hiram Berdan somewhere forward of the same sector. What transpired next would be a futile Confederate attack against strongly defended Malvern Hill, a "crushing repulse" for which Magruder would be blamed in many quarters.

How had things gone so badly wrong? After (and likely even *before*) the newly arrived Magruder dispatched a report to Lee by courier, confusion apparently reigned. "Back from Lee," wrote Gallagher, "came plain orders: 'General Lee expects you to advance rapidly. He says it is reported the enemy is getting off. Press forward your whole line and follow up Armistead's successes.'"

As Magruder then sent about a third of his fifteen thousand men into the advance in ragged spurts, brigades here, regiments there, three of his general officers also ordered their troops into the attack on Malvern Hill as well, but piecemeal, into the face of massed artillery—"and soon 5,000 Confederate bodies littered the slopes."

For the Confederacy, it was a horrific end to a difficult week in which "at a cost of 20,000 casualties, Lee had saved the capital and thoroughly overawed his cautious opponent without inflicting major physical damage on the Army of the Potomac." As one result, Lee came to the Confederacy's "center stage" as "the general who soon would personify the national strivings of his people."

As Gallagher also noted, that was the broad view of Seven Days'—in essence, Richmond saved, Federals in retreat.

For those interested in greater detail, however, there were other issues. What happened at Malvern Hill? On the tactical level, who should be blamed for the heavy casualties sustained in such a poorly managed attack? And on the broader, strategic level, why did the Confederates fail to close with a surprisingly compliant, withdrawing enemy and do him real damage?

The tenor of the recriminations to come was signaled that very evening, when Robert E. Lee himself appeared at Magruder's campsite even as the latter "prepared to lie down on blankets that had been spread for him." Here, Gallagher cited Magruder's staff aide John Lamb's recollection that Lee asked Magruder, "General Magruder, why did you attack?" And Magruder replied, "In obedience to your orders, twice repeated."

The very next day, apparently seeing the handwriting on the wall, Magruder told the Jefferson Davis administration he was ready to take up an earlier assignment to assume command of the Trans-Mississippi Department. "Without comment, Lee instantly relieved him of all duties with the Army of Northern Virginia."

Worse yet for Prince John, rumors now sprang up to the effect that Magruder had been drinking. Already on his way west, Magruder returned to Richmond to defend himself. Denying such talk, he produced a statement by a military doctor who had been with him and had seen no sign that he had been drinking. John Lamb likewise asserted that Magruder had been perfectly sober the day of the attack on Malvern Hill.

In the end, Prince John lost his opportunity to take over the Trans-Mississippi Department and instead was sent to the smaller, more distant District of Texas, New Mexico, and Arizona. Clearly, he had been "singled out for special blame after the Seven Days," Gallagher noted, while also pointing out that Stonewall Jackson escaped any such censure even though he hardly performed any better. It was Magruder who would be the scapegoat. "Magruder attacked at Lee's order on July 1 but failed to deliver a single powerful blow," wrote Gallagher. "That was unfortunate but typical of the overall Confederate effort throughout the Seven Days. The Confederate people may have settled on Magruder, and to lesser degree Benjamin Huger, as culprits because they could not believe Jackson, who had provided such magnificent news from the [Shenandoah] Valley in May and early June, capable of a less-than-sterling effort."

Then, too, given a choice between the flamboyant bon vivant Magruder and the ever-pious Jackson, it's easy to guess which of the two the staid Robert E. Lee would tend to favor and which he would prefer to blame for things gone wrong.

UNION
Lucky Pair

NAVAL OFFICER MOSES S. STUYVESANT was the luckiest Union sailor serving in the Civil War…or perhaps the unluckiest. Depends on how you look at it.

After all, his wooden sailing ship the USS *Cumberland* was shelled, rammed, and sunk by the Confederate ironclad *Virginia* the day before the latter clashed with the Union ironclad *Monitor* in the historic battle of Hampton Roads, the first such fight between two ironclads.

Then, again unprecedented, Stuyvesant's USS *Housatonic* was sunk by a torpedo delivered off Charleston by the Confederate submarine *Hunley*, also a first in naval history.

Once more aboard a historic vessel, this time the first ironclad to fight and capture another ironclad, he was the last man off when his monitor, the USS *Weehawken*, foundered in heavy seas and sank at Charleston with a heavy loss of life.

Just for good measure, shortly after the Civil War, his side-wheel steam gunboat, the USS *Wateree*, operating off Peru and Chile, was picked up by a tidal wave and hurled more than a quarter mile inland, there to stay...and to be turned into an inn.

All true, and all elements of Stuyvesant's colorful naval career before, during, and after the Civil War.

That career began when he entered the still-new U.S. Naval Academy at Annapolis in the 1850s, then graduated in 1860 at the age of nineteen. As a midshipman, he served aboard two warships before being assigned to the frigate *Cumberland*, which was the flagship for Commo. Garrett J. Pendergrast. Here, the young officer would serve as an aide to the commodore.

Stuyvesant still was serving aboard the aging, sail-powered warship when she was assigned to blockade duty off the Atlantic coast in 1861. "The *Cumberland*," he later wrote, "was one of the old sailing frigates, cut down or razed, as the term was, and rated in the Navy register as a sloop of war. She carried, for those days, a formidable battery, consisting of a 10-inch pivot gun forward on the spar deck, a rifled 80-pounder Dahlgren gun aft, and on the gun deck, in broadside, 22 9-inch guns." Her crew numbered a healthy 350 men.

"We had spent several months cruising, off [Cape] Hatteras, as part of the first blockading squadron organized, and upon being relieved from that duty, proceeded to Newport News [Virginia] for the winter. This was a newly formed camp on the east shore of the James River, where the latter empties into Hampton Roads, and about four miles from Fortress Monroe."

Here the powerfully armed *Cumberland* remained while, just ten miles away, at the former U.S. Navy base at Norfolk, Confederate workmen hustled to finish building the ironclad *Virginia* on the hulk of the Union's former frigate USS *Merrimack*, which had been scuttled and sunk at dockside just before the Federals burned and abandoned the Norfolk Navy Yard.

Aboard the *Cumberland* during those slow winter months, added Stuyvesant in a postwar paper for the Military Order of the Loyal Legion of the United States (MOLLUS; see http://suvew.org/mollus/warpapers), "life was made interesting, if not anxious, by almost daily reports of the progress toward completion of a powerful ironclad vessel being constructed in Norfolk."

When the newly built ironclad *Virginia* emerged on "a bright spring day" (March 8, 1862), she had a choice of engaging one or more of five Union warships standing by in the waterway, all wooden, two of them steam-powered. As her first victim, the *Virginia* chose the sail-powered *Cumberland*, although the iron-covered newcomer had to chug past the sail-powered frigate USS *Congress* to reach her.

The truly historic encounter that resulted minutes later, CSS *Virginia* versus USS *Cumberland*, was over in equally short time. The wooden *Cumberland*, both shelled and rammed by the iron-covered hybrid, never had a chance. "Our shot, striking the inclined sides of the *Merrimac*, bounded up and flew over, dropping into the water beyond." The ironclad's shot, on the other hand, penetrated the old wooden ship repeatedly, with terrible damage and carnage resulting at every salvo.

Even so, *Cumberland*'s flag—by Stuyvesant's order, apparently—was still flying as she sank, "by the head." More than a third of the *Cumberland*'s crew went down with their ship, Stuyvesant estimated, many of them fighting to the end.

Not yet through for the day, *Virginia* turned back to deal with the *Congress*, which had managed to run aground in the interim. Pounding the stricken warship almost at leisure, *Virginia* forced her surrender, then set her afire with hot shot. The resultant flames ate away at her innards for hours, until finally igniting her powder magazines and blowing up the ship about two o'clock the next morning.

The Confederate ironclad probably could have done similar damage to the steam frigate USS *Minnesota*, which also had run aground during the previous day's action, but after dealing with the *Congress* and then making what historians call a mere "demonstration" in the direction of the *Minnesota*, the *Virginia* returned to its berth with no more ado for that historic day.

One of the last to leave his sinking ship, meanwhile, Stuyvesant was promoted from master to lieutenant at age twenty-one. He next found himself aboard the Union monitor *Weehawken*, widely noted for her capture of the Confederate ironclad *Atlanta* off Georgia in June 1863, apparently as the first ironclad to capture an ironclad.

"After this victory, which made her the object of great fame," notes the Naval Historical Center (www.history.navy.mil/photos-/sh-usn/usnsh-w /wehawkn.htm), "*Weehawken* returned to the Charleston area, where she spent the summer of 1863 participating in regular bombardments of Confederate positions ashore. These greatly assisted in the capture of Fort Wagner on Morris Island and reduced Fort Sumter to rubble, although that position remained as strong or stronger than ever."

By December 1863, if not sooner, Stuyvesant was serving aboard the *Weehawken* as she was moored off Morris Island. She had undergone repairs after running aground during her attacks against Rebel positions the previous September and now, in rising seas on December 6, she "began to take on water forward," notes the Naval Historical Center account. "Due to faulty trim and debris in her bilges, the influx overwhelmed her pumps and the ship sank rapidly."

More than thirty of her crew, officers and men, went down with the stricken ironclad—and Stuyvesant, reports the MOLLUS account, was the last to leave the ship alive.

He then, just weeks later, managed to escape the blockading steam-powered sloop *Housatonic*'s grim fate when she was sunk by the *H. L. Hunley* off Charleston the night of February 17, 1864. Thus, notes the MOLLUS account, "With incredible bad luck, this survivor of the first ship sunk by an ironclad [the *Cumberland*] also became a survivor of the first ship sunk by a submarine."

A hop, skip, and a jump later, the Civil War well behind him by now, Stuyvesant was assigned to the steam gunboat *Wateree*, an oceangoing side-wheeler, as her executive officer when an earthquake in the area of the Port of Arica, Peru (later Chile), on August 15, 1868, created a gigantic tidal wave that lifted the 1,173-ton vessel more than five hundred yards inland. Although the gunboat was "deposited relatively intact," says the Naval Historical Center, refloating and repairing her "would have been impossibly expensive." As a result, she was sold. After which, adds the *Dictionary of American Naval Fighting Ships*, "apparently her hulk was converted to living spaces ashore, and the former warship served as an inn for some years thereafter" (www.history.navy .mil/danfs/w/wateree.htm).

Perhaps wisely, Stuyvesant left the navy later that year to become a lawyer, first in California and then Iowa, before finally settling down in St. Louis as a businessman. He died there in 1906.

★★★

Additional note: Oddly enough, Thomas O. Selfridge Jr., a fellow officer and shipmate of Stuyvesant from the *Cumberland*, also would have the bad (or extraordinarily good) luck to emerge from the Civil War as a survivor of three sunken ships, two of which he served as commanding officer. The first of course was the *Cumberland*, and the third was the timber-clad gunboat *Conestoga*. In between came the river gunboat *Cairo*.

Selfridge also had been one of the last officers to leave the *Cumberland*, for which he commanded the forward battery of guns. He made further history when he took temporary command of the ironclad *Monitor* two days later, or just one day after her historic battle in Hampton Roads against CSS *Virginia*. The Union ironclad's commanding officer, Lt. John Lorimer Worden, had been wounded and partially blinded when a shell struck the *Monitor*'s pilot-house in the fray of March 9, 1862.

Just weeks later, Selfridge, the son of a rear admiral, was commanding the Union gunboat *Cairo* on the Mississippi and its tributaries. He lost his ship a few months later (December 12, 1862) when he somewhat rashly steamed into the Yazoo River, waters known to be mined by the Confederates. He also was in command of the USS *Conestoga*, once a civilian side-wheel towboat and now converted into a timber-clad river gunboat, when she accidentally collided with the Union ram USS *General Price* (previously the *Confederate General Sterling Price*) and sank in early 1864.

"Thus," wrote Selfridge later, "for the third time in the war, I had had my ship suddenly sunk under me." He was struck by the "strange coincidence" that all three ships had names beginning with the letter *C*.

Selfridge, having survived these encounters, remained in the navy until retiring in 1898 at the same rank as his father, rear admiral. His last duty assignment was as commander in chief of the navy's European squadron. The forty-seven-year navy veteran produced a memoir for G. P. Putnam before he died in 1924, two days short of his eighty-eighth birthday.

CONFEDERATE
Monument to a Reb General

STANDING TALL AND RESOLUTE IN Judiciary Square in Washington, D.C., capital of the nation today, the Union capital during the Civil War as well, is the statue of Albert Pike, New England–born thinker extraordinaire, antisecessionist, poet, vigorous advocate of Freemasonry, teacher, lawyer, newspaper editor… and Civil War brigadier general.

Confederate general, to be precise, a rare creature to be found among the capital city's outdoor statuary.

That very same statue, by the way, proclaims Pike was "philosopher, jurist, orator, author, poet, scholar, soldier."

As the Smithsonian Institution's CivilWarStudies.org website adds, his many enemies could append the description with "libertine, traitor, glutton" and military "incompetent."

To that unappealing list, one could also add "wife-deserter" and possible (but unproven) creator of early Ku Klux Klan ritual.

And liar as well? According to the same Smithsonian source, Pike claimed to have attended Harvard, "but no record of it exists." Still, he undeniably was a brilliant scholar, even if self-taught, who "could converse in Sanskrit, Hebrew, Greek, Latin and French." And many years after the Civil War, Harvard apparently did grant him an honorary degree.

Pike was not always so brilliant at generalship. In the Mexican War, chiefly at the battle of Buena Vista, he "had taken a creditable part," conceded Ezra Warner in his definitive *Generals in Gray*, but Pike's later Civil War performance "was unfortunate to say the least."

In the first place, he only "incidentally" became a Confederate brigadier, added Warner, explaining, "An avowed Whig and anti-secessionist, he was a prominent lawyer and large land owner in Arkansas in 1861, and cast his lot with the South rather than desert his friends and property." Further, he was commissioned a general "to negotiate treaties with the Indians west of the Arkansas River and ally them to the Confederate cause."

With Pike leading them into battle in February 1862 at Elkhorn Tavern (Pea Ridge), his Indians "exhibited dubious conduct," Warner pointed out. They were accused of desertion and "scalping and defiling the bodies of the Union dead," added the Smithsonian account. Pike himself said that his Indian followers would not march with him until they were paid government allotments. Then, in the fighting that came later, some of his Indian allies mounted a charge "with loud yells" and captured a Union battery of three guns. Around the "taken battery" soon after, however, "was a mass of Indians and others in the utmost confusion, all talking, riding this way and that, and listening to no orders from any one," he noted in his after-action report. Pike added that he sent a captain "always conspicuous for gallantry and coolness" to the battery with orders to turn the guns toward another Union battery, "but he could not induce a single man to assist in doing so."

With two leading Confederate generals killed in the same battle, within minutes of each other (Ben McCulloch and James McQueen McIntosh, brother of Union general John Baillie McIntosh), the engagement was a significant defeat for the 17,000 attacking Southerners, even though the casualties of 800 on the Rebel side and 1,384 for the 11,000 Federals were fairly light in comparison to those of many battles yet to come.

For his part, Pike later argued that his Indians originally had been asked only to defend their own territory. In any case, fairly or not, Pike's wartime performance prompted at least one fellow Confederate general, Douglas Cooper, to complain that the Massachusetts native was "either insane or untrue to the South." Other officers, following a different tack entirely, had him temporarily imprisoned on charges of misappropriating funds, notes the Smithsonian report.

This was not the first alleged black mark against Pike's character, nor the last, it seems. A schoolteacher early in his adult life, he "left for the wilds of the west after rumors of affairs made it impossible for him to remain in Massachusetts," says the Smithsonian account. After the Elkhorn Tavern debacle, he resigned from the Confederate army and lived for the rest of the war in what Warner termed "semi-retirement." With the hostilities ended in 1865, he "abandoned his wife in Arkansas and roamed the east and the west practicing law, writing poetry, editing a newspaper, and reputedly creating the rituals of the Ku Klux Klan for Nathan Bedford Forrest," adds the Smithsonian.

He survived a postwar federal indictment charging him with treason, lived for a short time in Memphis (also the home of Forrest), and then, his civil rights restored, moved to Washington. There, a long-haired, giant figure at six feet and three hundred pounds, Pike "soon added more ammunition for his detractors to use against him by carrying on with the vivacious 19-year-old sculptress, Vinnie Ream, forty years his junior."

Far more positive is the viewpoint of the University of Texas's encyclopedic Handbook of Texas Online, which calls Pike "one of the most remarkable figures in American history." Citing his "adventurous spirit" rather than the Smithsonian's rumored scandals, the handbook reports that Pike left Massachusetts as a relatively young man to become an important Wild West pioneer. Traveling to Independence, Missouri, in 1831, he joined a party of traders and hunters headed for New Mexico. "On the trail, his horse broke away, leaving him to walk the remaining 500 miles to Taos," notes the handbook account. "His party was caught, as well, in a ferocious snowstorm that caused a layover of five days and froze many of the horses."

Undeterred by such hardships, Pike then joined another expedition traveling to Santa Fe, moved on in 1832 to the scarcely known Texas panhandle, next "crossed Oklahoma, and finally arrived at Fort Smith, Arkansas, having traveled 1,300 miles, 650 on foot, and experienced many hardships and exciting adventures."

What made it all so important, historically speaking, was that he wrote about his travels in narrative, short story, and poetic form, first for the *Little Rock (Arkansas) Advocate*, then in a book now considered "one of the most important descriptions of early New Mexico and far West Texas."

In Arkansas, meanwhile, Pike married, became owner of the *Advocate*, then turned to the law, and soon was "regarded as one of the most capable attorneys in the Southwest." He took time out for his "credible" service in the Mexican War and for his not-so-credible Civil War service. At Elkhorn Tavern–Pea Ridge, the handbook concedes, Pike's "Indian troops performed disgracefully, taking scalps and then routing in the face of federal artillery." By the end of the war, incidentally, the retired general had become an associate justice of the Arkansas Supreme Court. Along the way, too, back in the Mexican War, he had fought a harmless duel with future Arkansas governor (and later Civil War general) John Selden Roane.

As another aspect of his prewar days in Arkansas, reported Dr. Jack Welsh in his book *Medical Histories of Confederate Generals*, the usually overweight Pike "would starve himself when plagued with a troublesome [legal] case." On the other hand, "When the problem was resolved, he would fill a wagon with food and along with a cook go into the woods. There he would gorge himself around the clock for days."

As mentioned earlier ("Confederate: Song Is Born," page 30), the ubiquitous Pike, for many years an active Freemason, also managed to provide a set of poetic lyrics to "Dixie" that the Texas Handbook calls "perhaps the best of the many versions of the famous Southern anthem."

Almost all sources agree that in the immediate postwar years, Pike was viewed with some suspicion both in the North and the South. His property "confiscated," says the handbook, Pike became "something of a wanderer." Moving to New York in 1865, he feared arrest "for inciting the Indians to revolt and so fled to Canada." Pardoned by President Andrew Johnson, he returned to Arkansas, "but was charged with treason." Soon vindicated, "Pike moved first to Memphis, where he practiced law and edited the Memphis *Appeal*, and then to Washington, D.C., where he continued his practice and edited the *Patriot*."

By now he was well known for his work as a Freemason. "For many years he was engaged in rewriting the rituals of the society, and [his] *Morals and Dogma of the Ancient and Accepted Scottish Rite of Freemasonry*…remains one of the standard works on the subject," notes the handbook. In addition, "Pike's reputation as a poet was considerable, and his contributions to *Blackwood's Edinburgh Magazine* moved its editor to place him 'in the highest order of his country's poets.'"

Pike died, not so incidentally, in the house of the Scottish Rite Temple in Washington in 1891. According to the Smithsonian account, the Daughters of the Confederacy and the Masons joined forces to install his statue in Washington's future Judiciary Square in 1901, with at least one speaker predicting that "the name of Albert Pike will grow bright as the ages roll by." Today, however, probably few passing by the site realize who or what the name Albert Pike once meant.

UNION
Jules Verne and
an Alligator

JULES VERNE WOULD HAVE LOVED the Union submarine USS *Alligator*. In fact, it's quite possible that, from afar, he did.

After all, it was his own onetime math instructor, Brutus De Villeroi, who designed the Union navy's first submarine, the forty-seven-foot *Alligator*, launched at Philadelphia on May 1, 1862, at the height of the Civil War. And, it was just eight years later, in 1870, that science-fiction author Verne published his famous novel, *20,000 Leagues Under the Sea*.

Historians like to speculate that Verne's fictional submarine *Nautilus* possibly was inspired by De Villeroi's real-life submersible creations, such as the *Alligator*. Even without a Verne "connection," however, the story of the *Alligator* is a dramatic but often forgotten footnote to the long struggle between the Union and Confederate navies for control of the ocean, bay, and river waters of the Atlantic Coast.

Far better known these days is the fact that the Confederacy developed its own underwater boat, the *H. L. Hunley*, which then actually sank a Union warship off Charleston, South Carolina, in 1864 before carrying its crew to a deepwater grave in the aftermath of the same engagement. As a major coup by marine salvagers, the *Hunley* was located in the 1990s and then, in 2000, raised nearly intact.

The *Alligator* also was deployed for combat with an equally disastrous result for the vessel but fortunately *not* for its crew of twelve.

First, of course, came its creation by the French immigrant De Villeroi, who listed his occupation for a mid-nineteenth-century census as "natural genius."

He in fact was a printer's son, an inventor and underwater diver who immigrated to the Philadelphia area sometime before the Civil War. Genius or not, he had acquired the means to experiment with submersibles in the nearby Delaware River, but the Philadelphia police interrupted one such trial in 1861 by confiscating his boat on suspicion of "treasonable activities," according to a contemporary newspaper. The same excitable account in the city's *Evening Bulletin* said the strange thirty-three-foot vessel looked like an "enormous cigar" with bull's-eye portholes that gave it "a particular wide-awake appearance."

It turned out that the Union navy—at that initial stage, in the person of Capt. Samuel F. DuPont, commandant of the Philadelphia Navy Yard—was intrigued by De Villeroi's creation. The startling result, after various studies, followed by contract disputes and many construction delays, was the launch of the innovative *Alligator* (first called the Submarine Propeller) the next year as the U.S. Navy's first real submarine.

Wasting no time, the Union sent its submarine to the Hampton Roads area of Virginia in the same spring of 1862 for shallow-water rather than deepwater operations. The initial idea was to use the green-hued *Alligator* against the Confederacy's vaunted ironclad *Virginia* and, next, to clear river obstructions and blow up a railroad bridge on the Appomattox River just above its conjunction with the James at City Point (now Hopewell), close to Petersburg. That operation would have come during the Peninsula campaign, which climaxed in June 1862 with the Seven Days' battles just outside Richmond, but the water that far upriver left little room for the underwater boat to submerge, a drawback rendering it vulnerable to artillery fire and possible capture.

Still, the Union had a technological wonder on its hands, an operational prototype in many ways for the navy's submarines of today.

Among the firsts established by the *Alligator*, according to the National Marine Sanctuaries, the Union's underwater boat was the first submarine to boast onboard air compressors and an air scrubbing (purifying) system. It also was the first submarine ordered built for the navy; it was the first deployed to a combat area; it was the first to be commanded alternately by both a naval officer and a civilian; it soon would be the first to undergo overhaul in a U.S. naval shipyard, and it would set precedent as the first such undersea craft to have an "underway test" before the eyes of a sitting president—Abraham Lincoln, of course.

Looking like both a whale and a cigar, the boat boasted two hatches—one forward on the upper side of the hull for normal crew access and a second on the lower bow for a diver's exit and entry underwater. Just inside this hatch was the diver's airlock (a la Jules Verne's *Nautilus*, remember?).

Just in front of the upper hatch was a dome-shaped conning tower equipped with four glass windows, allowing a view in all four directions—forward, aft, and to both sides.

A few other innovations associated with the *Alligator* were a real disconnect from the norms of today, however. Most sensationally—incredibly when you think about it—the *Alligator*'s propulsion system, for both surface and underwater operation, at first consisted of nothing but oars. Thus, her crew of twelve would include "oarsmen."

Then, too, another surprise for most of us today, the underwater boat's mode of attack required a diver who would leave the underwater craft by means of the air lock, plant an explosive device on the side of the target, then return to his mother ship for a quick, undetected getaway. Thus the *Alligator*, say the experts at the National Marine Sanctuary agency, would go down in history as the first submarine to be armed with electrically detonated limpet mines. The South's *Hunley*, by contrast, was armed with a torpedo-like mine at the end of a spar protruding from the mother ship...but that sort of proximity to the explosion probably is what doomed the *Hunley* when she sank the USS *Housatonic* in 1864.

Meanwhile, the Union's new submarine wasn't quite ready for sea duty until after the Confederacy's *Virginia* had tangled with the USS *Monitor* at Hampton Roads—a historic and unprecedented collision of iron-skinned ships that ended essentially in a draw. With Union troops reoccupying Norfolk and moving up the peninsula toward Richmond, the Confederacy's *Virginia* was scuttled and blown up in the lower James River by her crew.

Even though the Union's innovative submarine could not now hunt down the *Virginia*, it proceeded to Hampton Roads anyway with a civilian, Samuel Eakin, as its acting master. Next placed under the command of the North Atlantic Blockading Squadron's Louis M. Goldsborough, *Alligator* for a short time was moored alongside the USS *Satellite*. The submarine would look to *Satellite* for meals and various supplies, also a significant innovation. As noted by former U.S. Navy submariner James L. Christley in an article for the Internet-based NavyAndMarine.org publication *OnDeck*, this established another first, the concept of "the forward area-based submarine tender."

Since the upper James was too shallow for safe operation of the undersea boat, the navy now sent it back to the Washington Navy Yard for further evaluation—and thought.

Lt. Thomas O. Selfridge (see "Union: Lucky Pair," page 81) "took the boat out several times…and issued a report on the 8th of August 1862," wrote Christley, a submarine historian who has been researching the *Alligator* story for years. "He was not optimistic as he had trouble controlling it while running submerged and could not get respectable speed surfaced or submerged." To this skeptical report someone—possibly Commo. Joseph Smith, chief of the navy's Bureau of Yards and Docks—hand-penned the notation "The enterprise is a failure."

As events turned out, however, the navy still had hopes for the *Alligator*'s usefulness. In the winter of 1862, a hand-cranked screw propeller replaced the oars as the submarine's still-primitive means of propulsion. Then, "in a test witnessed by President Lincoln, on the 18th of March 1863 the boat made four knots," double its previous best speed.

Now, Commodore Smith was told that the undersea vessel had performed admirably, noted Christley.

By chance, too, Samuel F. DuPont (the same who eighteen months before had been so greatly intrigued by De Villeroi's experimental underwater craft) was at this time off the coast of South Carolina with the federal ships enforcing the blockade of Charleston and preparing to attack the key harbor. But he was unhappy with the threatening appearance of two Confederate ironclads, the CSS *Chicora* and *Palmetto State*.

He needed a warship that could slip into the inner harbor and attack those dangerous foes at their moorings.

He realized this would be the perfect assignment for *Alligator*.

At his request, the Union submarine soon—by the end of March—was on its way south. After clearing the Potomac River and the Chesapeake Bay, the whalelike tube was under tow by a chartered wooden steamer that encountered gale-force winds on April 2. The port towline snapped. As the wallowing boat then heaved and pitched uncontrollably, the tow ship itself was in danger of foundering in the heavy seas.

With night coming, there seemed no choice but to let the *Alligator* go. And so, cast loose fifty or so miles south of Cape Hatteras, the Union's prototype submarine, at least forty years ahead of its time, disappeared in the tossing waters, never to be seen again. Thankfully, with none of the crew aboard, nobody was lost.

★★★

Additional note: With the CSS *Hunley*'s undersea grave located in recent years and that hull recovered from the watery depths, the navy's Office of Naval

Research, together with the National Oceanic and Atmospheric Administration (NOAA)'s Office of National Marine Sanctuaries and the Navy and Marine Living History Association (NMLHA), has mounted a cooperative search to "unlock the secrets of the USS *Alligator*" by locating its grave in the Atlantic. This would be a real needle-in-the haystack task, since the last known position of the *Alligator* and its tow ship together, taken at noon April 2, was lat 34.43, lon 75.20, but it wasn't until 6:00 p.m. that same day that the towed *Alligator* was cut free. Since the submarine was sealed tight against leaks, it presumably didn't go down on the spot but most likely floated and was buffeted for some time before finally sinking. Meanwhile, when the gale blew itself out at 6:00 p.m. the next day, the tow ship itself had been "beaten north and was near Cape Henry [Virginia], where she had begun her voyage," notes the Marine Sanctuaries website about the *Alligator* (www.sanctuaries.noaa.gov/alligator /report1.html).

The big news of recent years in this regard was Marine Sanctuary researcher Catherine Marzin's discovery in the French naval archives of De Villeroi's own sketches for his *Bateau Sous-Marine* ("Submarine Ship"). "It's like finding a photograph of a person you're doing historical research on, but you have no idea what they look like," said Christley. Finding those blueprints, he added, "was an absolute jewel in the crown."

The blueprints could provide clues as to how long the prototype submarine might have lasted in the storm-tossed seas off Cape Hatteras, clues in turn that could indicate where it might have gone under.

Meanwhile, as noted by Christley in his *OnDeck* article, the Confederate submarine *H. L. Hunley* was only a bit more than half as long as the Union submarine, but in so many other respects the two vessels are similar. As he points out, one possible explanation simply is that their parallel development at almost the same moment in time was strictly coincidental—the old story of great minds running along the same track. The other possibility would be that the Confederacy was relying upon spies who were providing details of the Union's work on *Alligator*.

"No documentary evidence has come to light as yet that either of the inventors/builders even knew of the other's design details," wrote Christley. Thus, in his view, "It is a unique testament to the American spirit and talent for technological innovation that the first two submarines used in wartime should look and operate so much alike."

CONFEDERATE

Dogged by Poor Health

AS THE CIVIL WAR PROGRESSED, it's a wonder that the leading Confederate generals could keep on their feet. Or, in some cases, their horse. Often they didn't.

Battle wounds of course were frequently to blame for the poor physical condition of this general or that one. But other health factors also took a toll. Take Robert E. Lee, for instance.

Only in his fifties during the war, Lee escaped the usual injuries inflicted by shot or shell, but he did have his mishaps, along with nagging and often debilitating ailments. Chief among the mishaps, he suffered a fall at Stewart's Farm, Virginia, on August 31, 1862, that resulted in one hand being sprained and a bone being broken in the other.

How did it happen? So simply, really. At someone's warning cry, "Yankee cavalry!" Lee's famous horse Traveller suddenly shied. The general, standing next to his mount, also startled, lurched forward to grab the horse's bridle, tripped, lost his balance, and fell forward. As anyone would have done, he put out his hands to break his fall. (And no Yankee cavalry in sight after all!)

His hands were placed in splints, but that meant Lee couldn't ride a horse for more than a week, and the timing couldn't have been worse. The injury came between the Union's retreat from Second Bull Run (Second Manassas) the night of August 30 and the battle of Chantilly on September 1, both in Northern Virginia and both quickly followed on September 4 by Lee's first invasion of the North at the head of the Army of Northern Virginia. By September 17 he was embroiled in the battle of Antietam, the bloodiest single day of battle during the entire war.

If Lee's hand injuries seemed to come at an inopportune moment, this wasn't the first time that physical impairment struck him during wartime. During the Mexican War, just before the American attack on Chapultepec, on September 13, 1847, "he was almost paralyzed by the strain," noted Dr. Jack D. Welsh in his 1995 book *Medical Histories of Confederate Generals*. That Lee was at one point that day "close to collapse," according to Lee's eminent biographer Douglas Southall Freeman, probably was due to the fact "he had been forty-eight hours without sleep." As the action proceeded, added Freeman's account, "strain and sleeplessness almost paralyzed Lee," and, "it was with the greatest difficulty that he kept his saddle." The then-young officer sustained a slight wound during the assault but "did not even stop to have it dressed." Shortly afterward, still on his horse but now as escort to Gen. Winfield Scott, Lee fainted dead away—"for the first and only time in his life," said Freeman.

Moving on to June 1862, right after Lee assumed command of the Army of Northern Virginia, he not only led the defense of Richmond by aggressively repulsing large Union forces during the Seven Days' campaign to the east of the Confederate capital, he also caught a bothersome cold, which he blamed on "being too heavily clad" for the hot weather that month, reported Welsh. Lee still didn't feel well for the first few days of July.

Then, in late August, came the injuries to his hands, from which he did not recover sufficiently to resume signing his name with his right hand until at least early October. But worse, far worse than such nuisance impairments, came a real emotional shock for the Confederate leader. Late that same month, October 1862, his second daughter, twenty-three-year-old Anne Carter Lee, came down with typhoid fever and died while visiting the springs in Warren County, North Carolina, with her mother and three sisters after a rare family reunion in Richmond.

Naturally, this was a terrible shock to all in the family. "I cannot express the anguish I feel at the death of my sweet Annie," the absent Lee wrote to his wife, Mary. The same letter underscored the pain and sacrifice that the long absences of his military profession imposed. "To know that I shall never see her again on earth," the general added, "that her place in our circle, *which I had always hoped one day to enjoy* [emphasis added], is forever vacant, is agonizing in the extreme."

Lee, who couldn't attend his daughter's funeral because of the press of his duties, nonetheless seems to have escaped additional medical problems of note for the next few months, but a "bad" cold developed in early April 1863, "aggravated by living in a tent," observed Welsh. Moving into a house to recuperate, Lee "did not feel very sick, [but] he had paroxysms of sharp pains in the chest, back and arms associated with some fever." Freeman and other historians have suggested the pain might have been indication of angina, heart-associated chest pain.

While confined, Lee did his daily paperwork, but he didn't ride a horse again until April 11, and even then "his legs were weak and his pulse was about ninety per minute." Both the pain and his cough disappeared the next day, April 12. Returning to camp—and the tent—on April 16, he "was still feeble and could do little."

History of course will record that just two weeks later, on May 3–4, 1863, he led his outnumbered army against a Union force entrenched at Chancellorsville, a major battle of the war...and a victory for Lee despite the loss of Stonewall Jackson in the same battle.

Now came Lee's second invasion of the North, capped by the three-day battle of Gettysburg, July 1–3, 1863. During the crucial battle, "Lee had diarrhea and possibly a recurrence of malaria [probably contracted in Baltimore in 1849]."

After returning to Virginia in retreat, Lee suffered a series of chronic health problems, while the Confederacy, after its watershed defeats both at Gettysburg in the east and Vicksburg in the west, conducted what amounted to a holding action until the war ended with Lee's surrender at Appomattox Court House in April 1865.

At the start of this difficult period, according to Welsh, the venerated Confederate leader suffered from "a rheumatic malady" and "experienced increasing failure of strength." He may not have recovered completely from his illness of the previous spring, and after futilely asking to be relieved of command, he contracted another "severe" cold in the fall of 1863 that "exacerbated the rheumatism in his back."

It was all downhill from there.

"The intense pain when riding his horse prompted him to use a spring wagon that on rough roads was almost as painful as horseback riding.... The violent back pains were attributed variously to lumbago, sciatica, or rheumatism. Attributing these symptoms to angina, as has been done by later writers, does not seem to be correct," Welsh observed.

Soon, Lee was confined to his tent, unable to mount his horse at all—"and when he did, every motion gave him pain." That was in October 1863, but in November he did ride "a great deal," albeit with some pain and stiffness.

In December, however, "he seemed to be aging hourly, and his hair and beard turned white." He intermittently suffered from "sharp paroxysmal pain" in his left side.

Moving on to May 1864, Lee apparently weathered the terribly trying battles of the Wilderness and Spotsylvania without obvious health impairment, but on the night of May 23, not long after those two bloodbaths and just days before the carnage at Cold Harbor, he "became very sick...with violent intestinal complaints that one observer said was bilious dysentery." He was even worse on May 25, staying in his tent, and on May 29, "he was so sick he could hardly leave headquarters." Two days later, just in time to brace for Ulysses S. Grant's attack at Cold Harbor, Lee "had improved enough…to get about in a carriage, and he was taking some brandy that had been sent to him."

As biographer Freeman pointed out, however, Lee's violent intestinal illness may have kept him from turning the tables on Grant at a key point during this same series of battles. Discussing their maneuvers at the North Anna River between the battles of Spotsylvania and Cold Harbor, Freeman said that for a few hours on May 24, "opportunity beckoned." More specifically, a Lee feeling well enough to organize a strong attack "perhaps" would have "crushed" the Union Second Corps on his right or the Union Fifth Corps to his left, but with every hour that passed, "as the Union entrenchments rose his chances of success grew less."

The next day, when he felt even worse and remained in his tent, he received reports and again continued with his correspondence, "in which there was not even a hint that he was sick." But his close associates knew better. As he felt his opportunity to close successfully with Grant "slipping away," he "had a violent scene" with his aide, Col. C. S. Venable. "We must strike them a blow!" he "broke out vehemently." And to his doctor he declared, "If I can get one more pull at [Grant], I will defeat him!"

There was a silver lining to the outcome, albeit a temporary one. Lee had failed to force Grant into battle under Lee's terms, true, but "strategically," Lee's operations on the North Anna forced Grant to relinquish any thoughts of assaulting Richmond directly from the north. Instead, he must continue to slide around Lee's eastern flanks until he fetched up, finally, at Petersburg, to begin the lengthy siege of that rail hub just below Richmond. Thus, a mixed blessing, Lee had bought himself—and the Confederacy—more time…but only prolonged the war in the process.

For the last months of war, during which Lee personally shared the deprivations of the months-long siege of Petersburg, "there was a continuation of the vague sciatica, lumbago, or rheumatism," reported Welsh. After the war, Lee grew progressively more feeble, may have developed rheumatic heart disease, often lived in pain, and finally died in late 1870. The doctors at the time blamed "congestion of the brain" as the cause of death. In Welsh's opinion, "Lee had heart disease, an ischemic stroke and probably had aspiration pneumonia as a terminal event."

Meanwhile, others among the major Confederate generals had health problems too.

- The unfortunate A. P. Hill, while a cadet at West Point, picked up an active case of gonorrhea that plagued him the rest of his life. Then, too, he contracted typhoid while serving in the Mexican War and possibly yellow fever while in Florida during the 1850s. During the Civil War, he was several times incapacitated by illnesses that likely resulted from his venereal infection and its later complications, such as impaired renal function and uremia. Often unable to sit on a horse due to pelvic pain, he was sick the first day of battle at Gettysburg. Hill was temporarily paralyzed in the legs when they were struck by a projectile at Chancellorsville. He was shot and killed at Petersburg in the last days of the war, struck through the heart.

- Pierre Gustave Toutant Beauregard, also a Mexican War veteran, entered the Civil War with a history of illnesses from fever and ague (malarial-type fevers and chills), especially in cold weather. He "was sick" when he took twenty thousand troops into battle at First Bull Run, July 21, 1861. He underwent throat surgery in Richmond in January 1862, set off for his new posting in Kentucky in February, and was twice laid up by throat ailments on the way. He was "still ill" when he took command of the Confederate troops at Shiloh after the death of Albert Sidney Johnston—who, incidentally, may have bled to death because he didn't tie off a leg wound with the tourniquet he carried in his pocket. For Beauregard, meanwhile, it was much the same story throughout the war—fevers, throat ailments, and colds that laid him low time after time.

- The unpopular Braxton Bragg "was very thin, stooped, and had a sickly, cadaverous appearance." He suffered from chronic migraine headaches, "stomach trouble, and generally poor health, in part due to "chronic dysentery." During the Mexican War, he was so disliked by his own troops that they "made two attempts to assassinate him," each time exploding an artillery shell next to his bed. Somehow Bragg escaped both incidents unharmed. During the Civil War, however, his staff apparently cared enough about him to worry "that his mental and physical condition would prevent him from eating adequately."

Then, too, in the spring and early summer of 1863, "a siege of boils and chronic diarrhea…culminated in a general breakdown of his physical condition." He asserted that he was recovered in July, "but in fact was in such poor health that he was barely able to continue his duties."

In further fact, "accompanied by Mrs. Bragg, he spent about a week in the middle of August in the hospital at Cherokee Springs, Georgia, in an effort to recuperate." Then came the battle of Chickamauga in the second half of September, a victory to Bragg's credit, followed by his loss at Chattanooga in October…followed by another recuperative period in December 1863, this time at Warm Springs, Georgia, many years later to be made famous as a restorative watering hole for the polio-stricken Franklin D. Roosevelt.

• Stonewall Jackson, as is well known, died after he was shot by mistake and wounded in the arm and hand by his own men at Chancellorsville, but he, too, had various health problems beforehand. According to Welsh's analysis, Jackson contracted malaria at the age of twelve, he was rendered partially deaf by a throat-and-ear infection in 1857, his eyes were so weak he had trouble reading in artificial light, and he was constantly bothered by indigestion. He also was a bit eccentric and even obsessive about his health. "He never ate pepper because it supposedly produced weakness of his left leg, and chronic constipation caused him to ingest large amounts of water. For a time he ate only while standing as an effort to improve his digestion by 'straightening the digestive tract.'" He probably suffered from acid reflux irritation of the esophagus, but many of his complaints disappeared once he took to the field during the Civil War. Even so, he still was often seen "sucking lemons, although no one knew how he obtained them."

For all his peculiarities, Jackson suffered more than one bona fide injury as a result of his wartime service, starting with a painful but relatively minor wound to his left hand at First Bull Run (First Manassas) in July 1861—the very time and place that he acquired the nickname "Stonewall."

"The ball had hit one side of the middle finger…and had carried off a small piece of bone," wrote Welsh. The upper part of the finger had been "split longitudinally," and the upper joint was left exposed.

The well-known doctor Hunter McGuire applied a splint held in place with adhesive plaster, then added a lint-and-water dressing. Told to keep his injured finger wet with cold water, Jackson later "was seen pouring cup after cup of water over his hand for several hours at a time." In another painful episode, Jackson was badly stunned in September 1862 when his horse reared and fell over backward with him in the saddle. The following January, "he developed a severe earache and had to move from his cold tent into a small office building for three months."

Then came Chancellorsville on May 2, 1863…and the unhappy mistaken shooting that led to his death eight days later. Suffering one gunshot wound to the right hand and two to his left arm, he lost the arm to amputation two inches below the shoulder. Moved to a safe location to the rear, he appeared to be recovering—his wounds definitely were healing—when he contracted pneumonia, weakened, and then died on May 10.

- Nathan Bedford Forrest, another Confederate general of note, managed to survive a series of health problems, gunshot wounds, and really serious bumps and bruises that would have killed many other men. The unschooled cavalry leader, a farm boy grown into a slaveholding plantation owner, already was a survivor of a rough life before he voluntarily entered the Civil War as a private. By 1861, he had survived a bout with typhoid that killed five of his siblings, a steamboat explosion, and a shoot-out in Hernando, Mississippi, in which he and three assailants all were wounded.

After raising a cavalry troop at his own expense in the early months of the war, he briefly was knocked out of action by chills and fever. Next, in late December 1861, he and a Union cavalryman collided (bruises); on February 15, 1862, a cannonball struck his horse right behind Forrest's legs (temporary numbness); a rifle ball at Shiloh, April 8, 1862, entered his torso above the left hip, traversed his back muscles, and lodged against his spine (the ball was removed surgically without anesthetic some weeks later; Forrest was in pain for six months); on September 17, 1862, he was "unhorsed" (dislocating his right shoulder); on June 13, 1863, an angry subaltern shot him at close range (he fatally injured the officer with a knife and missed two weeks of action; "The bullet entered just above his left hip joint and struck the outer edge of the pelvic bone…was deflected upward and passed back through his body without having touched either his intestines or any large blood vessels").

Back in the saddle by June 25, the ball still in his body, Forrest was bruised again when his horse fell in the fighting at Fort Pillow in April 1864; after the battle of Brice's Crossroads in June 1864, by now a major general and widely recognized by both sides as a cavalry wizard, he fainted and fell from his mount. Then, after a bout with boils, he was shot in his right foot at Tupelo in July 1864, his third combat wound and the most painful. "The ball ranged backward through his sole producing a flesh wound. When the severe hemorrhage was finally stopped, he mounted his horse and rode in front of his men. Healing of this wound was delayed, as Forrest was in poor health at the time and was plagued with boils…. Forrest rode around the camp in a farm buggy, looking sick and as thin as a rail, with his injured foot projecting over the front. He was incapacitated for some time, and when he took the field on August 9, he was still riding in a buggy."

Finally, in close, highly personalized fighting in Alabama during the final days of the war (April 1865), he suffered saber bruises around the head, arms, and shoulders. After the war, he continued to exhibit health problems possibly aggravated by diabetes and/or a gluten (wheat products) food allergy, continually losing weight, until he died in 1877, cause of death officially defined as chronic diarrhea.

UNION
Enduring Family Ties

FOR AUGUSTUS MOOR, OWNER OF a German beer garden in Cincinnati and first commander of the all-German Twenty-Eighth Ohio Volunteer Infantry, the early days of the Civil War presented one disaster after another. First, as he and his men crossed the Ohio River toward Point Pleasant in western Virginia on July 31, 1861, eight of his troops were drowned.

Next, ordered to attack Confederates encamped near Carnifex Ferry on the Gauley River, Moor and his men had to climb steep and rocky ground late in the day, then await the morning hours of daylight. As they were settling down in "the pitch darkness of the night," reports David Mowery in an article for the Cincinnati Civil War Round Table (www.cincinnaticwrt.org/28th_OVI _mowery), "they suddenly received rifle fire from their front left flank, killing and wounding several in their ranks." The Ohioans fired back "instantly with a volley that lit up the dense thicket."

Unfortunately, their opponents that night were fellow Union troops.

To make matters somewhat worse, both Colonel Moor and his second-in-command, Lt. Col. Gottfried Becker, fell off a rock ledge and hurt themselves so badly that a captain had to take command of the regiment. In sum: "In its first two months of service, the 28th Ohio had lost more men to accidents than it had lost to the enemy."

Plus, there had been the embarrassing incident involving the regiment's ten laundresses. According to a *Cincinnati Daily Gazette* article cited by Mowery,

"Col. Moor…thought it would be good for the men to have clean shirts once in a while, so accordingly when he left Cincinnati, he took with him ten stalwart Teutonic maidens—one for each company—whom he commissioned as laundresses." That of course would never do. When the regiment reached western Virginia, the "patriotic females" were ordered back home.

Then came the sad losses among the soldiery.

Not that Colonel Moor (see "Graveyard for Generals," page 235) was an absolute stranger to violent death. Just before the war he had been delighted to see his only daughter, Louisa, meet and marry German-born Godfrey Weitzel, a grocer's son who had been raised in Cincinnati's same Over-the Rhine neighborhood before going off to West Point and earning his commission as the second-ranking man in the class of 1855—Robert E. Lee's last year as academy superintendent.

Louisa's new husband in fact was returning to West Point as an assistant professor of civil and military engineering, notes Mowery in another article posted by the Cincinnati Civil War Round Table (www.cincinnaticwrt.org/weitzel). Just prior to their marriage, the promising young officer had designed and built the land defenses of New Orleans "under the supervision of P. G. T. Beauregard."

In November 1859, Weitzel and Louisa Moor married in Cincinnati and set off for West Point, "where they would enjoy their honeymoon while Godfrey started his new assignment at the Academy." But then came personal tragedy. Three weeks into their marriage, Louisa's skirt caught fire when she walked past a fireplace grate. Severely burned, "she died the same day."

Weitzel sent his in-laws the stark news by telegram that night.

Remaining close to the Moor family, Weitzel managed to put his own grief aside and continue on a path that would lead to recognition as an outstanding soldier and civil engineer. Promoted to first lieutenant in the summer of 1860, the widowed young officer was transferred in January 1861 from his teaching post to a company-sized unit in the Corps of Engineers in Washington, D.C. His Company A then was honored as the bodyguard unit for Abraham Lincoln's inauguration that March, Mowery adds.

With the Civil War soon ablaze, Weitzel briefly was posted at Fort Pickens, Florida; he then helped in the design of the fortifications of his hometown of Cincinnati. Next, while attached to George B. McClellan's Army of the Potomac, Weitzel built pontoon bridges and helped supervise the construction of the defenses of Washington.

Weitzel's reputation "as an effective military engineer becoming widely known," he soon moved on to an ironic coup. Dispatched to Maj. Gen. Benjamin F. Butler's side as his chief engineer for the campaign against New Orleans, Weitzel quite naturally was able to point the invading Union forces to the easiest path through the defenses of the port city. After all, as a young officer under Beauregard, he had built those defenses himself. As Mowery noted, "His intimate knowledge of the defenses contributed greatly to the successful capture of the Crescent City in the spring of 1862."

While in New Orleans as "Beast" Butler's second-in-command, even as acting mayor for a brief stint, Weitzel "helped raise the black regiments known as the Louisiana Native Guards." Soon promoted to brigadier general of volunteers, he also directed the construction of the land defenses for Baton Rouge and then led a division at the siege of Port Hudson. With other Western Department stops on the way, he next, in 1864, was sent to Butler's side again, this time both as commander of the Second Division, Eighteenth Corps, and as chief engineer of Butler's Army of the James outside Petersburg, Virginia.

As events then unfolded, Ulysses S. Grant would use one of Weitzel's pontoon bridges in the assault on Petersburg that led to the months-long siege of that city. Busy on other fronts as well, military engineer Weitzel, now a brevet major general of volunteers, took command of the Eighteenth Corps and then, as a full major general of volunteers, took over the all-black Twenty-Fifth Corps. In December 1864, the West Pointer from Cincinnati led the ground troops ashore at Fort Fisher, North Carolina, in an invasion whose failure would be blamed upon his commanding officer, Butler, rather than Weitzel himself.

For Weitzel, in fact, a singular moment of glory lay just ahead. After Grant gave him command of "all the Union forces north of the Appomattox River," it fell to Weitzel and nine thousand men to enter Richmond on the morning of April 3, 1865, as the first Union occupiers of the Confederate capital, a signal occasion marked by the German-born general's terse, no-nonsense telegram to Secretary of War Edwin M. Stanton: "We entered Richmond at 8 o'clock this morning." This bulletin "electrified the nation," noted Ezra Warner in his indispensable tome *Generals in Blue*.

As one immediate outcome, it fell to Weitzel to escort President Lincoln in his tour of the newly captured capital city. Fittingly, in the eyes of his Northern compatriots, the Cincinnati general took over Jefferson Davis's home—the White House of the Confederacy—as his headquarters, but Weitzel then "became embroiled in a scandal in which he was accused of allowing the Confederate Congress to meet in Richmond."

Soon escaping the whirlwind of war's end and associated controversy, Weitzel briefly took his Twenty-Fifth Corps to border-patrol duty in Texas—"a duty he considered as one of his most difficult assignments," says the Mowery account.

On a more personal note, Weitzel found time early in 1865 to marry again, this time to Louise Bogen, also of the German community in Cincinnati. But he remained close to his first wife's family, the Moors. So close were they that he and Louise would bury two children who died young in the Augustus Moor plot in the city's Spring Grove Cemetery.

As for Colonel Moor's Twenty-Eighth Ohio Volunteer Infantry, the war officially had ended with the expiration of the membership's original three-year enlistments in mid-1864, although more than 220 of the Twenty-Eighth OVI men would reenlist with the Twenty-Eighth Ohio Infantry *Battalion*, destined to "serve out the rest of the war performing guard duty in Wheeling, West Virginia."

Recovering from the misfortunes of their first days at war, the Ohio Germans compiled an impressive battle record in their three years of combat on behalf of the Union. When their first commander, Moor, took over an entire brigade, the Twenty-Eighth Ohio went with him as part of the brigade, with Lieutenant Colonel Becker now acting commander of the regiment. Soon after, the Twenty-Eighth "figured prominently" and "performed admirably," albeit unsuccessfully, in a flank attack against the Confederates in the May 15–17, 1862, battle of Princeton, West Virginia.

After a period of fighting "bushwackers and irregulars" that included "the famous McCoys of the Hatfield & McCoy feud," the Ohioans finally left the West Virginia mountains…just in time to take part in the battles of South Mountain and Antietam, where the Twenty-Eighth achieved some note as "the first regiment of the IX Corps to ford Antietam Creek above the infamous Burnside's Bridge."

Spending the next year back in West Virginia, the Twenty-Eighth then, on November 6, 1863, played a prominent part in the battle of Droop Mountain, as also noted in Mowery's painstaking account. "The soldiers of the 28th displayed great gallantry under fire at the 'Bloody Angle,' where they helped to roll up the Confederate left flank and forced the enemy to flee from the field."

Once more relatively quiet for some months, the Ohio Germans were destined to face fierce combat yet again before they could go home to a deserved hero's welcome in June 1864. First would come their difficult but peripheral role in the famous battle of New Market, during which they guarded German-born Gen. Franz Sigel's wagon trains near Strasburg, Virginia, to the north of the battle scene itself. Even as the boy-soldiers from Virginia Military Institute fought Sigel's men at New Market on May 15, 1864, however, five companies of the Twenty-Eighth found themselves under attack at Strasburg by Confederate cavalry. "After a vicious fight, the 28th successfully drove off the Rebels, but not before losing 2 men killed and 10 captured."

Next, on June 5, just days before most of the Twenty-Eighth's enlistments were due to expire, came the regiment's "bloodiest" encounter of the whole war. Also the regiment's "final glory," it would be the little-known battle of Piedmont, Virginia, where Colonel Moor's brigade lost five color-bearers "in quick succession" while mounting two unsuccessful charges against the Rebels. Then came a Confederate counterattack that drove back all the brigade's regiments *except* the stalwart Twenty-Eighth, "which was left alone to fight 6 Confederate regiments."

In arguably the unit's finest moment, acting commander Becker's men took full advantage of their artillery support to "single-handedly" repulse the attacking Confederates, then joined their brigade comrades in a third charge against the enemy. "This time the Confederate line crumbled, and victory fell upon the Ohioans."

The Twenty-Eighth alone paid a high price for the triumph—two officers and twenty-six men were killed and one hundred ten men were wounded, notes the Mowery account. These were significant figures when compared to the regiment's overall casualties for its entire time spent at war—two officers and sixty-six men killed or mortally wounded, aside from those lost to illness or accident.

Meanwhile, just four days after their last battle of the war, the regiment's surviving members were sent home to await a formal mustering out on July 23. (For the 220 reenlistment volunteers of the Twenty-Eighth Ohio Battalion who spent the next months on guard duty in Wheeling, West Virginia, of course, the war wasn't quite over yet.)

With peace and reunification of the nation finally in force after war's end, Godfrey Weitzel, for one, did *not* simply fade away. Not at all. Reverting to the rank of major in the Corps of Engineers, he had years of well-known and lasting works as a civil engineer still ahead of him. Probably chief among them was his solution to the Ohio River bottleneck at the Falls of the Ohio next to Louisville, Kentucky, long a "menace to Ohio River shipping and commerce." As Mowery explains in his profile of Weitzel, the Cincinnatian created an expanded canal, taking ships safely past the falls on the Indiana side of the river. "The feat was considered a civil engineering breakthrough, and Cincinnati business owners were forever grateful to Weitzel for the completion of the Louisville & Portland Canal."

In the postwar years, the former general found ways to improve navigation on more major rivers, the Cumberland, Tennessee, and Mississippi among them. Then came another engineering triumph, the 515-foot Weitzel Canal Lock for the Soo Canal on the St. Mary's River at Sault Sainte Marie, Michigan, at the time (1881), "the largest of its kind in the world." Even more visibly today, you might argue, he was the engineer behind the lighthouse rising from Stannard's Rock thirty miles out from the Upper Michigan shore in Lake Superior.

His health beginning to fail, Weitzel was assigned to desk duty in Philadelphia. He and his second wife, Louise, in the meantime were the parents of a third child, a daughter, Irene, who would live to age sixty.

She was only about eight years old, however, when her father was stricken by typhoid and died at their home on South Thirty-Sixth Street in Philadelphia. And now, in the year 1884, it would be Weitzel who would receive a hero's welcome from his hometown of Cincinnati, Ohio. "Although Weitzel had wanted a private funeral," writes Mowery, "the city could not hold back its emotion for this famous engineer and military hero. Awaiting the arrival of the remains were the 1st Ohio National Guard and [Civil War Gen.] Jacob D. Cox with fellow members of the Cincinnati Society of Ex-Army and Navy Officers. They accompanied the body to the English Lutheran Church on Elm Street… where the funeral was held in front of a capacity crowd. During the procession from the church to Spring Grove Cemetery, thousands of citizens lined the streets to do homage to the general. The city's newspapers touted the spectacle as the largest gathering seen for a funeral in many years."

As one of those newspapers also said, not only had the Corps of Engineers lost "one of its most capable officers," but society had lost "one of its best citizens."

★★★

Additional note: Weitzel outlived his former father-in-law Augustus Moor by only a year or so. The latter, after surviving several Civil War battles and a period of captivity, had been brevetted a brigadier general of volunteers. A native of Germany himself (Leipzig), Moor was not exactly a neophyte when he led his Twenty-Eighth Ohio Volunteers into battle. He had previously seen service in the Seminole War as a young officer with the First Pennsylvania Volunteers and then again, in 1846, as a captain serving with Ohio units in the Mexican War. He spent the years after the Civil War in his adopted hometown of Cincinnati. He was sixty-nine years old when he died in 1883. He and former son-in-law Godfrey Weitzel both are buried in the same Spring Grove Cemetery.

CONFEDERATE
Wesley Culp's Return

As a boy growing up in Gettysburg, Pennsylvania, young John Wesley Culp was familiar with the steep ground now known as Culp's Hill, since it was his Uncle Henry Culp's farm. But certainly, it never entered young Wesley's mind that in July 1863 he would be seeing the same hill one last time…as a Confederate soldier.

And yet, in the battle of Gettysburg, there he was, a private in a Virginia regiment soon to be advancing up Culp's Hill, just one of the tide in gray that was intent upon dislodging the men in blue from behind their defenses at the top.

The night before, the same young man had slipped through the town to a sister's home on West Middle Street for a clandestine visit, during which, surely, he asked about brother Bill's whereabouts as a Union soldier.

Just the month before, in one of the Civil War's many battles for control of Winchester, Virginia, Wesley's fellow Rebels of the Stonewall Brigade, a part of Richard Ewell's Second Corps, met brother William's Yankee compatriots of the Eighty-Seventh Pennsylvania Volunteers…but the two brothers themselves had not encountered each other.

More troublesome on this first weekend of July, Bill had not been seen since—*missing in action.*

Disturbingly also, at Winchester, Wesley had come across an old Gettysburg friend, Jack Skelly, lying mortally wounded. He of course was a Yankee soldier, from Bill Culp's own Company F of the Eighty-Seventh Pennsylvania, but no matter to these old childhood friends—the Rebel soldier Wesley listened intently and made a promise as Skelly intoned a message for his sweetheart back home. The promise was to see that she received the message.

Just how Wesley would convey Jack's thoughts across the miles, across the great divide between Confederate Virginia territory and the thoroughly Union precincts of Pennsylvania, neither man could say just then. Soon, though, fate would intervene and Wesley would find himself traveling north with his fellow Rebs on a track reversing Wesley's own travels south in the years before the war.

At age seventeen, Wesley had traveled south with a Gettysburg carriage maker relocating in Shepherdstown, Virginia. This western Virginia region was not known for great plantations tilled by slaves; it was no hotbed of secessionist thought; it in fact would emerge from the fratricidal war as a part of loyal West Virginia. Still, for reasons of his own, when war came, Pennsylvania-born Wesley Culp joined his new friends and neighbors who *were* attracted to the Southern cause. Only five feet tall and bearded like many of his brethren, the carriage maker's employee would serve as a private in the ranks of Company B, Second Virginia Infantry.

Now, as Ewell, Robert E. Lee, and their chief subalterns led the way through the countryside north of the Potomac River—in the South's second invasion of the supposedly sacrosanct North—the towns ahead or nearby were reminders to Wesley of an earlier life. "Late in June, he found himself in increasingly familiar country, around Greencastle, Chambersburg, Carlisle," noted Ashley Halsey Jr. in an article ("Brother Against Brother") for the April 15, 1961, issue of the *Saturday Evening Post*. "Then the Confederate march swung to the right, and the countryside grew even more familiar."

As fate would have it, his own hometown of Gettysburg suddenly lay just ahead.

And next, a "strange homecoming" for Wesley Culp on July 1, 1863, his fellow Confederates had driven a disorderly rout of bluecoats through the rows of tidy redbrick homes and neat stores "and taken over Wesley's old hometown."

All this came about as A. P. Hill's Third Corps banged into John Buford's Union cavalry between Cashtown and Gettysburg; as Hill then sent his troops swarming toward Seminary Ridge, running north to south just southwest of Gettysburg; as Ewell's corps came storming into town from the north in a successful effort to evict Union Gen. Oliver O. Howard's Eleventh Corps from its Gettysburg lodgings.

Outside of town, however, the Federals seized high ground to the south and southeast. One steep slope they occupied was Cemetery Hill and another, so familiar to the Second Virginia's Pennsylvania-born private, was Culp's Hill, an all-important anchor for the Union's right flank.

With darkness that evening, the fighting ebbed, and Wes obtained permission to visit his sister in town. "She greeted him warmly, but warned that some relatives had threatened to 'shoot the rebel on the spot' if they saw him. Wes smiled, ate his dinner, and told her of Jack Skelly's message for his sweetheart, a young woman named Jennie Wade. (Actually, Wesley may have visited his two sisters at once.)

When the sister offered to deliver it, Wes said no, he had promised to do so himself and would get around to it after the fighting ended." And soon he was gone, back to the ranks of the Second Virginia as it prepared to storm Culp's Hill late on the second day of battle at Gettysburg, July 2.

As fate would have it, the Confederate assault at Culp's Hill that night faltered and then failed. Sometime before the gray tide receded the next morning, leaving bodies behind, not only on Culp's Hill itself, but nearby as well, one was his own...dragged, they say, to the base of a tree that was itself "broken over by shell fire."

Wesley Culp—his body, that is—was never found, even though his family searched and searched. "We found dozens of broken down trees and dozens of bodies under them," explained a cousin later, "but we never found Wes." All they found was the stock of a rifle, his name plainly scratched into the wooden shoulder piece. (Some locals would wonder over the years, however, if the family did find Wesley's remains and bury them in secret.)

Considering the number of Confederates killed at Gettysburg (3,903) and the even greater number (5,425) reported missing, however, his presumed disappearance in the churned-up battleground wasn't so surprising.

As for Jennie Wade's message...events would dictate an unexpected outcome. On the third and final day of the great battle, she was at home, quietly kneading dough when Union snipers took refuge behind the house as their Confederate pursuers opened fire on them. "Five bullets tore through the door." Jenny would go down in history as the only civilian fatality of the battle of Gettysburg.

Far more happily, William Culp finally turned up four days after the watershed battle in their hometown. He "rejoined the Federal Army at Frederick, Maryland, and served out the war." (His and Wesley's friend Jack Skelly died of his wounds.)

★★★

Additional note: The story of the Culp brothers is only one example of the many brothers and other family members who fought on opposite sides during the Civil War. Abraham Lincoln himself was related by marriage to a Confederate general, Benjamin Hardin Helm, who was killed at Chickamauga...after which his widow, Emilie Todd Helm, came to visit her half sister, Mary Todd Lincoln, the president's wife, in the wartime White House. For that matter, the flamboyant Jeb Stuart renamed his son because the boy's namesake grandfather, Gen. Phillip St. George Cooke, remained loyal to the Union and even fought for it.

Among the war's additional warring brothers, meanwhile, were these:

- As mentioned earlier ("Union: Ringed by Rebellion," page 43), actually shooting *at one another*, opposing naval officers Franklin and McKean Buchanan, ages sixty-one and sixty-two, respectively, took part in the history-making clash of Franklin's ironclad CSS *Virginia* with McKean's USS *Congress* in Hampton Roads, Virginia, on March 8, 1862. Franklin's newly armored ship poured fire into the *Congress* as McKean, the stricken ship's purser, or paymaster, commanded the guns responding from her berth deck. Surviving the war and living into their seventies, the two brothers remained good friends despite their war experiences.

- Far less happy was the fate of Virginia's heroic two Generals Terrill, William and James, whose decisions to take opposite sides in the war may have stemmed from William's graduation from West Point, followed by U.S. Army service, and James's graduation from the Virginia Military Institute (VMI), followed by the beginnings of a law practice. However they arrived at their differing loyalties, unfortunately, each was killed in battle—Union General William at Perryville, Kentucky, and Confederate General James at Bethesda Church in Virginia. Their grieving father, it is said, erected a memorial to them both saying, "God alone knows which one was right."

Wesley Culp died on or near the hill in Gettysburg bearing his family's name.

- The Drayton brothers of South Carolina, Percival and Thomas, played out another heartrending family drama, apparently after attending church together one last time to seek guidance in the pending conflict. "They walked out, shook hands and went to serve as their consciences dictated—Thomas, the older, as a brigadier general, C.S.A., Percival as a Union Naval commander," wrote Ashley Halsey. Months later, Percival was in command of a Union gunboat taking part in a major attack against coastal defenses commanded by his brother Thomas. Neither brother would be among the casualties, and even later Percy would become a historical footnote as the Union officer (and fleet captain) to whom Adm. David Farragut gave his famous order at Mobile, Alabama, "Damn the torpedoes!...ahead...full speed!" Meanwhile, Percy had condemned slavery and explained his choice of Union over Confederacy by saying, "Their cause is as unholy a one as the world has ever seen, and mine just the reverse." He also predicted his brother Thomas, "like so many others," would lose "everything," but added, "Although sorry, I think he richly deserves it, even more than others, because he has not the excuse of utter darkness and ignorance of right." The prediction of economic devastation was correct, but a $27,000 bequest from Percival, who died in 1865, eased the financial pain of his "Rebel" brother, Thomas Drayton.

UNION
"Secession Is Rebellion"

BROTHER AGAINST BROTHER AGAIN, BUT this time big brother tried to reach across the metaphorical lines for a reconciliation with baby brother months before the shooting stopped.

As a professional soldier, a West Point graduate, a Union major general, and commander of division- and even corps-size forces during the Civil War, John Gibbon, badly wounded at Fredericksburg and again at Gettysburg, a veteran also of Second Bull Run, Spotsylvania, the Wilderness, and the Siege of Petersburg, had plenty to think about, aside from reaching out to his brother Nicholas somewhere in the Confederate ranks.

The older Gibbon had been born in Philadelphia but grew up in Charlotte, North Carolina, thanks to a family move south. He entered West Point in 1842 and graduated in the same class as the Union's Ambrose E. Burnside and the Confederacy's A. P. Hill. He then saw service in the Mexican and Seminole wars and taught artillery classes at West Point for five years.

When the Civil War broke out, there was no question of Gibbon's loyalty to the Union. Indeed, he once said, "Secession is rebellion and must be put down as such." His three younger brothers, all raised in the southern climes of North Carolina, thought otherwise, and all three—Robert, Lardner, and Nicholas—became Confederate officers, noted Ashley Halsey Jr. in his 1961 *Saturday Evening Post* article "Brother Against Brother" (see "Confederate: Wesley Culp's Return," page 107).

Halsey noted that young Nick's North Carolina brigade often clashed with older brother John's Union command. At Fredericksburg, "their lines veered but exchanged fire." At Gettysburg, on the third and final day, "Nick's unit swept forward with Pickett's great, forlorn charge which smashed in vain at an adamant Union line commanded by brother John." At Spotsylvania, however, the tables turned, and "Nick's gray brigade blazed away at the flank of John's attacking troops so furiously that it broke their nearly triumphant charge at the Bloody Angle 'with severe loss.'"

In the meantime, Robert Gibbon, brother to both, served in Nick's brigade—as brigade surgeon, or doctor. Thus, he repeatedly was treating young soldiers laid low by older brother John's troops. "At Gettysburg," wrote Halsey, "348 wounded trickled back to the brigade surgeon's field hospital."

But it was to Nick, youngest of all four Gibbon brothers, that John sent word across the lines from somewhere near Petersburg in the last year of the war…an invitation to meet in a neutral setting. He had Grant's permission, John Gibbon said.

Brother Nick was less than responsive, it seems. Scornfully, "he said that while General Lee no doubt would consent to the meeting, 'it is not agreeable that I meet you under the circumstances.'"

Undissuaded, John replied, "Under no circumstances could a meeting with one of my brothers prove disagreeable to me. Should we ever meet hereafter, you will find me, as ever, Your affectionate brother."

As events turned out, they survived the war, but "family tradition has it that Nick never again spoke to John."

Meanwhile, older brother John not only "became a famous Indian fighter after the war," he, more specifically, figured in Custer's Last Stand as the man in charge of the troops who arrived after it was all over and buried the dead. "The following year [1877]," noted Ezra Warner in his *Generals in Blue,* "he conducted a successful campaign against the Nez Perces." He retired to Baltimore, his wife's hometown, in 1891 and died there in 1896, while serving as commander in chief of the Military Order of the Loyal Legion.

CONFEDERATE
Dispute with Stonewall

HE ARGUED WITH HIS NOTORIOUSLY stodgy professor and for that was booted out of military school. He then challenged his professor to a duel...an added affront wisely turned down. Just a few years later, in the midst of raging war, he had to serve under his old nemesis...who now ended up endorsing his once-insubordinate student's promotion to brigadier general.

And the school? The school wound up giving the same argumentative student an honorary degree in place of the one he never received with his classmates.

For that matter, he survived the war, whereas the once-stodgy, wooden-faced professor did not. *Famously* did not.

Their shared story began, inauspiciously enough, in the professor's classroom. The time was May 1852, the students were gathered in Professor Thomas J. Jackson's natural philosophy class at the Virginia Military Institute, and cadet James Alexander Walker was called to come forward "to the board" and demonstrate his solution to a problem—determining the time of day from the angle of the sun.

To say the least, the demonstration did not strike Jackson as satisfactory.

In the court-martial resulting from their contretemps, both that day and the next, Jackson testified that Walker did not perform satisfactorily. "I sent him to his seat, he asked me in what his error consisted. I considered his manner disrespectful," Jackson testified.

But Jackson moments later realized he had fallen into an embarrassing trap for any teacher—a new edition of the class text gave a new method of solving the problem, whereas he had been relying upon an older edition. Thus, embarrassingly enough, "I saw that I could not reasonably expect from the accused the demonstration given in the old edition which I had studied."

Calling Walker to the board a second time, Jackson apparently went over the solutions, new and old, all over again, but his recalcitrant student "appeared to object to the investigation."

Jackson tried to smooth the waters. "I told him he was not expected to understand the subject but that it was my duty to explain it to him. I said this in what I considered a conciliatory tone."

Unmollified, Walker allegedly said that either he or Jackson must change his conduct.

Jackson said that he told Walker to stop talking and, "all I required of him was that he should behave himself."

So things stood, by Jackson's account, until they met again in the same class the next day. A class member then asked Jackson to repeat the lesson of the previous day…and if this cadet had hoped to goad Jackson into another confrontation, he succeeded admirably.

Jackson explained the problem and its solution all over again. He called "several students to the board" and asked another cadet to explain the solution.

Jackson then stepped into the predictable minefield. Stubbornly, he called on Walker again.

Cadet Walker responded that he did not know how to solve the problem despite Jackson's explanation the day before. He said that Jackson only *attempted* to explain it.

Said Jackson in a "conciliatory tone" again, "I told him that I did explain it but that he might not have understood it."

But Walker apparently wasn't willing to let it go at that.

"He again stated that I had attempted to explain it, and that I did not ask him whether he understood it or not."

At this point, their argument flared into open warfare. Again by Jackson's written account:

> I considered his manner improper. I considered it insolent. I called his attention to his manner being improper & as he continued to talk, I ordered him to stop—he disobeyed the order saying he would stop talking if I would stop, or words to that effect. I again ordered him to stop, saying "Silence, Mr. Walker," or words to that effect, in an imperative & authoritative tone. He again disobeyed the order & said he would stop talking if I would stop, or words to that effect. After I had given the last order I sent him to his seat. I subsequently reminded him of his assertion of the previous day—that his conduct must change or that mine must. I told him that mine would not

change. In reply I understood him to say that he had said that he did not intend to change his. After some reflection I ordered him to his quarters under arrest.

Walker, quite naturally, had a somewhat different story. Accusing Jackson of harboring "many singular and eccentric notions," the cadet insisted that his professor "entirely misconstrued my conduct." And then, "all my expressions of the most polite deference instead of convincing him of his error only served as new fuel to the flame." And finally, "he conformed his manner to his misconstruction of mine & his language becomes angry, imperative & harsh if not insulting."

So, who was right? Who was wrong?

As determined by VMI, the answer to the latter, no matter how stubborn or eccentric one might call Professor Jackson, was Walker. Thus, just weeks before his scheduled graduation, he was found guilty in his court-martial of disrespect and kicked out of school.

Before returning home to Augusta County, Virginia, it must also be noted, he managed to turn his wrath against VMI superintendent Francis H. Smith. Writing the insubordinate youth's father to inform him of his son's court-martial and dismissal from VMI, Smith complained, "This morning he called at my office and in terms in the highest degree disrespectful and insulting to the Supt., declined to take any appeal." Smith advised Walker's father to come "at once" to take the former cadet home, "as I have reason to believe he may involve himself in serious difficulty." By that perhaps Smith meant the challenge to a duel that Walker entrusted to a fellow cadet.

And now came the years leading up to the Civil War, with both men plodding along in near anonymity. Jackson, the future Stonewall Jackson, of course, remained at VMI (despite one alumni group's efforts to dislodge him from his teaching post). Walker, for his part, went to work for the Covington and Ohio Railway, progenitor of the giant Chesapeake and Ohio (C&O) of later years, then studied law at the University of Virginia, where he did earn a degree at last.

Settling in Pulaski County, Virginia, he began the Civil War as captain of the Pulaski Guard. But as fate would have it, Walker soon found himself serving at Harpers Ferry under his old nemesis, Jackson.

In short time, though, Walker rose to the rank of lieutenant colonel and then took the esteemed A. P. Hill's place as colonel of the Thirteenth Virginia Infantry while Hill also moved up the promotion ladder to brigadier general.

Finally, irony upon irony, as Jackson himself rose ever higher in rank and reputation, his once-difficult student wound up in charge of Jackson's own Stonewall Brigade. Walker, it seems, was making a reputation of his own. Indeed, wrote Ezra J. Warner in his *Generals in Gray*, "Walker rapidly made a reputation as a desperate fighter and took part in almost every battle and engagement of the 2nd Corps [which Jackson commanded from late 1862] from the Valley campaign of 1862 to Appomattox." Interestingly, too, it was "at the special request of Jackson, who had come to have a high regard for him," that former VMI cadet Walker was promoted to brigadier general as of May 15, 1863, just days after Jackson's death on May 10.

Later severely wounded at Spotsylvania, Walker managed to survive the war, which he ended in a divisional command. He then returned to Pulaski County "and put in a crop of corn with two mules he had brought home from the army," wrote Warner. Resuming his law practice, Walker six years later was elected to the Virginia House of Delegates. He then advanced to lieutenant governor of the state five years after that, only to part company with his long-standing Democratic Party base to become a Republican and win two terms in the U.S. House under the GOP label.

It was in the postbellum years that VMI relented and granted the exemplary war hero his honorary degree.

UNION
Honors for an Englishman

WHEN SIXTY-THREE-YEAR-OLD PHILLIP BAYBUTT WAS buried back home in his native England in 1909, no one bothered to inscribe his headstone with a fairly startling fact.

In the American Civil War half a century before, he had won the Medal of Honor.

An Englishman? The Medal of Honor?

Since he had joined the Union army, served and fought valiantly with the Union army, why not?

As for the specifics…only five-feet-two-and-a-half-inches tall, eighteen years of age, and a wagon driver from Manchester, England, by trade, he had crossed the Atlantic to the United States late in 1863 or early in 1864. "When he arrived, he was caught up in the whirlwind of civil war, the likes of which he had never seen," wrote Roger Willison-Gray, a leading British Civil War reenactor (Company H, Fourth Michigan Cavalry), in England's own *American Civil War Society* (ACWS) newsletter of August 2002.

Young Baybutt joined up in February 1864 and thus achieved the enviable distinction of serving in Company A of the Second Massachusetts Cavalry, otherwise and often known as the "California Hundred." The original Hundred, Willison-Gray explained, "all veterans of the gold rush and from a dozen different nationalities, had volunteered in San Francisco to fight for the Union" (see "Union: California's Crucial Role," page 121).

Weary of dull guard duty as homebound militia in unembattled California, they "wrote to the governor of Massachusetts and offered their services to fight in the east, where all of the action was." They then traveled east "at their own expense, providing all their own equipment in order to be in the thick of the action." At a later date, "Phillip Baybutt was recruited to fill the ranks of this depleted company."

As one result, Baybutt apparently took part in eight battles and many more skirmishes, with much of the unit's efforts spent in pursuit of "Gray Ghost" John Singleton Mosby's elusive rangers in the so-called lower (upper, on the map) Shenandoah Valley of Virginia. Before all was said and done, it seems, two of Baybutt's horses were "killed in action," and he was twice wounded and suffered a bad fall from a horse that would plague him in later years as a painful reminder of his Union service.

His supreme moment in the Civil War surely was in September 1864, near Luray, Virginia, when he and his Union comrades clashed with Col. W. H. F. Payne's Confederate cavalry brigade as it fell back toward the Page County town under pressure from Union troopers commanded by George Armstrong Custer.

As American Civil War reenactor Robert H. Moore II related the chain of events both before and after that point in his Heritage and Heraldry column appearing in the *Page County News & Courier* of June 3, 1999, "Somewhere between the county border and Luray, the clash of cavalry occurred. Badly outnumbered and outgunned, the Confederates were quickly overwhelmed, losing several men as prisoners."

Most important to young Englishman Phillip Baybutt, the Sixth Virginia Cavalry lost its regimental flag during the swirling melee at Yagers Mill—to him.

And that's exactly what his Medal of Honor citation says: "Capture of flag."

Moore and Willison-Gray both noted that Private Baybutt returned to

England after his discharge at Fairfax Court House at war's end, to work for his father, a Manchester merchant, and eventually to wind up a shipping clerk. Married to the former Harriet Jones, he would father eight children before his death in 1909 at the age of sixty-three.

But now comes the sad part of his life's story. As noted by Moore's 1999 Heritage and Heraldry column, "Baybutt suffered a great deal from the fall from his horse during the war and appealed for a veteran's pension from the United States in January 1904." Despite producing "at least three former comrades' written testimony as to the seriousness of the incident," added Moore's account, "his application was rejected." That was in 1906, three years before his death—"from 'exhaustion,' in addition to other ailments experienced as a result of the war."

By Willison-Gray's later account, the onetime federal cavalryman and Medal of Honor winner "was laid to rest in Manchester's Southern Cemetery with a headstone, which did not record his heroic deeds."

As the widow of a Union veteran, his wife then received a pension of eight dollars a month.

Albeit greatly delayed, kinder rewards eventually did come. "In September 2002," noted Willison-Gray, "the town of Luray erected a Civil War Trail marker to commemorate the battle of Yagers Mill to coincide with the 138th anniversary of the action. Phillip Baybutt's details were inscribed on the memorial." Fittingly enough, the American commemoration matched a similar ceremony at Baybutt's grave on the English side of the Atlantic, a memorial attended by his granddaughter, Edna Baybutt. By this time also, the U.S. government for which Baybutt once fought had provided recognition of his heroism in the form of the Veterans Administration's headstone designed exclusively for winners of the Medal of Honor.

None of which is to say that Baybutt was England's *only* Medal of Honor recipient of Civil War vintage…nor even the first Englishman so recognized. Indeed, listed close by in that alphabetically organized honor roll is George Bell, England-born and recognized as a Medal of Honor recipient as early as November 1861, for heroism displayed during a naval engagement off Galveston, Texas. In further fact, Roger Willison-Gray's ACWS newsletter reports, the overall count of English Medal of Honor winners "that are properly documented" comes to "at least" sixty-seven. For that matter, many nationalities are represented in the overall roster of Civil War Medal of Honor winners, as anyone sifting through the list can see.

CONFEDERATE
President's Son at War

AFTER HIS GRADUATION FROM YALE University, this Confederate general had strong ties with both the White House in the federal capital of Washington and the White House of the Confederacy in Richmond. He never attended West Point, nor was he *exactly* a veteran of the Mexican War, like so many of his general-ranked compatriots, yet he earned their plaudits for his performance during the Civil War and reached the rank of lieutenant general...all despite health problems that often relegated him to a horse-drawn ambulance, rather than his horse, for transportation during battle.

A Yale graduate, young Richard Taylor "went to war" in Mexico in the 1840s as a military secretary to his father, Gen. (and future president) Zachary Taylor. His father sent him back home to Louisiana after he developed inflammatory rheumatism, according to Dr. Jack D. Welsh's book *Medical Histories of Confederate Generals*. Young Taylor, born in 1826, then endured a return of his symptoms in the spring of 1847, and that summer, he sought relief at White Sulphur Springs in western Virginia, today the home of the Greenbrier resort hotel.

As a hero of the Mexican War, Taylor's father was elected president in 1848, taking his executive seat in March 1849. As one obvious result, Richard Taylor came to know the Washington White House from his father's term of office... the last president, incidentally, to bring slaves into the presidential mansion as part of his personal entourage. Then, too, during the Civil War to come, even an undistinguished Richard Taylor would have had entrée to the White House of the Confederacy by virtue of the fact that his late sister, Knox Taylor, had been the first wife of Jefferson Davis, the president of the Confederacy. Not only that, but Davis and his wife Varina had become close friends of President Taylor and First Lady Margaret Taylor during their White House tenure, which was cut short by Zachary Taylor's fatal illness in July 1850.

As events turned out, Richard Taylor, son of a former president of the United States, *would* be a distinguished participant in the battles of the Civil War...on the side of the seceding states that formed the Confederacy. His résumé would be impressive, even in skeletal form, without taking into account his personal battles against repeated illnesses.

Thus *this* General Taylor, born near Louisville, Kentucky, and raised in large part at his father's frontier army posts, studied in Europe, attended Harvard, and graduated from Yale just before the Mexican War. A Louisiana sugar planter and a state senator when the Civil War broke out, he first led the Ninth Louisiana Infantry as its colonel, arriving "at the field of First Manassas on the night of the battle," noted Ezra Warner in his *Generals in Gray*, then serving under Stonewall Jackson in the Shenandoah Valley campaign and in the Seven Days' battles outside Richmond, both in 1862. Promoted to major general that same year, Taylor took command of the District of West Louisiana. Here, "he made a notable record with a paucity of troops and supplies," noted Warner.

Still, his "most celebrated achievement" of the war wouldn't come until the spring of 1864. And that was "the complete repulse of [Nathaniel] Banks' Red River Expedition at Mansfield and Pleasant Hill."

Celebrated, yes, but with attendant controversy and disappointment, as also summed up in Warner's biographical sketch: "Prevented from following up his advantage by what he deemed to be the incredible stupidity of his superior, General Kirby Smith, Taylor asked to be relieved of his command. He was, nevertheless, promoted to lieutenant general to rank from April 8, 1864, and assigned to the Department of Alabama and Mississippi."

And finally, one last item for his military résumé: "He surrendered on May 1865 the last of the Confederate forces east of the Mississippi."

All very impressive, to say the least…but all the more so when his personal health record, as compiled by Welsh, is added. To wit: "He became ill after the Battle of First Manassas; a persistent low-grade fever was accompanied by loss of strength and the use of his limbs. To improve his health, he was ordered to go to…[a] springs some twenty miles south, where his sister joined him. With her nursing care and the sulphur water, he slowly regained his health."

But that would not be the end of his troubles. In September of the same year, 1861, he was "bedridden with arthritis" for a time, and in October he was given sick leave and again nursed by his sister. The winter of 1861–62 was "very hard on Taylor, who suffered from rheumatism and headaches."

That brings events around to spring of 1862, just before the Valley and Seven Days' campaigns. In April, in order to visit President Davis, his onetime brother-in-law, Taylor "had to travel in an ambulance because of his pain." Then, the night of June 25, the very day that the Seven Days' fighting began, practically at Richmond's doorstep, he suffered "severe pains in his loins and head." The next day, unable to mount his horse and "barely conscious enough to understand the messages sent to him," he lay on the floor of a vacant house while his brigade "marched off without him," leaving behind a small ambulance for his use.

He suffered "continuous pain in his head and neck and he had weakness of his extremities."

Recovering somewhat after a "few hours of sleep" on June 27 and hearing the distant sounds of battle, he struggled to his feet and used the small ambulance to follow his troops to Cold Harbor. "To preserve his strength, he used the ambulance throughout the Seven Days' battles. Paralysis of the lower extremities complicated his condition, and after the battles he was sent to Richmond, where he stayed a month."

Still an "invalid," he then was sent to Louisiana. The next health note cited by Welsh says that Taylor was ill on January 19, 1864, and that April he suffered from a low-grade fever—"although quite sick he was able to stay in the saddle." In May 1864, however, "his poor health made it almost impossible for him to conduct the affairs of his command, and he again requested that he be relieved from duty." Worse, "in June it was thought that his mind had been affected by his previous paralytic illness."

Even so, he managed to get through the last year of the war and then, in the four years of life still left to him, to seek leniency from President Andrew Johnson (Lincoln's successor) for Jefferson Davis, to appeal to the federal government for less-stringent Reconstruction policies, and to write a thoroughly cogent book, *Destruction and Reconstruction* (1879).

Briefly living in New Orleans and then Winchester, Virginia, after the war, he still suffered from attacks of arthritis that confined him to bed. Visiting a friend in New York City, ill now from dropsy and once more being nursed by his sister, he died there on April 12, 1879. He was fifty-four.

UNION
California's Crucial Role

THIS IS THE STORY OF how California won the Civil War...or something like that.

No, no, really! What other state, for instance, contributed more volunteer troops to the Union cause per capita than California? None.

What other state, Union or Confederate, contributed so much wealth to its respective cause? So much gold, that is? Add the silver from the Comstock Lode of Nevada passing through the port of San Francisco, and you've got probably $173 million shipped east from California in just the first three and a half years of the Civil War.

By contrast, noted Maj. Norman S. Marshall in the winter 1998 issue of the *Los Angeles Westerners Corral*, "at war's outbreak there was in the seven Confederate states only $27,000,000 in specie, [and] beyond that lay nothing save the dubious expedients of credit and confidence."

Another question: By war's end, what single Union state's forces held more square miles in the West than all the Union forces dispersed throughout the East?

As might be guessed, the answer again is California. But who would ever know?

Hardly anybody, notes Maj. Roger McGrath in an online article for the California Center for Military History (www.militarymuseum.org /HistoryCW.html).

"For most Americans," he declares, "the words California and the Civil War have nothing to do with each other."

And yet, McGrath adds, "California played a surprisingly important role in that epic conflict. Long ignored by most historians and documentary filmmakers, California's contributions and sacrifices, both in men and materiel, deserve a national audience."

Among the highlights, of course, was the gold. By 1861, the first year of the war, the great gold rush of 1849 had petered out to some extent, but the California mines still were pumping out a considerable amount of the precious metal by anyone's measure.

Then, too, while no other state could match California's contribution in that regard, neither could any other state quite match California's number of volunteers relative to the state's total population. "Nearly 17,000 Californians enlisted to fight," says McGrath. "Most of these men were kept busy in the West, but several companies of California volunteers saw action in the East as the California One Hundred or later the California Cavalry Battalion. These volunteers served with the 2nd Massachusetts Cavalry and fought in 31 engagements, many of them in the Shenandoah Valley. Other California volunteers served with distinction in New York and Pennsylvania regiments."

Indeed, as a member of Mosby's Rangers once ruefully recalled, the men of the California Hundred were "especially notoriously good fighters."

A surprise about California's proud volunteer rosters is the fact they came from a sharply divided state. In 1860, just before the war broke out, McGrath notes, the state's total of 130,000 registered voters broke down into 50,000 who were Northern born, 30,000 Southern born, and 50,000 foreign born, the latter "mostly" Irish, British, and German. "Thus, Southerners, most of whom were Confederate sympathizers, exercise[d] a good deal of influence in the state." Politically controlled by the Democrats—at both gubernatorial and state legislative levels—California nonetheless gave Republican Lincoln its vote in the 1860 presidential election.

As on the national level, the state's badly split Democrats wasted their votes on various candidates seeking Democratic support. Even so, California's Governor John Downey was both a Democrat and "a staunch Union man."

Meanwhile, the state's strong pro-Southern faction proposed that California secede and join an independent Pacific Republic that would include Oregon and Washington and perhaps even Utah and New Mexico, McGrath writes. In angry response, pro-Union Democrats held "a huge rally in San Francisco," with fifteen thousand participating, "a figure equal to the number of voters in the city."

All the more surprising about such fervor, California was so distant from events in the East that it took ten days to hear about the fall of Fort Sumter when the news was carried west by the Pony Express.

Interestingly, too, unlike their eastern counterparts, the California volunteers stationed in the West faced a two-front war of sorts. Not only did they have their engagements (limited in number, to be sure) against Confederate forces, they quite often faced the challenge posed by warring Indian tribes. "Quickly the regular Army was called to Eastern battlefields," wrote Herbert M. Hart in *Old Forts of the Far West* (1965). "Volunteer regiments were raised in the West and most of them stayed in the West. To them fell the job of preventing a Confederate takeover and of continuing the unceasing battle against hostile Indians. The latter took the division among the white man as good excuse to increase their depredations."

In the real war, though, the Yankee war against Johnny Reb, the highlight was the dispatch of the California Column, or First Infantry Regiment, California Volunteers, to the rescue of Santa Fe, Albuquerque, and Tucson in New Mexico and Arizona, all recently captured by Confederate Gen. Henry H. Sibley's forces out of Texas.

Col. James H. Carleton led his men eastward on the old Gila Trail, despite advice that the sheer number of his men would soak up and exhaust the scant water supplies to be found en route. He solved the problem by breaking his column into increments and marching them separately, with calculated gaps between the various segments.

As events turned out, Union volunteers out of Colorado met Sibley's forces in the battle of Glorieta Pass and sent the Confederates reeling back to Texas before the Californians could arrive. Still, "eighty miles up the Gila Trail," notes McGrath, at a place called Grinnell's Ranch, Carleton's scouts engaged in a skirmish with advance elements of the Texas-based Rebel force—"the westernmost action of the Civil War."

Carleton and his men then, in the little-known battle of Picacho Pass, "whipped the Texans thoroughly and retook Tucson." The Californians pushed on eastward as far as Texas itself, where, it seems, they captured Forts Bliss, Davis, and Quitman.

Typical of the "second front war" often facing the California volunteers, the last battle of the California column's campaign would *not* be fought against fellow whites in Confederate gray, but against hostile Apaches in southern Arizona.

All in all, adds McGrath, the California volunteers "occupied more than a million square miles of territory and had troops in the field from as early as August 1861 until as late as June 1865." Further, the state's pro-Union elements "were not only critical in keeping California part of the Union and in keeping the flow of gold to Washington uninterrupted but also in keeping the Far West [as] federal territory."

A final point: If California didn't quite "win" the Civil War all by itself, it is quite true, as McGrath asserts, that California's very solid contributions to the overall Union victory "have long been ignored or little understood."

★★★

Additional note: All that gold going to the aid of the Union cause certainly did not go unnoticed by California's pro-Southern sympathizers and others of like mind. "Those 'hot heads' were not slumbering malcontents," noted Marshall in his "Protecting the Gold" article for the *Los Angeles Westerners Corral.* "A real plot to seize the California gold shipments was discovered and thwarted by the seizure of the ship, *J. M. Chapman*, in San Francisco Bay by the USS *Cyane,* revenue officers and San Francisco police. A like effort was thwarted by seizure of the SS *San Salvador.*"

CONFEDERATE
War Baby

HE RODE INTO CAMP FELTON near Cartersville, Georgia, astride a blaze-faced bay pony.

This was in April 1861, he later related, "and I lacked one month being eleven years old." Thus, "Little Dave" Freeman—David Bailey Freeman, born May 1, 1851, in Ellijay, Georgia—apparently was the youngest of all Confederate soldiers, perhaps even of all Civil War soldiers, period.

His mother had let him go off to war.

Well...it hadn't become all-out war as yet. Then, too, by other accounts he may not have enlisted until *after* his birthday in May, making him all of eleven years in age. In any case, there was a special circumstance influencing his mother's decision.

That was his older brother Madison, who had helped raise a cavalry company in Gilmer County despite being partially crippled by "white swelling," or phlebitis of the legs. "Though hopeful, he was uncertain as to whether he could stand the service," related Little Dave many years later. "He asked our mother [Mary Ann Reynolds Murray Freeman] to let me go with him into camp if need be to be of help to him."

So off they went to Camp Felton, and there an infantry battalion and one of cavalry were formed into Smith's Legion. The infantry unit needed a drummer boy, and the cavalrymen needed a survey marker. "The latter place was offered me, and there, by my mother's and my brother's consent I enlisted."

As a result, young Freeman was present as the newly formed troop drilled in cavalry tactics, "including the leaping of fences, picking up handkerchiefs while riding at full speed, etc., in which I got my share of falls." At the beginning, it seems, "it was understood that I was to be allowed to return home any time the Colonel saw fit after drilling days were over; but, alas!, as we shall hereafter see."

"Hereafter" for Little Dave Freeman would mean roughly four years of wartime duty and service in the battle of Chickamauga and in the defense of Atlanta and environs against William Tecumseh Sherman's oncoming Union juggernaut, among other engagements.

But first, thanks to "the diminutive size of myself and steed," Little Dave attracted quite a lot of attention riding into strange towns with his cavalry troop, to be sure. "Some would give me presents, such as home knit socks, mitts, neck scarfs and comforters," he said, "and some would observe that I ought to be at home with my mother."

The troop's first long ride came toward the end of summer—over the Cumberland Mountains into Kentucky, where the boy-soldier caught his first glimpse of the famous Confederate raider John Hunt Morgan. "I thought General Morgan was the finest looking soldier I had seen, and he was. Robust, erect; well-fitting uniform; cavalry boots with spurs with immense rowels; white wide-brimmed hat, held up at the side with a star; dark hair and beard—all this, with his coal-black saddle mare, made him a picturesque figure."

At Bryantsville, the youth's unit was ordered to guard stores captured from the Federals in the recent battle of Richmond, Kentucky. "Acres of ground were covered with pickled pork in barrels." Nearby, a building packed with captured clothing and other equipment was set on fire, a sight he would never forget. "The heavens were lit up with the flames. Everything was on the retreat. Infantry had been passing in the day; artillery and wagons were moving at night. The demonical blaze, the stench from burning meat and clothing, the braying of mules, the cursing of teamsters, all made up a fiendish medley for the vision, the hearing and the olfactories."

All around, too, it appeared every soldier was carrying off "a huge chunk" of pickled pork meat "stuck on the end of his bayonet."

Young Freeman had been staying at a nearby home while his brother was busy elsewhere on detached service. But his brother returned for him late in the night—"right in the middle of this awful hubbub and confusion." They would have to catch up with their legion, which had gone on hours earlier.

Since someone had stolen the boy's pony, they had to share a single horse as, pummeled by heavy rains, they rode out among the wagons jamming the pike. At the next town, they stopped at an old blacksmith shop. They spread their wet blankets on the hard work benches "and stayed—not rested—till morning."

Come morning, though, the retreat was continuing. With the pike still jammed by a "seemingly unending line of artillery and wagons," they decided to take the back roads "through mountains full of bushwhackers." This took four days, with "sleeps in the woods well away from the roads." Even so, "we were fired on several times and narrowly escaped being captured or killed."

At the famous Cumberland Gap they came across a guard of Confederates who wouldn't let them pass because they didn't have official papers.

Withdrawing a short distance but staying out of sight, they waited until spotting a regiment they were familiar with, then passed through the gap hidden in the unit's wagons—"and thus we evaded the guards, finding our command over the mountain."

They also found Little Dave's pony, but it looked so poor and weak, it was fit only for the boneyard.

By now, the Georgia war baby had another mount…and other concerns. "At the gap—it was in October—a snow fell three feet deep. We built great log fires and laid down at night with our feet to the fire. I took sick from the exposure and was carried to a farm house, where I was placed on a pallet with my feet to the fire. My feet cracked open and ran blood."

Such was the "kindergarten" period of Little Dave's wartime career. He did recover, he did go home for a period, but he was soon back in tow with, now, the Sixth Georgia Cavalry, previously the cavalry element of Smith's Legion. And the "first great engagement" ahead for young Freeman would be the battle of Chickamauga in September 1863. Here, he proudly related, "the 6th and other cavalry had held the enemy back."

Next for his Georgia regiment came a "long night ride" of sixty miles from McFarland Spring, Georgia, to Panther Spring in east Tennessee. "We were engaged in a fight with Yankee Cavalry at Philadelphia, Tenn., and were with the [Gen. James] Longstreet forces in his fall and winter campaign '63–'64 in east Tennessee."

Now one of five regiments forming a Georgia cavalry brigade, the Sixth fell under the command of William T. Martin's division in "Fighting Joe" Wheeler's corps. "For privations and peril I am satisfied there was no more trying service in the war," said Freeman in a 1923 talk before the Atlanta Camp No. 159, United Confederate Veterans. "It seems to me we never had a whole night's sleep, the sharp notes of the bugle bringing us to saddle at all hours from dark to dawn." With snow "on the ground most all the time," the streams he and his comrades had to ford time and again—the Holston, the Clinch, and the French Broad rivers among them—were "filled with mush ice" that often posed the danger of "throwing a horse violently from its footing."

And of course there were the engagements fought, one after the other, most of them minor, but still potentially deadly for anyone caught up in them, much less a boy still looking forward to most of his teen years. One in particular stuck in Freeman's memory for six decades.

Encountering Yankees at a site called Bean's Station, Freeman's cavalry comrades were dismounted. He was stationed with the riderless "led" horses by the side of the road. As he watched, his men charged into a woods, "simultaneous with a broadside which sent shells and grape[shot] among our horses to panic them." Then came a rifle volley, apparently from a full corps of Yankee infantry concealed in the woods. That apparently was enough for the Confederates this day. "Seeing the odds they were against, our men went to horses and made their way back up the Holston, and on the night ride we slept in our saddles."

But there still was more of the war ahead.

Soon back in Georgia, where his own cavalry company was on escort duty with Gen. Joseph E. Johnston, he was again on the sidelines, watching, as his comrades prepared for a major battle. "At Resaca I saw the troops sling their knapsacks to be picked up by the wagons and on double quick, to enter the battle, and I will never forget the serious expression each man wore on his face as he pushed himself on to what he knew was danger, and perhaps death. Each countenance was as rigid as a stone."

Here, too, Yankee projectiles fell "thick as hail" around the headquarters wagons where Freeman and his comrades were eating breakfast. Shells came "crashing through the Jim Hill house, where General Johnston had his headquarters."

And then in the public square at Cassville, the shells again "fell thick where we were."

It was pretty much the same at the headquarters camp set up for the fighting at Kennesaw Mountain, where the general was wont to sit on a camp stool and watch the signal corpsmen on top of the mountain. "I thought I would like to move away from there every time a ball fell dangerously near, but the general was paying no attention to them," he recalled.

After John Bell Hood replaced Johnston in command of the Army of Tennessee outside Atlanta, the youngster's company no longer was a general's escort. Instead, "our company was put in charge of beef cattle for the army," Freeman related. "We turned cowboys."

Born into a family of at least five brothers and two sisters, the same Civil War "cowboy" not only would survive the war (apparently with the final rank of lieutenant), but he would grow up to become a newspaper editor and mayor of three Georgia towns: Calhoun, Cedartown, and Cartersville. His brother Madison survived the war but died shortly afterward, in 1869, due either to his phlebitis condition or to yellow fever, according to an online genealogical article by David Freeman's great-great-grandnephew, Alan Cole Freeman (http://homepages.rootsweb.com/%Eafreeman/davidb.htm). David himself, by now accorded the rank of brigadier general by the United Confederate Veterans, lived until 1929, succumbing to a heart attack at his Atlanta apartment at the age of seventy-seven.

UNION
Cheers for the Enemy

"HANDSOMEST THING IN THE WHOLE war," said a marveling James Longstreet.

"Never were men so brave," agreed Robert E. Lee, obviously moved as well.

"Brilliant assault," added George E. Pickett. And, yes, a sight surely "beyond description."

Before them, below the brow of their hill, one of the most memorable infantry charges of the Civil War was under way. It was an advance of brave men into the teeth of the enemy's murderous fire, with predictably horrendous casualties resulting.

It was so dramatic that possibly none of the three Confederate generals watching from a hillside had ever seen its equal. They certainly were stunned at what they saw unfolding below their vantage point.

If they were all together, watching from *above*, of course, it couldn't have been Pickett's own memorable uphill charge at Gettysburg, could it? A charge, ironically, ordered by Lee, doubted by Longstreet, and executed by Pickett.

But allow Pickett himself to explain: "We forgot they were fighting us, and cheer after cheer at their fearlessness went up all along our line."

And yes, it was the enemy they were watching with such great admiration. The Union. Specifically, at this moment, the Irish Brigade of New York in action at Fredericksburg, Virginia.

The date was December 12, 1862, when the Irish Brigade, as part of the Union's Second Corps, crossed the Rappahannock River on three pontoon bridges to enter the Virginia town. Up on the heights, Marye's Heights, Confederate Gen. D. H. Hill was made a bit uneasy by the sight. "There are those damned green flags again," he muttered.

It was the next day, December 13, when the Sixty-Ninth New York, the "Fighting Sixty-Ninth," took the brigade lead in the march down Hanover Street toward the heights. Just ahead of the New York Irishmen, Samuel G. French's division had been mauled and broken by the stout Confederate defense. And now, to the fore, came Brig. Gen. Thomas F. Meagher's Irishmen, thirteen hundred strong.

Their turn.

Up the hill they wheeled, up against the center of the Rebel line, while the likes of Lee, Longstreet, and Pickett looked down at them and marveled at the sight. One of French's men was watching too. "They pass just to our left, poor fellows, poor glorious fellows, shaking goodbye to us with their hats."

Into the storm they went. Almost all the way up the hill…but not quite.

Still watching in rapt attention was one of French's soldiers, Thomas F. Galway. Watching as the Irish "reach a point within a stone's throw of the stone wall." But then, not an inch farther. "They try to go beyond but are slaughtered. Nothing could advance farther and live. They lie down doggedly, determined to hold the ground they already have taken. There, away out in the fields to the front and left of us, we see them for an hour or so, lying in line close to that terrible stone wall."

That was it, their peak at Fredericksburg, recalled Gary Glynn in "Meagher of the Sword," *America's Civil War*, September 1995. By war's end, the Irish Brigade of the Army of the Potomac—its remnants—would be hailed for its performance in the Seven Days' campaign, at Antietam, at Chancellorsville… but its peak *was* Fredericksburg. By the time the survivors of the charge up Marye's Heights inched back down the hill, by the time some semblance of a brigade roll call could be taken that evening, only 250 of the 1,300 could be counted as alive, well, and present for further duty.

CONFEDERATE
Prayed with Stonewall

"IT WAS MY PROUD PRIVILEGE to know Stonewall Jackson personally, and to see a good deal of him during the two years of the war into which he crowded illustrious deeds which have filled two continents with his fame and make him one of the greatest soldiers of all history."

So stated former Confederate chaplain J. William Jones nearly forty years after he spent so many moments of those two years by Jackson's side…so many of them dramatic moments still burning in the aging clergyman's mind.

"I confess that I love sometimes to recall some of the great battle pictures in which he figured," wrote Jones, a lifelong apologist for the Lost Cause, in the December 1901 issue of the *Confederate Veteran* magazine.

One was that famous moment at First Manassas when hard-pressed Gen. Barnard E. Bee, "about to yield up his noble life," cried out: "Rally behind the Virginians! Look! There stands Jackson like a stone wall! Let us determine to die here, and we shall conquer."

Some may differ on the exact words, but all of course agree that's when the little-known professor from the Virginia Military Institute suddenly became the world-famous Stonewall Jackson.

Another favorite moment for Jones came from Jackson's brilliant Valley campaign—"that one at Winchester, when, driving [Union Gen. Nathaniel] Banks pellmell through the streets, he was surrounded by beautiful women, who hailed him as their deliverer, and cut off, as souvenirs, every button on his old gray coat."

Then, too, at Gaines's Mill, June 27, 1862, outside Richmond, "when he sat on his old sorrel horse sucking a lemon and gave the laconic order: 'Tell every one of my brigades to advance and sweep the field with the bayonet.'" (Note: the name of Jackson's horse was "Little Sorrel.")

Still more of the enthused chaplain's favorite scenes: "Cedar Run, where he rallied his broken legions and offered himself to lead the charge; Second Manassas, where, cut off for a time from the main army of Lee, he was every-where among his troops, the very personification of the genius of battle; Harpers Ferry, Sharpsburg [Antietam], Fredericksburg, and Chancellorsville, at all of which he proved himself worthy to rank among the great captains of history, and justified Lee's noble letter when he wrote his wounded lieutenant: 'Could I have dictated events, I should have chosen for the good of the country to have been disabled in your stead.'"

Clearly enough, Jones, a twenty-four-year-old native Virginian and Southern Baptist minister at the start of the war (he had been ordained in 1860), was *not* a witness to all the memorable scenes he cited, and in the words of Jackson biographer James I. Robertson Jr., he "always dramatized a good story." Still, Jones was virtually "embedded" for a good part of the war years with Jackson's forces, as indeed he was with other elements of Robert E. Lee's Army of Northern Virginia. "During the war, he helped form the Chaplains Association of the Army of Northern Virginia, and ministered to troops who served under Generals A. P. Hill, Stonewall Jackson, and Lee," notes the biographical entry on Jones from *The New Georgia Encyclopedia* (www.georgia encyclopedia.org/nge/ArticlePrintable.jsp?id=h-2898).

Says the same source: "He was indefatigable as a preacher and revivalist, once baptizing more than 220 men in a single year."

For many years after the war, Jones worked at compiling his book *Christ in the Camp: The True Story of the Great Revival During the War Between the States*, which drew upon his memories and those of his fellow Confederate chaplains. With four of his sons also joining the Baptist ministry, adds the *New Georgia* entry, "Jones became an influential leader of the Southern Baptist denomination" to the point that he and his sons "were affectionately known in Baptist circles as 'The Jones Boys.'"

At the same time, however, "Jones became embroiled in Lost Cause apologetics, arguing that the South had waged a just and holy war, and that the Confederacy produced 'the noblest army…that ever marched under any banner or fought for any cause in all the tide of time.' He held the powerful position of secretary-treasurer of the Southern Historical Society for more than a decade (1875–87) and edited fourteen volumes of the society's *Papers*, the major organ for the dissemination of Lost Cause ideology."

In his final years, adds the Georgia-based website, his "standard" prayer opening included the words, "God of Abraham, Isaac, and Jacob, God of Israel, God of the centuries, God of our fathers, God of Jefferson Davis, Robert Edward Lee, and Stonewall Jackson, Lord of hosts and King of Kings…"

"Never 'reconstructed,'" according to a fellow member of the historical society quoted in the *Georgia Encyclopedia* entry, Jones died in 1909 after devoting "his whole life to defending by tongue and poem the eternal righteousness of the 'Lost Cause' after it went down to defeat, and…at the last died not only in the 'faith once delivered to the saints,' but in the good old Confederate faith."

By his own account in the 1901 *Confederate Veteran*, Jones, as a young clergyman during the war, had drawn significant religious sustenance from his idol Stonewall Jackson:

> I love to recall him as announcing his great victories, "God blessed our arms with victory," and halting his victorious legions for a "thanksgiving service;" as sitting among his ragged soldiers and drinking in with kindling [kindly?] eye and beaming face the simple truths of the gospel; as dismounting one day from his war steed and walking with me for two miles to talk on the religious interests of his men and the subject of personal religion; as conducting a prayer meeting at his headquarters, and making one of the most appropriate and fervent prayers I ever heard; as delighting in religious conversation, as active for the salvation of others, and as so fully

committed into the hands of Christ his interests for time and for eternity that when cut down at Chancellorsville, in the full tide of his brilliant career, he could calmly say, "It is all right; I would not have it otherwise if I could unless I knew that it was my Heavenly Father's will."

For that matter, when mortally wounded on that very occasion, Jackson left behind "a record of his last days that showed beyond all peradventure that he had been taught by God's Spirit how to die, as well as how to live."

Moreover, he "spoke a prophecy of his own end as a stirring exhortation to his followers" with his final, dying words, "Let us cross over the river and rest under the shade of the trees."

In sum, "Determination to use his own best efforts, combined with his simple trust in Christ, and full confidence in the promises of God's word—these were the silent, potent influences which raised the penniless orphan boy into the world-famous Stonewall Jackson. 'Be ye followers of him, even as he also was of Christ.'"

UNION
At Home in Gettysburg

THE DAY BEFORE THE FIRST day of battle at Gettysburg, teenager Daniel Skelly, a clerk at a dry goods store, was at the Cobean corner of Chambersburg Street. He was standing, looking around, excited by all the recent troop movements in and around town. Just two days before, Confederate Gen. Jubal A. Early's men had occupied Gettysburg, but then they left peaceably enough. And now, well…sitting on a horse right before young Skelly was Union Brig. Gen. John Buford, whose cavalrymen had just trooped into town on the heels of the departed Confederates.

It was about four o'clock in the afternoon of June 30. And there the general sat, reported Skelly many years later, "entirely alone, facing to the west in profound thought."

In the next four days, the young Gettysburg resident would see many more soldiers, even a few more generals, but he never would forget this first, close-up view of a leader from among the Civil War combatants, blue or gray.

"I remember this incident very distinctly for it made a deep impression…. It was the only time I ever saw the general and his calm demeanor and soldierly appearance, as well as the fact that his uniform was different from any general's I had ever seen. He wore a sort of hunting coat of blouse effect."

For Skelly and his fellow townspeople, the sudden appearance of Buford's cavalry troopers that June 30 was reassuring. Two brigades of Federal horsemen had reached the Pennsylvania town, Skelly said. "I well remember how secure this made us feel. We thought surely now we were safe and the [main] Confederate army would never reach Gettysburg."

The previous days had been full of rumor and alarm, "for we knew the Confederate army, or part of it at least, was within a few miles of our town and at night we could see from the house-tops the campfires in the mountains eight miles west of us."

As a result, "We expected it to march into our town at any moment and we had no information as to the whereabouts of the [Union] Army of the Potomac."

Even on June 30, with Buford's cavalrymen trooping into town, the locals had no conception of the cataclysm about to burst in their midst. "On the night of the 30th the people of Gettysburg settled down in their homes with a sense of security they had not enjoyed for days and with little thought for what the morrow had in store for them."

The next morning, July 1, both Skelly and twenty-one-year-old Elizabeth Salome "Sallie" Myers, a schoolteacher on summer vacation, were up and out on the streets of Gettysburg early. "While our elders prepared food," said Myers later, "we girls stood on the corner near our house and gave refreshments of all kinds to 'our boys' of the [Union] First Corps, who were double-quicking down Washington Street to join the troops already engaged in battle west of the town." Until this day at Gettysburg, Sallie Myers couldn't stand the sight of blood.

Meanwhile, Skelly and a friend had walked out the Mummasburg road north of town as far as the encampment of Col. Thomas Casimer Devin's brigade, a part of Buford's division. "While we stood at Col. Dev[i]n's tent an order was handed him…directing him to move his brigade west of the town, as the Confederates were then advancing on the town by the Chambersburg Pike." The two friends headed for nearby Seminary Ridge, site of a Lutheran seminary, to watch events unfold from there. "The ridge was full of men and boys from town, all eager to witness a brush with the Confederates and not dreaming of the terrible conflict that was to occur on that day and not having the slightest conception of the proximity of the two armies."

Skelly climbed a "good sized oak" for a better view of the action.

Back in town, Sallie Myers and her companions "sat on our doorsteps or stood around in groups, frightened nearly out of our wits but never dreaming of defeat."

Then an injured horse was led by. It was bleeding at the head. The sight "sickened" the young schoolteacher. Worse, now came a man "supported by two comrades." His head had been bandaged, "and blood was visible." She turned away, "faint with horror."

More alarming, it wasn't long before "the artillery wagons began to go back and we couldn't understand that."

And next, late in the afternoon of July 1, a truly frightening order: "Women and children to the cellars; the rebels will shell the town."

With that, Myers and others took shelter in the cellar of her home on West High Street, close to Washington Street…"in the direct path of the retreat."

For two hours, from four to six o'clock, her cellar served as a refuge for many, while all hell broke loose outside. "The noise above our heads, the rattling of musketry, the screeching of shells, and the unearthly yells, added to the cries of the children, were enough to shake the stoutest heart."

Incredibly, too, it soon became evident that the Confederates were occupying Gettysburg again, taking over the whole town.

Some of the Union soldiers they had captured "were standing near the cellar window," Myers related. "One of them asked if some of us would take their addresses and the addresses of friends and write to them of their capture. I took thirteen and wrote as they requested. I received answers from all but one, and several of the soldiers [later] revisited the place of their capture and recognized the house and cellar window. While the battle lasted we concealed and fed three men in our cellar."

It had been quite a day for young Daniel Skelly also. After climbing to his oak-tree perch on Seminary Ridge, he could hear distant "skirmish fire" that gradually crept closer and closer, and he could see Buford's cavalry, "which had dismounted, some of the men taking charge of the horses and the others forming a line of battle, acting as infantry."

Trouble was, they steadily were falling back before the advancing Confederates, until the fighting reached the ridge just beyond his own. "Soon the artillery opened fire and shot and shell began to fly over our heads, one of them passing dangerously near the top of the tree I was on. There was a general stampede toward town and I quickly slipped down from my perch and joined the retreat to the rear of our gallant men and boys."

As Skelly crossed a field on his way to the Chambersburg pike, a cannonball struck not fifteen or twenty feet from him, "scattering the ground somewhat about me and quickening my pace considerably."

About the moment he reached the pike, a general and his aides "galloped past" on their way to the top of Seminary Ridge. "This I have always believed was General [Maj. Gen. John Fulton] Reynolds coming onto the field and going to the Seminary where he had an interview with General Buford... before going out where the battle was in progress." This was at nine o'clock in the morning or so. And indeed, by midmorning of that fateful day, First Corps commander Reynolds, a native of nearby Lancaster, Pennsylvania, was in the field northwest of town, leading infantry units to the aid of Buford's hard-pressed cavalry.

The ever-present teenager Daniel Skelly, in the meantime, found the streets of Gettysburg "full of men, women and children, all under great excitement."

He and others now went to the "observatory" on the roof of his dry goods store at the corner of Baltimore and West Middle Streets and across from the local courthouse for "a good view of the field where the battle then was being fought."

After a while, along came another Union general and his staff, coming up Baltimore Street from the south of town. "Upon reaching the courthouse, they halted and made an attempt to get up into the belfry to make observations, but they were unable to accomplish this. I went down into the street and going over to the courthouse told them that if they wished they could go up on the observatory of the store building. The general dismounted and with two of his aides went with me up onto the observatory."

From there, the general studied the field to the west with his field glasses, as well as the roads "radiating like the spokes of a wheel from the town."

In minutes, a scout galloped up West Middle Street at full speed, halted below, and shouted that he was looking for Maj. Gen. Oliver Otis Howard, commander of the Union Eleventh Corps.

Skelly recognized the scout as a local man, George Guinn, a member of Cole's Maryland Cavalry. And it turned out the general Skelly had escorted to the rooftop indeed was Oliver Howard, the very same whose right flank command at Chancellorsville had been rolled up by the late Stonewall Jackson just weeks before.

The scout's news was dire. General Reynolds—last seen going out to the battle scene about nine o'clock—had been killed while positioning his infantry in support of Buford's cavalry.

Howard reacted decisively, even if historically he has been saddled with the reputation of being *indecisive* after taking brief command of the Union forces in the field that first day at Gettysburg.

By Skelly's account, General Howard, his staff officers, and the teenager himself went to a third-story room downstairs. There, "General Howard stopped and gave orders to one of his aides to ride back and meet his corps, which was then on the march from Emmitsburg, Md., ten miles from Gettysburg." Auspiciously, too, it was here and now that Howard ordered the Union occupation and fortification of Cemetery Hill, such a key factor in the Federals' ultimate success at Gettysburg that he later was formally thanked by Congress.

According to Skelly, too, "General Howard, as he came into Gettysburg, had noticed the prominence of this hill, and riding up to the cemetery was impressed with its commanding position." Meanwhile, turning to another aide, Howard also ordered that "the bands should be at the head of the columns and play lively airs as they advanced." Throughout the episode, Skelly added, "General Howard was perfectly calm and self-possessed and I remember this made a lasting impression on me. His orders became so fixed in my mind that I have never forgotten them."

With Howard soon gone to the front in person, Skelly saw a large group of Confederate prisoners—Brig. Gen. James Jay Archer and many of his brigade—being marched to the rear. Shortly after noontime, an Eleventh Corps captain appeared and asked to be taken to Howard's rooftop observation post. "I learned after the battle that this officer's name was Frederick Otto Baron Von Fritche, and that he had written a book entitled *A Gallant Captain of the Civil War* in which he made mention of my taking him up on the roof and giving him some information in regard to the field and the battle then going on."

But now the day's activities for the Gettysburg youth took a new turn. He encountered his mother carrying two buckets of water for the wounded men who were beginning to stream back from the front lines. "We went down Carlisle Street to the McCurdy warehouse, just below the railroad, where the wounded were being brought in…. No provision had yet been made for their care in the town and they were laid on the floor. We remained there quite a while giving them water and doing what we could for their relief."

A while later, Skelly was again at the corner of Cobean and Chambersburg Street as Prussian-born Gen. Alexander Schimmelfennig's division of Howard's Eleventh Corps marched by in "quick time," with "all seeming eager to get to the front" despite the day's hot and sultry weather. Perhaps these were the same men seen hurrying forward along Washington Street by schoolteacher Sallie Myers. In any case, "All along Washington Street," said Skelly:

> the people of the town were out with buckets of water and the sol-
> diers would stop for a moment for a drink and then hurriedly catch up
> to their place in the line. They appeared to be straining every effort
> to reach the scene of conflict, and yet not an hour elapsed before
> the slightly wounded were limping back and those badly wounded
> were being brought back in ambulances to the improvised hospitals
> in the town. The hospitals were located in warehouses, churches,
> the court house and in various private homes. Many others were left
> dead on the field they were so heroically eager to reach such a short
> time before.

In actual fact, Schimmelfennig himself was separated from his corps as it and other Union forces fell back—and even apart—late that afternoon. He then was forced to spend the next two days hiding in a pigsty for fear of capture by the Confederates who swept into Gettysburg and occupied the town.

Nor was he alone in encountering such a predicament, since the Union by this time was in a real rout, with hundreds of blue-clad soldiers streaming

Sharpshooters ruled the streets of Gettysburg for most of the battle.

through Gettysburg, some seeking refuge wherever they could, others striving for sanctuary at the Union rallying point of Cemetery Hill, and still others falling prey to capture by the pursuing Rebels—or being shot down in the streets.

By late afternoon, too, the churches and warehouses closest to the fighting were filled to capacity by the wounded; next, the Catholic, Presbyterian, and Reformed churches, a schoolhouse on High Street, and the courthouse also ran out of space, and then private homes were pressed into service as makeshift hospitals.

Skelly visited the courthouse in company with Julia Culp, whose Confederate-soldier brother Wesley would visit her surreptitiously that night before suffering a mortal wound on or near Culp's Hill itself (see "Confederate: Wesley Culp's Return," page 107). Skelly and Julia Culp passed among the wounded men to give them water, but some "were so frightfully wounded that a lady could not go near them."

The teenager couldn't help but notice that "quite a number of our townspeople were there doing everything they could in the relief work as the wounded were carried in."

Then, too, "When our forces were being driven back through the town in the afternoon, I went home feeling that everything was lost and throughout my life I have never felt more despondent." (Worse yet for Daniel and his family, his brother Jack—Wesley Culp's friend—had been mortally wounded at Winchester, Virginia. See page 109.)

At the youth's home on West Middle Street, his mother intervened when Confederate soldiers took a wounded Union soldier prisoner right before her eyes. She asked if he could stay at the Skelly house in her care. "They allowed him to come [in] and then continued in pursuit of our retreating forces. My mother took him into one of the inner rooms and kept him there without the Confederates finding out. After the battle he was taken to one of the hospitals. In a week or more he was convalescent and came to see us on his way to join his regiment."

He gave young Daniel a pistol and a sword belt he had hidden before his brief detainment, said good-bye…and went off to war again. "We never heard from him afterwards."

Sallie Myers that same evening emerged from her cellar refuge about six o'clock to find that the Catholic and Presbyterian churches just "a few doors east of my father's home" had been turned into hurried hospitals…and with that, her life changed.

"Dr. James Fulton (143rd Pennsylvania Volunteers) did splendid work getting things in shape," she later said. "From that time on we had no rest for weeks. 'Girls,' Dr. Fulton said, 'you must come up to the churches and help us—the boys are suffering terribly!'"

Choosing the Catholic church, she found the wounded lying on pews or on the floor. Their groans were heartrending. She reported:

> I knelt beside the first man near the door and asked what I could do. "Nothing," he replied, "I am going to die." I went outside the church and cried. I returned and spoke to the man—he was wounded in the lungs and spine and there was not the slightest hope for him. The man was Sgt. Alexander Stewart of the 149th Pennsylvania Volunteers. I read a chapter of the Bible to him, it was the last chapter his father had read before he left home. The wounded man died on Monday, July 6.

He had been her first wounded man, but many others would follow. "The sight of blood never again affected me and I was among wounded and dying men day and night."

All during "that long, trying summer," she added, "I was treated with the greatest courtesy and kindness by the soldiers, not one, in either army, ever addressing me except in the most respectful manner. They were men. They bore their suffering in the hospitals with the same matchless courage and fortitude with which they met the dangers and endured the hardships of army life. Their patience was marvelous. I never heard a murmur. Truly, we shall not look upon their like again."

In a similar vein, young Skelly was struck by the conduct of the Confederate soldiers who had seized Gettysburg by dark that first day of battle. "We were now in the hands of the enemy," he noted, "and in passing, I want to pay a tribute to these veterans of the Confederate army. They were under perfect discipline. They were in and about our yard and used our kitchen stove by permission of my mother...gentlemanly and courteous to us at all times, and I never heard an instance to the contrary in Gettysburg."

That night, in contrast to the day's chaotic events: "We settled down quietly.... There was no noise or confusion among the Confederate soldiers sleeping on the pavement below our windows and we all enjoyed a good night's rest after the feverish anxiety of the first day's battle."

On this first day at Gettysburg, however, sixteen thousand men from both sides, blue and gray, had been killed, wounded, or captured. The battle would resume the next morning and rage on, of course, for another two days, with the Union at last emerging in possession of the small Pennsylvania town, the Confederates in retreat...but only after more artillery rounds had been fired back and forth, it has been estimated, than in all of Napoleon's battles... only after eighty-eight thousand Federals had engaged seventy-five thousand Rebels in all...only after more than seven thousand men had been killed, another thirty-three thousand–plus had been wounded, and nearly eleven thousand had been reported missing.

★★★

Additional note: Daniel Skelly may have encountered one more general of some note the second day of battle at Gettysburg, while the Confederates still held the town. He was talking that morning with a Confederate soldier when the latter asked if he had ever seen General Lee. "I replied that I had not. 'Well,' he said, 'here he comes up the street on horseback.'"

Lee, or whoever, "rode quietly by unattended without any apparent recognition from the Confederate soldiers along the street." At Baltimore Street, "about a square away at the court house," he turned into it and headed for High Street. "I was later informed...that he had gone to the jail, presumably for conference, but with whom has only been surmise."

So reported Daniel Skelly in his personal account of his experiences at Gettysburg, which was written with the encouragement of his children in 1932, the very year that he died at the age of eighty-seven after a successful business career in his hometown of seventy-two years. Sallie Myers, for her part, finished her account of the watershed battle by saying she would not want to repeat the experience, "yet would not willingly erase that chapter from my life's experiences." She in fact was "thankful" for the opportunity to minister to the suffering and the dying. Like Daniel Skelly, sadly, she lost a brother in the war. Later, she married a local doctor. Transcripts of their statements are available at the website for the *Gettysburg National Military Park Virtual Tour* (www.nps.gov/gett/getttour).

UNION & CONFEDERATE
Gettysburg Aftermath

IT WAS ONLY EVENING OF the first day, the battle not quite yet a staggering Civil War event, when Dr. Jonathan Letterman, medical director for the Army of the Potomac, began funneling tents, provisions, medical supplies, and of course, doctors—to Adams County, Pennsylvania.

Only the first day, yes, but already there were sixteen thousand soldiers from both sides killed, wounded, captured,…or missing.

As experience had taught the Union doctor, as long as the fighting continued, there would be more and more of the same…and at the watershed battle of Gettysburg, there certainly were. As noted on page 141, the end of the three-day engagement for 163,000 troops, all told, blue and gray, more than 7,000 were left dead and more than 33,000 had been wounded, to say nothing of the nearly 11,000 listed as missing. (The figures tend to vary a bit by source. These totals come from Dover's 1967 *Encyclopedia of Battles* by David Eggenberger.)

Most of the Union wounded would be staying on or near the scene, naturally, but the gray-clad wounded, thousands of them, posed a problem for Robert E. Lee and company. So did the four thousand or so Union prisoners his men had taken at Gettysburg. He wouldn't want to leave either group behind.

Then, too, as still another aspect of the Gettysburg aftermath for the locals to deal with, there was the ruinous impact on the town and surrounding Adams County. Their situation was unimaginable…but all too real. Bodies everywhere, crops and barns and homes destroyed, live ordnance lying around, churches and barns and private homes crammed with wounded soldiers, plus scores of horse carcasses to be disposed of. And it was summer…hot weather.

Still another factor for all to consider: With the failure of Pickett's Charge that third afternoon and the subsequent Confederate withdrawal from the slopes of the Union-held high ground at Gettysburg, was the battle really over? Would Gen. George Gordon Meade now mount a counterattack?

Not right away, as events turned out. On Seminary Ridge, the Confederates still held high ground of their own, and their line of short-range howitzers was fully capable of blunting any Yankee attack. For that matter, not only were the Union ranks badly depleted and far from organized after three days of intense fighting, but the Federals' stocks of artillery shells were dangerously low. Further, dark clouds warned that bad weather was on its way from the west.

All this, plus the simple exhaustion of his men and officers, was more than enough to give Meade pause. (Even so, the victor of Gettysburg would be severely criticized for allowing Lee's army to escape back to Virginia.)

Lee, of course, had no intention of waiting for Meade to regroup. Dealt a costly defeat deep in the enemy countryside, Lee had to bring home his invading army intact, if badly battered. He had many miles to cover, and quickly, in order to cross the Potomac River for the relative safety of Virginia. And not only with remaining units of his Army of Northern Virginia. In addition, as summed up by Civil War writer Jack Trammell in the *Washington Times* of December 24, 2005, Lee's mixed burdens, some good, some bad, included "nearly 13,000 wounded soldiers, thousands of wagons laden with Pennsylvania food and forage,…thousands of Union prisoners, and a very tenuous 40-mile line of retreat through enemy territory."

All this would mean a retreat composed of two elements. One would be the still-mobile components of the Army of Northern Virginia. And the other—a large, highly vulnerable wagon train requiring close guard all the way home.

Thus, late on the day of Pickett's disastrous charge, Lee ordered Gen. John D. Imboden to lead the wagon train taking the wounded, the fresh supplies, and the Union prisoners back to Virginia, as well as "a secret packet for Confederate President Jefferson Davis." Meeting with Lee that night, Trammell noted, the Confederate cavalryman found the storied general to be both exhausted and unusually pensive. "Fixing his eyes upon the ground [he] leaned in silence and almost emotionless upon his equally weary horse," Imboden observed.

By now it was about one o'clock in the morning of July 4, Trammell noted. The two men went inside Lee's tent, where both sat and Lee gave Imboden his orders. "He was to take his 2,100-man brigade and, supplemented by artillery, proceed southward with the entire train to Williamsport, Md. After crossing the Potomac, the column would continue to Winchester, Va."

Why would Lee entrust such a delicate mission to the little-known Imboden rather than his chief cavalry leader, Jeb Stuart? As is well known, Stuart "had sorely let him [Lee] down at Gettysburg, arriving late and failing to provide any worthwhile intelligence about the enemy's movements." As a leader of irregular cavalry raiders for the most part, Imboden himself was known for "self-aggrandizement and lack of discipline," but Lee did rely upon him "for situations like this and kept him under personal orders rather than placing him under Stuart's command." In any case, it was the lesser-known Imboden who, later on July 4, received orders from Lee in formal, written form that included this cautionary note: "I need not caution you as to preserving quiet and order in your train, secrecy of your movements, promptness and energy and increasing vigilance on the part of you and your officers."

The heavy rains signaled by the previous evening's dark clouds finally materialized in the early afternoon, a downpour that was no help to Imboden and his men in forming up their long column at Cashtown, west of Gettysburg proper, with artillery inserted "every one-third of a mile or so." The result of the soaking, said Imboden, was "one confused and apparently inextricable mass." Even so, the column began its march west and then southward by 4:00 p.m. Imboden himself, however, would be supervising its departure "until dawn the next day (July 5), when the last men and animals moved out." At that point, his wagon train stretched for seventeen miles.

"Imboden no doubt was exhausted, though the difficult portion of his task was just beginning," commented Trammell. The Rebel column first proceeded toward Chambersburg but then turned south to Greencastle, still in Pennsylvania, without actually entering Chambersburg. As the Confederates well knew, their wagon train would be a tempting target for the Union forces in the area, but in Greencastle, it was a group of angry citizens "who began breaking wagon wheels and smashing wagons with shovels or picks."

Union cavalry units also found the wagon train and struck at it here and there piecemeal, "before [Confederate] artillery or reinforcements could be brought to bear."

Unhappy with any loss, Imboden was disturbed by word that Williamsport, his proposed river-crossing point, was held by Union forces. But he "made the brave decision to ignore the report and continue moving." Fortunately for him, "the town was empty when the column arrived and between July 5 and 6, the complete train reached the safety of the defensive perimeter that Imboden set up."

Less fortuitously, he found that crossing the river would not be easy, since the recent rains had raised the water levels in the Potomac "beyond fording levels." Not one to wait around, Imboden "quickly put two small ferries into service, moving the walking wounded across the river as soon as they had eaten and had their wounds dressed." But now three brigades of Union cavalry approached. "Imboden positioned his artillery in the hills around the town and, with the help of other officers, drafted 700 wagoners into temporary service. Wounded officers voluntarily led the wagoners by company."

Soon a battle royal was raging between the two sides. "Imboden fully understood that his men had to hold out against a veteran force that certainly outnumbered them. As Confederate batteries began to run low on ammunition, companies of Union cavalry swept to within half a mile of the parked and concentrated wagons." Even so, Imboden's plucky makeshift force managed to hold off the Union troopers until they faded away, thanks to threats on their flank by men under Jeb Stuart. At that point, "Imboden's men, including the wagoners, slowly advanced and cleared the hills of the enemy."

As a result, Imboden was able to complete his special mission with the loss of only sixty wagons—and earn Lee's subsequent praise for "gallantly" repulsing the enemy at Williamsport.

Back in Gettysburg and surrounding Adams County, meanwhile, the citizenry faced a massive cleanup-and-rebuilding task. "Fields were trampled, livestock destroyed, orchards ruined, fences torn to pieces, their homes and barns filled with wounded men," notes a National Park Service website (www.nps.gov/gett/gettour/day4-det.htm). "Floors, walls, tables and chairs were stained with blood where the surgeon's saw and probe had done their work. Food stores were decimated. Graves were in every corner of their yards, gardens and fields, the air foul with the odor of death, mixed with the stench of human and animal waste."

The condition of the battlefields was so bad that Pennsylvania Governor Andrew G. Curtin was "appalled" when he came to see for himself, noted the NPS website. "Heavy rains had washed away the earth from some of the more shallow graves, exposing hands, arms and legs that stuck out of the ground like 'the devil's own planting…a harvest of death.'"

When several Adams County residents urged creation of a cemetery for proper burial of the scattered Union dead, "an enthusiastic Governor Curtin agreed that the state of Pennsylvania would provide funds to establish the cemetery and help finance reburials of an estimated 3,600 bodies." Soon land on Cemetery Hill itself was purchased and improved for that purpose—with the Soldiers' National Cemetery then taking shape on a significant part of the battlefield. The reburials began in the fall, with the recovered Union dead now placed in state plots in the national cemetery, "a final resting place for the defenders of the Union cause."

The dedication of the cemetery on November 19, 1863, would become one of the most hallowed moments in American history, thanks to one speaker's two-minute speech—Abraham Lincoln's Gettysburg Address.

★★★

Additional note: In addition to the dead, the still-living of course had required special attention of their own—from the first moments, to the very end, and even considerably beyond the epic battle. These were the estimated thousands of wounded of both sides, with the immediate care and long-term treatment of the most seriously wounded left to Union hands for the most part.

The wounded Rebels who were left behind when their army retired from the field added to the huge burdens of the doctors and citizen-nurses treating the wounded in all kinds of makeshift quarters—not only in field tents, but also private homes, churches, even barns. The brunt was carried by Jonathan Letterman's legions from the Army of the Potomac, but in short time he and the local citizenry were helped by charitable organizations such as the U.S. Sanitary Commission and the U.S. Christian Commission, along with Confederate doctors and chaplains who voluntarily remained behind to help out, even though they thus became prisoners of war. As early as July 5, the NPS website on Gettysburg noted, Letterman "issued orders...to establish a general hospital in the Gettysburg area and provide transportation and supplies to the site for treatment of the wounded."

The result was creation of a "vast hospital camp" on the George Wolf farm, a site a mile and a half east of town, affording access to road and rail transportation for resupply and transfer of patients to distant city hospitals once they were well enough to travel. Ready for use by mid-July, "Camp Letterman General Hospital" was "staffed with a small army of surgeons, nurses, cooks, quartermaster and supply clerks while a detachment of infantry was detailed as camp guards to look after stores and hospitalized Confederate prisoners." Sophronia Bucklin, a nurse at the temporary hospital, later recalled: "The hospital tents were set in rows, five hundred of them, seeming like great fluttering pairs of white wings.... The ground, now sodded, soon to be hardened by many feet, was the only floor in the wards."

Added the NPS account: "Camp Letterman was filled to capacity by late July and eventually hosted over 1,600 patients." Over the next weeks and months, its doctors steadily whittled down the hospital population, until fewer than a hundred patients were still on hand on November 10. The field hospital then "was officially closed a few weeks later."

CONFEDERATE
Texas at War

WITH A SMALLER FREE POPULATION than that of Maine and a legendary pro-Union governor in office at the start of the Civil War, Texas nonetheless would wind up joining the Confederacy and furnishing it an estimated seventy to ninety thousand military personnel, among them a raft of famous Rebel officers.

For a fringe state destined to host only a handful of Civil War battles, Texas made a dramatic show of support for its neighbors to the east. Then, as if to cap things off, Texas would be the locale of the last pitched battle of the war.

Not only that, but, by the estimate of early twentieth-century Texas historian Louis J. Wortham, the Lone Star State's weighty officer quotient in the Confederate armies included no less than 135 officers "above the rank of lieutenant colonel." Spelled out another way, that total included ninety-seven full colonels, thirty-two brigadier generals, three major generals, one lieutenant general, and one full general.

The amazing fact is that all those thousands of lower-ranks, plus the 135 colonels and generals, hailed from a state that had developed "in the short space" of just forty years "from a little group of three hundred families [settling] in the midst of a complete wilderness."

During that short span of time also, Texas had fought its own lonely war of independence against Mexico and had become an independent republic, with Sam Houston as its chief military hero and two-time president. It had been admitted to the Union as a slave state in 1845, and now, at the start of 1861, the same redoubtable Houston was its governor.

But not for long, as events turned out.

A slave state for real, Texas produced two population figures for the 1860 census—421,649 free persons and 182,566 slaves. Tiny Maine, by contrast, offered a population of 628,279 free persons. Period. No slaves.

More to the point, as secession fever swept through the South and into Texas after South Carolina's decision (December 1860) to leave the Union, Sam Houston, a Virginian by birth, fought to keep Texas out of the quickly forming Confederacy. When the secessionist leaders of Texas issued a call for a secession convention, he tried to block their move by calling the state

legislature into special session…only to see the legislators side with the secessionists by approving the convention effort, with the caveat that a proposed
secession ordinance would have to be ratified by popular vote.

In fairly quick order, the secessionists did meet—in Austin on January 28,
1861. They did vote for secession—on February 1, by the lopsided count of
166 to 8. Their proposal to leave the Union did win approval by the qualified voters of Texas—on February 23, by another lopsided count of 46,153
to 14,747. And the secession convention did then, in March 1861, formally
withdraw Texas from the Union and take the state headlong down the path
leading to war by joining the newly minted Confederate States of America.

Left high and dry by his own people, Governor Houston wouldn't swear
allegiance to the new order, and as a result, he was kicked out of office—
the secessionists now in charge declared the governorship to be vacant and
replaced Houston with his lieutenant governor, Edward Clark. So ended a
remarkable public career that had seen Houston go from congressman to
governor in Tennessee and to general, president, Texas Republic legislator,
U.S. representative, U.S. senator, and governor in Texas.

In the jubilant weeks and then the dreary months that came after secession, Texas not only provided the Confederacy with thousands of fighting
men, but also a cabinet officer (Postmaster General John H. Reagan), tons of
materiel, and millions in financial aid. As historian Wortham noted, "Texas
contributed an enormous quota of military supplies and provisions for the
armies of the South." More specifically, he added, "The state government
spent more than three and a half million dollars at home for military purposes
and paid more than thirty-seven million dollars of taxes, in Confederate
notes, to the Confederate government. The whole population was put on a
war basis throughout the conflict and all of the state's resources were unre-
servedly drawn upon to the limit to support the cause of the South."

The Texans moved quickly too. Within days of the firing on Fort Sumter
at Charleston, South Carolina, "Lieut. Col. John R. Baylor took possession
of [U.S.] army posts west of San Antonio, occupying the Rio Grande into
New Mexico. Col. William C. Young raised a cavalry regiment and captured Forts Arbuckle, Washita and Cobb, in the Indian territory beyond Red
river, and compelled the Federals to retire into Kansas."

Then: "Within a week after the fall of Fort Sumter the Confederate government made requisition on Texas for eight thousand infantry and these
were promptly furnished. In July Texas was called upon for twenty companies for service in Virginia, the enlistment to be for the period of the war,

and thirty-two companies responded. They later became famous as [Lt. Gen. John Bell] Hood's Texas Brigade."

By November 1, 1861, Governor Clark was able to report that "twenty thousand Texans are now battling for the rights of our new-born government." Meanwhile, Clark was succeeded in office by Francis R. Lubbock, who wasted no time in showing his own stout support for the Confederate cause. "Before his inauguration as governor," added Wortham, "Lubbock made a special journey to the seat of the Confederate government at Richmond, Va., to confer with President Davis and his cabinet on the question of how Texas could best serve the cause of the South."

On his return, Lubbock urged his fellow Texans to join the war effort as soon as possible, since Confederate success would depend on "quick and decisive action," whereas delay "would mean that the superiority of numbers in the North would be felt in the contest." Thus, historian Wortham added, as the war grew to "greater proportions than anybody had dreamed," Governor Lubbock "did all in his power to place the whole strength of Texas behind the Confederacy."

But then, that was only fair, since Texas was fairly safe from invasion by the Federals, "and the battles fought in other states were keeping Union soldiers from Texan soil."

Actually, in time, there certainly would be fighting in Texas proper as well— the island port city of Galveston, for instance, was captured by invading Federals and then recaptured by "Prince" John Magruder's Confederate forces.

Thus, in Lubbock's view, it was "fitting" for "every able-bodied man in the state" to "join the armies of the South." He proved such a persuasive recruiter that "within fifteen months more than 68,000 Texans were under arms." Even more were found when the Texas authorities tightened up their draft process. By some estimates, ninety thousand Texans may have served the Confederacy during the Civil War.

Unsurprisingly, considering the state's traditional horseback culture, most of those Texans preferred to serve in the cavalry. As the visiting British observer Lt. Col. Arthur James Lyon Fremantle later noted, "It was found very difficult to raise infantry in Texas, as no Texan walks a yard if he can help it." Governor Clark conceded that the same "predilection of Texans for cavalry service, founded…upon their peerless horsemanship" was "so powerful that they are unwilling in many instances to engage in service of any other description unless required by actual necessity." If there were relatively few Civil War battles in Texas, the state did have to guard against occasional Indian raids and even Mexican brigands striking from across the border. Thus, an estimated two-thirds of the state's military personnel remained close to home—in the Southwest—for the duration. They either were engaged in the policing work against border and frontier raids and building up the state's defenses, or they were thrown into the ultimately unsuccessful military campaigns aimed at subduing the New Mexico Territory.

Even so, thousands of Texans made their weight felt far to the east, in the really major battles of the war. Among the individual notables Texas contributed to the conflict were Albert Sidney Johnston, the army commander who bled to death at Shiloh; John Bell Hood, who fought on despite losing the use of an arm at Gettysburg and a leg at Chickamauga; and Hiram Granbury, one of the six Confederate generals killed (under Hood) at Franklin, Tennessee. The famous Texas Brigade, once commanded by Hood, was well known for its fierce performance at Gaines's Mill, Second Manassas, Sharpsburg, Gettysburg, and Chickamauga, while Terry's Texas Rangers and other Texas units also distinguished themselves on a host of battlefields.

With all that activity to the east, it was somewhat ironic that the last real battle of the war—Rip Ford's defeat of Union troops at Palmito Ranch (near Brownsville) on May 13, 1865—should be fought in Texas. Then, too, the date of Union Gen. Gordon Granger's reading of the Emancipation Proclamation in Galveston on June 19, 1865, has become known as "Juneteenth," first a Texas and now a nationwide commemoration of the end of slavery in America.

UNION
Unexpected Yankee Legacy

FOR THE MEN OF THE Fiftieth New York Engineers, leaving Upstate New York in early 1861 for the war down south meant the obvious expectation of building bridges, throwing up fortifications, digging trenches…and again building bridges, always more and more bridges.

But build a *church* in the enemy's desperately defended homeland? Who among these Yankees ever would have thought?

At first the engineering regiment's experience was fairly predictable, if not also tough and rigorous. From early duty in Washington (as infantry, apparently) and occupied Northern Virginia, the Fiftieth moved on to bridge building in

McClellan's Peninsula campaign and the Seven Days' battles outside Richmond. Next, in the late summer of 1862, the New Yorkers provided the Army of the Potomac with pontoon bridges across the Potomac River, allowing pursuit of Lee's army after the bloodbath at Antietam in Maryland.

Late in 1862, the intrepid construction men of the Fiftieth built bridges at Fredericksburg under repeated Confederate sniper fire…but build they did anyway.

They moved on to the Union disappointment at Chancellorsville in May 1863 and to the Confederacy's defeat at Gettysburg in early July. In 1864 they also were on hand for Ulysses S. Grant's Overland campaign, leading to the siege of Petersburg. Again, they laid bridge upon bridge—in one instance, they reportedly force-marched for eight miles, then threw up a passable bridge of 420 feet in just five hours.

During the subsequent siege of Petersburg, their job once again was to provide fortifications for the Union forces encircling the key railroad hub just below Richmond, although they deviated from time to time to destroy rail lines serving as Confederate supply conduits.

As the siege dragged on into late September 1864 and beyond (from its start in June), the engineers were among the federal units thrown into the minor battle of Peebles farm on the western edge of the siege lines. Here, Grant was hoping to seize the Boydton plank road and the South Side Railroad, both of them supply routes for the besieged Rebels.

At first, the Rebels were driven back by the Union assault across Squirrel Level road, their trench lines too lightly manned to offer really stout resistance. When the Union attack stalled, however, Confederate reinforcements struck back and drove the Federals in the opposite direction, toward Pegrams farm. The fighting ended at dusk that September 30, but it resumed the next morning with each side launching attacks and counterattacks.

In the end, the Confederates remained in their Boydton plank road fortifications, but the Union forces now held "key secondary roads leading into Petersburg…[allowing] them to extend their siege lines farther west," notes the website for the National Park Service's Petersburg National Battlefield (PNB).

Thus, "Grant did succeed in tightening his grip on the city but had failed to achieve his objectives. Lee, on the other hand, had failed to defeat the Union troops outright but had once more minimized the impact of their offensive."

In the meantime, for such minimal outcome to either side, men had been killed and wounded…and the local Poplar Springs church had been destroyed.

Now, with sporadic fighting seen at other sectors, the siege—destined to be the longest such standoff outside the perimeters of any American city—simply went on and on. Soon, the Fiftieth New York Engineers were setting up winter camp in the same vicinity as the Peebles farm skirmishing.

Weeks and then months staggered by.

Restless by early1865, the Upstate New Yorkers suddenly found a project to keep their spirits up, their hands and equipage busy—building a new church to replace the old one!

Capt. Michael H. McGrath of the regiment's Company F took to the proverbial drawing board to design the new edifice while many others ignored the February temperatures to scour the nearby woods for the necessary construction materials. "The new building, which seated about 225, was built entirely of materials gathered from the woods, including stripped logs, saplings, and bark," noted the Virginia Historical Society in a 2001 exhibition titled Lost Virginia: Vanished Architecture of the Old Dominion (see www.vahistorical.org/lva).

Actually, the new wooden structure didn't really "seat" anybody since it lacked pews. As the same exhibit noted, the Yankee soldiers gathering for worship in the newly created, newly named Poplar *Grove* (rather than Poplar *Spring*) church brought their own three-legged stools with them.

Actually, too, they didn't always gather exactly for worship, despite the tall steeple that clearly marked the handsome edifice as a church. "Intended as an auditorium for profane as well as sacred uses, it [the church] was first utilized for a strolling minstrel show," added the historical society's exhibit notes.

With the coming of March and then early April, the pace of the war again picked up, and the siege tightened then lapsed as Lee suddenly led his forces out of the city in a final, desperate dash for a supply rendezvous north of the James River. The Fiftieth New Yorkers were among the federal forces that followed in a hot pursuit, capped by Lee's surrender at Appomattox Court House just days later.

The Civil War virtually over, the New Yorkers soon would be mustered out of service and headed for homes far away from their little Poplar Grove church in Virginia. But then, the wooden Gothic that the Fiftieth built wasn't destined to last at the site for very long anyway—it was demolished in 1868, just three years later.

End of story? Not really…not with all the reburials of the widely scattered Petersburg dead still to be reckoned with. Reburials?

Absolutely, notes the website for the Petersburg National Battlefield. "During the siege, Union soldiers who were killed in battle were hastily buried near where the fighting took place, some in shallow pits, others in mass graves."

So primitive, hasty, and inadequate was this "system," the same account explains, "identification was as simple as a name carved on a wooden headboard, if there was time to leave even that."

Unsurprisingly, "most of these soldiers were not given a proper burial, save what their comrades could provide by saying a few words over them. Some units, like the IX Corps, had small cemeteries near their filled hospitals for soldiers who had died while in their care."

Clearly needed was a large cemetery in the general Petersburg vicinity for proper burial of the thousands of men killed in combat or struck down by disease during the great siege...and what better piece of land should turn up but the former campground of the Fiftieth New York Engineers, already "equipped," you might say, with the Gothic-style, pine-log church they had left behind.

With that very farmland just south of the city chosen as the future site of a cemetery for burial of the war dead, the next move was to find and transfer its many prospective occupants. Thus began the massive task of moving "approximately 5,000 Union soldiers from nearly 100 separate burial sites around Petersburg," says the Petersburg National Battlefield (PNB) account. In addition, "Bodies were moved from nine Virginia counties, reaching as far west as Lynchburg, Virginia."

This was tough, painstaking work, a truly daunting task, for all involved. "About 100 men comprised the 'burial corps.' With ten army wagons, forty mules, and 12 saddle horses, these men began their search and recovery mission."

Said an onlooker cited by the PNB: "A hundred men were deployed in a line a yard apart, each examining half a yard of ground on both sides as they proceeded. Thus was swept a space of five hundred yards in breadth.... In this manner the whole battlefield was to be searched. When a grave was found, the entire line halted until the teams came up and the body was removed. Many graves were marked with stakes, but some were to be discovered only by the disturbed appearance of the ground."

A grisly job for all hands, to be sure. "Those bodies which had been buried in trenches were but little decomposed, while [of] those buried singly in boxes, not much was left but bones and dust."

The task took three long years, with each of the recovered remains placed "in a plain wooden coffin" for reburial, the PNB account reported. "If there was a headboard, it was attached to it." By the end of the three years, the Petersburg burial corps had recovered and reinterred 6,718 bodies in all...but only 2,139 could be positively identified.

What finally emerged, however, still to be seen today, was the Poplar Grove National Cemetery, developed at the very site where the Fiftieth New York Engineers established their winter encampment of late 1854 and early 1865...where also these same "visiting" New Yorkers occupied their idle hours of early 1865 building their own Poplar Grove church.

★★★

Additional note: Buried not far away, at the historic Blandford Church Cemetery in Petersburg, are nearly thirty thousand Confederate dead...with only about two thousand of their names known. Both the Blandford Church Reception Center and the Petersburg National Battlefield maintain lists of the identified Confederate dead. The PNB has been compiling a database allowing public inquiry on the dead buried in the cemetery.

In addition, the Poplar Grove Cemetery, one of fourteen national cemeteries maintained by the National Park Service and the closely allied Petersburg National Battlefield, welcomes any information "regarding a soldier who is buried here or a soldier that was killed in the siege," says the PNB website. "Help us help others by e-mailing Petersburg NB with 'Poplar Grove' in the subject heading."

CONFEDERATE
Brother William's War

WHEN ROBERT E. LEE WAS engaged at Chancellorsville in May 1863, and William Barksdale's brigade was about to be overrun by Union troops back in Fredericksburg, the man who galloped, bareback, to warn Lee was a small, slightly built Confederate chaplain, William Benton Owen of the Seventeenth Mississippi Infantry.

One of at least three Confederate chaplains from obscure DeSoto County, Mississippi, Owen started the war as a private with Company I (Pettus's Rifles) in the Seventeenth. That was as of June 1, 1861, according to the DeSoto County website. By June 29, however, the Methodist minister had been named chaplain of the entire regiment. And once a chaplain, Owen "never felt it right that he should attempt to kill or wound a man, so he never fired another shot, yet he was seldom back of the actual line of battle," wrote Maj. Robert Stiles in his postwar book *Four Years Under Marse Robert*.

Owen's Seventeenth Mississippi certainly did see its share of notable engagements. The regiment's battles began with First Manassas (First Bull Run) in late July 1861 and continued with Ball's Bluff outside Leesburg, Virginia, in October 1861, followed by the Seven Days' battles outside Richmond in June 1862. The Seventeenth Mississippi then was absorbed into William Barksdale's Brigade, and together "they were in many battles," as noted by Tim Harrison, assistant DeSoto County coordinator on the county website. At Fredericksburg, Virginia, moreover, "beginning in December 1862 a great religious revival broke out in Lee's army. The same was true in Barksdale's Brigade. Maj. Robert Stiles of Virginia gave credit for starting these religious meetings, at least in this brigade, to Rev. William Owen, who was referred to as Brother William."

Stiles obviously knew and admired Owen for his selfless and utterly fearless ministry as a chaplain. "Of all the men I ever knew," wrote Stiles in his *Marse Robert* book, "I think he was the most consecrated, the most unselfish, and the most energetic, and that he accomplished more than was really worthy of grateful recognition and commendation than any other man I ever knew, of his ability."

To explain what he meant about "ability," Stiles added, "By this I do not mean to imply that his ability was small, but simply that I do not include in this statement a few men I have known, of extraordinary abilities and opportunities."

In any case, the same Brother William was "a man of the sweetest, loveliest spirit, but of the most unflinching courage as well," wrote Stiles.

For Stiles, it wasn't enough to say that Brother William was seldom to be found *behind* the lines during battle. "It may give some faint idea of his exalted Christian heroism to say that his regular habit was to take charge of the litter-bearers in battle, and first to see to the removal of the wounded, Federal as well as Confederate, when the former fell into our hands; and then to attend to the burial of the dead of both sides, when we held the field and the enemy did not ask leave to bury their own dead."

By Harrison's website account, the Mississippi chaplain took a more activist role when Barksdale's Brigade faced a Union onslaught at Fredericksburg in May 1863 while Lee was busy at Chancellorsville about twenty miles away. Reacting quickly, "Brother William rode all the way to Chancellorsville on a horse without a saddle and reported this development to General Lee, himself, who then sent troops to correct the situation."

At Gettysburg just weeks later, Barksdale was killed in his brigade's attack on the Union-held Peach Orchard the second day of the battle, while the Seventeenth Mississippi alone lost forty killed and counted one hundred sixty wounded. Chaplain Owen came through the maelstrom unscathed but stayed behind to tend to the wounded when Lee's battered army retreated to Virginia. For this, naturally, the Mississippian was taken prisoner.

Released in November 1863, Brother William just as naturally went back to war, his kind of caretaking war, with the Seventeenth Mississippi. Thus he was present when Lee and Grant collided at the Wilderness in May 1864, not far from the Chancellorsville battlefield, and he was on hand again for another ghastly collision of the Union and Rebel armies at nearby Spotsylvania just days after the Wilderness.

This, though, would be the Methodist minister's last battle.

After one Union attack, wrote Stiles years later, "Brother William was, as usual, out in front of our works, utterly unconscious of his own heroism or his own peril. He had removed the wounded of both sides and taken note of our dead, and was making his memoranda of the home addresses of the Federal dead, when a Minié ball struck his left elbow, shattering it dreadfully."

He was taken to a field hospital, and meanwhile some of Barksdale's men sent word to Stiles. "As soon as our guns were disengaged I galloped to the hospital to see him; but when I arrived he was under the knife, his elbow being in the process of resection, and, of course, was unconscious."

Soon removed to Richmond, the Reverend William Benton Owen eventually was sent home to Mississippi. His comrades left behind had their hopes for his recovery.

"But, no," wrote Stiles, "he was never really a strong man; indeed he was one of the few small and slight men I remember in the entire brigade, and, besides, he was worn and wasted with his ceaseless labors. He never really rallied, but in a short time sank and passed away. Few servants of God and man as noble and consecrated, as useful and beloved, as William Owen have lived in this world or left it for Heaven."

★★★

Additional note: DeSoto County's two other chaplains in gray created memorable legacies of selfless, high-risk ministries of their own.

One, Episcopalian minister M. L. Weller, was killed at Shiloh in April 1862 while serving as chaplain of the Ninth Mississippi Infantry. His original company commander, Brig. Gen. James R. Chalmers, described the slain chaplain as "a pure man and ardent patriot and true Christian."

The county's third known chaplain was Methodist minister Benjamin Crouch of the Seventh Tennessee Cavalry, with which he served as acting aide-de-camp to Brig. Gen. W. H. Jackson. Sadly, the Reverend Crouch was also killed in the line of duty—at Thompson's Station, Tennessee, on March 5, 1863. He fell while riding along the line to pass on an order for a charge. Maj. Gen. Earl Van Dorn later said he had been a brave soldier and a good man.

UNION
Out of Uniform

Surrender? Not me, sir!

Galloping down the road near Cabletown in the Shenandoah Valley with thirty or forty of Mosby's Rangers in hot pursuit, Union cavalryman Henry Pancake was not about to join his commander, Capt. Dick Blazer of the Fifth Virginia's Blazer's Scouts, in halting to surrender.

For one thing, Pancake had looked back just in time to see one of their pursuers stop to shoot a wounded Union officer dead.

For another, Henry Pancake was out of uniform. Unlike Blazer, he was not in his Union blue. Instead, he was dressed in Reb gray.

"You see," he explained to a reporter from the *Ironton (Ohio) Register*:

> We were organized to fight Mosby's Guerillas, and as we had to fight them as they fought us, and wearing each others' uniforms was part of the game. Why, I've got in with the rebels and rode for miles without their suspecting I was a Union soldier. One time, Mosby's men captured a mail wagon and some of us wearing rebel uniforms caught up with them and helped guard the wagon until our pursuing force came in sight. That's the way we had to fight Mosby, and it was part of the regulations that some of us wore gray.

It was some time late in 1864 that Pancake was wearing his gray at the wrong moment. "We had gone down on a scout from the neighborhood of Winchester into Luray Valley," he revealed for the *Register*. "We had ridden two days and nights and were returning toward Winchester again. We had crossed the Shenandoah River at Jackson's Ford, about daylight, and rode into Cabletown, about a mile from the ford, and back on the Harpers Ferry road a short distance, where we stopped to cook a little breakfast."

Minutes later, Pancake was busy boiling some coffee near Captain Blazer and a second officer, a Lieutenant Coles. Just then, "a colored boy came up and said about 300 of Mosby's Guerillas had crossed the ford and taken position in the woods, halfway between the ford and Cabletown, and were watching us." The child explained that he had been sent to warn them by "a Union woman near the ford." And now, the Confederates were only a half mile away—three hundred of them to Blazer's sixty-five or so.

A quick reconnaissance from a nearby hilltop confirmed the boy's report. Told the Rebels were in "good position" and "it wouldn't do to attack them with our little force," Captain Blazer quite inexplicably decided to attack anyway. That decision was all the more incomprehensible in view of the fact that sixteen men in the company that morning were dressed in "rebel uniforms" and thus subject to execution as spies if captured.

Nonetheless, Blazer led his scouts across the road and into a field next to the woods where Mosby's men were hiding. There was a necessary delay while the Union horsemen took down two rail fences. They then, still inexplicably, rode "deep into the field," where they were in full view of the enemy. "It was a desperately daring deed, and we hurried up the job [taking down the fence rails], coming round into line like a whip cracker. Just as we got into line, here came the rebs down on us with a yell. We fired one volley, and then they were on us, blazing away."

In seconds, Pancake found himself in a wild melee, with Rebels and Yanks all mixed together...but with the Rebels, in their greater numbers, "shooting our boys down and hacking our ranks to pieces." Now, the object, the only object, was to escape. "To get through the gap in the fence and get out of the scrape, and into the road, was the aim of all."

In such an "awful, nasty fight," it was every man for himself, with those managing to reach the road then flying "in all directions, some across the fields, some up toward Cabletown and some toward the ford."

Pancake was among the last to squeeze through the gap in the fence, with "the rebs all around me and after me." At this point, his Rebel uniform was his salvation...he looked like one of them. But his ruse was not destined to last very long.

He immediately turned his horse for Cabletown and in seconds was pelting down the road with Coles and Blazer just ahead and "another of our boys" just behind.

The "another of our boys" promptly was caught and made a prisoner as the pursuit took up in earnest. "The balls whizzed all around me."

Close to Cabletown, the unfortunate Lieutenant Coles suddenly fell from his horse, "his head resting on his arm as I passed by." Seconds later, "I looked back and the foremost reb...stopped right over him, aimed his carbine and shot Lieutenant Coles dead."

That left only Blazer and Pancake as the quarry for thirty or forty of Mosby's men in hot pursuit. "I gained on Blazer and soon caught up with him. The captain asked, 'Where's the boys?' I replied, 'All I know is one just behind and I guess they got him by this time.'

"'I'm going to surrender,' he said. And I said, 'I'm going to get out of this.'"

When Blazer surrendered, he just may have saved Pancake's life.

"The rebs were not over 30 yards away from us and were peppering away. The surrender of the Captain stopped them for a moment, and I gained a little."

The Southerners took up the chase "mighty soon again," but the brief respite had been crucial for Pancake—he stayed ahead of the briefly delayed posse. After another two miles, his pursuers finally dropped back in frustration. "The pursuing party was reduced by ten, and then finally gave up the chase by sending a volley that whizzed all around me. When I looked back and saw they were not pursuing me, I never felt so happy in my life."

Momentarily happy, perhaps, but not yet ready to stroll on home. After all, his unit had been broken up. Men had been killed, wounded, taken prisoner, or scattered all over...and still the countryside crawled with Johnny Rebs.

In fact, just ahead and off to one side, Pancake spotted a lone man leading a horse on an intersecting side road. The enemy? A trick luring him into ambush?

But no, "I soon observed he was one of our men. He had been wounded and escaped."

When they approached the Union lines near Winchester about dusk, however, Pancake finally was "captured sure enough." Thanks to his enemy uniform, it took until eleven o'clock that night to persuade his comrades that he was one of them and not a Confederate.

As Pancake, a grocer after the war, told the *Ironton Register*, Captain Blazer could afford to surrender..."and live." But not Pancake in his Rebel uniform. "I had to beat in that horse race or die, and as there were 40 horses on the track after me it looked every minute like dying."

Summing up, the Civil War veteran added, "There were 16 of us in Blazer's company who wore rebel uniforms, and I was the only one who got out of that scrape alive. Of the entire number in the company, 65, only 13 escaped and five of these were wounded."

In sad fact, too, "That was the last of Blazer's Scouts."

Pancake returned to the scene of the fight the next day. "Twenty-two of our boys were buried near the road. The colored people buried them. Lieutenant Coles' body was exhumed and sent home and now sleeps in Woodland Cemetery near Ironton. He was a brave fellow."

CONFEDERATE
Agony for Atlanta

TERMINUS AT FIRST, MARTHASVILLE NEXT, and Atlanta (short for the suggested Atlantica-Pacifica) as its final and lasting name, this rail town in Georgia still was backward and surprisingly small just a few years before the Civil War.

In 1842, two decades before war came to Georgia, the future state capital consisted of six buildings and boasted all of thirty local residents. *Thirty*.

By 1844, the town had grown to seven streets. A young U.S. Army officer came through town on the way to his posting at nearby Marietta. Twenty-three-year-old *William Tecumseh Sherman*.

By 1847, things were booming—thirty stores in town, a handful of hotels, at least one church, and twenty-five hundred persons now living here.

The next year, 1848, a majority of the 215 voters reporting to the town's single polling place elected the first mayor, Moses Formwalt.

In 1850, the city council hired two night watchmen to make the nightly rounds, ten o'clock to dawn, at twenty dollars each per month. By this time, the town could boast a population of 2,058 whites, 493 slaves, and 18 free blacks. The predominant occupation among the local residents was carpenter (seventy of them), with merchants coming next...and, at a total of thirty-eight, not even close in number.

Meanwhile, as the town's population shot past six thousand in 1853, the council went ahead and created a police force. *Three men*.

In addition, oil-burning street lamps would be okay if the residents provided the oil. A single public school and a hospital opened for business.

The next year, the city council banned hogs on the streets while approving the prospect of gaslighting for the same streets. A major passenger depot of brick now would serve the four railroads coming to town. And the first gaslights fed by William Helme's gasworks would wink on as of Christmas Day 1855.

In 1856, just five years before the war, the growing town's population hit eight thousand.

Then, with less than a year to go, the crucial presidential elections of 1860 found John Bell of Tennessee and his running mate, Edward Everett of Massachusetts, both of the pro-Union Constitutional Union Party, leading the ballot in Atlanta with 1,070 votes. Running next, with 835 votes, according to the online *A Short History of Atlanta*, was the Southern Democratic ticket consisting of John Breckinridge of Kentucky, candidate for president, and Joseph Lane of Oregon, running for vice president. (Breckinridge was the outgoing vice president, in partnership with outgoing President James Buchanan.) Following them, with a mere 336 votes, was the "straight" Democratic ticket headed by Senator Stephen Douglas of Illinois and including, for vice president, Georgia's own immediate past governor, Herschel Johnson. The national winners, Abraham Lincoln of Illinois and his running mate, Senator Hannibal Hamlin of Maine (both also pro-Union of course), "were not on the ballot."

And now, with the advent of 1861, *fateful* 1861, in January came Georgia's secession vote, making it the fourth state to abandon the Union. Quickly, too, the state's own Alexander H. Stephens, a former U.S. House member, became vice president of the Confederacy. Soon also, Jefferson Davis, the newly installed Confederate president, came to visit…to be feted at a party at the Trout House Hotel.

Next? Seemingly a backwater war zone for many months, left out of the running for capital city of the new Confederacy (that dubious honor, with all the glory and pain that it would bestow, going from Montgomery, Alabama, to Richmond, Virginia), Atlanta in fact was becoming a major manufacturing center and storehouse for the Confederacy—"the war supplier of the south," in the terminology of the online *Short History*. Manufactured here were "railroad cars, revolvers, cannon, knives, saddles and spurs, buttons and belt buckles, tents and canteens." Although the war at first seemed rather distant, Atlanta soon came under martial law, and hired slaves earned their owners a dollar a day by building defenses around the city. At one point, Mayor James Calhoun asked "every citizen able" to bear arms. As yet another "war measure," the sale of whiskey in retail stores was banned.

But worse, far worse, was still to come. For suddenly the year 1864 was at hand.

The first hint of pending trouble came as Sherman, now a Union major general, began moving his army southeast from his base at Chattanooga, Tennessee, along the railroad tracks leading eventually to Atlanta. The distance was 147 miles, but Mayor Calhoun now appealed for all able-bodied men to join military units and told any shirkers "not willing to defend their homes and families" to "leave the city at their earliest convenience, as their presence only embarrasses the authorities and tends to the demoralization of others."

The brave Confederate stand at Kennesaw Mountain northwest of Atlanta on June 27, a repulse of a Union attack, failed to stop the Sherman juggernaut. Here, too, at adjoining Pine Mountain, actually, a Confederate casualty was the Episcopal Bishop-General Leonidas Polk. A Yankee hero (and survivor) was future army chief of staff Douglas MacArthur's father, Arthur MacArthur.

After Sherman, his sights clearly fixed on Atlanta, began crossing the Chattahoochee above the city on July 9, the Rebels were forced to fall back. In just days, another Confederate casualty of sorts would be Jefferson Davis's old nemesis of West Point days: Gen. Joseph E. Johnston…replaced on July 17 by Davis with John Bell Hood of Texas. Expected to be more aggressive, Hood still would have a force only half as large as Sherman's one hundred thousand men.

All told, three Union armies now were closing on the Georgia city that had grown into the South's major supply, transportation, manufacturing, and medical center—to the north, Gen. George H. Thomas's Army of the Cumberland advanced on Peachtree Creek, while from the northeast and east came John M. Schofield's Army of the Ohio and James B. McPherson's Army of the Tennessee.

In Washington, meanwhile, the same series of events were boding well for the politically embattled Abraham Lincoln in his bid this presidential election year to win a second term. His prospects looked even better as Hood attacked Thomas at Peachtree Creek on July 20 but then had to fall back into the city itself after suffering twenty-five hundred casualties to the Union's sixteen hundred in a fierce three-hour battle.

Among the Union survivors this time was future president Benjamin Harrison, grandson of Virginia-born president William Henry Harrison. Here, too, Michigan's own 1st Lt. Frank Dwight Baldwin earned the first of his two Medals of Honor—for outdistancing his own men in a countercharge, penetrating the Confederate line by himself, and returning with two Rebel officers as his prisoners, plus a Georgia guidon. He would later win a second Medal of Honor as an Indian fighter in the West, one of only two regular army men to earn two Medals of Honor during the nineteenth century. (The other was George Armstrong Custer's brother Tom, who earned both of his medals in the Civil War. Like his brother, however, Tom Custer would die at the Little Big Horn in 1876.)

Next in the Atlanta campaign, as McPherson's army moved southeast, sent there in mistaken pursuit of a supposedly retreating Hood, the Texan boldly struck back at the Federals' southern flank on July 22. But to little avail, since Hood now lost eight thousand men to the Union's thirty-seven hundred, although one of them was McPherson himself.

While personally grieving over McPherson's death, Sherman kept up the pressure. With Oliver O. Howard replacing the slain army commander, Sherman shifted the Army of the Tennessee to the right, southwest of town. The subsequent battle of Ezra Church brought yet another lopsided Union victory—this time, the Yankees suffered only six hundred casualties to the South's three, four, or five *thousand*. (As a grim parallel, but in reverse, incidentally, the Federals at Kennesaw Mountain the previous month had lost two thousand in casualties to the South's mere four hundred–plus.)

As the campaign for control of Atlanta ground on through the weeks of July and August, the Union's superior numbers couldn't be stopped. One by one the city's rail lines from the south were cut off; the city was enveloped from nearly all sides, and in the end it was isolated. By September 1, Hood was forced to retreat, after "setting fire to major supply dumps on his way out of town." The present-day corner of Marietta Street and Northside Drive in Atlanta marks the spot where Mayor Calhoun then, at the head of an official delegation of city officials, sought out the advancing Union troops and surrendered the city to them.

Overall, the capture of the great Confederate supply center had cost Sherman more than twenty-one thousand casualties; its defense had cost the Confederacy more than twenty-seven thousand. And still the war—and Sherman's campaign—would go on. For Atlanta itself, in fact, the agony was not yet over. Far from it. For now, after brief occupation, Sherman would be leaving Atlanta for his March to the Sea aimed at Savannah.

But first, rather than leave a possibly viable and resurgent city of Atlanta at his back, he gave his dread order: burn Atlanta.

The civilian population had been told to leave, fortunately, and much of Atlanta already had suffered extensive damage from artillery fire, but this...this would be altogether too much. So decided—and pleaded—Father Thomas O'Reilly, pastor of the downtown parish served by the city's Roman Catholic

Shrine of the Immaculate Conception. Well known for his ministry to the soldiery of both sides, as well as to his own civilian flock, recalled the Shrine's centennial anniversary commemorative program of 1969, Father O'Reilly was stunned to hear of Sherman's November 9 order calling for the destruction of any building or facility of possible military usage. "Father O'Reilly interceded with General Henry Slocum, commander of the 20th Corps, then in top command of the city, to save what he could," added the centennial program.

As a result, Confederate Gen. W. P. Howard was able to report just weeks later, the city hall, a handful of churches, and nearby homes were spared the Union torch, "all attributable to Father O'Reilly, who refused to give up his parsonage to Yankee officers who were looking for fine houses for quarters, and there being a large number of Catholics in the Yankee army, who volunteered to protect their church and parsonage, and would not allow any houses adjacent to be fired that would endanger them."

In sum, Howard said, "to Father O'Reilly the country is indebted for the protection of the City Hall, Churches, etc." Or, as the online *A Short History of Atlanta* explained the priest's role, the four hundred structures left standing after Sherman left town included five churches, "thanks to the personal pleadings of Father Thomas O'Reilly." One of them of course was the priest's own, although it was damaged and would be replaced by a new one that is still standing and in use today.

In the meantime, Lincoln had been reelected on November 8 and Sherman was gone, now embarked upon his notorious march. As recalled by the city's online *Short History*, with its citizenry returning to their city and vowing to rebuild, newly reelected Mayor Calhoun looked into his city treasury and found exactly $1.64.

UNION
Tie Askew

"THE FIRST TIME I SAW the President was on September 3, 1864." So begins the story of a young Virginia woman who, with her mother, traveled to Washington to seek a pardon from President Abraham Lincoln for her younger brother after he was arrested in Norfolk for running the federal blockade.

A general in federally occupied Norfolk had given the two women a pass for their travel to Washington, but there were obstacles to overcome—chiefly a lack of travel money. And once in Washington, there still would be the question of obtaining a personal audience with Lincoln.

First, the money. According to the daughter, Helen Coleman, later to be known by the stage name Helen Truman: "Our worldly goods at that time consisted of a barrel or two of Confederate money which would buy us virtually nothing. We had lived in the South for many years, our plantation had been the scene of several battles and our slaves had been taken from us."

But "Mother was fighting for the life of her son...and the lack of funds would not stop her." Pawning every bit of the family jewelry, "we finally secured enough money to buy our tickets to Washington."

Arriving by train on August 20, they took a carriage straight to the White House, no appointment made, no prior arrangements whatsoever.

Exhausted emotionally and physically, Helen's mother had to be helped from the carriage and then up the White House steps by a soldier who was standing on guard. "I was fearful lest she collapse before we could see the President."

Even in the midst of the horrendous war, all the two women had to do to gain entrance was to ring the doorbell. A "sentry" then appeared to ask their business, but his response was a shock. "I told him we had come seeking an interview with the President and was informed that Mr. Lincoln was out of the city."

Stunned at the news, "Mother gasped and fell in a faint at the sentry's feet," recalled Helen. "A soldier rushed to her assistance and, lifting her from the floor, placed her on a haircloth sofa in the hall near the door and handed me a palm-leaf fan from several on a nearby table. Water was brought and the soldier set out to get a doctor."

One thing led to another as a kindly White House staff swung into action on behalf of the two Southern women. The sentry, who was unable to leave the door, pressed a bell. In moments, a black man "in uniform" appeared. He was asked to send his wife "to attend Mother." The wife turned out to be "an experienced nurse," and she "quickly revived her patient." Next, the sent-for doctor also appeared, "and finding we were strangers in the city and from the South he took us to a private house where we awaited the return of the President to Washington."

It would be more than a week before the two women could return to the White House in hopes of gaining an audience with the president. Once they heard he was back "from the front," however, they hurried over to the Executive Mansion again "and fortunately happened to find the same sentry on guard at the door."

The discouraging word now was that Lincoln was busy. And yet there apparently was hope, for they were ushered into a "private room" and told they would be called when the president "was at leisure."

Half an hour later, the helpful sentry reappeared and escorted them to Lincoln's office. "He was sitting at his desk, but turned as we entered and inquired pleasantly if he could be of any service to us," said Helen Truman as part of a story by L. D. Hotchkiss that appeared in the *Los Angeles Times* in February 1924. "Mother was nervous and could scarcely speak, her sobs making her language incoherent.

"The President spoke to her in a calm, low tone and told her to rest a bit before telling her mission. In a few minutes she regained her composure and told him the story of her only son in prison in Norfolk as a blockade runner and of her efforts to get him released.

"All the while she spoke, the President listened intently and did not interrupt until she had finished. He then told her he would look into the matter and have it investigated. He further advised her to get some rest and cease her worry. We were told that a decision would be reached within a week or ten days and that she would be notified."

Concerned for both her mother and brother as she was, Helen did not fail to notice details in her close observation of Lincoln. "One thing I noticed at this time and on later occasions when I saw him," she said, "was that his tie was always askew. But for this detail his dress was always immaculate."

He of course was tall "and perhaps ungainly in appearance," but he gave no impression of awkwardness. His voice was "moderate and kindly." In fact, "he was possessed of the most kindly face I have ever looked upon."

Helen's mother, meanwhile, knelt at Lincoln's feet and said a prayer of thanks. "Mr. Lincoln helped her to her feet and assured her it would be all right. He shook hands with both of us at our departure."

The two women then left the White House, unaware that Lincoln was about to find out the young man of their family also had been accused of being a spy.

For the next eight days they waited "in terrible suspense" for further word, but none came. Finally, "Mother could stand it no longer, and in addition, our supply of funds was nearly exhausted, so we decided to again visit the White House."

This time, their visit once again spontaneous and unannounced, they had to wait on the haircloth sofa just inside the door for "an hour or more."

Finally ushered into Lincoln's presence once again, "We were informed that my brother's case had been investigated and that another accusation had been found against him." The spy charge.

But not all was lost…far from it.

With no conclusive proof found to back up the spying charge, Lincoln said, he had granted the young man a pardon and forwarded the necessary papers to the federal authorities in Norfolk. "Mother's gratitude then knew no bounds. The President stated that he appreciated her thanks, and wished us a safe journey on our departure. Our joy was so great that we were both in a near state of collapse as we left the White House."

It was a hot day, and Helen was quite thirsty and felt "afraid." Lincoln, on the other hand, "did not seem to mind the heat…and appeared very cool and comfortable during the interview."

As the immediate aftermath to their adventure with the president, Helen's mother returned to Norfolk, but Helen stayed in Washington…to find work. "Our family had lost everything during the war and I felt that I had no choice but to earn my own way. In those days the status of women was much different from that of [1924]."

As the young Virginia woman, still in her teens, saw the situation, there was just one hope for her—the stage. She accordingly applied to John T. Ford of Ford's Theatre on Tenth Street and was hired, thus beginning a stage career that would last for more than three decades. It would be just days before she saw Lincoln again—repeatedly, in fact—as a frequent theatergoer. Up to and including the night of his assassination in April 1865, he always sat in the same box. "This box when not used by the President or his wife was always occupied by Cabinet officers or other members of the President's official family."

★★★

Additional note: Helen Coleman-Truman, by then the wife of fellow actor Frank Wynkoop, died at her home in Los Angeles in May 1924 at the age of seventy-eight. Her death, said the *Los Angeles Times*, apparently left only two survivors from the Ford's Theatre troupe present the night of the Lincoln assassination. Meanwhile, possibly Mrs. Wynkoop had mixed up the dates of her White House visits with Lincoln. According to E. B. Long's painstaking Civil War almanac, *The Civil War Day by Day*, Lincoln apparently was in Washington at the very time she allegedly was told he was "out of the city."

CONFEDERATE
Cadets to the Defense

IT WASN'T EXACTLY NEW MARKET, Virginia, all over again…but it at first did appear that way as three hundred teenage cadets at the State University of Alabama were rousted from their beds the morning of April 4, 1865, to fight a Union cavalry brigade storming into town by way of the six-hundred-foot covered bridge spanning the Warrior River between Northport and Tuscaloosa.

Ironies upon ironies…far to the north, Robert E. Lee was abandoning Petersburg and Richmond, Virginia, to their respective fates for his retreat westward. In five days, April 9, he would surrender to Ulysses S. Grant at Appomattox Court House. The Civil War was just about over…done, finished.

But in Alabama at this precise time, what did they know about this?

Ironies again…the bridge that carried Kentucky-born Brig. Gen. John T. Croxton's tough troopers into the university town had replaced a tornado-damaged span built in 1834 by a slave, Horace King, and his onetime master, John Godwin. Freed from slavery *before* the Civil War and soon to be known throughout Georgia and Alabama as a master bridge builder, King would engineer yet another replacement span at the same site in 1872.

Part black, part Indian, part white, King—with the help of Godwin and Tuscaloosa's Alabama legislator Robert Jemison—was freed by an act of the state legislature in 1846. King later was a reportedly "reluctant" supporter of the Confederacy; he built a three-story spiral stairway in the state capitol at Montgomery, Alabama, that today is still considered an engineering marvel, and he served two terms in the "Reconstruction" legislature of Alabama, although he had been born in South Carolina and would make his last home in LaGrange, Georgia.

At the bridge site, meanwhile, the Federals on the night of April 3, 1865, fought off the local Home Guard and entered Tuscaloosa. About that time, an emissary from the nearby Alabama Insane Hospital rushed to the University of Alabama grounds to give the alarm.

In response, notes an Alabama historical marker at the battle site, "University President Landon C. Garland ordered the guardhouse drummers to 'beat the long roll' to awaken the 300 sleeping cadets."

Quickly forming into three companies, they marched from the campus into town. There, cadet commandant Capt. John H. Murfee's platoon from Company C skirmished with elements of the intruding Sixth Kentucky Cavalry. "In the ensuing firefight, Capt. Murfee was wounded along with three cadets." But they had achieved at least a temporary victory. "The Union pickets then retreated down the hill back toward the bridge."

The advance cadets now rejoined their main body on the brow of River Hill, a vantage point from which they could fire "several volleys down on the Union enemy by the river."

But a freshly released Confederate prisoner then reported they faced a Yankee force of fifteen hundred men and two captured cannon. President Garland and Commandant Murfee "decided that an attack with teen-aged boys would be a useless sacrifice."

As a result, the cadet corps was marched the mile and a half back to the campus and even beyond, to Hurricane Creek eight miles to the east. There they took planks from the flooring of the Hurricane Creek bridge "and entrenched themselves on the east bank."

The fact is, though, Union General Croxton wasn't all that interested in the cadets. Instead, in an action parallel to Union Gen. David Hunter's firing of Virginia Military Institute after the VMI cadets fought (and in ten cases, died) at New Market, Croxton now torched the University of Alabama campus and blew up the university's ammunition supplies. Explains another state historical marker in Tuscaloosa, "After the mayor, accompanied by a Catholic priest, surrendered the town, the Union troops burned the main buildings of the State University, the foundry, factories, warehouses and over 2,000 bales of cotton."

Seeing the destruction of their school "from afar," says another historical marker, the cadets were marched even farther away then told to disband and "re-form in one month's time." But…no need, no point. The war by then had ended.

If it seems that the affair was somewhat bloodless, the Federals did suffer casualties before, during, and after the skirmishing at Tuscaloosa, while a single member of the town's Home Guard, fifty-three-year-old Capt. Benjamin F. Edins, is memorialized by additional historical markers noting that he alone was fatally wounded while leading "about a dozen old men and young boys" in defense of the covered bridge on the Warrior River on the night of April 3.

"This Home Guard removed 30 feet of the bridge's flooring in a delaying action as they retreated, returning fire with their single-shot weapons," adds one of the markers. By contrast, the 150-odd Union troopers (from the Second Michigan Cavalry) rushing the bridge that night were armed with seven-shot carbines. In addition to Edins's fatal wounding (he died ten days later), fifteen-year-old John Carson was wounded "and crippled for life by a bullet."

The Michigan horsemen, for their part, came away with twenty-three unspecified casualties.

As one final punitive action, the raiding Yankees destroyed the two captured canon and burned down the covered bridge as they left the area on April 5.

★★★

Additional note: Destructive as it was to the South, the Civil War did little to diminish former slave Horace King's reputation as a widely respected bridge builder. He earned his place in history, noted the *Atlanta Journal Constitution* not long ago, "for the legacy of more than 100 covered bridges he built throughout Georgia and neighboring states."

According to Bill Osinski's article in the December 7, 1997, issue of the Atlanta newspaper, King's career began while he was still owned by Godwin, "an entrepreneur who studied bridge building with some of the leading New England experts of the times." What Godwin, a brother named Wells, and King specialized in was Ithiel Town's "art of lattice bridge building," explains the website of the Georgia Transportation Department.

A key to their combined success came in 1832, when Godwin, Wells, and slave King moved to Columbus in west Georgia, "where bridge builders were needed, especially to help open up the Chattahoochee Valley region," added Osinski. Despite his slave status, Horace King even now "functioned more as Godwin's junior partner."

Their 560-foot covered bridge connecting Columbus with Phenix City (then, Girard), Alabama, was the first span across the Chattahoochee and thus was "crucial to the development of the region."

When a flood destroyed the bridge in the 1840s, it seems King and Godwin won the contract to build a new one for a high bid coupled with an early completion deadline. King salvaged sections of the destroyed bridge to help build the new span in time to beat the deadline.

"It was this kind of cooperation," added Osinski, "that led Godwin to give King his legal freedom in 1846. The Alabama legislature, likely influenced by an important legislator [Robert Jemison] who was a business associate of Godwin and King, passed a bill making King's freedom official." Osinski noted, "It is also likely that Godwin's failing finances and ill health contributed to the timing of his decision to make King a free man." Godwin, who died in 1849, "wanted to ensure that King could not be considered part of his estate that could be claimed by creditors."

The former slave was so grateful to his former master, he placed an expensive headstone over Godwin's grave in Phenix City—it cost him $1,000, "an incredible sum in those days." Said the inscription, "This stone was placed here by Horace King in lasting remembrance of the love and gratitude he felt for his friend and former master."

As a free man, King now "moved about the South building covered bridges in Georgia, Alabama, Mississippi and Tennessee," along with "homes, commercial buildings, a state hospital in Alabama, and a three-story textile mill… near Columbus." And that "magnificent self-supported wooden staircase that is still one of the most outstanding features of the Alabama Capitol building."

After the Civil War (and his two terms in the Alabama state legislature), King moved to LaGrange, with his four sons now active in the construction business he had started. Between them, they continued building bridges, private homes, commercial structures, and part of a school for black children. He enjoyed "raising and riding fine horses" and often walked about town "wearing a velvet-lapeled jacket." At the time of his death in the late 1880s, a long procession of mourners wound around the center of LaGrange.

His obituary in the local newspaper indicated that he had "risen to prominence by force of genius and power." To which today's website for the Georgia Transportation Department adds: "Horace the 'Bridge Builder' as he was often called had lived at the right time for his skills and resourcefulness to be fully utilized."

UNION
Secret Ally in Richmond

AMERICA'S GREATEST SPY EVER? HOW about Ulysses S. Grant's "mole" operating in the very heart of the Confederacy's capital city?

For here was a spy who lived all four war years in the bosom of the enemy, who placed an agent in the home of Confederate president Jefferson Davis, who sent the Union a steady stream of important military information, who brushed aside enemy suspicions by acting just a wee bit crazy, who maintained a "secret room" at home to hide escaped POWs, who developed cooperative agents in the enemy's own governmental apparatus, who "co-opted" even a prison official or two, who developed a cipher system for coded messages and learned to send them in hollowed-out eggs or the bottoms of a man's boots, and all with absolutely no training in so-called spycraft whatsoever...nor even any urging to begin spying in the first place.

Who admittedly went to bed every night fearful of discovery and yet began all over again the next day. Who once wrote, "From the commencement of the war until its close, my life was in continual jeopardy."

Was it a help or a hindrance that the Union's greatest spy in Richmond was a woman?

That's an imponderable, but we know without a doubt that Elizabeth "Crazy Bet" Van Lew was highly effective. We have Grant's word for it. "You have sent me the most valuable information received from Richmond during the war," he told her.

Indeed, it is sometimes alleged that during the siege of nearby Petersburg, Grant could enjoy flowers from her garden at his breakfast table in the Union headquarters across the James River. More important, the same possibly exaggerated story goes, she also provided Richmond newspapers on a daily basis.

More certain as fact is her longtime activity as a repeated visitor to the Union POWs in town, chiefly to those held at Libby Prison, below her family's mansion on Church Hill, visits during which the prisoners gave her valuable information while she handed out books, foods, and basic necessities. Certain, too, as time went on, she developed five relay stations to forward her intelligence. At her own large house, wrote William Gilmore Beymer in the June 1911 *Harper's Monthly*, "she received and harbored the secret agents who stole in from the Federal army; when no Federal agents could reach her she sent her own servants as messengers through the Confederate armies."

Then, too, "clerks in the Confederate War and Navy departments were in her confidence," and further, "counsel for Union sympathizers on trial by the Confederacy were employed by her money." Amazingly also, she was able to conceal escaped Union prisoners "in the Van Lew house in the heart of Richmond." Here, too, "she planned aid for those who remained in the prisons, to whom she sent or carried food and books and clothing; for their relief she poured out her money—thousands of dollars—until all her convertible property was gone."

One time during the war, a mean, widely hated clerk at Libby Prison, Erasmus Ross, growled instructions for a POW to meet him after roll call at the clerk's office. Others given the same terse instruction never had been seen again, so it was with considerable misgivings that the Union officer reported as ordered. "Ross was the clerk who called the rolls and superintended the prison under Major [Thomas P.] Turner," the same Union officer would explain after the war. "He never called the rolls without swearing at us and abusing us and calling us Yankees, etc. We all hated him, and many a man said that the time might come when we could get even with the little scamp."

Said the onetime POW also: "Our attention had been frequently called to the fact that officers had been called out and never returned. We had no knowledge of what became of them."

As events turned out (and, no doubt, as they had many times before), Ross merely pointed his "prisoner" in the direction of a Confederate uniform…and then left the officer to his own devices.

Naturally, the POW slipped into the uniform, walked past a strangely deserted guard post, and in a moment's time, stepped out onto a Richmond street. There, according to the story later told by Col. D. B. Parker of Chautauqua County, New York, a wartime aide to General Grant, "a black man accosted him and asked if he desired to find the way to Miss Van Lew's house. He replied that he did, and was guided to her residence, on Church Hill, where he was secreted until an opportunity was found to get him out of Richmond."

The fact is, the hated Ross actually worked for Elizabeth Van Lew—and the Union. Furthermore, "Miss Van Lew kept two or three bright, sharp colored men on the watch near Libby Prison, who were always ready to conduct an escaped prisoner to a place of safety."

A petite spinster in her forties, Crazy Bet lived in the mansion with her aged mother. Educated in her mother's hometown of Philadelphia, she abhorred slavery. After the death of her father, owner of a hardware business in Richmond, she freed nine family slaves, and sent one of them, Mary E. Bowser, to school in Philadelphia. It was Bowser who later infiltrated President Davis's household as a servant to the first family…and spy for her benefactor.

The spy network included more of the freed Van Lew slaves, men and women who worked at her Richmond house or at the Van Lew farm outside the city and across the James River from City Point (today's Hopewell, Virginia), where the Union established a headquarters and huge supply depot during the siege of Petersburg in 1864 and early 1865. The farm provided a good excuse for the comings and goings of her domestics, many of whom wore brogans with extra-thick soles secreting messages, even maps. Others would be burdened with baskets of farm goods—but some of the eggs had been hollowed out to carry information to the Federals just beyond the Confederate lines.

During the last year of the war, the farm was visited on a regular, even nightly, basis by federal agents from across the river.

The Van Lew retinue also included a little-known circle of hidden Unionists in Richmond who provided the occasional safe house needed as a way station for a newly escaped prisoner.

Meanwhile, Libby Prison clerk Erasmus Ross was so successful at his role as a gruff, uncaring keeper that he was afraid in the first hours after the war ended to be seen by former POWs. "Perhaps some officer who had been a prisoner in Libby Prison might recognize me and put a stop to my career," he told Colonel Parker immediately after the federal occupation of Richmond. This was at a dinner at Van Lew's house two days after the Confederates evacuated the capital city in April 1865.

According to the same Grant aide, Van Lew herself confirmed, "I have had him in Libby Prison for years doing my bidding."

All during that time, Van Lew, frequently muttering or singing to herself, encouraged the general impression in Richmond that she was a harmless eccentric seeing to the wants of the POWs for humanitarian reasons…misguided perhaps, even unpopular because of her apparent Union sympathies, but basically harmless.

The actual fact of course was that these POWs were a mother lode of military intelligence. As noted by Beymer in his *Harper's* article, "The Federal prisoners furnished her with much more information than might be supposed possible." From their prison windows, stockade apertures, or hospital wards, they saw military traffic passing back and forth. They could estimate the numbers and even the destinations from the directions taken. Further, they heard the conversations of prison guards and doctors. In addition, after capture, just about every POW was marched through layers of Confederate forces simply to reach Richmond. Thus, from "mere scraps" combined with other such scraps, the clever Van Lew could send her Union contacts a steady supply of valuable information.

As probably her most astonishing feat of all, she made the arrangements, lining up exactly the right personnel (more of her supportive Unionists), for the hasty exhumation of federal raider Ulric Dahlgren's body from a secretly dug grave in Confederate territory and its removal to another secret resting place on a farm near today's Laurel Station, Virginia; to remain there until its return to the slain colonel's father, Union Rear Adm. John A. Dahlgren, after the war.

Van Lew paid a price, to be sure. For her well-known antislavery views, plus her "humanitarian" work in the prisons, she was roundly despised by

The Van Lew home in Richmond was the base for the Union's best spy network.

her neighbors—and even suspected as a spy by the authorities. But she was never caught, and some years after the war, newly inaugurated *president* Grant appointed her as postmistress of Richmond, a post she held for eight years, followed by a government clerkship in Washington.

After that, she returned to Richmond and the old mansion on Church Hill… but not to a happy ending. Stalked by poverty, bereft of friends, seemingly forgotten, and bitter in her old age, she wrote: "For my loyalty to my country I have two beautiful names—here I am called 'Traitor,' farther North a 'Spy'— instead of the honored name of 'Faithful.'"

Not totally forgotten, actually, she for some years before her death in 1900 (at age eighty-three) benefited from a helpful annuity organized by friends and relatives of Col. Paul Revere, grandson of the famous Revolutionary-era Paul Revere, in gratitude for helping him when he was a prisoner of war in Richmond.

★★★

Additional note: For most of the time that Elizabeth Van Lew operated as a Union spy in the nest of the enemy, her brother John was busy running the family hardware business in Richmond…and turning over some of its meager profits for her use among the Union POWs. The day finally came when his military deferment for poor health no longer was a protection. He was drafted into the Confederate army.

Rather than serve, he deserted and went into hiding at a safe house on the outskirts of the city. As he awaited a good opportunity to cross the lines into federal territory, his sister came to visit one night in disguise.

For once, her intelligence-gathering capabilities failed her. That night more than a hundred Union POWs broke out of Libby Prison in a mass escape by tunnel.

That meant the authorities were certain to search the properties of any and all suspected Unionists, like those with whom her brother was hiding. It also meant her own home on Church Hill would be a likely target—indeed, some of the escapees had knocked on her door during the night and "begged to come in," a servant reported. Fortunately for Van Lew and her spy operation, they had been turned away for fear they were Confederate agents trying to entrap her and her servants.

As she later wrote, "Brother then had to give up all hopes of escape, because we knew vigilance would be redoubled, and we were in great trouble for the family he was with; for it was to be expected that their house would be searched...and it would have gone very hard with them had a deserter been found secreted [there]."

After they returned to Richmond, Van Lew tried to have her brother declared physically unfit for duty, wrote Colonel Parker. When that effort failed, she persuaded a friendly Confederate general to take John into his own regiment, "and there he was able to give such effectual protection that John Van Lew never wore a Confederate uniform, and only once shouldered a Confederate musket (as a 'figurerhead guard' at a governmental department door on a 'panic day')."

By the summer of 1864, the desperate Confederacy did its best to scoop up any and all potential soldiers such as the reluctant John Van Lew. He deserted again, this time safely reaching the federal lines. The *Richmond Whig* on July 28 reported that he "has gone to the Yankees," but a day later reported that Van Lew's friends and associates claimed he was captured by the Yankees. Either way, he was gone, as they say, for the duration.

Note: Excellent sources for the story of Elizabeth Van Lew are the book *A Yankee Spy in Richmond: The Civil War Diary of "Crazy Bet" Van Lew* by David D. Ryan and the Internet site titled Civil War Richmond, available at www .mdgorman.com/Other%20Sites/van_lew_house.htm.

CONFEDERATE
Distaff Defenders Ready

RIDING INTO TOWN IN THE Deep South one day late in the war, the Yankees making up a column of Union Brig. Gen. James H. Wilson's raiders were startled to notice that the Confederate defenders blocking the way forward not only *looked* like a bunch of women, they *were* women.

Although this was the Civil War, the brave women of LaGrange, Georgia, had drawn upon the eighteenth-century American Revolution to name their apparently unique all-distaff company the Nancy Harts.

Remember her? The legendary Georgia woman accosted in her home by British soldiers who shot her family's best turkey and forced her to cook it up for their dinner? Who then shot one of the unwary Redcoats and held the others at gunpoint until she was rescued?

Well remembered by the ladies of LaGrange, Nancy Hart became the namesake for the forty or so women who responded early in the war to a local woman's suggestion that the ladies of LaGrange should form a militia unit as a Home Guard, replacing the able-bodied men who had gone off to war as members of the Fourth Georgia Infantry's LaGrange Light Guard. As explained by Chris Cleaveland in the June 1994 issue of *Civil War Times*, the LaGrange women's militia that then came into being was unique among the smattering of all-distaff Home Guards formed around the South, "because their group would become a well-organized, disciplined, commissioned military company that would train regularly for almost three years."

As additionally noted in the book *Touring the Backroads of North and South Georgia* by Frank Logue and Victoria Logue, the female militiamen at first were such bad shots, they once managed to shoot and kill a cow belonging to Judge Orville Augustus Bull, father of two of the company's members.

In time, though, the LaGrange women became excellent shots. One of them, Mrs. James Allen Morris, wrote: "It was an open question whether the muzzle or the breach was more dangerous. I have yet a feeling of how the flint lock fowling piece of my grandfather got in its vigorous kicks. But we soon became expert and didn't mind shooting."

According to the Logue book: "Every capable woman of LaGrange, married or single, enlisted as a Nancy Hart.... They had no uniforms and twice a week they were drilled in their long skirted dresses by Dr. H. C. Ware, who could not fight with the Confederates because of a physical disability."

Cleaveland's account agreed that they met twice a week, "usually at Harris Grove, for drills and target practice," while also noting that "the men of the town had taken most of the good firearms when they left to fight the war." Thus, "the women were left with old guns, including some flintlocks." In time, not only their marksmanship, but also their marching improved, as a "dividend of many hours spent practicing in the town's streets to the beat of a tattered drum."

Since LaGrange, situated far behind the lines, soon became a hospital town, men did reappear in town—but for the most part, they were wounded, maimed, or dying men sent back from the front. As one result, the Nancy Harts put in many hours nursing their male compatriots.

And so it went, all through a good part of the war. No combat, but practice, practice, practice, and frequent hospital duty…until, finally, that day *after* Lee's surrender at Appomattox Court House, when the Yankees at last showed up.

First there did come a warning, and *not* from very far away.

Wilson's rampaging cavalrymen, fresh from a raid on Selma, Alabama, were en route to the nearby rail center of West Point, Georgia—three thousand of them, plus artillery, said a telegram from Confederate Brig. Gen. Robert Tyler. Any and all able-bodied men available were desperately needed to help defend the fort guarding that town's railroad bridge.

"All the walking wounded soldiers and aged men in LaGrange gathered and rode a train to the fort," wrote Cleaveland, himself a modern-day LaGrange resident. "The exodus left the town with no men capable of fighting."

As expected, Wilson's raiders attacked the fort at West Point; his three thousand soon overwhelming its three hundred or so defenders. The rampaging Yankees destroyed "hundreds of railroad cars loaded with war supplies," along with nineteen locomotives. "The defeat was troubling news to the Nancy Harts. Many had family and loved ones at the fort."

Among many others, General Tyler was killed.

In LaGrange, the women feared the Federals would move on to their town, as indeed was the case. "Sure enough," wrote Cleaveland, "retreating Confederate cavalrymen brought news that a federal column was coming up the road from West Point."

Dismayed at the news but undeterred from their sense of duty, the women assembled, rejected the pleas of their onlooking compatriots to go home, and instead marched in the direction of the oncoming Yankees. "At the sight of the blue uniforms, the Nancy Harts formed a line and prepared for the worst."

As events turned out, fortunately, the Confederate ladies of LaGrange were met by a group of Yankees commanded by Colonel LaGrange—Oscar H. LaGrange—who had the good sense to defuse the tense confrontation by promising no harm to their homes or fellow citizens if they would disarm peacefully. That did not stop his men from burning the town's railroad depot and cotton warehouses, among other buildings, and looting local stores, but it did result in his invitation to dine at a Nancy Hart's home and his parole for some of the local men he held prisoner to attend the same dinner party.

LaGrange himself, it seems, had been held prisoner in or near the town after being seriously wounded and captured a year earlier and then exchanged in the fall of 1864 to go back to war again.

Since it still was war during these spring days of 1865—or so everybody in LaGrange thought—the colonel dutifully rounded up his wards the morning after the dinner and rode off toward Macon, Georgia, to turn them over as POWs. Now the scene was of "teary-eyed women" bidding their farewells to "husbands and sons marching away as prisoners of war." Still, their homes had been spared, and in a sense, "the Nancy Harts had prevailed in their only confrontation, without firing a shot."

Even more happily, as soon as Colonel LaGrange's column reached Macon, he was told of Lee's surrender and immediately freed his prisoners.

End of story? Not quite. According to the Logue book, Colonel LaGrange was smitten by a young woman he met in Macon—he married her "and took her back north with him." Meanwhile, the same Mrs. James Allen Morris who had to use her grandfather's flintlock rifle later acquired her married name from a resident of Morristown, Pennsylvania, after meeting him at the home of former Confederate Gen. John B. Gordon in Atlanta. During her Civil War service with the Nancy Harts of LaGrange, she had been 1st Cpl. Leila Pullen. And it was she who entertained the Yankee Colonel LaGrange, his officers, and his prisoners the fateful day and night Wilson's raiders visited her hometown of LaGrange, Georgia.

UNION
Plantation Spared

WILLIAM TECUMSEH SHERMAN, WHO GREW up in the same household in New Lancaster, Ohio, as his future wife, Ellen, once played the romantic young squire with a winsome Southern belle, then years later made sure to protect her columned manse during his march through Georgia.

According to the book *Touring the Backroads of North and South Georgia*, by Victoria Logue and Frank Logue, the young lady who caught West Point cadet Sherman's eye was Cecelia Stovall, the sister of his onetime (1836) roommate Marcellus Stovall, son of a well-to-do Augusta cotton merchant. Young Sherman allegedly was smitten when Cecelia attended dances at the military academy.

That was when she reportedly told the future Union general (and Civil War nemesis of her own state): "Your eyes are so cold and cruel, I pity the man who ever becomes your foe. Ah, how you would crush an enemy."

To which he gallantly replied, "Even though you were my enemy, my dear, I would ever love and protect you."

All well and good, except that their lives took quite separate paths shortly after. "Marcellus resigned from West Point because of ill health the following year, and decided to make the Grand Tour of Europe," said the Logues. "Cecelia accompanied him and managed to be in London to witness the coronation of Queen Victoria."

Returning to Augusta, she "became interested in another West Point graduate." But "unfortunately, Richard Garnett, stationed at the U.S. Arsenal there, did not have a large enough salary to suit Cecelia's father, so he packed her off to South Carolina to visit relatives and to let distance kill the blossoming romance." (Garnett, a valiant career soldier and future Confederate general, was destined to disappear in the stormy climax of Pickett's Charge at Gettysburg.)

Meanwhile, "who should be stationed in Augusta but Sherman," the Logues observed.

But no matter. "Chances are the young lieutenant wouldn't have suited Cecelia's father either, as he was looking for someone wealthy to marry his daughter."

Still, "one must wonder…if Sherman's heart didn't beat a little faster when he was told where he was to be stationed."

Faster heartbeat or not, an irreversible destiny carried the young man and woman on their separate ways. "While in South Carolina, Cecelia met and fell in love with Charles T. Shelman, who was a native of Cass (now Bartow) County." Married in 1848, they eventually lived in "a beautiful white home with six Doric columns atop a bluff overlooking the Etowah River."

Young army officer Sherman, for his part, briefly returned home to Ohio to marry Ellen Ewing, with whom he had grown up from age nine after his widowed mother allowed the Thomas Ewing family to raise her son, one of eleven children.

Fast-forward now to the Civil War, and one day in 1864 Maj. Gen. William Tecumseh Sherman pulled up before the front gate to Shelman Heights, near today's Cartersville, Georgia, at the head of his army. "When the home was brought to his attention, Sherman decided to see what it had to offer despite the fact it was slightly off his course." For the moment, he apparently was unaware of the home's connection with his own past.

An elderly, somewhat agitated slave met him and a fellow Union officer at the front gate. As the old retainer repeatedly said, he sure was glad that "Miss Cecelia" wasn't home to witness the visitation by Union troops.

"Miss Cecelia?" Sherman apparently repeated. "Not Miss Cecelia Stovall?"

Naturally, it *was* one and the same…only now she was Mrs. Shelman, wife of a captain in the Confederate army, and neither one was waiting at home for a visit by Sherman's marching army. "This aged servant was the only one left to take care of the place."

Then Sherman ordered his men to replace any items they had taken and posted a guard to safeguard the property until his army had passed.

He told the slave to tell his mistress she could have stayed home in safety. He also left a poignant note "that still remains in the family today."

Cecelia found it waiting when she returned to her home on the Etowah River.

"You once said that I would crush an enemy and you pitied my foe," Sherman had written. "Do you recall my reply? Although many years have passed, my answer is the same. I would ever shield and protect you. That I have done. Forgive all else. I am only a soldier."

★★★

Additional note: Cecelia and her husband spent many postwar years at their striking Shelman Heights home—together until his death in 1886, and she as a widow until her death in 1904. Unfortunately, the antebellum home burned down and was lost to posterity on New Year's Day 1911.

NEITHER UNION NOR CONFEDERATE
Lunged with a Knife

SHE LOOKED UP FROM THE stage and saw him standing by the president's box. He looked down and returned her "nod of recognition." She turned to go to her dressing room for a quick change of costume…but after a few steps clearly heard a pistol shot.

"I stopped, remembered instantly there was no shooting in the play and was about to make inquiry when I heard a woman scream."

She would never forget "that shriek of horror," said actress Helen Truman years later. "It was terrible. Looking toward the President's box I saw that something had happened. It was Mrs. Lincoln who was screaming."

But Truman hardly had time to realize the implications. For here came the same theatrical acquaintance she had seen moments before at the corner of the president's box. "Just then I noticed a man rushing toward me. His face pale and drawn. I recognized him as John Wilkes Booth. Jennie Gourley—now Jennie Gourley Struthers—another actress, had by this time reached my side. As Booth passed us in his flight he lunged at us with a knife in his right hand. He slashed the gown worn by Miss Gourley and continued madly on his way."

The scene the fleeing Booth left behind was a nightmare. Truman, a young Virginia woman not yet twenty-one years old, was so shocked she couldn't move. "The audience was in a panic. They all seemed to sense a terrible happening but did not know what it was. Laura Keene, the leading lady, rushed to the scene of the shooting and I saw her hold the head of the President in her lap. The blood from his wound fell on her gown but she seemed to be the coolest person in the house, giving directions for the summoning of physicians and in many other ways helping to aid the wounded President."

In the meantime, all around her, Truman also would say later, was a scene never to be matched—not in her lifetime at any rate. "The shouts, groans, curses, smashing of seats, screams of women, shuffling of feet, and cries of terror created a pandemonium that through all the ages will stand out in my memory as the hell of hells."

Total chaos reigned even after the fatally stricken Lincoln was carried down from his box at Ford's Theatre and across the street to a hastily procured bed in the Petersen House. "It was difficult to get the people out of the house even after the President had been removed," she told the *Los Angeles Times* in 1924, just before Lincoln's birth date of February 12. "All seemed to be groping for a way to lend a helping hand, but no one had any definite idea as to the actual situation."

As a member of the theatrical troupe putting on *Our American Cousin* that fateful night in April 1865, Helen Truman—by 1924, Mrs. Frank Wynkoop—had met John Wilkes Booth, she had seen Lincoln sitting in the presidential box many times, and she had seen Mary Lincoln in attendance at many of the plays produced at Ford's Theatre in Washington, as well. Oddly, she never saw the president and his wife come together...until the terrible night of his assassination.

"One remarkable thing about the President as I remember was the fact that although he seemed to thoroughly enjoy the plays he seldom applauded. His smiles were infrequent too and he would generally sit in the corner of the box away from the stage and held the curtain so that people would not stare at him. He was among the few theatergoers of the day, however, who always remained for the farce, it then being the custom to stage a farce or comedy after the drama."

Mary Lincoln, on the other hand, was much more visible and emotive. The first time Helen Truman (a stage name, by the way) saw the first lady at Ford's Theatre, "she was dressed in white brocaded satin with a wreath of white roses in her hair and was accompanied by two women and an officer in uniform." Sitting in the highly visible center of the presidential box, she "bowed and smiled to those she knew throughout the audience." The play was *Fanchon the Cricket*, and between acts she sent her large bouquet of flowers to its star, actress Maggie Mitchell.

Another time, appearing with a large group of women to see *Camille*, Mrs. Lincoln and her friends all "enjoyed a good cry." But that wasn't a bit surprising. "Matilda Herron was the actress in the leading role, and I think she was one of the greatest emotional actresses of the day. She had a great effect on her audiences and it was a rare sight of her performances to see a woman in the audience that was not crying."

As for the assassin Booth, Helen Truman first met him at a Christmas Eve dinner party given by John T. Ford, owner of the theater. "It was Mr. Ford's custom to give a dinner to members of his company after the performance of that evening, and each member was permitted to bring a friend. Someone of the troop, I can't recollect now, brought John Wilkes Booth. I was introduced to him and recalled I had heard of him before. He appeared to be a very pleasant man but was somewhat nervous. The dinner was a gay affair and we all enjoyed it. Little did I think then that one of our guests would a short time later end the life of our great President."

Nor did the young Virginia woman have the slightest notion that she would be a witness. Indeed, when she first saw Booth standing by the president's box on the night of April 14, 1865, she did, for a moment, think it "peculiar that he should be standing there." But then she remembered "it often was the custom of actors and actresses to go to the President's box for introduction to the Chief Executive and [I] really dismissed the incident from my mind."

Booth, for that matter, saw her "gazing" at him and rather coolly "returned my nod of recognition."

The performance of *Our American Cousin* had begun "smoothly and quietly," with both the president and the first lady making their rare joint appearance in the presidential box together. "We were all notified of the fact and I managed to look into the box and see that Mrs. Lincoln had on a new spring dress of a small pinhead check gray silk with a bonnet of the same material. Previous to this time she had appeared always in evening dress and we all remarked of the change."

Fresh from Lee's surrender, Gen. Ulysses S. Grant, together with his wife, Julia, had been invited to attend the play with the Lincolns that night, but they declined. "A box had been reserved for him [Grant] and it was decorated in flags and banners. It was not occupied. As it had been announced that the President and the commanding officer of the Union forces would appear, the house was crowded."

Helen Truman had just finished a scene at front stage and "tarried for a moment in the wings" when she looked up at the president's box and spotted fellow actor Booth standing at its corner. It was mere seconds later, as she turned for her dressing room and a change of costume, that he shot Lincoln in the back of the head, slashed the arm of a nearby army officer with a knife, then leaped onto the stage Helen Truman had just left, only to slash at her and her companion Jennie Gourley Struthers as he fled, presumably with the same bloodied knife.

Flag-raising ceremonies at Fort Sumter on April 14, 1865

PART 3
★ AND AFTER... ★

UNION
Return to Sumter

THEY WERE THE SAME. THE same U.S. Army officer, now aging a bit. The same faithful sergeant. And the same "dear flag."

On the same day of the month, the same month of the year, they were back at the same site in Charleston Harbor—Fort Sumter.

Where it all began…

"I am here," began the officer, former Maj. Robert Anderson, now fifty-nine, now *Brigadier General* Anderson. "I am here," he said, "to fulfill the cherished wish of my heart through four long years of bloody war, to restore to its proper place this dear flag, which floated here during peace, before the first act of this cruel rebellion."

It was a short but obviously heartfelt speech to a small crowd in the parade ground of the shattered island fort. "I thank God I have lived to see this day, and to be here to perform this duty to my country," he declared.

With that and a few added words, he then "seized the halyards," as Bvt. Maj. Gen. Edward D. Townsend, adjutant general of the U.S. Army, later recalled. Faithful Sgt. Peter Hart joined in the ceremonial flag raising by passing the halyards through his hands, and "the general's young son, Robert, held on to the end of them."

The dear flag then went up "to the peak by Anderson's own hand," added Townsend in his book *Anecdotes of the Civil War in the United States.* "He refused the proffered aid of every one, and seemed determined that his own strength alone should restore 'this dear flag' to its old place, if it were to be the last effort of his life."

Four years before, to the day, on April 14, 1861, U.S. Army Maj. Robert Anderson had surrendered his shattered outpost in Charleston Harbor after thirty-four hours of artillery bombardment by Confederate batteries on shore—the opening salvos of the Civil War. His own historic dispatch to Washington told the story succinctly and dramatically:

HAVING DEFENDED FORT SUMTER FOR THIRTY FOUR HOURS UNTIL THE QUARTERS WERE ENTIRELY BURNED THE MAIN GATES DESTROYED BY FIRE. THE

CORCE WALLS SERIOUSLY INJURED. THE MAGAZINE SURROUNDED BY FLAMES AND ITS DOOR CLOSED FROM THE EFFECTS OF HEAT. FOUR BARRELLS [CQ] AND THREE CARTRIDGES OF POWDER ONLY BEING AVAILABLE AND NO PROVISIONS REMAINING BUT PORK, I ACCEPTED TERMS OF EVACUATION OFFERED BY GENERAL BEAUREGARD...AND MARCHED OUT OF THE FORT SUNDAY AFTERNOON THE FOUR-TEENTH...WITH COLORS FLYING AND DRUMS BEAT-ING...AND SALUTING MY FLAG WITH FIFTY GUNS.

In response to Anderson's conditions of surrender, which included saluting the flag, P. G. T. Beauregard had sent him this message: "Apprised that you desire the privilege of saluting your flag upon retiring, I cheerfully concede it, in consideration of the gallantry with which you have defended the place under your charge."

But now it was four years later. Aside from scattered outbreaks, the war was over. Lee had surrendered. And Washington had "determined to celebrate the anniversary of the fall of Fort Sumter, Charleston Harbor, by hoisting the Stars and Stripes, with imposing ceremonies, over the ruins of the fort," reported Townsend, who as adjutant general was placed in charge of the ceremonies.

This time it was April 14, 1865, not 1861. And Anderson, the very officer who had been forced to surrender Fort Sumter at the start of the war on that earlier April day, now was under the orders of Lincoln's war secretary Edwin M. Stanton to "raise and plant upon the ruins of Fort Sumter...the same United States flag which floated above the battlements of that fort during the rebel assault, and which was lowered and saluted by him and the small force at his command when the works were evacuated on the 14th day of April, 1861."

Although so much was to be the same as it was at the sad leave-taking four years before, this time, also at Secretary Stanton's order, the flag, when raised, would be saluted by one hundred guns from Fort Sumter, rather than a mere fifty, and all to be accompanied by "a national salute from every fort and rebel battery that fired upon Fort Sumter."

In addition, the noted preacher and abolitionist Henry Ward Beecher would be the principal speaker.

With a select party invited to attend the return-to-Sumter ceremonies, Townsend wrote later, many were transported to Fort Sumter by the char-tered passenger steamer *Argus*, which set sail from New York on April 8, then stopped at Fort Monroe at Old Point Comfort overlooking Hampton Roads, Virginia, to pick up a few more guests. Among those invited, said Townsend, were "some of the noted orators and prominent abolitionists of the time."

Another stop was made at Hilton Head, South Carolina, with side trips provided to Savannah, Beaufort, and Fort Pulaski, as well as to Mitchelville, "where a sort of impromptu town had been established for the 'freedman,' as they were beginning to be styled." Added the politically correct Townsend: "At this last place there was an abundance of speech-making." But not by the Reverend Beecher, who, it seems, "preferred to remain in quiet at Hilton Head, and employed himself in preparing his address." Here, too, Townsend himself, with General Anderson's help, was able to formulate and to have printed, for free, a program for the ceremonies at Fort Sumter.

On the evening of Thursday, April 13, the *Argus* set sail again, this time directly for Charleston. The next day of course would be Friday, April 14— Good Friday, it happened, and a black day for the nation.

But first, the next morning brought a minor snag for the Sumter-bound travelers. The day broke with high winds and high seas. The master of the *Argus* thought it too dangerous to cross the Charleston bar, so he anchored and transferred his passengers to the small steamer *Delaware*. "The rolling of both vessels made it a hazardous undertaking for the ladies," commented Townsend, "but, being safely accomplished, it rather added to the interest of the occasion."

Then arriving at the fort (note: some invitees also came aboard the chartered steamer *Oceanus*), the party found it to be "a perfect mass of ruins." Since Anderson had left Fort Sumter four years earlier, Confederate troops had occupied the island fort, and federal gunners had rained down an estimated thirty-five hundred tons of explosives on the island, reducing its overall size by two-thirds.

"Hardly any trace of its character, except broken gabions and shattered casemates, was to be seen," Townsend added.

Sprucing things up a bit, however, was a temporary platform built in the center of the parade ground for the ceremonial return to Sumter. It was "covered" with myrtle, evergreens, and flowers beneath an arched canopy draped with an American flag. The ensemble, reported the *Baltimore American*, "was the combined taste of six Union ladies of Charleston."

The dramatic moment of the ceremonies came when General Anderson "received the old flag, packed in the Fort Sumter mail-bag, from Sergeant Hart, the soldier of Anderson's command who hauled down the flag," related Townsend.

A word here on Sergeant Hart, who four years previously had given up his job as a New York City policeman to voluntarily join Anderson, his old Mexican War commanding officer, on Sumter Island as a civilian. Contacted by Anderson's wife when hostilities appeared imminent at Charleston, Hart had traveled to the secessionist hotbed, but he wasn't allowed to join Anderson and his small garrison as a newly sworn soldier. So, assuming the role of a carpenter, he joined a work party sent out to Sumter before the bombardment began.

The rest of his story is told in my book *Best Little Ironies, Oddities, and Mysteries of the Civil War*:

> A volunteer all the way, he willingly stayed at Fort Sumter beyond the final ultimatums that preceded the artillery barrage launched by South Carolina. Acting the role of a sergeant again, Hart then led work parties putting out the fires started by the shelling.
>
> On the second day of the thirty-four-hour bombardment, the garrison's American flag was blown down. And it was Peter Hart who responded by nailing the colors to a spar fastened to a gun carriage... who thus briefly raised the American flag over Sumter again.

Now, in April 1865, the two old friends and comrades-in-arms unfurled the same old flag together. As they then adjusted the halyards and prepared to haul up the colors, Townsend wrote, "some one handed to Anderson a bright wreath of roses, which he fastened to the top of the flag." It was then that Anderson, "as soon as he could control his emotion," addressed the onlookers as "My friends, and fellow citizens, and brother soldiers" and declared how thankful he was to be raising "this dear flag" over Fort Sumter once again.

Moments later, the flag flew.

It flew from atop the brand-new flagstaff erected for the occasion in the parade ground. The shout that then arose from those assembled "must be imagined; it can scarcely be described," added Townsend. "Then came the booming of the guns from the fleet, and from half a dozen batteries, and the playing of several bands vying with each other in rendering the national airs."

For all who came, saw, and took part, it had been a glorious day.

They didn't know, they couldn't and wouldn't know, as they sailed for points north on the *Argus* and *Oceanus* later in the day, that Abraham Lincoln that very evening would be attending a play at Ford's Theatre in Washington...that he would be shot and fatally wounded by John Wilkes Booth.

★★★

Additional note: Maj. Robert Anderson, son of a Revolutionary War officer, began his duty tour at Charleston late in 1860 as commander of three army forts there, not only Sumter, but also Castle Pinckney and Fort Moultrie. Since he was born in the Border State of Kentucky, was considered proslavery, was married to a Georgia woman, and yet was expected to remain loyal to the Union, his selection on the eve of the Civil War was, we would say today, politically correct in every way. He then surprised the pro-secession firebrands of Charleston, and undoubtedly quite a few of his pro-Union peers, when he suddenly moved his command on December 26 from the vulnerable Moultrie bastion to the incomplete Fort Sumter in Charleston Harbor. Tensions between North and South rose as South Carolina strenuously objected, but done was done...and there he was, isolated but also much less vulnerable in his island fortress.

The surprise move bought him time but was no permanent solution to the possibility of real hostilities erupting in this center of secessionist excitement. "When the steamer *Star of the West* appeared to reinforce him [in early January 1861]," noted Ezra Warner in his *Generals in Blue* compendium, "Anderson—not wishing to provoke war and having only vague instructions from Washington—permitted it to be driven off." The ship, a slow-moving paddle-wheeler, was actually fired upon and struck three times before it turned back.

There was no further action until April, but it really was only a matter of time before the impasse would end, either in violence or with somebody backing down. The bombardment of Sumter, beginning April 12, 1861, and ending on April 14, finally came after Anderson refused a formal demand he surrender the island fort.

Anderson returned to the North as a gallant hero—indeed, wrote Warner, "his conduct served to unify the North."

Promoted to brigadier general in the regular army by Lincoln, Anderson next was posted to his home state of Kentucky, "where he helped maintain the state's nominal allegiance to the Union." After falling ill, he formally retired in 1863, without further Civil War action.

After his brief return to Sumter in 1865, and now accorded the rank of brevet major general, Anderson died in Nice, France, in 1871. He was buried at West Point, from which he had graduated in the class of 1825.

CONFEDERATE
"Yankee George's"
Secret Love

FROM OUT OF THE CIVIL War comes a bittersweet tale of long-smoldering love at last requited.

It begins with two young men, both Virginia residents, both named George, good friends and first cousins, making their way side by side through the Virginia Military Institute (VMI) and graduating in 1852 and 1853, respectively. It continues with their brave and honorable service for the Confederacy as colonels and regimental commanders, the one rescuing the other at New Market, it so happens. And it ends, years later, in distant California.

In the meantime, of course, there is the woman they both would love. *Susan*.

Susan was descended from a Virginia family so old and distinguished that it had ties to Edward I of England, Philip III of France, and possibly even some of the English barons who signed the Magna Carta in 1215.

Oddly, the two cousins were *not* both Virginians by birth. One, an Episcopal minister's son, was born in Philadelphia, but he and his family moved to Virginia when he still was young. Friends and cousins teased him as a "Yankee," but he truly loved his adopted state and was a Virginian at heart. When Virginia seceded, he seceded.

So did his Virginia-born cousin, of course...the very one who had married Susan in 1855 and fathered her four children.

By this time, 1861, both VMI graduates had spent some time teaching, had become up-and-coming lawyers, and had moved to western Virginia to practice law. The Virginia-born George, a year older than his "Yankee" cousin, formed a flashy militia company soon to be known for its drills and dash as well as its leader's strict military discipline and training. This George sensed the coming of war and was determined to be prepared.

Yankee George, on the other hand, restless and unsettled as yet, left for the still-sparsely populated Northwest, then took part in a survey for a proposed road stretching all the way from the Oregon Territory to Fort Benton on the Missouri River, almost the same distance as that covered by the Lewis and Clark expedition of 1804–6.

The moment he heard of John Brown's raid on the arsenal at Harpers Ferry, however, he headed for his home state of Virginia and joined its fledgling provisional army.

His cousin George, meanwhile, had led his militia company to Harpers Ferry as part of the state and federal response to John Brown's brief rebellion. Now convinced war was coming, this George moved his wife and children back to the family homestead near Culpeper Court House.

Soon enough, when war broke out in 1861, both Georges were in the thick of the fighting as infantry officers. Both were captured in 1861, and both were paroled to fight another day. As the war ground on, not only did each become a colonel and regimental commander…each also suffered significant wounds. And each was known for his bravery and fighting skills.

In the battle of New Market, where the VMI cadet corps joined Confederate compatriots in a rousing victory against the hated Yanks, the slightly older George was called upon to lead his regiment to the rescue of Yankee George's regiment when it was trapped in a ravine under galling Yankee canister fire.

Both Georges survived that day, along with other major battles and any number of the nasty little skirmishes that took a few lives here, a few lives there.

The day finally came, though, when one of the two close friends would *not* survive.

Mortally wounded at Winchester, Virginia, in 1864 (as the city changed hands for the seventy-third time in the war) and dying days later was Susan's husband. He would be the second of two brothers in his immediate family to be killed before all the shooting stopped.

Then, for those surviving the war, for their families, too, came the terrible letdown of defeat, a double blow felt both economically and emotionally.

Yankee George, still a single man, was so embittered, wrote historian and biographer Carlo D'Este, he never would, "to the end of his life," swear allegiance to the restored United States.

Like his slain cousin, D'Este noted, he experienced visions "so clear they could not be dismissed as mere fantasy." As one example, he once "found himself in a large ballroom filled with officers attired in the gray uniforms of the Confederacy." After each came up to him and shook his hand in total silence, he realized every one of them had "served under his command and all had died in the Civil War." It should be no surprise, then, to learn that Yankee George in 1866 departed for Mexico, taking his unrequited feelings of love with him…and leaving the still-grieving widow Susan behind.

She, for her part, had been through ordeal after ordeal all her own. She had learned of her husband's death at Winchester in the Union press four days after the fact. That's right, the *Union* press, too late to attend his funeral in Winchester.

She eventually would have found out anyway. For one thing, her husband's black "batman-slave" Peter left Winchester with his master's horse, saddle and saber and, "riding only at night," eluded Union pickets and foraging units just long enough to reach a brother's home. Surviving family members, "in recognition of this act of faith and devotion," provided the loyal slave their support for the rest of his life.

Susan, of course, was left to raise her four children on her own.

Well, not only that…with the end of the war, so devastating to the Virginia countryside and farmlands, she also would be caring for her blind father and a brother, Confederate navy Capt. William T. Glassell, once a daring hero of the Confederacy's torpedo boats but now a former POW who had contracted tuberculosis in a Union prison. First living in Goochland County, Susan and her entourage moved to Orange County, where they were fortunate enough to take over a mansion once belonging to the late Founding Father and President James Madison's brother.

There they were all but destitute…as was nearly the entire state, site of more battles and skirmishes (two thousand–plus) than any other state, Confederate or Union.

As even more family members moved in, including Susan's mother-in-law, they extracted a meager living by farming some river-bottom land. Fortunately, the same brother-in-law visited by the slave Peter gave them a young steer to eat. That was a red-letter day, since they were close to starving, said Susan's young son (also named George).

Then came real emancipation for Susan and family—another brother, attorney Andrew Glassell, wrote from his home in Southern California and invited all to come west. Wonderfully, too, he sent Susan $600 to finance the trip. "Although it was a princely sum for the time," wrote biographer D'Este, "it was not enough for eight people." But never mind, it was too good an opportunity to pass up. Susan set about selling "everything the family owned," except her late husband's Bible, sword, saddle, and gold watch. A young brother-in-law, Willie, also gave up his worldly goods as Susan's entourage prepared for the move west.

And no wonder, since in Virginia, "there was nothing left for them in the ruins of their politics and their plantations—and their way of life," wrote Susan's great-granddaughter, Ruth Ellen Patton Totten, years later.

Thus, "in November 1866," added biographer D'Este, "the impoverished family of Col. George S. Patton left its beloved Virginia for the long and difficult journey to California. The Pattons sailed on the SS *Arizona* to Panama and then traveled overland across the Isthmus to the Pacific coast, where another ship took them to San Francisco. At San Francisco the Pattons boarded yet another vessel for the final leg of their journey to Los Angeles."

Like many others in her day, Susan, twenty-six years old, found the Panama crossing to be a dangerous ordeal—she was prostrated by a raging fever and nearly died. Then, too, the voyage from San Francisco to Los Angeles was undertaken in "such rough seas that their vessel was eleven hours overdue and feared lost."

Still, all the family members who left Virginia weeks before did arrive safely, to begin a new life in Southern California…at first a mixed blessing, it seems. "Although relieved to be freed of the oppressive burden of life in post-war Virginia, Susan Glassell Patton nevertheless found Southern California, with its bare hills, wide-open spaces, strange customs, and mostly Spanish and Indian population in stark contrast to the lush green hills and valleys of her native Virginia. 'I can never feel so much at home anywhere as I did in old Virginia,' she nostalgically wrote her sister in 1867."

Also in 1867, the young widow added a plaintive note on the third anniversary of her husband's death. "This is the saddest time of all the year," she wrote to her sister. "I feel like a stricken, broken down woman when I remember the fell blow that came upon me just three years ago, blotting out the light of life for me and sending me and mine forth in the world homeless wanderers."

Quite the opposite of a "broken-down" woman, however, Susan put aside her sadness to deal with the realities of her new life. Seeing that her family's presence was "an intolerable imposition" on her brother Andrew, who indeed was feeling the financial strain, she soon moved to a small adobe house and established a private school for girls in a nearby schoolroom. "Her first class consisted of only eleven students, who each paid $3.00 per month, but eventually Susan Patton gained a reputation as a superb, no nonsense teacher who could handle even the most ill-behaved pupil."

The school eventually grew to fifty pupils, but financially Susan and her children still lived "on the thin edge of privation." Eventually, the sale of the family property near Charleston, West Virginia, symbol of far happier days, produced a boon in the form of $500. Her "financial constraints were eased somewhat," added D'Este in his biography, *Patton: A Genius for War.*

Even so, she remained a single woman in a strange land; she "suffered from a throat infection that eventually forced her, in December 1868, to stop teaching for a time, and in the 1870s her health continued to decline."

But in the late 1860s, newfound happiness for both Susan and her children lay just ahead. It came in the form of her late husband's cousin, good friend, and fellow VMI graduate, Yankee George Smith.

Last seen, Smith, still harboring his seemingly fruitless love for the widowed Susan, had fled devastated Virginia in 1866 to seek a new life in Mexico. He spent a year there "surveying" and another year "attempting to grow cotton." In 1868, he turned up in San Francisco, where he spent another year.

Naturally, he knew of Susan's relocation to California, and now he was "drawn" to Los Angeles himself. Never married "because of his love for her," George Smith now openly courted the widow Patton, grandmother of the twentieth century's famous World War II general, George S. Patton Jr. "In 1870 his hopes were realized with their marriage," added D'Este. "Smith adopted Susan Glassell Patton's children, who adored him, particularly young George Patton [future father of the World War II general]. A kind and gentle man, Smith was very protective of the family of his late first cousin and became the father George had never really known."

In their thirteen years of marriage, Yankee George and Susan produced two children of their own, both girls, Annie Ophelia and Eltinge, but Eltinge died of tetanus as a child. Sadly, Susan herself, stricken for some years with cancer, died in 1883. Her second husband George lived until 1915...after becoming a California state senator, prominent attorney, and commissioner of the state's supreme court.

Both before and after Susan's death, former Confederate Col. George Hugh Smith "brought up the Patton children as his own," wrote D'Este. Added Susan's great-granddaughter Ruth Ellen Totten, daughter of the twentieth-century general: "He was a noble and generous man, and he raised George Smith Patton II (and later his son, George Smith Patton Jr.) on stories of the heroism of George Patton, the real father and grandfather whom they never knew."

★★★

Additional note: To keep the descendants clear, the first George Patton (Civil War era) cited in the foregoing was the grandfather of Gen. George S. Patton Jr. (World Wars I and II). The George who came in between, George Patton II, born on the eve of the Civil War, was the son of the first George Patton and father of the third George Patton cited herein.

UNION & CONFEDERATE
Working for the Khedive

OUTSIDE A GREEK RESTAURANT IN Alexandria, Egypt, one day in 1872, shots flew among three former Confederate officers and a party of civilians headed by a nephew of notorious Union Gen. Benjamin "Beast" Butler, widely hated in the South for his harsh rule of occupied New Orleans.

The Civil War all over again, albeit on a minor scale?

Not really, but the odd and little-known fact is that Khedive Ismail's Egypt in those days had become home base to a number of former Civil War officers (and a few enlisted personnel), both Union and Confederate in persuasion. And they usually weren't shooting at each other, despite the hostilities of the recent past.

As explained by historian and multimedia writer Michael Butzgy in his own website on the subject (http://atomic_rom/egy/ptho.htm), most if not all were recruited by Union Col. Thaddeus Mott, a favorite of the Turkish court who met and impressed Ismail shortly after the Civil War. Given a major general's commission in the Egyptian army himself, "Mott quickly convinced Ismail to add more American veterans to the Egyptian staff," says Butzgy's website. "With the Khedive's blessing he returned to the United States, and with the help of General of the Army William T. Sherman, began enlisting recruits. The situation presented a new chance for dozens of Civil War veterans. About fifty former Union and Confederate officers would make a three-week journey to Egypt. In addition, at least four active U.S. officers were given leaves of absence, allowing them to gain experience in Egypt."

Some of the fifty would turn around and go right back home after just a few days in their new surroundings. Others stayed on for months and even years.

For the most part, the former Civil War adversaries were able to put aside their differences and work together. Their perhaps surprising accord was signaled from the very start by the fact that Union officer Mott's first two "Egyptian recruits" were former Confederate Gens. William Wing Loring and Henry Hopkins Sibley (see "Confederate: Sibley's Ubiquitous Tent," page 59). "The pair were given uniforms, introduced to the Khedive and put to work inspecting Egypt's defenses," says Butzgy's website called "Americans in the Egyptian Army."

Also writing separately for the *Handbook of Texas Online* (www.tsha.utexas
.edu/handbook/online/articles/LL/f1077), Butzgy notes that the one-armed
"Blizzards" Loring "was subsequently put in charge of Alexandria and the
country's coastal defenses." As a result, "he thus became the only American
ever to command Egyptian troops."

Meanwhile, not only Loring, but all the Americans were sworn to fight for
Egypt against any adversary but their own country. As events turned out, the
only real war that came up was an abortive expedition the Khedive mounted
against Ethiopia, with Loring taking part in the invasion as second in command.

The outcome was a disaster due to transportation and supply problems—"and
the Egyptian army was almost wiped out during the initial battle." Unhappily,
"Loring and the other Americans were subsequently blamed for the debacle,
and in 1878 all but one were dismissed."

North Carolina native Loring, for one, returned to the United States, ran for
the U.S. Senate, but lost, then settled in New York, where he wrote a book
about his recent experiences titled *A Confederate Soldier in Egypt*. A soldier off
and on from the age of fourteen (in the Florida territorial militia fighting the
Seminole Indians), he died in New York on December 30, 1886, at the age of
seventy-eight.

Back in Egypt, meanwhile, his recruiter, Thaddeus Mott, had fallen out of
favor with the Khedive after a short time, with the result that former Union
Gen. Charles Pomeroy Stone was named chief of staff of the Egyptian army,
even though he technically was outranked by Mott.

The idea of importing the Americans initially appealed to Ismail because
they had experienced "the most highly technological war the world had yet
seen," Butzgy's website points out. With his country made wealthy by selling
cotton on world markets in place of the embattled South's cotton during the
Civil War years, with construction of the ambitious Suez Canal soon to be
completed, the Khedive was in an expansive mood. As the burden of the
canal project grew and grew, however, he also became desperate to avoid
dependence on the French and/or British to bail him out. In the end, with
Egypt deeply in debt, he and Egypt did lose control of the canal. Indeed, all of
Egypt was on its way to becoming, instead of a satrap of the Turks, a British
protectorate as of 1914.

Before all those events could take place, American military men made idle
by the end of the Civil War had looked to the Khedive's Egypt as a fresh, hotly
beckoning opportunity in an exotic setting, with possibly boom times ahead.
After all, here was employment in their specialty, plus, as further lure, the great

canal project, the Pyramids, the famous Sphinx, the storied city of Cairo, the historic Nile, even a new opera house for which Verdi had written *Aida*.

But the two military cultures, American and Egyptian, were fated to clash rather than to click. As explained by Butzgy, Stone's general-staff way of doing things "conflicted with the Egyptian pasha system, in which each commander (pasha) was completely responsible for his unit, overseeing such matters as supply, discipline, and transport, as well as leading it into battle."

To the Americans, Butzgy observed, the pasha approach "seemed rife with corruption." And the Egyptians "did not understand why it was necessary to divide these tasks among a headquarters staff, thinking it confusing and irresponsible. Nor did they share the American love of paperwork."

The result was "frequent" friction between the two cultures. "The Americans could be headstrong and blunt, the Egyptians obstinate and inscrutable."

While there was the briefly "notorious" but-in-actual-fact minor shooting incident in Alexandria "involving" three Southerners (Loring was one of them, apparently) and U.S. Consul G. H. Butler (nephew of Benjamin F. Butler), the Americans usually got along with each other. Stone, notes Butzgy's website, sometimes found himself "a lightning rod for the discontent of several of his officers," but "such cases were the exception, and many of the officers made lifelong friendships, regardless of which side of the Mason-Dixon line they hailed from."

If the Americans left Egypt with no great military victories to their credit, they did leave behind a record of success in other endeavors.

"The Americans," notes Butzgy, "established schools to train officers and enlisted men, and even conducted classes for the children of soldiers. Because of this, the literacy rate soared." But their "most spectacular contributions" stemmed from their wide-ranging explorations on behalf of the Khedive. Thus "several of the officers led expeditions through unexplored regions of East Africa. Charles Chaille-Long undertook a perilous journey to Uganda, and discovered Lake Kioga, through which the Nile flowed north toward Egypt.... Alexander McComb Mason mapped the White Nile all the way to Lake Albert, and discovered the Semliki River. Other expeditions explored and mapped the de Darfur and Kordofan."

One of those noted for his explorations, onetime Union officer Erasmus (or Erastus) Sparrow Purdy, never returned home from Egypt. After expeditions taking him as far as Uganda and to the iron mines of Kordofan and Darfur in western Sudan, he retired from the Egyptian army in 1878 and held a "modest" civilian job until his death three years later, noted an Associated Press dispatch from Egypt in 2000. The occasion then was the dedication of a new tombstone—"a ten-foot-high obelisk of gray marble"—at his grave site "in a leafy Anglican cemetery in Cairo's old Christian quarter." Purdy had died in Egypt as apparently the last still-remaining Civil War veteran hired by the Khedive in hopes of building an empire.

CONFEDERATE
A Most Prolific Author

ONCE THE CIVIL WAR ENDED, some veterans went back to farms, banks, or stores at home. Some became soldiers of fortune overseas. One, Union Col. Washington Roebling, built the Brooklyn Bridge. Others, such as Union Gen. Grenville Dodge, led in the construction of the transcontinental railroad. Union Gen. Lew Wallace wrote his famous *Ben Hur*. Confederate veteran Prentiss Ingraham, on the other hand, found his niche and achieved literary fame as the author of hundreds of novels or novelettes (some estimate nearly a thousand!).

The undisputed king of the dime novels that were popular in the second half of the nineteenth century, Ingraham wrote more than two hundred about Buffalo Bill alone, a major chunk of the four hundred–odd novels and six hundred or so novelettes that made up the thousand. The mathematics of his incredible thirty-four-year writing career—not begun until *after* the Civil War—has been parsed this way: he spun out the equivalent of 1,350,000 words annually, or 3,708 words a day, 154 words an hour.

Easily the most prolific author ever to emerge from his native Mississippi, Col. Prentiss Ingraham wrote about adventurers of all kinds—cowboys, soldiers, pirates, Buffalo Bill, even the real-life "Texas Jack," a.k.a. John Burwell Omohundro Jr., a Virginia-born frontier scout, actor, and cowboy. Ingraham often wrote under various pen names, some of them a bit bizarre, such as Dr. Noel Dunbar or Midshipman Tom W. Hall and Dangerfield Burr.

Ingraham himself was quite an adventurer. He also was the son of another prolific writer, the Reverend Joseph Holt Ingraham, whose own adventure stories sometimes became the basis for many of the son's dime novels.

The younger Ingraham, his father's only son, was born in Natchez, Mississippi, in 1843. He was a classmate of young John Wilkes Booth, Lincoln's future assassin, at St. Timothy's Military Academy School in Maryland, then he attended Jefferson College in Mississippi and was taking classes at the Mobile Medical School when the Civil War broke out less than twenty years after his birth. He joined the Confederate army as a private in Withers's First Mississippi Light Artillery and attained the rank of ordnance sergeant before suffering a wound in his foot and being captured at Port Hudson, Louisiana, in 1863. He subsequently was paroled or escaped… In either case, the injury to his foot would prove to be a problem for life.

When the war ended in 1865, Ingraham joined those Confederates seeking sanctuary or further action in Mexico. There, he sided with the forces of Benito Juarez in ousting imported Emperor Maximilian of Austria, the puppet ruler installed by Napoleon III, but Ingraham's activities as a soldier of fortune did not end in Mexico. He soon was to be seen at the battle of Sadowa, Austria, in 1866; in Crete fighting on the side of the Greeks against the Turks; even in Cuba on the side of the rebels more than two decades before the Spanish-American War.

Acquiring his title of colonel in Cuba, he was captured by the Spanish and condemned to death…but escaped. Not long after, he popped up in the West, most notably, it might be said, at the side of Buffalo Bill, soon to be a favorite subject of Ingraham's dime novels under titles such as *Buffalo Bill's Slim Chance* or *Buffalo Bill's Fight for Right*. "For a time," says an online summary of notes from an Ingraham exhibition at the University of Mississippi, "Ingraham worked as a press agent for Buffalo Bill's Wild West Show" (see www.olemiss .edu/depts/gener…bits/past/ingraham.html).

But first the superprolific author had begun writing his dime novels in the early 1870s for the New York publishers Beadle and Adams, often basing his stories "on his own military experiences, as well as on themes devised by his father." In the latter category, the younger Ingraham "reworked a number of his father's sea stories into a pirate series, which were reprinted many times well into the twentieth century."

Naturally, the busy author's enormous literary output is easily dismissed today as "hackwork written quickly and produced cheaply," notes the same exhibition material…but perhaps too easily, since Ingraham did capture a "substantial popular audience," with the significant result that he "is credited with popularizing the cowboy hero and in shaping America's popular perception of the Western frontier."

A New York City resident for most of his adult life, ironically enough, Col. Prentiss Ingraham lived to the age of sixty-one before checking into the Confederate Soldiers Home established at Beauvoir in Biloxi, Mississippi, the last home of Jefferson Davis, on August 12, 1904…and dying there just four days later of Bright's disease. The Civil War veteran was buried in Grave no. 62 in Beauvoir's Confederate Cemetery.

★★★

Additional note: Before becoming a man of the cloth, Prentiss Ingraham's father himself had written more than eighty short paperbound novels suspiciously similar to the classic dime novel. "Many of the novels had nautical themes, while others contrasted the bucolic pleasures of country life to the evils of the city," notes the Ole Miss library site.

A Maine-born Yankee transplanted to Holly Springs, Mississippi, he previously had written a travel book called *The South-West by a Yankee.* His life and his writing both took a new turn when he decided, "in mid-life," to become an ordained Episcopal deacon. Now, his adventure stories reflected a religious tone. "In 1855, Reverend Ingraham published his most successful book, a novel set in the biblical era entitled *The Prince of the House of David.*" Over time, it would sell nearly five million copies.

No longer a Yankee in thought, he later wrote a "pro-Southern piece" called *The Sunny South* as a response to Harriet Beecher Stowe's *Uncle Tom's Cabin.* It appeared posthumously in 1860, the very eve of the Civil War.

Additional point: Some years after Jefferson Davis's death in 1889, his widow, Varina, moved to New York with daughter Winnie and sold Beauvoir to the Mississippi Sons of Confederate Veterans for a minimal fee with the understanding it would remain a shrine to his memory. The veterans then enlisted the Mississippi state government as operator of the property as a home for Confederate veterans. With twelve barracks built on the grounds, it accommodated 250 war veterans, wives, or widows at its peak population between its opening in 1903 and its closing in 1957. "With the end of state operation of Beauvoir, control of the entire property was returned to the Mississippi Division of the Sons of Confederate Veterans, which operates the property as a shrine to the memory of Jefferson Davis," noted James West Thompson in his book *Beauvoir: A Walk Through History.*

A popular historical shrine, Beauvoir for many years was open to the public…until Hurricane Katrina came along in August 2005 and left the old home heavily damaged both by waves and wind. "Severely damaged but not destroyed," was the word from the historic site's faithful wardens as they announced a fund-raising campaign and plans to make the necessary repairs for the last home of Jefferson Davis and his on-grounds library. "The positive news is that both of these will be repaired, with adequate time and funds," said a press release issued by Beauvoir's overseers. (For latest updates or information on the fund-raising effort, see http://beauvoir.org.)

UNION
Valor Seemingly Ignored

THE OLD GENERAL, WINNER OF the Medal of Honor in the Civil War, was obviously aghast.

The official after-action report on the battle of Piedmont, Virginia, prepared by his commanding officer, Gen. David Hunter, made no mention of the old-timer's signal contribution to the Union victory.

Told of the omission, the octogenarian was obviously staggered.

"Suddenly, his face grew white," his companion later wrote. "He arose, breathing shortly, trembling." And no wonder. "For fifty years Gen. Julius H. Stahel had believed that the story of his charge at Piedmont was set forth in the official reports of the battle, and now he discovered that Gen. Hunter had utterly ignored him, barely referring to the cavalry and giving by name to Stahel's subordinates all credit for the success of the cavalry movement," wrote Phillip H. Dillon in the *New York Times* of August 10, 1913.

It was the very action for which General Stahel—Hungarian Count Sebastiani in an earlier life—was awarded the Medal of Honor in 1893, nearly thirty years after the battle.

As explained by Dillon, Stahel/Sebastiani once was a young nobleman who "rode with Louis Kossuth over the plains of Hungary…in the battle for the independence of his native land." Born in Szeged, Hungary, in 1825, he had joined the Austrian army as a private, reached the rank of lieutenant, but then went over to the revolutionary cause led by Kossuth.

"They lost—those chivalrous horsemen of Kossuth's guard—and many were exiled. Count Sebastiani, or Julius Stahel, came to America in 1856. He discarded his rank. He became a plain American citizen." A teacher and journalist before reaching America, he went to work in New York City for a German-language weekly newspaper.

With the start of the Civil War, however, his fighting spirit found a new outlet—he and Louis Blenker organized the Eighth New York Infantry, also known as the First German Rifles, as the unit's lieutenant colonel and colonel, respectively. Their regiment "aided in covering the fleeing Union forces" at First Bull Run. His service from then on—as successor to Blenker in command of the German Rifles in the Shenandoah Valley, at Second Manassas in command of the cavalry assigned to the defenses of Washington—had been commendable enough, if not spectacular.

But then, in 1864, came the battle of tiny Piedmont, Virginia, near Port Republic in the Shenandoah Valley, not a major engagement but one that meant the world to General Stahel. As he told the *New York Times* correspondent Dillon: "It is true some of the most stirring scenes in the great Virginia campaign of 1864 took place in the Shenandoah Valley. It is also true that the great moments of a soldier's life might be in a minor battle or skirmishes which are hardly mentioned in history."

His own most meaningful moment in battle came exactly in that sort of footnote engagement. "The battle of Piedmont was not one of the big battles," he said. "Gen. David Hunter, who commanded the federal army, had about 8,500 men, of whom about two brigades, numbering some less than 2,500 men, were cavalry under my command. The Confederates had about 6,000 men under Gen. W. E. ["Grumble"] Jones."

After advancing all morning on June 5, Stahel related, he dismounted some of his cavalrymen and led them across an open space in support of Ohio Brig. Gen. Augustus Moor's (see "Union: Enduring Family Ties," page 101) infantry brigade, "which was engaged on our right."

Out of the blue, he suddenly was struck in the left shoulder... For the moment, though, he just kept going. "It was only a gunshot which struck the bone and glanced off, giving me a great shock—but I did not fall."

He did at some point walk back to the rear for treatment of his wound. There, he gave in and lay on the ground while a surgeon applied a bandage. His whole left arm turned "black" and "of course it pained."

About this time, General Hunter came up to him "and expressed great regret and disappointment, saying that he had wanted me to charge the enemy's flanks and dislodge him, while he, Hunter, would at the same time attack the enemy's line in full force."

Despite his limp black arm, Stahel said he would lead the charge Hunter had planned.

He ordered one brigade to charge the Confederate right flank and the other to charge the left. He himself would ride with the men going left. "At 2 p.m.

I was assisted to mount my horse, my left arm being bandaged." Then, as the infantry moved across an open field against the Confederate line, Stahel's two cavalry brigades attacked both flanks. "The whole movement was entirely successful. The enemy was routed and we captured 1,000 prisoners." In addition, Grumble Jones died a soldier's death while rallying his frontline infantrymen in the same little-known battle.

After a period of recuperation, Stahel served on court-martial duty until resigning his commission in February 1865, noted Ezra Warner in his *Generals in Blue*. As a civilian again, Stahel in the postwar years would represent U.S. interests in the consular service in Japan and China before going into the insurance business in New York.

It was there that Dillon raised the issue of the old Civil War battle at dinner one evening shortly before the aging Hungarian's death in 1912.

After Dillon elicited details of the minor Virginia battle that earned Stahel the Medal of Honor, he said he would write a story about it. The general then "insisted" they go to the library the next day and look up Hunter's official report on the battle—in order to "verify all I have told you."

That was when they discovered—as Dillon read the report out loud to the old gentleman—that it contained no mention of his role whatsoever. "No reference to Gen. Stahel, nor any single word about his cavalry charge," wrote Dillon later.

Stunned, the old man asked in a hoarse whisper, "Did you read it all?"

Told yes, he cried, "Let me read it!" so loudly that "those below in the great reading room looked up, startled."

When he then looked for himself, he obviously didn't understand. Neither did Dillon the writer. "Why should General Hunter do you this injustice?" he asked.

"He was a strange man—a very strange man," said Stahel. "Perhaps he forgot."

Indeed, Hunter raised many an eyebrow during the Civil War for burning the Virginia Military Institute (VMI) and for issuing an emancipation order that Lincoln immediately repudiated. Earlier, he had became a general after striking up a correspondence with president-elect Lincoln and riding to Washington on Lincoln's "inaugural train" in February 1861, Warner 's book noted. Later, Hunter would preside over the trial of the Lincoln conspirators—after accompanying the assassinated president's body back to Springfield, Illinois, for burial.

Strange or not, however, it turns out that he did *not* totally ignore General Stahel's heroic charge at Piedmont, Virginia, that June day in 1864.

As Dillon and Stahel considered the surprising omission in the official battle report, Dillon suggested that Congress "must have known the facts" when it acted to award Stahel his Medal of Honor. "I suppose so," said the aggrieved old-timer, "but we shall drop the matter."

Not so, insisted Dillon. "Let us look further."

Thumbing through the thick war records volume, Dillon found a letter from Hunter to Union army Chief of Staff Henry W. Halleck that in fact did pay *some* homage to his subordinate for his valor at Piedmont. Without going into great detail, it noted General Stahel suffered a wound there and added that "he displayed excellent qualities of coolness and gallantry."

The letter did *not* point out that Stahel led his cavalry charge after suffering his wound. Still, it was Dillon's clear impression that the old soldier was "very glad" to find even these cursory references, "because I again had full faith in the truth of his story on Piedmont."

In fact, Dillon eagerly said he would like to write the story of Stahel's heroism at Piedmont.

But no, insisted the old general, "not a word!"

Impulsively, Dillon cried, "When you are dead, if I remain, I shall tell the story!"

Stahel smiled whimsically. "Well, after I am dead it does not matter!"

Less than a year later, Stahel had died, and Dillon published the story—in the *Times*. Not simply the battle story, but also the story of the after-action report, Stahel's shock at learning he was not mentioned in it, and the subsequent discovery of Hunter's letter somewhat alleviating the omission.

★★★

Additional note: Here's the text of Hunter's letter to Halleck: "I have the honor to inform you that in consequence of a wound received while gallantly leading his division in the recent battle of the 5th inst [June 5, 1864] at Piedmont I have relieved Maj. Gen. Julius Stahel from service with the forces in the field and have ordered him to Martinsburg and Harpers Ferry for the purpose of collecting and organizing all troops that can be spared from the defense of the B&O R. R. [railroad]. It is but justice to Maj. Gen. Stahel to state that in the recent engagement he displayed excellent qualities of coolness and gallantry, and that for the happy result the country is much indebted for his services."

Meanwhile, Stahel's Medal of Honor citation says that he "led his division into action until he was severely wounded." Again, a bit off the mark, since the real essence of his brave conduct was that he roused himself and led his troopers in a charge *after* he was severely wounded.

CONFEDERATE
His Last Home

THE VISITOR HAD ARRIVED ON the Gulf Coast at night and taken a room at a small inn in neighboring Mississippi City. He was there to look over properties, vacant lots his wife had selected while he was still a U.S. senator from Mississippi, but now…now, why not turn the hired horse and buggy in the direction of old friend Sarah Dorsey's nearby home on the Mississippi Sound called Beauvoir (meaning "beautiful view")?

The year was 1875, and so far as is known, Jefferson Davis, former president of the Confederate States of America, was about to have his first look at his last home.

He had been acquainted with Sarah Ann Ellis Dorsey, daughter of a plantation owner and a childhood friend of his wife, Varina, in Natchez, Mississippi, for many years. During that time Sarah had married a Maryland man, Samuel Dorsey, who managed the plantation properties she inherited from her parents until his death. Once she became a widow, Sarah Dorsey moved into the waterfront home, best described as a Louisiana "raised cottage" done in Greek revival style. (Note: It was raised to accommodate the occasional hurricane surge, but, as mentioned earlier, the structure was heavily damaged by Hurricane Katrina in 2005; see "Confederate: A Most Prolific Author," page 201.)

Situated between the villages of Biloxi and Handsboro, accessible both by road and by steamboat, the coastal retreat began life in 1851 as the centerpiece of wealthy Mississippi planter James Brown's waterfront complex consisting of two flanking pavilions, a kitchen, a carpenter's shop, chicken coop, and barn or carriage house, plus a cottage home for his foreman. Sarah Dorsey later would add a railroad station, but that's getting ahead of the story.

As events first unfolded, the Civil War forced Brown and his family to flee inland. He died and financial problems forced an auction sale of the property. It then was purchased by Frank Johnston, later attorney general of Mississippi, but he retained ownership for only two months before selling the estate in 1873 to the Widow Dorsey, writer, socialite, intellectual. It was she who gave the coastal cottage its name, Beauvoir, and she who added a railroad stop on a main-line track already running across the rear of the property.

When old friend Jefferson Davis came calling two years later, she was away, but he looked around anyway…and liked what he saw. A "fine place," he called it, a "large and beautiful house, and many orange trees yet full of fruit."

In front, as an endless vista of usually calm waters, lay the Mississippi Sound, a part of the Gulf of Mexico. The orange grove was to the rear, and beyond, a small stream meandered through a stand of pine, with wild azalea and yellow jasmine growing on the banks of the brook. In addition, notes James West Thompson in his book *Beauvoir: A Walk Through History*, "the house was surrounded by live oaks, magnolias, and cedars, with Spanish moss festooning the live oaks." Then, too, six acres of the property were covered with scuppernong grape vines.

In late 1876, just a year after his first visit, the none-too-young Jefferson Davis (born in 1808) was back on the Gulf Coast of Mississippi, both to visit relatives in the Biloxi area and, more important, in search of a quiet retreat where he could gather his thoughts and write all that he had seen, heard, and experienced in his truly unique role as president of the Confederacy. He had in him a book that had to be written soon, before the memories faded away or would be lost forever with his death.

Beauvoir in 1936

He was attracted by the sparsely populated coastal strip at the bottom of his adopted state of Mississippi, but he faced a quandary. "He considered putting a small cottage on his lots, and he hired a man to clear the bushes, although he remembered that before he left her in England, Varina had told him not to get a house on the Gulf Coast," wrote Thompson. Varina, it seems, did not care for the climate.

Actually, she did not care much for Sarah Dorsey, but that, too, is getting ahead of the story.

This time Jefferson Davis found Sarah Dorsey at home. This time, in fact, hearing that her old friend was in the area, she invited him over.

"When Dorsey discovered that Davis was seeking a place to write his long-delayed book, she showed him her east cottage, which consisted of one room with a pillared gallery completely surrounding it," wrote Thompson.

The rear gallery could be enclosed to become a bedroom and dressing room, while she proposed that the existing room could be turned into a combination library and office. In short order, for a rental fee of fifty dollars a month, and with Davis footing the carpentry costs, it was a done deal. By February 1877, the former Confederate leader, his secretary Maj. W. T. Walthull, and—who else?—Sarah Dorsey "were all hard at work on Davis's book," she as a helpful writer-editor.

Somewhat inexplicably (but pleading illness), Varina Davis, still in Europe, wouldn't return to the United States until October, but their twenty-year-old son, Jefferson Davis Jr., moved into one of the newly created small rooms at the back of the east cottage and joined in the book effort by taking dictation. Again inexplicably, except for her expressed dislike of the climate, when Varina Howell Davis suddenly did return to New York from Europe—unannounced—she traveled only as far south as Memphis.

She stopped there "and made her home" with her married daughter, Margaret Hayes, despite her husband's entreaties to come to Beauvoir.

As Burke Davis noted in his book, *The Long Surrender,* Varina already had written to her husband that she had no desire "ever" to see Sarah Dorsey's home on the Gulf.

When he went to Memphis in an effort to dissuade her, "she told him flatly that she would never live under the same roof with Sarah Dorsey."

In the midst of this unhappy standoff, the gossips of the world of course were thoroughly titillated, "and there was much speculation about the relationship between Jefferson Davis and his attractive landlady and patron as they worked in such intimate circumstances to complete his book," added Burke Davis.

"Some of this gossip may have reached Varina's ears, for she appeared suddenly and unexpectedly at Beauvoir."

In hopes of "luring Mrs. Davis to her home," Sarah Dorsey had invited Varina to a party in her honor. Varina had declined—emphatically and more than once.

But now, again "without warning," came a sudden change of heart. "She arrived unannounced at the plantation house, only a few moments before the first guests were to arrive for the party. Sarah Dorsey greeted her effusively, but something set off Varina's explosive temper and she lashed out at her hostess, screaming and sobbing uncontrollably. She then ran from the house into the woods, but Sarah Dorsey followed and managed to placate her distraught guest of honor before others arrived."

The party now proceeded, apparently with none of the guests aware "that the mercurial First Lady of the Confederacy had so recently recovered from a tantrum." Indeed, Varina was decorum itself as she received one admiring guest after another.

Even more surprising, "Varina remained at Beauvoir, where she, too, became a paying guest." She was, to be sure, at first touchy about Sarah Dorsey's earlier help with the book, which now passed into Varina's capable hands. Then, too, "as the weeks passed and her confidence and serenity returned, Varina grew fond of her old friend Sarah. Their reconciliation seemed to be complete." As Thompson added in his *Beauvoir* book, Varina wrote to a friend that their hostess "makes us very comfortable" and went so far as to say, "I am very fond of her."

Just a year later, however, a rampant disease greatly and justly feared in the nineteenth century would intervene, with its frequent grim result—Jeff Jr., the couple's only living son, contracted yellow fever and died in Memphis. Of the Davis couple's four sons and two daughters, Jeff Jr.'s death left only the two girls, Maggie and Winnie, still living. (The Davises' toddler son Samuel had died in 1854; their four-year-old son Joseph had been killed in a fall from a balcony at the Confederate White House in Richmond during the Civil War; their eleven-year-old William died in 1872.)

Still another blow was pending. Sarah Dorsey had cancer, as she apparently had known or suspected for some time. In late 1877, related Thompson, she told visiting Confederate Gen. Jubal Early that Davis was "almost destitute," that she didn't have long to live, and she "intended to leave her entire estate to Davis."

Some months later, in February 1879, she followed up by offering to sell

Beauvoir to Davis for $5,500, payable in three installments. Thus, with his payment of the first installment, he acquired title to the handsome beachside cottage on February 19, 1879.

After moving to New Orleans, Sarah Dorsey died on July 4 of that same year.

Her will, drawn up on January 4, 1878, bequeathed Beauvoir to Davis…but somewhat unnecessarily, as events turned out. As explained by Thompson: "It is noteworthy that after her death, Davis paid the two remaining installments due on Beauvoir in order to liquidate debts owned by Dorsey's estate. Consequently, Davis did buy Beauvoir, and he paid for it in full."

Noteworthy, too, was the statement in Sarah Dorsey's will: "I do not intend to share in the ingratitude of my country towards the man, who is in my eyes, the highest and noblest in existence." From that and all her actions, it is obvious that she adored her old friend.

Meanwhile, he now finally had a quiet corner in which to write his two-volume work, *The Rise and Fall of the Confederate Government*. However dry, even wooden, it may have been in style, it quite naturally gave the world—and America's later generations—an invaluable and unique look at the inner workings of the short-lived, independent Confederacy as seen by its one and only political leader.

Still, if Jefferson Davis now had a home, he still was denied a country, thanks both to his own refusal to ask for pardon and to congressional refusal to include him in a blanket restoration of U.S. citizenship to Confederates of various stripes. "Many people urged Davis to apply for a pardon so that the Mississippi legislature could elect him United States senator," added the Thompson account of Davis's days at Beauvoir. "At the time, all senators were elected by their state legislature, not by the people. But Davis would not apply, and he avoided politics."

He did travel around the South; he did make occasional speeches—one of them to the Mississippi legislature, before which he did react to his exclusion from the citizenship measure. As noted by Thompson, he said: "I have not repented. Remembering, as I must, all which has been suffered, all which has been lost, disappointed hopes and crushed aspirations, yet I deliberately say, if I were to do it all over again, I again would do just as I did in 1861."

On the other hand, sounding much like Robert E. Lee, he went on to urge peaceful acceptance of the Civil War's outcome. "Our people have accepted the decree," he said. "It therefore behooves them…to promote the general welfare of the Union, to show the world that hereafter, as heretofore, the patriotism of our people is not measured by lines of latitude and longitude, but is as broad as the obligations they have assumed and embraces the whole of our ocean-bound domain."

According to Beauvoir historian Thompson, "He always spoke of the fact that the United States was now one country and on the theme of reconciliation." Clearly though, the denial of resumed citizenship was a barb that stung to his last days. In March 1889, following a serious illness, he spoke of it in one of his last speeches. Agreeing to address a group of young men gathered in Mississippi City, just miles from Beauvoir, Jefferson Davis first greeted them as "friends and fellow citizens," then remembered that wasn't quite accurate. "Ah, pardon me," he added, "the laws of the United States no longer permit me to designate you as fellow citizens, but I am thankful that I may address you as friends."

With a hint of the old defiance, however, he added that he felt "no regret" to stand before them as "a man without a country," because "my ambition lies buried in the grave of the Confederacy."

He then went on to acknowledge, "The past is dead; let it bury its dead, its hopes and ambitions." Before his far younger audience, he added, lay a future of "golden promise," of "expanding national glory, before which all the world shall stand amazed." He beseeched his listeners to "lay aside all rancor, all bitter sectional feeling, and to take your places in the ranks of those who will bring about a consummation devoutly to be wished—a reunited country."

It was one of his last public appearances. Ten months later, eighty-one-year-old Jefferson Davis, former president of the Confederacy, died of natural causes. Beauvoir had been his home for the last twelve years of his life.

***

Additional note: Far too late to be of any comfort to Davis, Varina, or their nineteenth-century contemporaries, Congress finally restored his citizenship in 1978. Senator Mark Hatfield of Oregon set the ball rolling with the introduction of a Senate joint resolution to that effect. Then-representative Trent Lott from the Mississippi House district encompassing Beauvoir introduced the measure in the House. Fellow Southerner and president Jimmy Carter signed it into law. Thus, noted Thompson, "Jefferson Davis no longer was a non-citizen in the land of his birth—a nation he had served as an army officer, a Congressman, a wounded Mexican War hero, a United States Senator, and a secretary of war."

UNION
Lost at Sea

WHEN THE GREAT SHIP SAILED on her maiden voyage to America, he was a first-class passenger quartered in Cabin E38. He was an officer of the American Academy in Rome, a native of Massachusetts, a former war correspondent of some note, a book author, and a fairly well-known artist.

Last seen helping others after his ship struck an iceberg in the North Atlantic the night of April 14, 1912, sixty-five-year-old Francis Davis Millet also was a Civil War veteran—possibly the only Union veteran, if not the only Civil War veteran of either side, to have been lost in the sinking of the superliner *Titanic*.

And no, Col. Washington Roebling, chief builder of the Brooklyn Bridge, was *not* among those lost. That was his young nephew by the same name. Thus, the retired colonel's wife (at one time his foreman for the bridge project) started getting condolence calls from friends misled by the early newspaper reports.

The unfortunate nephew's body was never found, but Millet's was.

Unlike most of the *Titanic*'s more than fifteen hundred victims, he didn't go down with the ship. Instead, his body was recovered by the cable ship *Mackay-Bennett* out of Halifax, Nova Scotia. His remains were carried to Boston and buried at St. John's Central Cemetery at Bridgewater, Massachusetts, according to the online *Encyclopedia Titantica* (www.encyclopedia-titanica.org /biography/207/).

His last home was in *East* Bridgewater, Massachusetts, although he had been born (November 3, 1846) in Mattapoisett, Massachusetts, and had not spent much time either there or in any of the four neighboring Bridgewater townships. To the contrary, he had lived in Washington, D.C., where he maintained an apartment and studio on Wisconsin Avenue in Georgetown, and he spent a quarter-century at the quaint village of Broadway in the British Cotswolds as impresario of a small, informal art colony that included John Singer Sargent. The father of four children, Millet was married in Paris, France, to the former Elizabeth Merrill, known as Lily, of Boston—the writer Mark Twain and the sculptor Augustus Saint-Gaudens were witnesses at their wedding. Sargent, for his part, later painted a striking portrait of Lily in addition to his paintings and sketches of the Millet children.

The multifaceted Millet earlier in life also had been a war correspondent covering the Russian-Turkish War of 1877–78 for newspapers in England and the United States. "He was decorated by Russia and Rumania," notes the *Encyclopedia Titanica* website, "for bravery under fire and services to the wounded." Managing to juggle more than one career at a time, he also was a member of the international art jury for the Paris Exposition of 1878 and, some years later, director of decorations at the World's Columbian Exposition of 1893 in Chicago. He wrote short stories and books on his travels, he translated Tolstoy's *Sebastopol* into English—"and in 1898 at the age of 52 he went to the Philippines again as a [Spanish-American] war correspondent," notes a website for the JSS Gallery (www.jssgallery.org).

Despite so many apparent distractions, he could boast quite a few impressive credits as a working decorative artist. Among them were murals at the state capitols of Wisconsin and Minnesota, the Baltimore customhouse, Trinity Church in Boston, and a mural in the Newark, New Jersey, courthouse called *The Foreman of the Grand Jury Rebuking the Chief Justice, 1774.* His paintings also found their way into the Metropolitan Museum in New York and the Tate Gallery in London.

He began his career in art after studies at Harvard and an early stint in journalism as first a reporter then as city editor at the *Boston Courier*. Encouraged by his aptitude for lithography and portraiture of friends, says the *Encyclopedia Titanica*, he entered the Royal Academy of Fine Arts at Antwerp, where "he won an unprecedented silver medal in his first year and a gold medal in the second."

All this of course was totally unknown, probably not even suspected, when he entered the Civil War in 1864 as a sixteen-year-old drummer boy with the Sixtieth Massachusetts Volunteers. Frank, as he was called, apparently accompanied his surgeon father, Asa, and the youngster allegedly wound up an assistant army surgeon himself. The Sixtieth, one of five Massachusetts militia regiments formed to replace regular Union troops tied down by garrison duty in the final year of the war, spent most of its time in service at Washington, D.C., and Indianapolis. Young Millet, enlisting for a one-hundred-day period, served from July 14, 1864, to November 30, 1864, according to the local history, *Bridgewater in the Rebellion* (see http://freepages.genealogy .rootsweb.com).

Immediately after the Lincoln assassination just months later, incidentally, it was the young man's father, Asa Millet, who would direct a procession leading to a memorial service held by all four Bridgewater townships. According to a Millet family genealogy website (www.greggmillet.com/Millet_family_in_America.htm),

Asa Millet began a family history later supported by his son's further research while he was living in England.

Despite Francis Millet's many career moves, he was best known at the time of his death in 1912 for his artistic endeavors—so much so that the *Washington Times* of the day wrote, "As an artist and as an architect, he was one of the most noted in his particular kind of work in the world." Citing contributions to the "beautification of Washington," the *Times* of 1912 (no relation to the present-day *Washington Times*) described Millet as "one of the city's most picturesque characters," adding, "soldier of fortune, adventurer, war correspondent, art student, and artist, he seems to have been constituted of the stuff which makes dramatic events possible."

Millet was great friends with Maj. Archibald Butt, an aide to both former president Theodore Roosevelt and sitting president Howard Taft and, like Millet, a former newspaperman. Butt and the Millet couple had been in Rome before the greatly ballyhooed sailing of the "unsinkable" *Titanic*, and now the two men were returning to America together aboard the legendary liner.

In a letter to designer Alfred Parsons, founder of the Parsons School of Design, which was posted at Queenstown on April 11, Millet said that the great ship "has everything but taxicabs and theaters." With considerable asperity, he wrote about the "obnoxious ostentatious American women" aboard, describing them as "the scourge of any place they infest and worse on shipboard than anywhere." Many of them, he added, "carry tiny dogs and lead husbands around like pet lambs."

He was happy with his accommodations, however, saying the cabins "are larger than the ordinary hotel room and much more luxurious with wooden bedsteads, dressing tables, hot and cold water, etc., etc., electric fans, electric heater and all." He closed, "I have the best room I have ever had in a ship and it isn't one of the best either."

The night the ship sank, one survivor noticed both Butt and Millet in the smoking room with two other male passengers. Col. Archibald Gracie later said, 'They seemed to be absolutely intent upon doing what they were doing and disregarding anything that was going on the decks outside." Others said both Butt and Millet were last seen giving up their life preservers to women passengers aboard the doomed ship.

The two friends are remembered by the Butt-Millet Memorial Fountain, an eight-foot-high marble fountain on Washington's Executive Avenue next to the White House.

CONFEDERATE
His Faithful Companion

IN A BOX ONCE BURIED somewhere in the front yard of Beauvoir, Jefferson Davis's last home, lay, and perhaps still lies, his old friend, walking companion, and bodyguard, Traveler.

His exact parentage unknown, beyond having a Russian bulldog for his father, Traveler could be a killer when he had to be.

But he also could be gentle as a lamb with children. He could be playful as a puppy, chasing after the fiddler crabs that scurried and scuttled across the white beaches in front of the Beauvoir home on the Gulf Shore of lower Mississippi.

As a dog, he bore no relationship to Robert E. Lee's famous horse of nearly the same name, Traveller. This Traveler, born and raised in Europe, originally was *not* a faithful companion to Jefferson Davis in his declining years, but instead started his connection with Beauvoir as a pet and staunch bodyguard for Sarah Dorsey, who owned Beauvoir before both selling and bequeathing the beachside cottage (see "Confederate: His Last Home," page 208) to her friend and idol, Jefferson Davis.

Traveler's history can be traced to the time Sarah and her husband, Samuel, acquired him as a mere puppy while traveling in the Bernese Alps, according to an article that appeared in the *Confederate Veteran* in April 1909 and was reprinted in the 1988 book *Beauvoir: A Walk Through History* by James West Thompson. "They carried the young dog everywhere with them, and he was trained to be Mrs. Dorsey's special bodyguard," says the *Confederate Veteran* account.

And bodyguard he was…with a vengeance.

First, to go by the *Veteran* account, there was the would-be thief and assassin.

Encountered in the Dorsey couple's travels to "the Arabian Desert," he was an Arab servant who had been beaten on Samuel Dorsey's orders for attempted theft. "The next day, Mr. Dorsey and some of the Arabians went on a two days' journey, leaving Mrs. Dorsey and the camp in the charge of an old Arab."

Big mistake. "That night, while asleep under the tent, Mrs. Dorsey was awakened by a spring and a growl from Traveler, then the shriek of a man."

Jumping to her feet and obtaining a light, she found the recently beaten thief pinned to the ground by Traveler, a "huge" knife lying on the floor next to the intruder. "He had cut his way into the tent and crept in, evidently determined to wreak his vengeance upon her for the stripes he had received."

Next to run afoul of the protective Traveler was a would-be diamond thief in Paris, France. For him, the outcome would be a good deal more serious than for the Arab. The issue this time was the tempting glitter of the diamonds that Sarah Dorsey had worn to a reception. Back at their Paris hotel, she went to bed while her husband and some friends "walked out to smoke."

A short while later she awoke to the sounds of a disturbance in her room—the sounds of yet another "desperate struggle" on the floor.

Traveler this time had thwarted the designs of "one of the worst characters in Paris," it seems. He in fact had gone for this intruder's throat, with a fatal result for the would-be diamond thief.

Thus, the canine was a proven protector with a killer instinct when Jefferson Davis acquired him from Sarah Dorsey after taking up residence at Beauvoir. Thus, too, Traveler "allowed no one to come on the place whose good intent he had any reason to suspect. The entire place was under his care; not a window or door was locked or barred, for everything was safe while Traveler kept his sentry march on the wide porches that surrounded the house on every side."

Fortunately, Jefferson Davis had only to say the word for friends, family, or associates to pass inside safely. "If Mr. Davis wished to safeguard the coming and going of any one and give him the freedom of the place, day or night, he would put one hand on the person's shoulder and the other on the dog's head and say: 'Traveler, this is my friend.' The dog would accept the introduction very gravely, would smell his clothes and hands, and 'size him up' generally; but he never forgot, and henceforth, Mr. Davis's 'friend' was safe to come and go unmolested."

Also absolutely safe with the fierce guard dog were children. "Mrs. Davis's small niece, a child about two years old, made the dog her chosen playmate, and the baby and dog would roll together on the grass in the highest glee. She would pull his hair, pound on his head or ride around the place on his back, the dog trotting as sedately as a Shetland pony. This child lived some little distance down the beach; but it went home day after day in perfect safety, guarded and guided by Traveler."

The playful side to Traveler also came out in his romps on the beach, where he loved to chase fiddler crabs. He "would bark and throw up the sand with his paws in wild glee when he had succeeded in driving a number of the ungainly objects into the sea."

What really struck onlookers, however, was Traveler's absolute devotion to his new master, Jefferson Davis. Not even the fiddler crabs could gain his attention while he was on a walk with the former president of the Confederacy. "He was then a bodyguard, pure and simple, and had all the dignity and watchfulness of a squad of soldiers detailed as escorts."

If the former president fell into such deep thought that his feet wandered toward the water's edge, the ever-watchful Traveler "would gently take his trousers leg in his teeth, or, by bounding between him and the sea, he would manage to call attention to the big waves coming in."

In sum, no dangerous person or like threat to Jefferson Davis ever eluded the faithful Traveler…instead, Traveler became the apparent target of someone's evil intent.

The Davis household first became aware one day when Traveler struck them as uncharacteristically "droopy" and even "in pain."

As time passed with no improvement, Jefferson Davis sought the advice of a good friend and doctor who lived in the area. "The doctor came, but nothing seemed to relieve the dog's suffering. All night he moaned and cried, looking up into Mr. Davis's face with big, pathetic eyes, as if begging help from the hand that never before failed him."

Even Sarah Dorsey herself joined the vigil for the stricken dog, noted the *Confederate Veteran* account by "L. H. L.," but it turned out to be a "hopeless watch."

Sadly, "[T]he work of the vile poisoner had been too well done for remedy."

He died at daylight, "his head on Mr. Davis's knee and his master's tears falling like rain upon the faithful beast."

"I have indeed lost a friend," said Davis as he carefully placed Traveler's inert form on a nearby rug.

With the household gathered as mourners, Traveler was laid to rest in a "coffin-like box" in the front yard of Beauvoir. "Mr. Davis softly patted the box with his hand, then turned away before it was lowered into the ground."

For years a "beautifully engraved" stone marked the spot where Traveler was buried, but the stone eventually disappeared…and today there is no telling exactly where lies Traveler, old friend, walking companion, and bodyguard to Jefferson Davis in his declining years.

UNION
Not Really a General

BY CAREER'S AND LIFE'S END, he had held many titles: attorney at law; member, West Virginia House of Delegates; U.S. attorney; secretary of the navy; U.S. House member; U.S. circuit court judge; U.S. senator; and brigadier general, Union army.

The troublesome fact is that neither during the Civil War nor at any time thereafter was he ever a general.

He was, however, a veteran of mean fighting in the mountains of western Virginia, the Shenandoah Valley, and Northern Virginia. He had been a POW held in Libby Prison in Richmond and later at a sister facility at Salisbury, North Carolina. And for a time he was a cause célèbre whose plight in solitary confinement became a concern to Abraham Lincoln.

Outside of West Virginia circles, the name Nathan Goff Jr. is hardly known today…but there he was, back in 1861, a callow youth of eighteen years, a freshman that spring at Georgetown College in Washington, D.C., who left school after Virginia's formal secession on April 17 to rejoin his family at their home in Clarksburg (once Stonewall Jackson's hometown) of today's West Virginia.

At the time, the western mountains and hardscrabble rivers he knew so well from his youth were a part of Virginia, and no one quite knew what might happen next. "The Goffs were pro-Union in sympathy and Union sentiment was rather strong in the town," recalled G. Wayne Smith in a paper published in the January 1953 issue of the *West Virginia History Journal*, "but the outlying districts [of adjoining Harrison County] contained many supporters of the new Confederacy."

With many in this part of the state strongly opposed to secession, and many others just as adamantly in favor of the break, "law and order were in danger of breaking down completely."

Indeed, when a group of Confederate militiamen, the Harrison Rifles, assembled in Clarksburg in early May, an opposing group of Union Guards threatened to seize them. Trouble was averted when Goff's father, Waldo, a prominent local merchant, former Virginia legislator, and oddly, a pro-Union slave owner, took charge of the Rebels' weapons until they marched off the next morning.

By the end of May, Clarksburg had been taken over by George B. McClellan's army and made into a "military supply depot of some consequence," Smith reported. It wasn't long before young Goff joined the newly formed Third Virginia Volunteers as, first, a private, then as a second lieutenant. "The regiment's first duties were uninspiring," Smith noted. "To protect western Virginia, headquarters were maintained in Clarksburg, but individual companies were soon scattered from Grafton to Sutton to guard the area against Confederate sympathizers and bushwhackers."

Fall came and went, then the winter also. Finally, in May 1862, Goff saw action at the battle of McDowell, Virginia—the first in the series of battles that comprised Stonewall Jackson's famous Shenandoah Valley campaign. The engagement literally was an uphill fight against Jackson's men that lasted from late afternoon to eight o'clock. Their ammunition about gone, the Union soldiers in the end had to back off.

Not only was the result a defeat, it was inflicted in part by Confederates from Goff's own Harrison County. Still, he "could take comfort in the fact that his regiment had fought well and bravely against what was thought to be a superior force, entrenched on a mountain top."

Next for Goff and his compatriots came Maj. Gen. John C. Frémont's pursuit of Jackson "up" the Shenandoah Valley ("up" meaning southward), with a series of engagements adding up to a severe testing period for the neophyte Third Virginia Volunteers. At one point, young Goff wound up as the acting commander of the regiment's Company G and indeed as its only officer "present for duty." In August 1862 he was promoted to first lieutenant and named adjutant of the regiment. This, quite naturally, "put him in much closer contact with regimental affairs." Thus, he was "with the regimental command" for the August 9 battle of Cedar Mountain and then for a series of engagements punctuating John Pope's Northern Virginia campaign that month, capped by Second Bull Run on August 29 and 30.

Held in reserve at Bull Run, the Third Virginia tried "to stop the retreating Union forces on both days," but to no avail. The Third Virginia was "forced to retreat with the rest of the army across Bull Run to Centreville." For the West Virginians, the unhappy debacle at the very doorstep of Washington, D.C., ended a spring and summer campaign that at least "made veterans of previously untried troops."

And now it would be back to the West Virginia mountains for dreary months of guard duty "against Rebel bushwhackers and guerrillas." In late April and early May 1863, however, the war came to the Third Virginia's home base in earnest as Confederate Gens. John D. Imboden and William E. "Grumble" Jones launched a two-pronged raid into the mountainous terrain. After they briefly threatened Clarksburg itself, destroyed rail facilities, and made off with captured cattle and new recruits for the Rebel cause, the Third Virginia, now mounted as part of a new command, joined in Union raids against the Rebels.

"In this, his third summer of the war," wrote Smith, "Goff saw action near Hedgesville and Martinsburg, West Virginia, on July 18–19. He was with his regiment on [Gen. A. W.] Averell's first cavalry raid from August 5 to 31, through Hardy, Pendleton, Highland, Bath, Greenbrier and Pocahontas counties, which resulted in engagements with the Confederates at Jackson River on August 5, and at Rocky Gap near White Sulphur Springs on August 26–27. Goff's reports as adjutant indicate that this was now a veteran fighting regiment, strictly disciplined, one of which he could be very proud."

At this point, a still-young Goff left his original regiment to join the brand-new Fourth West Virginia Volunteer Cavalry as a major, and it, too, then spent months based at Clarksburg, followed by redeployment to New Creek, West Virginia, while its organizers acquired equipment, sought to fill the ranks with qualified recruits, then searched high and low for the horses they would need. "This was the situation on January 28, 1864, when the regiment was ordered to guard a supply train of eighty wagons which had been dispatched the previous day to reprovision the garrison at Petersburg, an exposed Union outpost in the South Branch Valley, some fifty miles south of New Creek."

The wagon train, guarded by Goff's regiment, never made it…and neither did Goff himself. Attacked en route by Thomas Rosser's brigade, an element of a new Confederate raiding force led by Jubal A. Early, the supply convoy was abandoned to the Rebels by its teamsters. Goff, his legs pinned beneath his horse when it was shot dead, was among the forty Union men taken prisoner in the clash.

Thus began a new and quite different phase of Goff's *genuine* Civil War service on behalf of the Union. Arriving at Libby Prison in Richmond on February 10, 1864, the day after 109 Union POWs had escaped by tunnel, he found the detention facility in "an uproar." Eighteen days later, Smith noted, "Two Union columns [led by cavalryman H. Judson Kilpatrick] tried to push into the city to free the prisoners. They were repulsed but Richmond was thoroughly frightened and the prison was mined by the guards and the prisoners were warned that any attempted break would result in the blowing up of the prison."

For some weeks, Goff was treated the same as the other Union officers held at Libby, but early in May, "he was singled out for special treatment." He now was to be held as a hostage for the release of a Southern officer, Maj. Thomas D. Armsey, apprehended in the Clarksburg area and held "on the charge of recruiting men for the Confederacy within Union lines." As luck would have it, both Armsey and Goff were from the same Harrison County encompassing Clarksburg.

With the Union holding firm against exchanging Armsey for Goff, the appeals began to fly—from Goff himself, from his parents, from West Virginia political figures. Goff, in the meantime, was "placed in solitary confinement in a small damp basement cell."

Rather than give in to the pleas, Secretary of War Edwin M. Stanton took a step in reverse: not only would he refuse to release Armsey, he would place a Confederate major, also a prisoner of war, in "close" confinement as retaliation for Goff's treatment.

In part, Goff's predicament was a matter of bad timing. As Smith explained in the *West Virginia History Journal*, it was "an inopportune moment" for pleas on Goff's behalf. "Retaliation instead of exchange seemed to be the proper course of action for the War Department to follow at the time." Early in the war, "prisoners were liberally exchanged," but then the exchange system broke down for "various reasons, not the least of which was General B[enjamin] F. 'Beast' Butler's execution of a Louisiana citizen in the summer of 1862 for tearing down the Union flag in New Orleans." Thus, "by the time of Goff's capture, bad blood on both sides had ended any system of general exchange."

Still, Goff's adherents kept trying, with his mother writing to Lincoln on behalf of her "brave and noble Boy," a plea given added weight by the fact she and her husband already had lost an older son, Henry Clay Goff, to the war effort. Then, too, there was a letter from Waldo Goff to a well-placed close friend pointing out the father's feeling that "it was unbearable to lose one son as a result of 'this wicked rebellion' and have the other mistreated because 'infamous scoundrels' in the Confederacy from West Virginia had singled him out in retaliation for the conviction of 'a miserable wretch who fled from this County and came back with a Major's commission in the rebel army' to enlist men for the Confederacy."

Waldo Goff's understandable question: "Can it be good policy for our government to let my son die in that loathsome [c]ell rather than give up that contemptible creature 'Tom Armsey'?"

But then the sun broke through the war clouds. President Lincoln not only granted the suffering couple a personal interview, he sent electrifying word down his chain of command: "Let it be done." Or, more precisely, "If General [E. H.] Hitchcock [commissioner for the exchange of prisoners] can effect a special exchange of Thomas D. Arm[se]y, now under conviction as a spy, or something of the sort, and in prison…for Maj. Nathan Goff, made prisoner of war and now in prison in Richmond [actually Goff had been moved to Salisbury by this time], let it be done."

Ironically, just days later, orders to bring about the special exchange would go to none other than Butler himself, along with the cautionary word that Lincoln was personally interested in the case, as now was Secretary of War Stanton.

So it was, on happy note at last, that Nathan Goff returned home, spent the last months of the war recuperating from the deprivations of prison life, and then embarked upon his highly successful career as lawyer, judge, and leading politician from the newly created state of West Virginia.

To the public, added Smith in his biographical paper, Goff "was a glamorous figure."

As a bona fide veteran of the Civil War, he certainly had appeal to his fellow Union veterans. "He had fought for over two years until captured by the enemy. The story of that capture and subsequent confinement could be told over and over again to evoke an emotional response among other veterans hardly obtainable any other way." He had gone to war in 1861 a "boy of eighteen"; by 1865, "he was a veteran soldier and practicing attorney ready to enter a man's estate."

But still, the "General Goff" of future years never was a general, not even a brevet (unofficial) general. As Smith wrote, "In later years his military career was exaggerated in several respects for political purposes." As one of those respects, "Goff allowed his supporters to refer to him as 'General Goff,' and newspaper sketches appearing in loyal Republican papers [for he was a Republican] during the campaigns usually mentioned that he had been 'made a brevet brigadier general of volunteers, for gallant and meritorious service on the field.'"

The completely erroneous references appeared as early as 1870, the Civil War only five years distant. "By 1876 the references were commonplace and by 1882 they had received the stamp of authenticity by Goff himself."

What to think? The key word here may be *commonplace*. It wasn't all that unusual in Goff's day to see such easily challenged exaggeration of the facts. Such exaggerations, noted Smith, "unfortunate from the present point of view, were understandable in light of the political tactics of the period." Feelings generated by the Civil War still ran high: "Democrats constantly recalled the improper methods by which West Virginia had been formed, and Republicans vigorously waved the 'Bloody Shirt.'" Moreover, the public "was more gullible in some respects than now [1951], and standards of political morality not as highly developed."

In Goff's case, however, the seemingly commonplace art of exaggeration went even further than his appropriation of a general's rank. "To illustrate his courage, justice and magnanimity toward a defeated foe, the story of his imprisonment and release was changed in several details. Major Armsey became a spy who had been 'condemned to death by Union authorities' for his recruiting activities and for whom Goff would be put to death if the sentence were carried out." And Goff allegedly had called for a guilty Armsey's execution, "regardless of its consequences to me."

Even more embellished was a later version of the Goff story asserting that he arrived home right at war's end in April 1865, just in time to step before an angry mob and save a recaptured Armsey's life. By this totally spurious account, "Goff stayed the anger of the crowd by saying: 'Let no friend of mine lay a hand upon this man; he is entitled to our protection as a prisoner of war.'"

Whatever the motives and/or customs of the day, the fact is that Goff served his country honorably and well. He learned enough of leadership to become a political leader himself, not an easy task in a newborn state torn straight from the bloodstained fabric of fratricidal war.

By a possibly accurate account as well, he personally met with Lincoln after his release and made a plea for a continued exchange program to hasten the release of comrades still suffering in the prisons of the South. According to the source of this story, Frank A. Burr's *General Nathan Goff, Jr.: A Biographical Sketch* (1882), "His eloquent recital of their hardships brought tears to the eyes of the great-hearted President, and even moved the stoical Stanton, who was present." The alleged result was the start of a broad exchange program, "promptly afterwards carried into effect."

The tale sounds a bit melodramatic, true, and it certainly is doubtful that Goff's plea alone would have fostered such a sweeping policy change. Still, the likely exaggerations aside, researcher Smith said he could not prove or disprove the claim that such an interview with Lincoln and Stanton took place.

CONFEDERATE
His Last Trip

A STORIED COUPLE, AND THEIR ships *almost* did, in *his* last few days, pass in the night.

They each were on the Mississippi, he, a man still without citizenship, returning to New Orleans after being taken ill upriver, and she hurrying upriver to be at his side.

He, a man who still refused to ask forgiveness, was aboard a steamer commanded by the storied riverboat Captain Leathers, and she was hastening northward on another steamer with *another* Captain Leathers in charge. Father and son, Mississippi steamboat captains Thomas P. and Bowling Leathers, respectively.

The elderly soldier–statesman just days before had left Beauvoir, his beachfront cottage on the Gulf Coast at today's hurricane-battered Biloxi, Mississippi, to visit his old plantation, Brierfield, on the Mississippi River just below Vicksburg.

It was early November 1889, and the weather was nasty when he set out from his last home for his last trip. "He went by train to New Orleans, arriving in sleety rain," according to James West Thompson's book *Beauvoir: A Walk Through History*. "Although he caught a severe chest cold, he boarded the steamer *Laura Lee* for the trip to Brierfield."

It was late at night when the *Laura Lee* pulled abreast of Brierfield on the eastern side of the great river. But the passenger felt too poorly to disembark just then, so he remained on board until the steamer reached Vicksburg the next day. By the time he finally reached his beloved antebellum plantation that same day, however, it again was nighttime. And all he could do was fall into bed for the next four days.

In the meantime, the plantation manager "secretly" telegraphed the man's wife, who left at once for New Orleans.

Back at Brierfield, the elderly patient rallied enough to arrange passage downriver aboard his old friend Capt. Thomas Leathers's steamer named *Leathers*. Miles south of Brierfield, meanwhile, the ailing passenger's worried wife had boarded a steamer commanded by the younger Leathers. It now plowed upriver against the current.

The two Leathers-commanded steamers might have passed each other in the night, except that Bowling Leathers learned who was aboard his father's steamer. In quick order, he brought his riverboat alongside his father's and transferred the wife to the *Leathers*.

The wondrous result for this historic couple—loved in some quarters, hated in others—was that he awoke and was "amazed" to find his concerned wife at his bedside. As she herself later wrote, "He was asleep…but waked very soon and seemed better for meeting me."

Sadly for them, and their many admirers, this was not quite the end of the story.

A pair of doctors examining her husband at Bayou Sara above Baton Rouge diagnosed acute bronchitis, "complicated with grave malarial trouble," the man's wife later explained.

Making matters worse, the weather still was miserable—a cold, cold rain—as they disembarked at New Orleans. He was too ill to travel to their beachfront home on the Mississippi Sound east of New Orleans. They instead would stay here at a friend's home.

The old soldier—still, in 1889, refusing to ask pardon, still being denied restored citizenship—apparently felt well enough to tell an attending physician: "It may seem strange to you that a man of my age [eighty-one years old] should desire to live; but I do…. There are still some things that I have to do in this world."

As the patient now lingered on for some days, a magazine editor was in touch about an article he had written. The wife wrote back on November 28 that her husband was able to do "absolutely nothing." Said she also: "We sit up with him every night and he is a very ill man. He could not write his name, still less read a proof…. He is weeks, it may be months, it may be for ever, from being 'out.' I do not want the household told, but am miserably anxious."

Surprisingly, her husband rallied, shook off his fever, and began eating again. "The doctors here [have] every hope of his recovery," she exulted…briefly, "but it must be nearly two weeks, if not more under the most favorable circumstances before we can come home."

Recovery, did she say? Her husband politely begged to differ. "I want to tell you I am not afraid to die," he said. That very evening he was seized by a deep chill and suddenly was failing again. His wife encouraged him to take his medicine, but he never finished doing so. "Pray excuse me," he said. "I cannot take it."

Three hours later on that same December 6, 1889, Varina Howell Davis later wrote, "his brave, true heart had ceased to beat."

Thus died Jefferson Davis, West Point graduate, heroic Mexican War veteran, former U.S. House and Senate member, former secretary of war…but also former Confederate president and man technically without a country until posthumously granted restored citizenship by Congress in 1978, nearly a hundred years later.

★★★

Additional note: The elder of the two steamboat captains named Leathers was a famous veteran of the Mississippi River and connected waters, both as owner and skipper of steamboats and for his race in 1870 against the *Rob't E. Lee*, a contest described by the National Rivers Hall of Fame as "the most legendary steamboat race in history" (www.mississippirivermuseum.com/fame /leathers.htm).

As noted by the same source: "He had great financial success in the lower river cotton trade and built many steamboats, among them seven named *Natchez*. The *Natchez (VI)* made 401 trips without accident in the New Orleans-to-Vicksburg trade route—a great accomplishment in an era with little or no safety regulations." It was as captain of the side-wheeler *Natchez (VI)* that Thomas P. Leathers seemingly lost his epic race to St. Louis against the *Lee*…but then, Captain Leathers made all his customary stops to discharge and take on passengers, whereas the *Lee* never stopped, took on no passengers and even refueled in midstream with the aid of another steamboat. In addition, her Capt. John W. Cannon lightened his craft by stripping her of various doors, windows, and shutters.

Even so, Leathers pulled in at St. Louis only six hours behind the speedy *Lee*, in an event "immortalized by Mark Twain in *Life on the Mississippi*," noted the *New Orleans Times-Picayune* on August 14, 2004.

In 1861, ironically enough, and as also noted by the *Times-Picayune,* it was one of Captain Leathers's *Natchez* steamboats (number five) that "picked up Jefferson Davis at Brierfield Plantation near Vicksburg and ferried him to his swearing-in [in Montgomery, Alabama] as President of the Confederate States of America." Two years later, "the crew set the boat on fire to prevent its capture by the Union."

In 1891, three decades later, Captain Leathers at age seventy-five was still going strong when he, "his son Bowling and Bowling's wife Blanch (one of the very few women to earn a master's license) launched and captained the eighth *Natchez*," the *Times-Picayune* noted. In 1896, unfortunately, Captain Leathers, now eighty years old, died from injuries suffered when he was "run over" by a bicyclist. Buried "on Steamboat Lane in the Natchez City Cemetery," he is included in the National Maritime Hall of Fame as well as the Rivers Hall of Fame.

"He was a staunch supporter of the Confederacy," says the latter's website, "and is said to have defiantly flown the 'Stars and Bars' on his boats for many years after the Civil War."

UNION
Confusion over Reno

IF THE NAMESAKE OF RENO, Nevada, hadn't died in a Civil War battle, instead of fighting the Sioux and their allies with Custer at the Little Big Horn more than a decade later, the confusion over the real Reno behind the name of America's famous city of broken marriages would be somewhat laughable, a lame joke.

Unfortunately, Maj. *Marcus* Reno became much better known publicly for his connection with George Armstrong Custer and the Little Big Horn than Union Maj. Gen. *Jesse Lee* Reno, despite the latter's stellar leadership—and sudden death—during the Civil War.

Thus, it may be only natural for the American public to assume the better-known, albeit lesser-ranking Reno was the Nevada city's namesake, even though he was harshly criticized, court-martialed, and dishonorably discharged for his role in the massacre on the Little Big Horn in 1876.

To make matters worse, a Nevada history published in 1913 included an article by a former army major and director of the state chamber of commerce that credited the naming of Reno to Marcus Reno instead of the Civil War Reno.

In actual and contradictory fact, Reno was founded and named for Jesse Reno in the year 1868, eight years before the massacre known as Custer's Last Stand. "Charles Crocker, the railroad construction superintendent for the Central Pacific Railroad, and his partners, at the behest of Gen. Irvin McDowell, officially named the new town at Laker's Crossing on the Truckee River for Jesse Reno, not Marcus Reno," noted Nevada state archivist Guy Rocha in the *Reno Gazette-Journal* of January 7, 2003. "The public first learned of the naming in the April 23, 1868, issue of the Auburn, Calif., *Stars and Stripes*."

Rocha began his explanation by posing the key question: "Who was the city of Reno named after? And for that matter, Reno County, Kan., and El Reno, Okla.?"

He answered: "Those who don't know generally say Maj. Marcus Albert Reno, the officer who, until his exoneration in recent years, bore the blame for the defeat of Lt. Col. George Armstrong Custer's troops at Little Big Horn in June 1876."

A popular misconception, it turns out, that is woefully wrong.

As Rocha additionally pointed out, the Kansas legislature "created Reno County near Wichita," even before the founding of the Nevada city by that name, also in honor of "the fallen war hero, who also had served in the Mexican War." Then, too, "El Reno, founded in 1889 in central Oklahoma, was named after Fort Reno, which also was named after Union Gen. Jesse Reno."

So who was the real Reno behind the naming of Reno, Nevada, and other American places? What did he do to deserve such lasting recognition by his nineteenth-century contemporaries?

During the early months of the Civil War, Reno's West Point classmate Thomas J. Jackson could have answered that question in considerable detail. Reno "led men facing or chasing his friend and West Point classmate Gen. Thomas 'Stonewall' Jackson at least three times," noted John E. Carey on the Civil War page of the *Washington Times* on June 11, 2005.

In one such confrontation, taking place at Second Bull Run (Manassas) on August 29, 1862, just days after Reno was promoted to major general and placed in charge of the Union Ninth Corps, Reno and his men "forced Jackson to leave behind his dead and wounded and flee the field." Then, "the next day, after Gen. James Longstreet's corps arrived, a flanking movement on the Union left caused the Army to crumble. When Union forces broke and ran under the withering Confederate fire, Reno's stoic stand near the center proved memorable."

As recalled by Carey's account, that was a highly charged moment. "Maj. Gen. Philip Kearney, commanding the 1st division of the Union III Corps, rode up to Gen. John Gibbon and shouted, 'Reno is not stampeded. I am not stampeded, you are not stampeded. That is about all, sir. My God, that is about all!'"

The ultimate fact is that the Federals, under the overall command of John Pope, eventually retired behind the defenses of Washington, leaving the battlefield to the Confederates, but not before a stiff fight at Chantilly in which the Union paid a heavy price—thirteen hundred casualties to the South's eight hundred—while holding off Jackson's superior numbers.

Reno came through unscathed physically, but surely he suffered emotionally when he saw what happened to two fellow generals. "Taken ill, Reno temporarily transferred his command to Maj. Gen. Isaac Stevens," wrote Carey. But Stevens then was killed, and Reno had to take over again. His attack against Jackson repulsed, he "moved back in good order," it seems.

Next, "Reno summoned Kearney...to come immediately to assist the IX Corps. Kearney responded, only to die by enemy fire as he moved up." After that, Carey added, Reno would be "credited with masking the Union Army's retreat."

Reno had graduated from the U.S. Military Academy in 1846, with George B. McClellan and George Pickett, along with the future Stonewall Jackson as classmates. As a green artillery officer he earned plaudits from Winfield Scott for his performance in the Mexican War, during which he won brevets to first lieutenant and captain for his gallantry at Cerro Gordo and Chapultepec. He then moved on to teach at West Point, to an artillery command for Albert Sidney Johnston's Utah expedition against the Mormons, and to two federal arsenal commands.

As the Civil War unfolded in 1861, Reno was by now a brigadier general of volunteers and led a brigade under Ambrose E. Burnside in the winter Carolinas campaign against Roanoke Island, New Bern, and Camden. Indeed, at Second Bull Run in 1862, he was directing Burnside's Ninth Corps while Burnside himself was busy with his command of Pope's right wing.

After the fighting on the Virginia flanks of Washington that August, attention turned to the Maryland countryside to the west as Pope's replacement, McClellan, confronted the invading Robert E. Lee at South Mountain and Antietam Creek. Both Burnside and Reno were on hand for this bloody clash of armies. And on September 14, Reno fell mortally wounded while leading reinforcements to another general's aid in Fox's Gap at South Mountain.

As his men carried him to the rear, wrote Carey, Reno saw yet another West Point classmate and friend, Gen. Samuel D. Sturgis, and said, "I'm dead."

Thus, added Carey's account, "Reno, at 39, faced death the way he had always faced battle: with bold, sure determination and matter-of-fact practicality."

Burnside, announcing Reno's death to the men of the Ninth Corps, said, "By the death of this distinguished officer the country loses one of its most devoted patriots, the army one of its most thorough soldiers." Obviously moved, Reno's men, crossing Antietam Creek near Burnside's Bridge, chanted, "Remember Reno!"

★★★

Additional note: Marcus Reno, born in 1834, also was a West Pointer and a Union officer taking part in the 1862 Antietam campaign. Twice brevetted for his performance during the war, he reached the temporary rank of brigadier general of volunteers. Later, as an officer in Custer's Seventh Cavalry, he reverted to the regular rank of major. Officially accused but cleared of cowardice and widely criticized for not going to Custer's aid at the Little Big Horn, he was court-martialed for minor infractions by the same General Sturgis who had greeted the dying Jesse Reno at South Mountain...and whose son had died with Custer. Many years after Marcus Reno's dishonorable discharge and death, a board of review changed his discharge to honorable, and he was reinterred at the Little Big Horn cemetery.

Incidental: Just to confuse the city of Reno's naming issue a bit further, it turns out that Jesse Lee Reno's original surname wasn't Reno at all—it was Renault.

CONFEDERATE
"That Vagabond Soldier"

BORN OF A VIRGINIA MOTHER who was on the high seas aboard a ship off the coast of Virginia and then spending his first ten years in Virginia, Henry Ronald Douglas MacIver did later fight for the Confederacy...but not until after defending British rule in India against the Sepoy mutiny of 1857 and then, on a contrary tack, fighting in Italy with Giuseppe Garibaldi's rebel Redshirts.

Later to become a naturalized U.S. citizen, even a U.S. consul as part of a truly checkered career, the onetime Confederate major would serve under at least eighteen different flags as probably the epitome of the nineteenth-century soldier of fortune.

Only sixteen years old at the time of the Great Indian Mutiny and an ensign with the East India Company, he was lucky to survive that first taste of warfare. "He was wounded in the arm, and, with a sword, cut over the head," wrote the famous American correspondent Richard Harding Davis in his book *Real Soldiers of Fortune*. "As a safeguard against the sun the boy had placed inside his helmet a wet towel. This saved him to fight another day, but even with that protection the sword sank through the helmet, and towel, and into the skull."

The result was a scar visible for life.

"He was left in the road for dead, and even after his wounds had healed was six weeks in the hospital."

From India, the young man traveled to Italy, where he "was a volunteer and wore the red shirt of Garibaldi."

Still ahead would be military service or campaigns in Egypt, Cuba, Spain, Mexico, Brazil, Argentina, Crete, Greece, Serbia…and his onetime home base of Virginia. Serving the Confederacy under Jeb Stuart, Stonewall Jackson, and Edmund Kirby Smith, he emerged from the Civil War four times wounded and officially described as "an officer of great gallantry." In addition to his eighteen stints at soldiering by age sixty, said Davis, MacIver survived capture by hostile Indians in the Southwest, spent days adrift at sea off Cuba, foiled "several attempts to assassinate him," and "fought several duels, in two of which he killed his adversary."

From among those duels, however, comes a Civil War tale with an ugly outcome. "At the close of the war duels between officers of the two armies were not infrequent," Davis asserted. Then citing an account sent to an unnamed Northern newspaper by a correspondent in Vicksburg—"who was an eyewitness to the event"—Davis explained that MacIver, for reasons not given, engaged in a duel by swords with a Captain Tomlin, a Union artillery officer from Vermont.

MacIver, said Davis, "ran Tomlin through the body."

Then, reported the newspaper account quoted in Davis's book,

> the Confederate officer wiped his sword on his handkerchief. In a few seconds, Captain Tomlin expired. One of Major MacIver's seconds called to him: "He is dead; you must go. These gentlemen will look after the body of their friend." A Negro boy brought up the horses, but before mounting MacIver said to Captain Tomlin's seconds, "My friends are in haste for me to go. Is there anything I can do? I hope you consider that this matter has been settled honorably."
>
> There being no reply, the Confederates rode away.

Years later, in a dueling episode with a happier outcome, MacIver was appointed to serve as the U.S. consul in Denia, Spain. But there was a problem. "When MacIver arrived at this post the ex-consul refused to vacate the Consulate," wrote Davis. MacIver's reaction was "to settle the difficulty with dueling pistols."

Fortunately, Stephen Bonsul, U.S. chargé d'affaires in Madrid, hurried to Denia, "to adjust matters." As a result, "without bloodshed he got rid of the ex-consul, and later MacIver so endeared himself to the Denians that they begged the State Department to retain him in that place for the remainder of his life."

Meanwhile, soon after his fatal duel with the Vermont officer, MacIver tried to leave the former Confederacy for Mexico, where he planned to join Emperor Maximilian's royalist army. On his way across Texas from Galveston to El Paso, however, he was captured by Indians. "He was not ill-treated…but for three months was a prisoner, until one night, the Indians having camped near the Rio Grande, he escaped into Mexico." After joining the royalists, he took part in various skirmishes and a battle at Monterrey—"and for his share in it received the title of Count and the order of Guadalupe."

With the subsequent collapse of Maximilian's "empire" and the latter's execution, MacIver fled by boat to Rio de Janeiro. "Two months later he was wearing the uniform of another emperor, Dom Pedro, and, with rank of lieutenant-colonel, was in command of the Foreign Legion of the armies of Brazil and Argentina, which at that time as allies were fighting against Paraguay."

But now an outbreak of cholera in Buenos Aires killed thousands, including about half of MacIver's seven-hundred-man legion. The epidemic also sent the commander himself to a hospital bed for six weeks…and the legion, carried to the front under a junior officer, simply dissolved.

Returning to his father's homeland of Scotland, MacIver soon departed for new adventures. He and former Confederate naval officer Bennet Burleigh (later a well-known newspaperman) organized an expedition to help insurgents on the island of Crete in a revolt against their Turkish rulers. The irrepressible MacIver next moved on to nearby Greece, where he fought "brigands" in Kisissia on the borders of Albania and Thessaly as an aide to his commander from Crete in the fight against the Turks.

After three months spent "potting at brigands" in the mountains, the wandering soldier repaired to New York, where he prepared for fresh services with an abortive rebellion against the Spanish in Cuba.

When that failed, the rebels scattered, and MacIver escaped the Spanish "only by putting to sea in an open boat, in which he endeavored to make Jamaica."

Rescued by a passing steamer three days later, he made his way back to New York once again. Here, he was recruited anew by an agent—a former Union officer—for the Egyptian ruler Khedive Ismail as part of the contingent of former Union and Confederate soldiers rounded up to help run the Egyptian army (see "Union & Confederate: Working for the Khedive," page 198).

But the climate in Cairo "did not agree with MacIver," and after six months as inspector general of the cavalry, he moved on...this time to plunge into Europe's Franco-Prussian War.

Serving on the staff of French Gen. Antoine Chanzy, cavalry Colonel MacIver was wounded at Orleans...after recovering and seeing the French lose their war, he followed his usual pattern and moved on. Thus the year 1873 saw him in league with the followers of the Spanish pretender Don Carlos, often serving as a "bearer of important messages from the 'King,' as Don Carlos was called, to the sympathizers with his cause in France and England."

When this latest crusade failed, and never fond of the Turks anyway, he next found common cause with the Montenegrins and Serbians fighting against the Turks in Bosnia and Herzegovina. He now organized and commanded his own cavalry brigade, the Knights of the Red Cross. He soon was a highly decorated "general de brigade," explained by Davis as "not what we know as a brigade general, but...one who commands a division, a major general." As such, "he was a great favorite both at the palace and with the people, the pay was good, fighting plentiful, and Belgrade gay and amusing."

Indeed, "Of all the places he has visited and the countries he has served, it is of this Balkan kingdom that the general seems to speak of most fondly and with the greatest feeling."

He for a time still would be organizing yet more foreign legions, reorganizing "small armies" in Central America, becoming a naturalized U.S. citizen, even offering to fight in the Spanish-American War of the late 1890s, but at age sixty in 1901, after serving so many countries, Henry Ronald Douglas MacIver was a "rolling stone" without a pension or real home to call his own. After forty years of "selling his sword and risking his life for presidents, pretenders, charlatans and emperors," noted correspondent Richard Harding Davis, MacIver truly and only was, as even the king of England once fondly said, "that vagabond soldier."

UNION
Graveyard for Generals

IT'S NOT A NATIONAL CEMETERY full of veterans' graves, but the Spring Grove Cemetery and Arboretum in Cincinnati, Ohio, nonetheless is final home for forty-one Union generals, among them a popular veteran whose untimely death paved the way for another general's path to the presidency of the United States.

As a percentage, 41 ranks low in comparison to the 1,950-odd generals, of permanent rank or temporary, who served the Union cause, but still…41 Union generals buried in one place? And not even in a battlefield or military park, at that. (Arlington *National* Cemetery, on the other hand, holds more than 100 Union generals…but then, it *is* Arlington.)

Here, you see the graves of the four **McCook Brothers**, just half the eight sons that Ohio's Daniel McCook gave to the war. Here, too, lies **Daniel** himself.

Over here lies a general named Lytle, a congressman's son, himself former speaker of the Ohio House, a poet of some note in his day…and, alas, as an only son and single when killed in battle, the last of his line. Severely wounded at Carnifex Ferry, West Virginia, then wounded again and captured at Perryville, Kentucky, he was paroled, went off to fight again, and was killed at Chickamauga. By chance **William Haines Lytle**, grandson of an early Cincinnati settler, had published a narrative poem before the war in which the protagonist also was a soldier killed in battle. For Lytle's funeral in late 1863, throngs lined the Cincinnati streets between the church and the cemetery.

Here, too, in yet another grave, meet **Jacob Dolson Cox**, not only a Civil War general and division commander of some note, but later, after the Civil War, governor of Ohio, secretary of interior under Ulysses S. Grant, a one-term U.S. House member, and later president of the University of Cincinnati. Also of real note, here lies **Joseph "Fighting Joe" Hooker** of Chancellorsville fame. While he didn't fare well there, he did prove himself an able combat leader at other significant engagements both before and after that disappointing outcome.

Many of the Spring Grove generals are not nearly so well known, of course… fair to say, in fact, some are hardly known today at all, even though they led interesting lives or contributed materially to the Union cause as officers. Maine-born **William Henry Baldwin**, for instance, a lawyer, briefly served under Giuseppe Garibaldi in the Italian civil war of the mid-nineteenth century. When he heard that civil war had erupted in his own country, he "hastened" back home to take part as lieutenant colonel of the Eighty-Third Ohio at Vicksburg and Mobile, noted James Barnett in an article about the Union generals of Spring Grove Cemetery for the Cincinnati Civil War Round Table (see www .cincinnatiwrt.org/forty.html).

Another, **Stephen Joseph McGroarty**, Irish-born and initially serving as an officer in the Irish Tenth Ohio Volunteers, certainly was determined to continue despite any setbacks encountered. Shot through the right lung in West Virginia, he recovered and moved on to leadership in the Sixty-First Ohio Volunteers. He then lost an arm in the battle of Peachtree Creek in 1864, but nonetheless moved on to a fresh leadership role with the Eighty-Second Ohio. In all, he suffered a reported total of twenty-three wounds before war's end.

Since it was the custom to reward wounded war heroes like McGroarty with election to public office, added Barnett, McGroarty promptly sought the Republican nomination for Hamilton County auditor in 1866, only to be defeated by another widely respected war hero. Not quite yet daunted, he next sought and won the Democratic Party's nomination for county prosecutor, but then lost in the general election. In 1869, vindication at last seemed on hand when he won the office of county recorder. But alas, two months before taking office the following January, McGroarty, only thirty-nine years old, died suddenly.

As a compensating gesture to his family, wrote Barnett, "in later years his friends secured the job of postmistress of the College Hill station for his wife, Mary McGroarty, who held that position for many years."

A real and antebellum political veteran was **Elisha Bassett Langdon**, an attorney who had served in both the Ohio House and Senate before going off to war as another regimental leader. He survived the battles of Shiloh, Perryville, Chickamauga, and Missionary Ridge, but it was his unexpected and sudden death at age forty in 1867, apparently from the effects of his wartime wounds, that opened the way to the presidency for still another war hero from Ohio. As Barnett explained, "General Langdon was highly respected by both Republicans and Democrats and was almost certain of victory as the Republican candidate for governor of Ohio in the fall elections of 1867." With his sudden death the previous spring, however, that pathway opened up for U.S. Representative (and former Civil War hero) Rutherford B. Hayes. "Compelled" by Langdon's death to find a substitute candidate, the party chose Hayes, "who went on to serve two terms as governor of Ohio and eventually was elected the nineteenth president of the United States."

Overall, it might also be mentioned, the forty-one generals at final rest in the Cincinnati cemetery predominantly were lawyers or law students. Seven were West Point graduates, but only four were regular army officers when the Civil War broke out, and only four could claim combat experience—Generals Lytle, Baldwin, Hooker, and **Augustus Moor**. Importantly, in Barnett's view, "twenty-three had advanced from no military experience whatsoever to attain the highest rank in the Union Army." Such "a remarkable feat," added Barnett, "underscored" the fact that the initial core of the Federal army was "a force of 'inspired volunteers' rather than a standing army in the European tradition."

At the start of the Civil War, the regular army consisted of only nineteen regiments, boasting a slim 1,098 officers and 15,279 enlisted ranks in personnel. "Needless to say, this minuscule force was not much of a factor in the formation of the Union Army, precisely as the framers of the [U.S.] Constitution had planned." With the firing on Fort Sumter and newly installed president Abraham Lincoln's call for volunteers, however, everything changed dramatically. By war's end, "More than two and a half million men would serve in the Union Army, yet only six per cent of them were draftees."

Among the Spring Grove generals, meanwhile, a surprising number—eight—were war survivors who lived beyond seventy years in age, two of them into their nineties, in fact. Seven, on the other hand, died before reaching the age of fifty, but only four of the forty-one were killed in action or by combat-related injury. Ten more died between the ages of sixty and seventy.

If most of the Spring Grove forty-one died peacefully of natural causes long after the shooting was over, not so for one of the McCook Brothers. **Edwin Stanton McCook** (yes, named for Lincoln's future war secretary Edwin M. Stanton, then law partner to an older McCook brother) was assassinated in 1873. In his role as acting governor of the Dakota Territory, he had been speaking in Yankton when a member of the audience shot and fatally wounded him. He was only thirty-six years old.

In the view of many, another of the four McCook generals buried at Spring Grove also was murdered...but during the Civil War itself. An extremely ill **Robert Latimer McCook** was fatally wounded by Southern irregulars who attacked his party while he was being transported in a horse-drawn ambulance. His brother **Daniel McCook Jr.**, for that matter, another of the Spring Grove generals, was fatally wounded while leading a Union assault at Kennesaw Mountain, Georgia, during William T. Sherman's Atlanta campaign. A lawyer before the war in the same legal firm as Sherman and his foster brother Thomas Ewing (both future Union generals), twenty-nine-year-old Daniel McCook died in mid-July 1864 after being transported all the way north to a brother's home in Steubenville, Ohio.

Thus, of the four McCooks buried in the Spring Grove cemetery, only **Alexander McDowell McCook**, a West Point graduate and career army officer, was destined to reach old age and a peaceful death. Before passing in 1903, he achieved a major general's rank in the regular army, retired in 1895, and represented the United States at the coronation of Russian czar Nicholas II in 1896, Barnett noted.

Two more brothers buried at Spring Grove, both Union generals, were Civil War survivors: **Jeptha Garrard** and **Kenner Garrard**. Older brother Kenner was a West Point graduate and regular army officer serving in Texas when the war broke out. "Making known his loyalty to the Union cause," wrote Barnett, "he was imprisoned by the Confederates, but was exchanged on August 27, 1862." He then was named colonel of the 146th New York and served in a string of major battles—Fredericksburg, Chancellorsville, and Gettysburg—before taking part in Sherman's Atlanta campaign as a division leader. He returned to the Garrard family home base of Cincinnati after the war and died in 1879 at age fifty-one.

Younger brother Jeptha, on the other hand, was a lawyer with no military experience before taking command of a New York cavalry regiment. Like his brother Kenner, he returned to Cincinnati once the hostilities ended. He lived to the age of seventy-nine. A third Garrard brother, Israel, *not* buried at Spring Grove, also was a Union general—and all three were grandsons of Kentucky's second governor, James Garrard.

Among the remaining Union generals buried at Spring Grove is the once-suspect Irishman **Peter John Sullivan**, whose Democratic Party allegiance made him a suspicious character of doubtful loyalty to the Union in the eyes of Ohio governor William Dennison, a Republican. As events turned out, Sullivan, at his own expense, organized four regiments and won the backing of Abraham Lincoln for a commission as lieutenant colonel of the Forty-Eighth Ohio Volunteers. Soon taking part in the battle of Shiloh, he had four horses shot out from under him and was wounded three times.

Never able to return to combat, he, like many of the "generals" buried at Spring Grove, was made a brevet, or temporary, brigadier at the end of the war. He later served Presidents Andrew Johnson and Ulysses S. Grant as minister to Columbia before dying in Cincinnati in 1883 at the age of sixty-one.

George W. Neff, another of the Spring Grove brevet brigadiers, somewhat ironically spent a year as prisoner of the Confederates, then wound up his war career as colonel of an Ohio regiment guarding Confederate prisoners at Camp Chase in Columbus, Ohio. In the interim, he had taken part in the pursuit of Confederate raider John Hunt Morgan during Hunt's foray into Ohio itself. He lived to 1892 before dying at age fifty-nine.

Also somewhat ironical was the sad demise of **Frederick William Moore**, once "the youngest colonel in the [Union] volunteer army." Moore led his

Eighty-Third Ohio Volunteers in the siege of Vicksburg among his various Civil War engagements, then returned to a law practice and two judgeships (in the common pleas and superior courts, respectively) in his native Ohio before retiring. In 1905 he planned to return to Vicksburg to help dedicate a monument to his regiment, but he suddenly died, age sixty-five, before he could make the trip.

Meanwhile, serving at Shiloh, in the Atlanta campaign, and in Sherman's March to the Sea was not exactly exclusive territory for any single Civil War veteran, but only **Thomas Tinsley Heath**, of all the brigadiers in the entire Union army, could claim the "unique distinction" of commanding the Union flag detail in the official ceremonies attending Joseph E. Johnston's surrender to Sherman after the battle of Bentonville, North Carolina, essentially the last surrender of any significant Confederate force at the end of the Civil War. Heath then returned not only to a law practice in Cincinnati but also to a new career as an inventor—chiefly as the man behind the newspaper printing method known as stereotyping. He lived to the age of ninety before his burial at Spring Grove in 1925.

Arthur Forrester Devereux, Massachusetts-born and a heroic brigade leader at Gettysburg, left a "legacy" of an entirely different kind—his wife, Clara Rich Devereux, for many years was society editor of the *Cincinnati Enquirer* and "originator" of the city's "Blue Book." His daughter Marion, moreover, succeeded her mother as society editor—"and became the undisputed 'tsarina' of Cincinnati society for thirty years."

Notable family ties were a hallmark of **Nicholas Longworth Anderson's** background, since he was a nephew of Ohio governor Charles J. Anderson and Maj. Robert Anderson, who commanded the Union garrison at Fort Sumter in Charleston Harbor when it was shelled by Confederate shore batteries in the first real action of the Civil War. The younger Anderson's mother, Catherine, was a Longworth, the same family that later produced U.S. Rep. Nicholas Longworth, who was destined to marry Theodore Roosevelt's daughter Alice and serve as Speaker of the U.S. House.

A law student and then a volunteer private at the start of the Civil War, Nicholas Anderson soon claimed a colonelcy and "served in western Virginia and in most of the major campaigns in the West, but was wounded severely twice and was mustered out of service in June 1864, having attained the rank of brevet major general." He lived to the age of fifty-four before his death and burial in 1892.

While many of the Spring Grove generals began their military careers as privates and then quickly advanced to a more exalted officer's rank, **Jacob Ammen** did it in the space of one day to the next. Already a hoary fifty-three years old when he volunteered as a private at the start of the war, the civil engineer "was named captain the next day." By July 1862, just over a year later, he was appointed as a brigadier general of volunteers. He would survive a bout with typhoid as well as combat. He lived to 1894, dying at age eighty-six.

Moving from the first to almost the last on the Spring Grove roll call of generals, alphabetically speaking, regular army **Maj. Gen. Godfrey Weitzel**, best known for his occupation of Richmond the day the Confederate capital fell to Union forces (see "Union: Enduring Family Ties," page 101), joined the deceased here in 1884, at age forty-eight, after a distinguished career as both a soldier and a civil engineer.

★★★

Additional note: The history of Spring Grove Cemetery goes back to early nineteenth-century cholera outbreaks in the Cincinnati area. With so many persons stricken, often fatally, says the cemetery's online history (at www .springgrove.org/SpringGrove/history.htm), "the crowded and sometimes unkempt appearance of many small church cemeteries...offered little comfort to bereaved families." Members of the city's horticultural society then stepped in to search for a site "suitable for creating a picturesque park-like institution, a rural cemetery, contiguous to the city yet remote enough not to be disturbed by expansion." They visited cemeteries in the United States and in Europe "as they planned a cemetery that would equal the famed beauty of Pere la Chaise in Paris and various outstanding cemeteries on the East Coast of the United States." Opened in 1845 and now officially known as the Spring Grove Cemetery and Arboretum, the burial grounds cover a beautifully landscaped four hundred acres of lawns, "native and exotic plant materials as well as...State and National champion trees." Another as-yet-undeveloped 333 acres await the cemetery's future expansion needs.

CONFEDERATE

Forever Unreconstructed...

THAT SURELY WAS JUBAL A. Early, combative Southern general during the Civil War and outspoken as the South's chief defender of the faith after the war. So unforgiving and still combative a defender was he after the fighting stopped, that he once said, "I have got to that condition that I think I could scalp a Yankee woman and child without winking my eyes."

Born in Franklin County, Virginia, an 1837 West Point graduate, a U.S. Army veteran of the fighting in the Seminole Wars and of largely garrison duty during the Mexican War, a practicing attorney, and a one-term Virginia legislator in the years immediately before the war, he voted *against* secession in the Virginia convention of April 1861.

But that did not impede his quick decision to join the Confederate army once Virginia did secede, followed by his command of the Twenty-Fourth Virginia Infantry at First Manassas as its colonel. His progress up the promotion ladder was rapid from there on—he served in the Army of Northern Virginia's every battle from 1862 to 1864, by which time he was a lieutenant general and prominent as one of Robert E. Lee's most dependable and trusted lieutenants. During this time he had been at Gettysburg, temporarily had taken over A. P. Hill's corps, served at the Wilderness, and taken over Richard S. Ewell's corps for a time. In the end, this fierce Rebel fighter was given command of his own Second Corps, with instruction to clear the Shenandoah Valley of federal Gen. David Hunter's forces and to draw off Union attentions from the Richmond–Petersburg hub.

This he did so admirably that he chased Hunter into West Virginia, then swept north to appear suddenly at the gates to Washington, D.C., itself. Held up for two days at Monocacy, Maryland, by Union Gen. Lew Wallace's smaller force, Early's command briefly entered the streets of the Union capital on July 11, 1864, his men within shooting distance of an onlooking Abraham Lincoln at Fort Stevens.

Early's escapade came to a halt once Ulysses S. Grant sent two corps hustling north to defend Washington, but for weeks to come Early still had a free hand in the Valley, ranging far north into Pennsylvania and burning Chambersburg on July 30. Grant now dispatched his own attack dog in the form of Phillip

H. Sheridan, who wasted little time in confronting and defeating Early at Winchester and Fisher's Hill in late September, then sent his fellow West Pointer reeling at Cedar Creek a month later. The coup de grace came on the second day of March 1865 as Sheridan smashed the last remnants of Early's corps at Waynesboro.

Such a crushing defeat was bad enough, but this also was a critical moment in Early's relationship with his fond mentor, Lee. As Civil War historian Gary W. Gallagher noted in his book *Lee and His Generals in War and Memory*: "[Lee] appreciated Early's talents as a soldier and displayed a personal fondness for his cantankerous and profane lieutenant. Only Stonewall Jackson among Lee's corps commanders received more difficult assignments from Lee, a certain indication of the commanding general's high regard."

Still, after Waynesboro, Lee felt he must relieve Early from command, a delicate task he managed gently, Gallagher noted, so as to ensure his feisty subordinate's continued "utter devotion." Expressing his regrets, Lee "noted that defeats in the Shenandoah Valley had alienated that vital region's citizens and raised doubts among Early's soldiers." Choosing his words with great care, Lee added, "While my own confidence in your ability, zeal, and devotion to the cause is unimpaired, I have nevertheless felt that I could not oppose what seems to be the current of opinion, without injustice to your reputation and injury to the service."

Even as Lee added his thanks for Early's "fidelity and energy," his "courage and devotion…in the service of the country," the cause they shared was very nearly moot—utter and final Confederate defeat was just days off.

With Lee's surrender at Appomattox Court House in April, Early fled westward, "with the hope of joining Confederates in the trans-Mississippi theater." Hearing that they, too, had laid down their arms, he simply kept going…to Havana, Cuba, first, then to Mexico, and finally to Canada. He felt constrained to leave the reunited country, he said, "to get out from the rule of the infernal Yankees…I cannot live under the same government with our enemies. I go therefore a voluntary exile from the home and graves of my ancestors to seek my fortunes anew in the world."

In four years, though, he was back in Virginia, where he would take up the verbal cudgels of war to carry on the vision and myth of the Lost Cause as probably its greatest postwar advocate. In a memoir and many other writings, he built an image of the beleaguered South that would last until our own time. As summarized by Gallagher, Early's major points were these: "(1) Robert E. Lee was the best and most admirable general of the war; (2) Confederate

Jubal A. Early, permanent apostle of the "lost cause"

armies faced overwhelming odds and mounted a gallant resistance; (3) Ulysses S. Grant paled in comparison to Lee as a soldier; (4) Stonewall Jackson deserved a place immediately behind Lee in the Confederate pantheon; and (5) Virginia was the most important arena of the conflict."

Familiar, isn't it? While serious students of the Civil War might well argue this point or that, isn't that basically the image of the Civil War held by the American public in our own times, nearly 150 years later?

Early's scenario was especially kind to his hero, Lee, and of course highly critical of James Longstreet, along with various lesser beings in the Southern pantheon. In his view, unkind circumstances singly or in combination conspired to undermine Lee's best efforts to garner victories for his Army of Northern Virginia. "Defending his subject at every turn," added Gallagher, "Early explained Gettysburg as an instance where Lee's subordinates (especially James Longstreet) failed to execute a sound plan of battle. The public misunderstood the campaign only because Lee's magnanimity had prevented his revealing the true causes of that defeat."

Additionally, "Early explained the fall of Richmond in April 1865 and the surrender of Lee's army as 'consequences of events in the West and Southwest, and not directly of the operations in Virginia.'" Naturally, too, the North and its leadership, even the manhood of its soldiers, also came in for considerable Early criticism. "I might multiply the instances of the attempts of our enemies to falsify the truth of history in order to excuse their manifold failures, and to conceal the inferiority of their troops in all the elements of manhood, but I would become too tedious," Early commented.

Possibly tedious to some, Early in fact maintained his unreconstructed barrage of pro-Lee, pro-Confederate talking points to the end of his life (he died in Lynchburg, Virginia, on March 2, 1894). "In lectures, writings and personal correspondence over the last twenty-five years of his life," wrote Gallagher, "Early put his impressions of the war on record." As one result, he "achieved a position in the South as a leading arbiter of questions relating to Confederate military history. He orchestrated the effort to isolate James Longstreet—Lee's senior subordinate throughout the war—as a pariah because he had dared to criticize Lee in print."

In fact, Early's active pen discouraged others from expressing any negative reviews of Lee. Gallagher noted, "If Early could savage a soldier of Longstreet's wartime accomplishments and reputation, scarcely anyone would be safe criticizing Lee." And of course Lee "towers above all other Civil War figures in Early's writings."

With the war lost, though, any realist could see there was no hope that the South of old could rise again...so, why persist? As Gallagher observed, Early wrote to Lee in 1868, saying, "The most that is left to us is the history of our struggle, and I think that ought to be accurately written. We lost nearly everything but honor, and that should be religiously guarded." Then, too, "Apart from his concern about future perceptions of Lee and his army, Early also sought to guard his own long-term reputation." Either way, he clearly hoped to influence the perceptions of what he called "the rising generation."

And he did leave strong impressions, not only upon the immediately "rising generation," but upon many a generation thereafter...*if only because much of what he said was actually true*. Noted Gallagher: "Robert E. Lee *was* a gifted soldier who inspired his army to accomplish prodigious feats on the battlefield. The Army of Northern Virginia and other Confederate forces consistently fought at a disadvantage in numbers and often of materiel." In addition, even Northern opinion makers were critical of Grant's "hammering" tactics of 1864 that won battles but cost so much in Union lives. And Stonewall Jackson indeed was a great general and right arm to Lee. And Virginia, in the eyes of many both then and now, certainly was viewed as a "crucial arena" of the Civil War.

But in Early's scheme of things, there also was distortion, which "came when Early and other proponents of the Lost Cause denied that Lee had faults or lost any battles, focused on northern numbers and material superiority while ignoring Confederate advantages, denied Grant any virtues or greatness, and noticed the Confederacy outside the eastern theater only when convenient to explain southern failures in Virginia."

Distortion or not, many of the views espoused by the die-hard Early and others of like mind are still with us today. Is it not true, for instance, as Gallagher points out, that "the rebel Lee rather than the Union's protector Grant has joined Lincoln as one of the conflict's two great popular figures?" Food for thought...and perhaps Jubal Early had greater long-lasting effect than even he could have predicted.

UNION
Amazing Postwar Résumé

BEGINNING MILITARY LIFE AT AGE seventeen as a private with the Nineteenth Massachusetts Volunteers, this young man compiled more than an adequate record for his time spent in Union uniform—several major battles and three serious wounds endured and the rank of brevet major achieved. But the still-young Adolphus Greely, a native of Newburyport, Massachusetts, had only begun building one of the most amazing lifetime military careers ever put together by an American soldier.

With a very special Medal of Honor as a final capstone for all his achievements, the résumé he compiled over the years is all the more amazing considering the absolute disaster that struck when he led a twenty-five-man exploratory expedition into the then little-known Arctic in the 1880s…and staggered back into public view many months later with only six of his men still alive.

But then, what does one expect from soldiers and a leader who had never been to the Arctic before?

What to expect especially when, for two consecutive summers, their supply ships never showed up? When also they lived for two years near the North Pole in a large rectangular structure built of wooden boards covered with tar paper and requiring tons of coal to stay heated? When they found themselves in total isolation, no local peoples nearby to help, no radio yet invented to allow an SOS? And when, finally, dissension riddled their ranks, and as the starving expedition members began to die off, their commander Greely ordered the execution of a man for stealing precious communal rations?

The fact is, ill-prepared in the extreme, they were stuck in "a region of which civilized man knew next to nothing even while it exerted a grip on his imagination," per Leonard F. Guttridge in his book *Ghosts of Cape Sabine: The Harrowing True Story of the Greely Expedition.*

Apparently involving cannibalism by some expedition members, it truly was a horror story, with Greely and his six fellow survivors nearly dead by the time they were rescued by Navy Cmdr. Winfield Scott Schley in 1884. (One man died soon after the rescue.)

Widely criticized, both at the time and sometimes in the years since, Greely nonetheless managed to transcend what would have been a career-ending blot for most. He, in fact, carved out such an amazing military career that, when he reached his ninety-first birthday in 1935, Congress voted him the Medal of Honor not for any specific brave deed but "for his life of splendid public service."

That service had resumed soon after the Civil War with the regular army's signal service. As now a mere lieutenant, he spent "many of his next 14 years... constructing transcontinental telegraph lines under hostile conditions," noted Lt. Col. Charles M. Hall in the article "When Honor Conflicts with Duty," which appeared in the *Air University Review* of September–October 1980. "At the end of this period, he advocated and was appointed leader of the successful but ill-fated Lady Franklin Bay Arctic Expedition of 1881–1884."

With two supply ships unable to reach the Greely party on the eastern shore of Ellesmere Island two years in a row due to ice conditions (they did try) and nothing more heard of the expedition, Greely was presumed lost and so was passed over for promotion to captain. Confronted, as he was, with life-or-death issues for his party, Greely of course had more on his mind than rank.

And there were successes for the inexperienced Americans in their Arctic foray—among them the record for farthest northward travel yet achieved by any of the hostile region's explorers, an honor going to a three-man sledge party headed by Lt. James B. Lockwood and including Sgt. David Brainard. Of the three, only Brainard survived, later to become a brigadier general.

Meanwhile, Greely's party mapped newly discovered geographic features while also taking important meteorological, oceanographic, and geophysical measurements before abandoning its Fort Conger base after two years without supply and, by standing orders, moving southward by boat to Cape Sabine to await rescue there. Sadly, that meant spending another winter in the freezing cold with inadequate shelter and few provisions, the weakest men dying off one by one.

While initially greeted in the aftermath with recriminations and considerable shock as the expedition's problems became known, Greely received his captaincy in 1886 but then leaped in rank—no, vaulted!—in less than a year to brigadier general as he became chief of the army's Signal Corps.

From there Greely went on to a truly remarkable career. As Billy Mitchell's mentor, Greely "laid the foundation for the Army's assumption of an air service," noted Hall. Long before that, however, in 1898, *before* the Wright brothers flew at Kitty Hawk in 1903, according to the National Park Service, Greely obtained a fifty-thousand-dollar congressional appropriation for development of a "flying machine for war purposes."

Further, he briefly was head of the U.S. Weather Service, at one time an army agency. He was a founder of the National Geographic Society. As Signal Corps chief, he directed the laying of twenty-five thousand or more miles of telegraph lines and submarine cables during the Spanish-American War, thus providing communication links with Cuba, Puerto Rico, Alaska, and the Philippines.

Later advanced to the then still-rarified rank of major general and based at the Presidio in San Francisco, the onetime Civil War private found himself in charge of the army's relief efforts in the wake of the 1906 San Francisco earthquake.

It's not too clear when he had the time, but in addition to his many scientific and official reports, he also turned out at least six books—one of them on a theme he personally knew all too well: *True Tales of Arctic Heroism*.

CONFEDERATE
"Fighting Bishop"

THIS CIVIL WAR GENERAL'S REMAINS reside in a cathedral—Christ Church Cathedral in New Orleans. But then, Confederate Lt. Gen. Leonidas Polk, killed by a cannon shot at Pine Mountain, Georgia, during William Tecumseh Sherman's Atlanta campaign, also was a bishop, the first Episcopalian bishop of Louisiana.

Born in Raleigh, North Carolina, he first, like his good friend Jefferson Davis, was a military man. He graduated from West Point in 1827, a year ahead of Davis, but at the military academy he had felt the call to a different kind of service. Converted and baptized while still a cadet, he left military service soon after his graduation to become a man of the cloth. He studied at the Virginia Theological Seminary in Alexandria, Virginia, and served as a deacon at the Monumental Church in Richmond, future capital of the Confederacy. Soon ordained and married to the former Frances Ann Devereux, he traveled in Europe—perhaps for health reasons, since he was prone to respiratory illnesses— then became, with his wife, owner-operator of a plantation in Tennessee while he also served as an Episcopal minister.

In his late twenties and his thirties, noted Dr. Jack D. Welsh in his book *Medical Histories of Confederate Generals*, the Reverend Polk "was in poor health." One day in March 1836, just short of his thirtieth birthday, "he woke up

The death of Gen. Leonidas Polk

partially paralyzed and with his speech impaired." That episode was succeeded by "a similar attack" the next month, followed by a "slow" recovery.

Despite such health problems, Polk served as the Episcopal Church's missionary bishop for the Southwest, a post calling for often-strenuous travel in the primitive and undeveloped areas of Arkansas, Louisiana, the Indian Territory (future Oklahoma), and Texas. He then became the first bishop for the diocese of Louisiana. And he and his wife then operated a plantation in Thibodaux.

As the Civil War approached, meanwhile, he had survived bouts with cholera in 1849 and yellow fever in 1854. Important, too, it was about this time that Bishop Polk wrote a letter to his fellow Southern bishops of the church proposing creation of a great educational institution, a church-supported university of the South. He thus planted the seeds that would grow into today's University of the South at Sewanee, Tennessee. "He studied universities at home and in Europe; he spread the need for a place of Christian learning; and he had persuasive gifts," noted Andrew Lytle in a Founders' Day address at Sewanee in 1964. As a major element of Polk's vision, he hoped to benefit the South's slaves by making sure their masters were schooled well enough to eventually educate and even free their slaves.

Apparently he had something like this in mind back in his cadet days at West Point. "The beginnings of the idea of a great liberal university can be traced back to Polk's conversion at West Point in 1826 and his interest in [an] invitation to become a professor," said the Reverend Moultrie Guerry in an article for the *Historical Magazine of the Protestant Episcopal Church* in 1938.

Whatever or whenever the genesis of the concept, with the support of the Southern bishops, Polk led a fund-raising drive that amassed half a million dollars for the proposed school by late 1860. But the advent of the Civil War put a stop to the proceedings. And now the man of the cloth, himself a slave owner, once more took up the sword, on behalf of the Confederacy led by his old West Point companion, Jefferson Davis.

Quickly given the rank of major general, he was placed in command of Department No. 2, a region stretching from the Red River to Paducah, Kentucky. He assembled the Army of Mississippi, later absorbed into the Army of Tennessee, and was a corps commander at the battles of Shiloh, Perryville, Murfreesboro, and Chickamauga. In the interim, he escaped harm from the enemy—instead, it was the "Lady Polk," a cannon named for his wife, that almost did him in.

The incident took place at Columbus, Kentucky, in November 1861. The cannon, an eight-ton rifled Dahlgren, had been allowed to cool with a shot left in it after a round of firing. As the metal cooled, it contracted and tightened on the round left inside. General Polk was standing nearby some time later when the gun was prepared for renewed firing—at the first shot, it burst, killing several soldiers also gathered nearby and knocking Polk to the ground. "Stunned, he was carried to his headquarters," wrote Welsh in his medical histories book.

At first it appeared that only Polk's eardrums were injured. Two weeks later, however, it appeared his "system was shocked, and there were indications of a more serious injury than was first supposed." After a period of rest, though, he was able to resume his duties in the field.

Promoted to the rank of lieutenant general in 1862, he apparently was popular with his men. One of them, Pvt. Thomas Jefferson Walker of the Ninth Tennessee Infantry, later wrote that Polk's troops at first feared "that he, being a preacher, would be afraid to fight." They called him "Granny Polk." But then Walker and his comrades one day saw Polk in battle. "Then suddenly there came riding down in front of our lines," Walker wrote, "as magnificent a specimen of noble, courageous manhood, mounted on his magnificent roan charger, I then thought and still think, as I have ever seen. With his sword unsheathed and with fire flashing from his eyes, he pointed toward our retreating and broken lines. He rode in front of us with the Federal line in pursuit. Then wheeling his horse as he reached the center of our regiment and raising himself in his stirrups and shouting, 'Follow your Granny!' he led the charge."

After that, his troops never again called their general "Granny."

"From that moment," added Walker, "his corps loved and worshipped him until his deplored death and still revere him as few heroic commanders have been loved and worshipped in the world's history." In the same vein, but more dispassionately, British observer Lt. Col. Arthur James Lyon Fremantle agreed that Polk was "much beloved" by his troops "on account of his great personal courage and agreeable manners."

Eighteen sixty-two was the same year, during the actions at Perryville, Kentucky, that Polk one night found himself on the wrong side of the front lines. Challenged to identify himself by a Yankee officer and hoping that in the dark the color of his uniform wouldn't betray him, Polk said, "I'll show you who I am. Cease firing at once!"

To continue his deception, he turned his horse and rode down the Union line, shouting the order to stop firing. He expected at any moment to be cut down by a fusillade of bullets from behind, but in moments he was able to steer his steed into some trees and then gallop back unharmed to his own lines. There he gave the order to his men to open fire on the now-quieted Yankee line—with tragic results for the Twenty-Second Indiana Infantry. Said Polk later, "I assure you, sir, that the slaughter of that Indiana regiment was the greatest I had ever seen in the war."

At the same time, Polk wasn't always considered a great strategist by his peers and he had a falling out with his commander at Chickamauga, Gen. Braxton Bragg, also a close friend of Jefferson Davis. "His [Polk's] performance upon some occasions was judged to be hardly commensurate with his rank, and he was particularly censured by General Bragg for dilatory tactics at Chickamauga," noted Ezra Warner in his book *Generals in Gray*.

Even so, on November 7, 1861, Polk managed a small coup that many of his Confederate peers later might have found difficult to match—in the little-noted battle of Belmont, Missouri, he fought a still-hardly-known Union general named Ulysses S. Grant to a standstill or narrow victory, depending on one's definition. More specifically, Grant withdrew, but he did so by fighting off the Rebel force that Polk sent to trap him. Almost a balance also, the Confederate losses of 642 out of 4,000 engaged were almost the same as the Union casualty count of 607 out of 3,114 engaged.

More significant, nearly three years later, in the midst of Sherman's Atlanta campaign, came the day, the rainy June day, that Sherman himself noticed a group of Rebel generals studying his deployments in the area of Kennesaw, Lost, and Pine mountains outside Marietta, Georgia. They were within the range of his artillery, but the Union batteries, under orders to conserve their ammunition, were quiet for the time being. Not liking what he saw, Sherman told his gunners to fire and force the Rebel onlookers to take cover.

The first Union round to hit had the desired effect—almost. "The first shot scattered most of the generals, but Polk, for some reason known but to him, took his time," notes Randy Golden on the About North Georgia website (http://ngeorgia.com/history/polk.html). "A second round struck nearby and the third round entered Polk through the arm, passing through his chest and exiting through the other arm."

It was a Parrott shell, and it didn't explode until it struck a chestnut tree close by, according to Welsh. But no one could have survived such a terrible wound.

Polk's fellow West Point graduate and Confederate general Joseph E. Johnston stood over the "Fighting Bishop's" body and cried, adds the Golden account. Polk had baptized both Johnston and John Bell Hood earlier in the campaign.

When Polk was buried in Augusta, Georgia, Bishop Stephen Elliott said in a eulogy that the day would come "when this martyred dust shall be carried in triumphal fashion procession to his own beloved Louisiana, and deposited in such a shrine as a loving, mournful people shall prepare for him." And so it was…in 1945, when the remains of both Bishop Polk and his wife were reinterred below the chancel of Christ Church Cathedral in New Orleans, with appropriate, reverential ceremony.

★★★

Additional note: Another Confederate General Polk, Bishop Polk's nephew Lucius, took part in the same Kennesaw Mountain battles that June—and came away so badly wounded in the leg by a cannonball that he had to leave military service.

He and his slain uncle each had an unusual connection with the Confederate Gen. Patrick Cleburne. Lucius served under the Irish-born general and, in an odd way, was partially responsible for the latter's wounding at Richmond, Kentucky, in 1862. According to Welsh, Lucius was wild and disoriented after suffering a head wound there. "While he was being taken to the rear…Cleburne stopped to talk to him and was wounded himself." As for the connection with Leonidas Polk, the North Georgia website says that he gave the land for a church that Cleburne admired so much that he once remarked, "It is almost worth dying for to be buried in such a beautiful place." Killed in the battle of Franklin, Tennessee, Cleburne actually *was* buried there…"until later disinterred."

UNION & CONFEDERATE
A Soldier's Legacy

WASN'T IT A NICE GESTURE when Charles Strahan, editor of the *Martha's Vineyard Herald*, one June day in 1891 announced in the paper that "all new subscriptions…this season will be turned over to the purchase fund for the monument"?

What he meant by "subscriptions" was the proceeds from all new subscriptions.

What he meant by "the monument" was the proposed statue to be erected in the central square of the island's town of Oak Bluff to commemorate the brave Union soldiers of the not-so-distant Civil War. Under the heading BOYS! IT'S GROWING, he ran a sketch of the proposed monument and the added lines:

THIS
SOLDIERS' MEMORIAL
WILL BE ERECTED IN HONOR OF
THE GRAND ARMY OF THE REPUBLIC
BY THE
MARTHA'S VINEYARD HERALD

Further, the handsome pedestal with a Union soldier's figure on top was to be erected "about August 1" of the same year.

Nice indeed…especially considering that the same Charles Strahan in the not-so-distant past had himself been a Civil War soldier—a *Confederate* soldier.

A Marylander, he served with the Twenty-First Virginia Infantry. Strahan was wounded in the battle of Seven Pines near Richmond in late May 1862. As a result, he later told postwar *Union* veterans, he would always "carry the mark of a Federal bullet on my body."

After recovering from his wound, according to an obituary cited by Martha M. Boltz in an article for the *Washington Times* (July 23, 2005), he served at Gettysburg on the staff of Brig. Gen. Isaac R. Trimble, who was wounded and captured on the third and last day of the watershed battle. From there, apparently an officer by now, Strahan briefly drops out of historical sight. The reason probably lies in the fact that Maryland was a Border State that never seceded or joined the Confederacy. Thus, Strahan's service is not easily verified by official records. And that wouldn't be unique, noted Boltz, "given the strange situation of Maryland soldiers, who frequently affiliated with whatever unit needed their services."

But he does turn up again—and in a key post at that. "Strahan's next verified appearance is as the head of the [Confederate] Bureau of Conscription under Gen. John Smith Preston," Boltz discovered. "Strahan remained in this position until the end of the war."

Tracking his postwar travels, she learned that he spent a brief time in Louisiana as a coffee importer but then moved with his family to Martha's Vineyard, the popular island summer resort off Cape Cod. There, in the community then called Cottage City but more recently known as Oak Bluffs, he purchased the *Cottage City Star*, a weekly. Changing its name to the *Martha's Vineyard Herald*, he began publishing year-round instead of in the summer season only, "soon surpassing the *Vineyard Gazette*, an older publication."

His Confederate service during the recent war was no secret…and was obviously resented in some quarters. As late as 1887, according to Boltz, with a Memorial Day program about to take place, "the locals sent word to Strahan that if he attended, they would not be present."

Rather than cause trouble, Strahan "sent a reporter to cover the event." Not long after, however, editor-publisher Strahan printed a letter from a Union veteran chiding others for their hard feelings. "So the seeds of reconciliation were sown," wrote Boltz.

When Strahan next suggested that his now-defunct newspaper could begin raising money for a monument in town honoring the Grand Army of the Republic (GAR), "the idea was received enthusiastically by the local GAR post." In short order, Strahan was invited by the Henry Clay Wade GAR Post to speak at a Memorial Day observance in 1891. Introduced as a former Confederate soldier who nonetheless had proven his loyalty to the community, Strahan reportedly said, "The mists of prejudice which have hung like a cloud over me, in this, my adopted home, are fast disappearing under the sunlight of your affection and brotherly hearts."

A total of $2,000 was needed to fund the monument, which would include a fountain with water pouring from two lion heads. In just two months, it seems, Strahan had raised $700 of the money needed. By midsummer of 1891, "he lacked only $500, which, it appears, he contributed personally."

At the formal dedication of the monument in August of that year, Strahan's five-year-old daughter Louise was given the honor of ceremoniously pulling off the American flag draped over the proud Union soldier figure. Acknowledging his own Confederate background, Strahan said it only signified "that we are once more a union of Americans; a union which endears with equal honor the citizen of Georgia with the citizen of Maine; that Massachusetts and South Carolina are again brothers; and that there is no North nor South, no East nor West, but one undivided, indivisible Union." As at Valley Forge and Yorktown, he observed, "so the sons of the Gray will stand with the sons of the Blue" against "any foe, domestic or foreign," that dared attack the flag of the reunited nation.

Still, the erection and dedication of the monument would not be the end of the story. In the first place, Strahan took note in a subsequent editorial that one of the four tablets on the base of the monument had been left blank—on purpose. "Who knows," he went on to suggest, "but that, as the Grand Army of the Republic becomes smaller, and the passions of war are lost in forgetfulness, these few remaining veterans may yet inscribe on the blank tablet a token of respect to their old foes in the field…thus lifting up and keeping the American name and nation the brightest and most magnanimous in the galaxy of nations."

It would be another thirty-four years before his strong hint was acted upon. But finally, in 1925, the blank tablet was inscribed by members and associates of the old GAR Wade Post to say, "The chasm is closed," and to dedicate the tablet itself in honor of the soldiers of the Confederacy. Not only that, but one of the other tablets was changed to note that the monument had been erected "by Charles Strahan, Co. B, 21st Virginia Regt.," a reference of course to his old Confederate regiment.

Since he died six years later at the age of ninety-one, the wise old editor missed one final tribute to his spirit of unity and forgiveness—in 1980, notes the online *Insiders' Guide to Cape Cod*, "the town of Oak Bluffs repainted the Union soldier atop the memorial in Confederate gray colors to pay homage to Strahan."

In the interim, Boltz added, the advent of modern-day traffic had made it necessary to move the monument from its original site in the town square to "a plot that overlooks Nantucket Sound, at the head of the Oak Bluffs wharf." And there it stands today, a somewhat-amended tribute not only to the soldiers of both sides in the Civil War but also to the man who would close the chasms created by that same war.

Soldiers at East during Lincoln's funeral procession in Washington

PART 4
★ FINAL GLIMPSES ★

UNION
The Long Way Home

ALL THE CITIES SEEN BEFORE would be the same. But in reverse.

Springfield, itself a capital, would be waiting at the end of the line, rather than Washington, D.C.

This time, too, the depots, the stations great and small, and even the long rural stretches of nothing but track assuredly would be crowded with onlookers...and they were.

This time, however, no smiles, no cheers greeted the slow-moving train. The music was solemn, the songs were dirges, and often there were bells tolling and guns measuredly firing.

"The train," said a rider, also a member of the official honor guard, "started on its mournful journey at eight o'clock a.m., Friday, April 21, 1865, preceded by a pilot-engine to guard against accident." The train consisted this time of two "elegant" cars, one a funeral car, the other for the guard of honor. Six more cars were filled with mourners. "The funeral car was heavily draped, within and without, with black, while silver stars and tassels relieved the somber festoons." The car was divided into three parts. In the center was a sleeping compartment and at each end a sitting room. The coffin was on a bier covered in black in the rear sitting room. Another, smaller coffin was placed in the front sitting room for the long, roundabout journey home.

"The depots everywhere were draped in mourning, and many had mottoes conspicuously displayed," wrote honor guard member Edward D. Townsend, assistant adjutant general at the time and on board to represent War Secretary Edwin M. Stanton. He noted, "The cities vied with each other in the elegance with which their buildings, public and private, were draped. Crowds thronged the depots and streets, but there was no jostling, no noise; all was solemn and sad."

From Washington the train moved northward, arriving at ten o'clock in Baltimore, where leading state officials waited for it and "an imposing procession was formed." The open coffin, surrounded by flowers, was on display in the rotunda of a grand city building until time to depart for Harrisburg, state capital of neighboring Pennsylvania, at 3:00 p.m.

At Harrisburg that evening a "driving rain" and the dark of night "prevented the reception which had been arranged." But the remains went anyway, by horse-drawn hearse, through muddy streets to the state capitol, there to be on view until eleven o'clock the next morning, then to be escorted back to the depot by "a very large procession."

In the meantime, "guns were fired and bells tolled through the morning, and trains came in from the surrounding country, laden with people who sought to do honor to the occasion."

And next, on to Philadelphia and its historic Independence Hall...exactly where he had spoken on his way to Washington in 1861, where he in fact spoke of standing up for the nation's ideals, even if it meant his own assassination. "And now his lifeless body had come to make that utterance prophecy."

Meanwhile, the *Philadelphia Inquirer,* in many columns of type, described the event and the scene:

> The hall at large was completely shrouded with black cloth, arranged in a very graceful and appropriate manner. The old chandelier that hangs from the center of the room, and which was directly over the coffin of the deceased, was entirely covered, and from it radiated in every direction festoons of black cloth, forming a sort of canopy over the entire room. The walls of the room presented the appearance of having been papered with black.... The statue of Washington, at the east end of the room, stood out in bold relief against the background. Wreaths of immortelles were hung on the black drapery that covered the walls, and were placed about midway between the floor and ceiling.

As the silent throngs passed by the coffin, noted Townsend in his 1883 book *Anecdotes of the Civil War in the United States*, many expressed the desire, "in some cases amounting almost to insanity, to touch the face, as if virtue would flow from the contact." But of course this would not do. A balustrade erected on either side of the coffin served as a barrier to keep people from approaching too closely.

More than two hundred thousand persons, many of them African Americans, made the pilgrimage to and through old Independence Hall from 10:00 p.m. Saturday to 1:00 a.m. Monday.

Double lines here, three miles long.

At the leave-taking from Philadelphia, mothers held up their babies "above the heads of the multitude" so they could say in later life that they saw it all, even if the scene didn't really register with them.

The train departed for New York at 4:00 a.m.

But first, Jersey City, where the hearse "moved out of the depot to go on board the ferry boat." A chorus of "two hundred voices" performed the dirge here.

As the ferry docked in New York, guns fired, bells tolled, and the flags aboard nearby ships were at half-staff. Greeting the remains as escort for the trip to city hall was the same New York Seventh Regiment that had been such a relief to Washington when it appeared in the first days of the Civil War.

At city hall, the body was placed on an inclined dais in the city council room, at the head of two flights of steps. Thus "persons ascending one flight of steps would have a perfect view of the features while crossing the platform [in between] to descend by the other flight." The stream of people was constant, unending. "Probably more than half a million souls passed across that platform while the doors remained open."

Remarkably, too, when time came for the remains to move on to the depot for the train trip to Albany on the afternoon of Tuesday, April 25, a procession of fifty thousand to seventy thousand persons followed on foot. Reported the *New York Herald*: "In solemn silence, unbroken by the slightest expression of applause at the drill of the soldiery or by the appearance of various popular men and societies, the mournful pageant moved through miles of magnificent dwellings hung with black; and, when the impressive ceremonies were over, the vast assemblage dispersed so quickly and quietly that in a couple hours no trace of its existence remained."

On the way to the Hudson River Depot, Townsend spotted his old commander, former general-in-chief of the army Winfield Scott, still alive, "though pale and feeble." He was present, like everyone else, to pay his parting respects to the deceased.

The Hudson River rail line north "seemed alive with people," and as the train reached one small town after another in the dark, "the darkness of night was relieved by torches, which revealed the crowds there assembled."

The train reached Albany in the middle of the night. "It was long after midnight when the coffin was placed in the State Capitol at Albany. Yet the stream of visitors began the instant the doors could be thrown open."

At 4:00 p.m. Wednesday, it was on again, on again, still by rail, still attended by all the silent crowds. Through Rochester, Herkimer, Little Falls, Utica, and Syracuse, where, close to midnight, "a hard rain did not deter over thirty thousand people from turning out to witness the passing of the train, with torches and bonfires, bells and cannon." And now on to Batavia and Buffalo, where former president Millard Fillmore was among the mourners, where "we first received intelligence of the capture and death of Booth, the assassin."

From here on, closer and closer to his Midwestern political origins with every clack of the rail ties beneath the wheels, "the intensity of feeling seemed if possible to grow deeper." In Cleveland, reached the morning of April 28, a huge canopy structure thirty-six feet in length, twenty-four feet across, and fourteen feet high had been erected in the town square to allow public viewing of the coffin. The lines entered at one end and left at the opposite end. "So great was the influx of persons from the neighboring towns and country, that hundreds were unable to find a resting place for the night." A bishop at one point conducted "solemn religious services at the canopy."

From Erie to Cleveland, the locomotive called the *William Case* was the same that had borne him eastward in 1861. The conductor, E. D. Page, was the same as in 1861. And the fireman of 1861, George Martin, by now an engineer, had reverted to fireman again for the somber trip west after asking for the privilege of doing so.

And now on to Columbus for a twelve-hour stay, followed by Indianapolis, reached at 7:00 a.m. Sunday, April 30. "At midnight, the route was resumed for Chicago. While the darkness prevailed, the approach to every town was made apparent by bonfires, torches and music, while crowds of people formed an almost unbroken line." At Michigan City at 8:30 a.m. on May 1, the funeral train was greeted by a series of floral arches, "beautifully trimmed with black and white," that had been erected over the railroad track itself.

In Chicago, the decorations again were somber but profuse. The remains were taken in a procession to a courthouse rotunda, to lie in state "from early afternoon, all through the night, and until eight o'clock the following evening." Here, too, the crowds were immense, reverent, and awed to be in his presence.

Down the line, toward the last stop, someone in Lockport was preparing a sign that would be seen from the train. "Come home," it said. And from Chicago, he would.

"The cortege left Chicago, the last stopping place before Springfield, at half-past nine o'clock p.m. As usual night was forgotten by the people in their anxiety to show all possible respect for him whom they expected."

After Lockport came Joliet at midnight. Once again, rain—"but, just the same, ten thousand persons were gathered at the depot."

Here, there was an illuminated portrait with the motto, "Champion, defender, and martyr of liberty." Here, the train passed beneath another arch. Here, "sweet" voices were heard singing: "There is rest for thee in heaven."

At Lincoln, named for him, an arch bearing a portrait with the motto, "With malice for none, with charity for all."

And finally, at 9:00 a.m., May 3, he was back in Springfield, Illinois, the very place he had left on the morning of February 11, 1861, on a train following the same route to Washington, D.C., where on March 4, 1861, he was sworn in as president of the United States. Here, back home among his old friends and neighbors, the slain Abraham Lincoln would be buried, as would his young son Willie, who had ridden the same train home to Springfield in the small coffin carried in the funeral car. (Twelve-year-old Willie had died of a fever in 1862.)

For one last time, Lincoln would lie in state in Springfield, as he had at other state capitols on his way home. First, though, after the arrival of his funeral train, "a large procession, in which were many of the most distinguished men in the land, escorted the body, which was conveyed in a splendid hearse, brought for the purpose from St. Louis, drawn by six black horses." He was taken to rest on a catafalque erected in the Representative Hall of the capitol, which now became "truly the hall of mourning." And there is hardly any doubt, as Townsend surmised, that it was "hard for these, his old time neighbors and friends, to realize the dreadful fact that he had come back to them in this guise; and still harder that all that was left of him must, in a few brief hours, be closed from their view forever."

In the meantime, the town that was Lincoln's home "had become classic ground." His old law office, along with his and Mary Todd Lincoln's former home here, "were freely thrown open to the thousands eager to see the places which had known him, and should know him no more."

The funeral services, with all appropriate ceremony, religious and secular, would take place at the city's new Oak Ridge Cemetery the afternoon of May 4, but first the doors to the hall in the capitol were closed "while the undertaker and embalmer renewed some of the trimmings of the coffin, cleansed the dress and face, and reverently sealed the coffin-lid."

It was just then that a small vestige of the long train ride home unexpectedly turned up. "At this moment," Townsend wrote, "a little rose-bud attached to a geranium leaf, which a woman had dropped upon the body at Buffalo, was found nestling directly over the heart."

Townsend did not say if the dried flower was cast aside as they closed the coffin or if it stayed there, next to Abraham Lincoln's heart, for all eternity.

★★★

Additional note: The twelve-member guard of honor accompanying Lincoln's body to Springfield was composed of military officers, most of them army generals (including Brevet Brigadier General Townsend himself), although the navy contributed an admiral and a captain, and the Marine Corps a major. In addition, "twenty-five picked men, sergeants of the Veteran Reserve Corps," also rode the train and acted as the coffin's bearers at all the stops made en route to Springfield.

"In every city where the remains were exposed to view," Townsend related, "a guard of honor was selected to be present while the crowd passed through the hall." Even so, he added, "throughout" the entire journey, at every stop, at least two of the honor guard riding the train with Lincoln's body were always by the side of his coffin. And, "No bearers, except the veteran guard, were ever suffered to handle the President's coffin."

CONFEDERATE

Final Chapter for Jefferson Davis

WITH A BAND PLAYING "DIXIE," the cortege proceeded in stately style from the capitol in Richmond, once the Confederacy's capital city, to the city's history-laden Hollywood Cemetery. It was the afternoon of May 31, 1893, and this would be the final and official burial of the onetime president of the Confederacy.

After his death in December 1889, Jefferson Davis had been interred in the Metairie Cemetery in New Orleans, the city where he died. As explained by Mary H. Mitchell in *Hollywood Cemetery: The History of a Southern Shrine*, the president's widow, Varina Howell Davis, wanted to see him buried on the grounds of their last home, Beauvoir, on Mississippi's Gulf Coast (see "Confederate: His Last Home," page 208). But she realized (wisely, in view of the destruction wrought by Hurricane Katrina in 2005) "that flooding and erosion might ultimately destroy the site."

Deciding upon an alternate burial place for her husband was not all that difficult a choice. To many, in fact, it seemed obvious. "Large numbers of veterans wrote Mrs. Davis asking her to chose Richmond, where 'that

President was loved and honored during the most eventful and trying years of his useful life.'" Indeed, back when Davis died, Hollywood's own directors had offered his widow "any lot she wished in the cemetery," wrote Mitchell. In response, Varina Davis had asked for a year's time to confer with her children and other family members. "In the meantime," she replied, "be sure that heroic and affectionate memories never will be lacking, or fail to speak for Hollywood or Richmond."

So compelling were those memories, it turned out, Hollywood certainly would be the appropriate and final resting place, not only for her husband, but also for their four deceased sons. Thus, three of them would be reinterred beside their father on June 3, 1893—little William, who had died at the age of ten in Memphis, Tennessee; Samuel, who died in Washington, D.C., another capital with compelling memories for the Davis family; and little Joseph, who fell to his death at age four from a portico at the Confederate White House during the Civil War and already was buried in Hollywood. The fourth Davis son, Jefferson Davis Jr., who also preceded his father in death when stricken in Memphis with yellow fever, would be reinterred at Hollywood in 1895.

At Hollywood, Davis and his sons would "rest among the dead of all states who fell for the South," the Mitchell book pointed out. Those included notables

The Davis family plot at Richmond's Hollywood Cemetery

such as Jeb Stuart, George E. Pickett, John D. Imboden, and Henry Heth, all generals who served the Confederacy (but *not* all of them battlefield casualties), plus many other generals, lower-ranking officers, and enlisted men…even Gen. John Pegram, whose funeral at St. Paul's Episcopal Church in Richmond in 1864 came just three weeks after his wedding in the same church. He was "the last Confederate general killed in battle to be buried in Hollywood Cemetery during the war." Also buried here were many of the Confederate dead from Gettysburg, along with Gen. James Longstreet's three children who died of scarlet fever in January 1862, and Presidents James Monroe and John Tyler, who died "in his rooms" at the Ballard Hotel in Richmond while serving as a member of the Confederate House of Representatives.

Just before the Jefferson Davis reinterment ceremonies in May 1893, "the remains of fifty soldiers exhumed at Drewry's Bluff were brought to Hollywood for burial," with a marker to their memory erected in the soldiers' section.

The real pomp and ceremony of that same month, though, took place after the arrival of the slow train from New Orleans bearing the former Confederate president's remains, accompanied by "an official escort and three hundred family members and guests." The special train from the Deep South "had been stopped many times along the way for people to view the coffin of the only president of the Confederate states." In Richmond, the deceased president lay in state for a day in the rotunda of Thomas Jefferson's capitol. On the afternoon of the thirty-first a caisson covered with black netting and drawn by six white horses bore the coffin to Hollywood. "A band played 'Dixie' as the cortege—including Mrs. Davis, her daughters Varina Anne Davis and Margaret Howell Davis Hayes, the governors of other southern states, and [Confederate Gens.] John B. Gordon, Charles J. Anderson, Fitzhugh Lee, and John Glynn Jr.—moved from the Capitol to the cemetery. Richmond composer Jacob Reinhardt wrote 'The Jefferson Davis Funeral March' for the occasion. The whole city was draped in mourning for the fallen chieftain."

In the years ahead, more endings would be noted. Hollywood Cemetery's Davis Circle would be completed and its set-asides would be filled. In time… Varina would be buried here (1906), as would her two daughters, Varina Anne "Winnie," who had been born in Richmond in the final year of the war and who died in 1898 ("Thousands of Richmonders attended her funeral"), and Margaret, who died in 1909.

UNION
Grant's Last Battle

LEE, YOU COULD SAY, DID the expected, and Grant the unexpected. Lee lost, and Grant, put up against Lee, won. But it was Lee who came out of it as the legend today and Grant as the far less respected today…in some quarters, even disrespected.

There are explanations, of course. Lee, considered close to saintly in his conduct by his admirers, carried on brilliantly as the leader of the underdog South. Grant, his detractors would argue, hardly could lose, given his massive and superior numbers in manpower and materiel. The North, given its industrial power and population edge, in the long run, no matter who was commanding general at the end, hardly could lose.

Handsome, soft-spoken, aristocratic, genteel to the core, Lee did have a slow start. But from the time he took over the Army of Northern Virginia in the Seven Days' campaign in June 1862, he clearly was the Confederacy's man to watch in the all-important East.

Grant, pegged as a slow learner, an alleged drunkard, a man without a career between the Mexican War and the Civil War, a stubby blue-collar contrast to Lee, was stuck for the longest time out *there*…somewhere by those rivers—the Tennessee, the Cumberland, the Mississippi—far away from the two capitals of Richmond and Washington. People didn't *know* him—that is, people who counted didn't know him.

McClellan was the fair-haired boy of the eastern establishment. McClellan and then quite a few others…all fated to be no better than tryouts.

And true, it would take a while for Grant to be noticed by those who counted. At the start, going from clerk in a Galena, Illinois, leather goods store to colonel of a volunteer regiment overnight wasn't all that startling for a West Point graduate and Mexican War veteran such as Grant…no matter how undistinguished his record as a civilian. By August 1861, though, he had scrambled upward to brigadier general of volunteers.

Then, for months thereafter, still no thunderbolts…until he seized Forts Henry and Donelson on the Tennessee and Cumberland Rivers, respectively, in February 1862, thus giving Lincoln and the North their first major victory of the war. Now, at least two key people in Washington did sit up and take notice.

One was Lincoln himself, and he appointed Grant a major general of volunteers. The other was the army's top general, Henry W. Halleck. Then came Shiloh, the war's major battle so far in terms of casualties…so many casualties. "Rumors that Grant's misconduct was the reason for the high casualty rate reached the President," noted Mark E. Neely Jr. in *The Abraham Lincoln Encyclopedia*. Halleck "defended his subordinate, though he had his private doubts about Grant's abilities anywhere but on the field of battle."

For the record, the standard assessment of Grant's performance at Shiloh says he was slow to see the battle coming and slow to react…but on the second day, he came away the clear victor, even though the cost in men killed and wounded was a shock (and yet a mere portent of things to come) in that still-early stage of the war.

Next, "As Lincoln began to plan the campaign to capture the Mississippi River line," noted Neely, "he overlooked Grant for two political generals: Nathaniel P. Banks and John A. McClernand. By early 1863, however, Halleck convinced Lincoln that Grant should direct the Vicksburg campaign." As several months then passed with only minor progress made, an impatient Lincoln "wanted Grant to move his army south of Vicksburg to join with Banks' forces." And Grant did send a fleet downriver, "past the Confederate forts"; he did "march his army south on the opposite bank"; and he did ship his troops across the river in boats. "However, he did not march south to join Banks but instead turned north to lay siege to Vicksburg. By May 26 [1863] Lincoln saw that the campaign was 'one of the most brilliant in the world.'"

When Vicksburg then fell on July 4, the eyes of the East were fastened upon the great Union victory at Gettysburg (July 1–3, 1863), but Lincoln a few days later wrote Grant in praise of his "inestimable service" and "to make the personal acknowledgment that you were right, and I was wrong." Grant now was given the rank of major general in the regular army.

Up until this time, and for many months yet to come, Grant and Lincoln never met. And one of Grant's irritating faults was his lack of communication with his superiors. As Lincoln himself remarked later that same month, "Gen. Grant is a copious worker, and fighter, but a very meagre writer, or telegrapher."

Meanwhile, with the Mississippi now under total Union control, Grant late in 1864 went to the relief of the Union forces trapped at Chattanooga, Tennessee, in the aftermath of the defeat at Chickamauga and drove off Braxton Bragg from his strong points on Lookout Mountain and Missionary Ridge.

Following these masterly developments, none too surprisingly, Grant would become Washington's darling. "In February [1864]," noted Neely's account of the Grant-Lincoln relationship, "Congress revived the rank of lieutenant general, last held by Winfield Scott and before that only by George Washington." And it was done for Grant, unexpected hero of the West. "Grant received his commission at Washington on March 9, 1864. At a reception at the White House the night before, he met [Lincoln] for the first time."

More important, Grant now became *Lincoln's* darling (and commanding general of all Union armies). Discounting a detail here, a detail there, they saw eye to eye on the blunderbuss war strategy about to emerge. In the view of Michael Korda, author of *Ulysses S. Grant: The Unlikely Hero*, Grant had in mind the winning strategy for the war from the outset. "He understood that it could not be done by successfully winning a battle, or even several battles...but that it depended strategically upon splitting the South by descending the great rivers deep into Confederate territory and once that had been achieved, by forcing on the South a war of attrition that the Confederacy could not sustain," Korda wrote in *American Heritage* magazine in October 2004. Further, "in the final analysis the North's superior manpower and industrial might would need to be brought to the battlefield."

Grant saw and he persuaded Lincoln to see "that the war would therefore be long and bloody...but it could be won that way and no other, and he knew how to do it."

As another aspect of this new partnership, noted historian Mark Neely, "Grant's plan to send Benjamin F. Butler toward Richmond from the James River, to instruct General George G. Meade to follow Lee wherever he went and to send William T. Sherman to attack Atlanta was congruent with Lincoln's idea that there should be a general move to attack the enemy's armies on all fronts."

As Grant then began his sledgehammer blows against Lee himself in the Virginia campaign of spring 1864, at the Wilderness, Spotsylvania, and Cold Harbor, followed by the siege of Petersburg, the tremendous casualties that Grant's strategy cost the Union again were a shock to the North, but he persisted...and, as noted by Neely, "Lincoln telegraphed: 'I begin to see it, you will succeed.'"

As history would record, Grant did...he forced Lee into surrendering his army in April 1865, a final blow to the Confederacy, forcing it to give up the war altogether shortly thereafter. And yet today Lee is the legend while, for the most part, Grant gets but grudging respect here and there. Not totally fair. Or, as Michael Korda stated the case: "Lee is the more glamorous figure, but Grant was the better general, and what is more, he defined American generalship for all time. Eisenhower won the war in Europe by using Grant's strategy and methods."

Fairly ranked today or not, Grant in any case had achieved the unexpected. Rising from humble beginnings and near-total obscurity, in contrast to Lee, who was so well regarded even before the war that he was offered command of the *Northern* armies, Grant did the unexpected by winning through at the end and, in the eyes of the nineteenth-century North, emerging from the Civil War as its chief military hero.

So much the hero was he that Congress gave him the rank of full general, an honor previously conferred only on George Washington. Grant then won two straight terms as president of the reunited nation, but as chief executive he unfortunately suffered in reputation by allowing his chief subordinates to indulge in corrupt schemes, albeit apparently behind his back. After a two-year round-the-world trip with his wife, Julia, in which he won great acclaim, he would attempt a political comeback, but his own Republican Party refused to nominate him again and chose James A. Garfield, a far-lesser Civil War general, as its ultimately successful nominee for the 1880 presidential election.

For Grant, a business venture in New York then proved a disaster, wiping out his financial assets—he even lost his swords and other personal memorabilia put up as surety for a loan he was unable to repay. Awarded full army retirement status with a small salary attached, Grant still was desperate for income. When the *Century* magazine asked him to join the crowded field of Civil War veterans writing articles for the periodical, Grant—the "meagre" writer of Lincoln's day two decades before—saw his opportunity once more to achieve the unexpected: he would become a writer.

But not in the usual sense. He would write his memoirs, a two-volume work, that would be widely acclaimed both as Civil War history and as literate history. Destined to be published by Grant's friend Mark Twain, of all people, the book emerged from a race against the clock—not to meet a publisher's deadline, but to finish before throat cancer would take the author's life. Completed just days before his death on July 23, 1885, *The Personal Memoirs of U. S. Grant* would be a publishing coup that earned his estate and family a most helpful $450,000. And so, Ulysses S. Grant, far better known during his days at West Point for horsemanship than for academic excellence, once again had done the unexpected.

UNION & CONFEDERATE
Last Great Reunion

SOMETHING ABOUT THE PLACE WAS magic. Fifty years after the great battle, its veterans (and then some) came back. So many, they made the gathering of July 1913 the largest combined reunion of Civil War veterans ever held…anywhere. Fifty years after the fact, and more than fifty thousand came to the party.

It was not exactly what the good-hearted leaders of Pennsylvania expected when they first issued their invitation for any and all honorably discharged Civil War veterans, both Union and Confederate, to come visit for the fiftieth anniversary of the battle. No one quite realized the magic of Gettysburg when Governor John K. Tener first suggested that Pennsylvania should be the host and cover the costs of rail transportation for its own veterans. He also urged other states to do the same for their aging veterans. And then came the rude awakening. "The expense of sending hundreds of old soldiers to the reunion from as far away as California was overwhelming," notes a National Park website on the great event (www.nps.gov/gett/getttour/sidebar/reunion13.htm), "and many states could not provide cash donations either to the reunion or to their veterans."

While various states and organizations, such as the United Daughters of the Confederacy, scrambled to raise the monies needed to send the veterans to the reunion, Pennsylvania's Governor Tener found himself in a thicket of problems. "The projected cost of the reunion rose as plans changed, and with it grew opposition in the legislature as more state money was appropriated," notes the NPS website. "Several legislators argued that hosting two large veteran organizations without compensation was fruitless and was eventually going to put a strain on the state budget. Tener finally approached the Federal government, which agreed to step in and appropriate funds to feed and provide tents for the veterans during the encampment."

In addition, the army would provide cooks and bakers. Thus assured, the Pennsylvania legislature assigned $500,000 to the reunion.

As detailed plans were laid—two years in advance—the army became more and more involved. Added tents and equipment would be needed. And "personnel from the…Quartermaster Corps and the Engineer Corps arrived at Gettysburg National Military Park in 1912 to plan military and civilian support for the encampment."

The encampment site would be a field adjacent to the scene of Pickett's fateful charge on the third and final day of battle. The "Great Camp" established here in 1913 would be divided into Union and Confederate sections. "Soldiers installed utility systems, erected hundreds of tents to house the veterans, built picnic tables, benches and boardwalks throughout the camp. By the first of June, the sprawling Great Camp occupied 220 acres, included 47.5 miles of avenues and company streets, was lit by 500 electric lights, and 32 bubbling ice water fountains were installed. Over 2,000 army cooks and bakers manned 173 field kitchens, ready to provide three hot meals a day for veterans and camp personnel alike."

Ranging in age from 61 to a claimed 102, the veterans began arriving on June 25, 1913. They walked, talked, and ate from the very start, with several hundred Boy Scouts acting as their escorts, aides, and messengers. In addition, two battalions of the U.S. Fifth Infantry, plus a cavalry detachment, plus Pennsylvania state police, plus Pennsylvania National Guardsmen, plus the American Red Cross and the army medical corps, all were on hand to provide security and support as needed.

And a good deal of support indeed was needed, since nearly ten thousand of the aging veterans had to be treated for "ailments ranging from heat exhaustion to stomach disorders," reports the National Park Service. (Still, over the entire week, only nine of the old-timers died during the encampment.)

Part of the 1913 Gettysburg encampment with a view of the railroad depot

Among other kinds of support furnished by the organizers of the grand event were cots, bedding, tents (eight men to each one), with 688,000 meals served by week's end from kitchens situated at the end of each company street. The food ran from "fried chicken suppers to pork roast sandwiches with ice cream for dessert."

Aside from such logistical facts and figures, the real story for the veterans returning to Gettysburg from all over the country was the intangible. The Park Service website account by John Heiser tells it well:

> Despite the heat and often dusty conditions, nothing could keep the aged men in camp and hundreds wandered the battlefield. Many visited battle sites where they or their comrades had been fifty years before. Confederate veterans especially were pleased to find old cannon mounted on metal carriages to mark the locations where their batteries had been during that fateful battle.
>
> Invariably, the presence of khaki-clad U.S. Army personnel caused a lot of excitement. The soldiers were there to guard camp supplies, give demonstrations, and provide services to the veterans who delighted themselves discussing the modern weapons of war. Many an aged veteran was eager to explain how much things had changed in fifty years to any soldier who was handy and army personnel were entertained by old soldiers at every turn.
>
> In spite of their advanced years, the old soldiers walked for miles through the battlefield park and packed into the Great Tent erected in the field of "Pickett's Charge" adjacent to the camp for daily meetings and ceremonies.

Naturally, there were many speeches made—by various dignitaries, by various state governors, even by President Woodrow Wilson, who was persuaded to come only at the last minute. Among other highlights of this last joint Civil War reunion for most of the old soldiers, members of the Pickett's Division Association and the Philadelphia Brigade Association met at the stone wall that was the "high water mark" for the relatively few participants in Pickett's Charge of July 3, 1863, who actually reached or even momentarily breached the Union line that terrible day. "Despite the torrid heat [in 1913], the veterans made speeches, traded ceremonial flags and shook hands over the stone wall that outlines the Angle where fifty years before the two groups met in mortal combat," notes the NPS website. The same line often is called the "high water mark" of the Confederacy itself.

As for the *then-somes*, many Civil War veterans, other than strictly *Gettysburg* veterans, came too. One was Melvan Tibbetts, a private in Company H, Fifteenth Maine Volunteer Infantry, accompanied by his daughter Elsie.

Maine's website (www.state.me.us/sos/arc/archives/military/civilwar.htm) notes:

> The 15th Regiment did not fight at Gettysburg, so Melvan was not entitled to go on the special train at state expense. But so many veterans like Melvan, as well as family members, were determined to go anyway that a second train was organized and chartered at private expense. Eventually 452 Gettysburg participants traveled on the special train, followed by a second train bearing 102 family members and veterans who did not fight at Gettysburg. These folks had to pay for their own accommodations as they were not allowed to camp on the field.

Heading up Maine's official Gettysburg contingent was eighty-five-year-old Joshua L. Chamberlain, former governor, former college president, former brigadier general who had earned the Medal of Honor at Gettysburg…but he wouldn't be able to go in person. "It was the last great undertaking of his life, and he threw himself into it," explains the Maine website. "Six weeks before the Reunion he made his last trip to Gettysburg to see that all was well with the arrangements for the Maine delegation. He wanted to attend the Reunion, of course, but his health was rapidly failing and his doctor forbade him to make the trip." He died within the year.

Meanwhile, Melvan Tibbetts and his daughter returned home with the tale of a Pennsylvania veteran who also had been forbidden to attend the reunion by his doctor (and family). The story was that he escaped his home by climbing out a window, somehow reached the encampment site on his own "and was now hiding 'incognito' in the Pennsylvania camp lest his family catch up with him."

Wrote Elsie Tibbetts on her return home, "So strongly did the bugles of Gettysburg call."

Overall, the reunion had been "a great success," per the Maine archives account. "Only one Maine veteran died during the encampment, while the rest of the delegation got back to Maine safe, sound and exhausted."

★★★

Additional note: Twenty-five years later, in July 1938, the last and final get-together of Civil War veterans, blue and gray, would come on the seventy-fifth anniversary of the battle. The fiftieth had taken place on the eve of World War I; this one would come just before World War II. This time, instead of Woodrow Wilson, the ranking speaker would be President Franklin Delano Roosevelt. And this time, while an estimated 150,000 spectators came to Gettysburg to look and listen, only 1,845 Civil War veterans were on hand—average age, ninety-four.

Julia Grant also would become a president's wife

PART 5

★ GENERALS' WIVES ★

by Ingrid Smyer

CONFEDERATE
Mary Anna Randolph
Custis Lee

LIKE HER GREAT-GRANDMOTHER, WHO WAS sometimes known as the Lady of Mount Vernon, this general's wife also would become associated with a historic mansion standing tall on the Virginia banks of the Potomac River.

Born Mary Anna Randolph Custis, she was the idolized only child of Arlington, the grand estate overlooking Washington, D.C. As child or grown woman, her very name reflected an enviable station in life, for she was connected to every Virginia family of substance and in particular was heir to a fortune that came from that same Lady of Mount Vernon—her great-grandmother, Martha Washington—and then was passed along to Mary Anna through her father, George Washington Parke Custis. Martha, of course, was the wealthy widow of John Parke Custis and mother of two Custis children when she met young George Washington, the future hero of the Revolutionary War and first president of the United States. After they married, the future president became a tender stepfather to John Parke Custis and Martha Parke Custis.

Young John was married at the age of nineteen to Eleanor Calvert, sixteen-year-old daughter of Benedict Calvert of Mount Airy, Maryland. They had four children, and the youngest, George Washington Parke Custis, named in part for his famous step-grandfather, was only a few months old at the time of the battle of Yorktown, where his father was serving as an aide to Washington in October 1781. Falling ill with a violent attack of camp fever, the young aide was obliged to leave his post. When General Washington heard that his stepson lay dying nearby, he rushed to the young man's side, but too late. In tears, he vowed—on the spot, it is said—to adopt his stepson's two children as his own.

George Washington Parke Custis thus became known as the adopted son of George Washington. As such, he not only carried an illustrious name, but he would inherit from his grandfather Custis (Martha's first husband) vast Virginia landholdings that included the White House plantation on the Pamunkey River in Tidewater Virginia, where the widowed Martha had been living when she met the dashing young Washington. The latest in the Custis line also was heir to other plantations…and the large Arlington tract across the Potomac River from the Federal City, as Washington was once called.

Here, over a period of years, Custis built his grand mansion, Arlington House, on a height three hundred feet above the Potomac and half a mile back from the river frontage. As a visitor in 1853 described it:

> The building is of brick and presents a front, the center and two wings of one hundred and forty feet. The grand portico, which has eight massive Doric columns, is sixty feet in front and twenty-five in depth. It is modeled after the Temple of Theses at Athens. In front, sloping toward the Potomac, is a fine park of two hundred acres dotted with groves of oak and chestnut, and clumps of evergreens; and behind is a dark old forest, with patriarchal trees bearing many centennial honors and covering six hundred acres of hill and dale. Through a portion of this is the sinuous avenue leading to the mansion. From the portico a brilliant panorama is presented—the Capitol, the Executive Mansion, Smithsonian Institution, the growing, magnificent Washington Monument, and almost every house in the Federal City may be seen at a glance from this point, while between them and Arlington flows the bright flood of the Potomac.

Not only were the house and grounds magnificent, but the estate was imbued with the atmosphere of Southern hospitality. Here family and friends were always welcomed and made comfortable—indeed the many bedrooms were often filled with visiting cousins.

Custis began the estate soon after Martha Washington died in 1802, and he named it Arlington for a family plantation on the Eastern Shore. In 1806 he brought his bride, Mary Lee Fitzhugh, to the beautiful setting, then showing only the very beginnings of the grandeur to follow. His young wife was the daughter of William Fitzhugh of Chatham, another grand manor, this one gracing the hills across the Rappahannock from Fredericksburg. Chatham was the gathering place for the gentry from all the great houses in Tidewater, an apt setting for a lifestyle of grand parties and like gatherings to dine, drink, meet cousins, even to arrange marriages.

Mary Lee Fitzhugh and George Washington Parke Custis had three girls and a boy, but only one of their four children survived infancy. That was Mary Anna Randolph Custis, who was fated to live as a central figure in the most turbulent and tragic years of American history.

Although Mary Anna was raised as an only child, she never was lonely. She not only had a loving father and mother, but she was surrounded by many servants—often fond or even loving, but still, slaves. In addition, her many cousins and friends were ever welcome and were often visitors in the grand house for a week or more at a time. And Arlington was a wonderful place for a young girl to grow up. She was allowed a great deal of freedom to roam the grounds, enjoy the changing seasons, wander among the flower gardens, frolic with her pets.

The atmosphere at Arlington also was conducive to exploring American history firsthand since Mary could wander into the library, where she often found her father perusing family papers inherited from his grandmother Martha. Sometimes, if he thought she would be interested, he read aloud to her from the valuable Washington collections. Many years after the Civil War, now aging and truly lonely as a widow, she would find solace working on these valuable historical papers as she prepared to publish her father's *Recollections* and enlarge her own *Memoir* of her father.

Other relics inherited from Mount Vernon were the family portraits that hung along the walls of the great hall. Surprisingly, though, it was not the furniture or china that captured the imagination of the little girl of Arlington, but rather the army tent and personal effects that had once been used by the hero of the Revolution. On very special occasions, Washington's tent was set up on the lawn at Arlington. As an artifact of a not-so-distant war that won the nation its independence from England, the tent fascinated adults and children alike.

Every day at Arlington began with prayer, and on Sundays serious Bible study and prayers occupied Mary, her mother and father, as well as the servants. Promptly at ten o'clock the carriage arrived to take the family to the Episcopal Christ Church in nearby Alexandria, or sometimes to the chapel of the Episcopal Theological Seminary, then in the countryside, but today within the greatly expanded boundaries of the same city. Grace was said before every meal, and Mary was expected to learn a hymn and the collect (short prayer) for the day. Mrs. Custis also devoted time to religious instruction for the servants.

As mistress of a great plantation, Mrs. Custis held an important position of honor and distinction, but her duties would seem without end to the modern homemaker. A kind woman possessing practical sense and strong family ties, she spent time just about every day supervising kitchen activities and menus, overseeing many important decisions of the plantation in general, seeing to the gardens and their management, nursing the sick, managing the house servants and directing the housekeeping, doing the sewing and generally acting as counselor, teacher, or confidant for all, while always also being available to her husband and daughter as needed.

In this home of bountiful hospitality, Mrs. Custis must have seemed in perpetual motion, yet she graciously saw to her guests, while her husband, somewhat of a dilettante, prided himself on playing the charming host. The beautiful house and majestic setting attracted distinguished visitors from far beyond Virginia. One outstanding guest was an old comrade-in-arms of George Washington who had returned for a visit and tour of the United States by invitation of Congress. Mary, a young girl of fifteen, surely saw the pride in her father's eyes as he welcomed General Lafayette, whose own reverence for Washington was and still is legendary.

A few days later, on October 19, 1824, Lafayette was a guest of the city of Alexandria and honored with a parade. He led the grand event in a splendid barouche, and in the next carriage rode George Washington Parke Custis with the visiting general's son, George Washington Lafayette. Mary and her mother were among the many onlookers admiring the famous visitor, but according to biographer Rose Mortimer Ellzey MacDonald in *Mrs. Robert E. Lee*, Mary really had eyes only for a young marshal in the parade: Robert Edward Lee.

Ravensworth, a lovely plantation in Fairfax, not terribly far from Arlington, was the home of Mrs. Custis's brother, William Henry Fitzhugh, who was a distant cousin of the Lees of Virginia. Very often the Fitzhughs entertained Mrs. Henry Lee, widow of Henry "Light-Horse Harry" Lee of Revolution fame, who had lost the family's fortune through speculation. Quite frequently, Mrs. Custis also would be visiting her brother and sister-in-law at Ravensworth. Thus, the widowed Mrs. Lee's youngest son, Robert, and Mrs. Custis's daughter, Mary, were often thrown together to play hide-and-go-seek or other games on the lawn of the great house.

So there they were the handsome but impoverished young man and the lovely but privileged young heiress who together were destined to play a leading role in the great war lying but a relative few years ahead. For the moment, though, they simply were two children enjoying time together with cousins and friends…completely unaware.

But now, fast-forward to 1829, the year Robert E. Lee graduated second in his class at West Point. Although soon to be an accomplished lieutenant in the elite Engineer Corps of the U.S. Army, the young officer realized that he had to overcome his lack of fortune—and the shame brought on the family name by his older half brother, Henry Lee (born to his father's first wife, Matilde), who allegedly had seduced his own wife's younger sister. At first only whispered, the scandal became public knowledge when Henry Lee, who carried his famous father's name, was nominated by President Andrew Jackson for the ambassadorship to Morocco. In the furor that followed, no member of the Senate voted for confirmation, and Henry left the country…to die in Paris seven years later. Perhaps, as Robert E. Lee's well-known biographer Douglas Southall Freeman suggested, "the stern morality of Robert E. Lee was stiffened by the warning of his half-brother's fall."

In any case, after completing a posting in Savannah soon after his graduation, the handsome young lieutenant went to visit friends in Northern Virginia, where he had lived (in Alexandria) until his invalid mother's death. Already determined to win the hand of his childhood sweetheart, Robert would ride his horse up the hill to the stately Arlington mansion as often as he could. He had an understanding ally in Mrs. Custis, but Mary's father was not happy when he saw the same horse so often tethered by the grand house. Even so, the young lieutenant was not deterred from laying siege to Mary's heart. Thus, when Mary daintily reached for a slice of fruit cake one afternoon, intending it for her beau, he too leaned forward and quietly posed the consuming question…which indeed was answered in the positive. "If he ate his fruit cake," wrote Freeman, "it was with a happy heart."

Finally winning his future father-in-law's consent, the prospective groom and his bride-to-be began making plans for the nuptials. She chose six of her favorite cousins as bridesmaids and he six of his friends to stand with him.

The wedding was held at Arlington House on June 30, 1831, with every planned detail, every memorable aspect unfolding smoothly—almost. All the bridesmaids and groomsmen were present, and the groom arrived on time as well. The Rev. Reuel Keith from Christ Church was to officiate at the ceremony, and he was on his way well in time, too. But riding the short way from Alexandria, he was caught in a sudden summer shower and drenched to the skin. Still, no major problem. The bride's decidedly short, somewhat stout father offered the lanky minister his wardrobe, noted historian Emory Thomas in his essay on the Lee marriage for *Intimate Strategies of the Civil War*. Fortunately, the Reverend Keith could don his cassock and surplice to hide the short pants and sleeves he wore underneath for the ceremony.

In the fashion of the day, most of the wedding party remained at Arlington until July 5, though some of the bridesmaids lingered until two or three days later than that. At last the lovers were alone—almost, since the bride's parents still were around and about. By July 11, however, the young couple had begun their journey (accompanied by Mary's mother) to his new posting at

Fort Monroe, which overlooked Hampton Roads. They made stops to visit relatives at Ravensworth, then proceeded to Loudoun and Fauquier Counties for additional visits.

Robert and Mary were blissfully happy, and the bridegroom "seemed already to bear unconsciously the air of a man destined to achievement," wrote Freeman.

Lee's marriage to Mary Custis was one of the major influences of his life. While it was undoubtedly a love match, the additional fact is that her family estate freed him from the worry of establishing a permanent home for his family, which would grow to seven children over a period of fourteen years. Arlington offered a seemingly safe and permanent haven between his army assignments, and it was here that the children were born and largely raised with the tender help of Mrs. Custis, who proved to be a conscientious and loving grandmother.

Throughout their thirty-nine years of marriage, Mary and Robert lived a peripatetic life. They started life together at Fort Monroe and from there would move on to St. Louis, Missouri; Brooklyn, New York; Baltimore, Maryland; West Point, New York; Washington, D.C.; Richmond, Virginia; "Derwent" in Powhatan County, Virginia; and finally, little Lexington, Virginia. Such were the places Mary Custis Lee traveled with bag, baggage, babies, toddlers, growing children, or teenagers. Sometimes, however, Mary's army husband was sent to far-flung outposts that were inappropriate or too uncomfortable for the whole family. When he was stationed in Washington with the Corps of Engineers, of course, Lee and his growing family resided for extended periods at Arlington. The grand manor on the Potomac not only served him as a home from time to time, but here he gained a deepening reverence for George Washington and his father-in-law's close link to the first president, even though Lee always had been acutely aware that his wife was the great-granddaughter of Martha Washington.

Never out of Virginia before she married Lee, Mary may have been reluctant to travel west, but when her husband was assigned to St. Louis, she went along with her two boys and left baby Mary at Arlington. She seemed happy being with her husband and was welcomed by the other army wives. She spent her time sewing for the children, gathering various wildflowers, in her daily study of the Bible, or pursuing her best talent, painting. The letters she sent back home were cheerful and uncomplaining, always looking on the bright side. To her mother soon after settling in St. Louis, she wrote:

> We are much more comfortable now. Our rooms have been white-washed and painted—quite cool & pleasant, looking out on the water; and being small, they require less furniture.... We have two small closets, in one of which I have arranged my books & shall now commence the *Life of Washington*, as I feel more settled. I have been reading some beautiful poetry of Coleridge, Shelley, Wordsworth, some French books lent me...& other little things, among them Goldsmith's Life & poems.

She continued on about the children's activities and bank and business matters, noting that there is "plenty of silver out here, we never see a bank note of less than $5."

These comments, among the many letters cited in MacDonald's biography, illustrate Mary Lee's inquisitive mind and intelligence as well as her interest in current events and in literature. It is interesting to note that in another letter, however, there was a distinct hint of homesickness: "Mee [Mary] must keep up her spirits & think of me out here almost devoured alive with moschetaes [mosquitoes], for they are as thick as a swarm of bees every evening."

Nineteenth-century travel at best was long and tiresome, but travel to the West could be treacherous. For the still-young army officer, his wife, and two little boys, the first leg of their journey to St. Louis and its Jefferson Barracks took them from Washington to Baltimore, thence on to Philadelphia. At six o'clock the next morning they boarded a train that took nine hours to reach Harrisburg, Pennsylvania, just in time to take the canal boat that would reach Pittsburgh in three days. At Pittsburgh it was necessary to wait a week for a steamboat to take them down the Ohio River to Louisville and from there on to St. Louis.

After all that, though, Lieutenant Lee later wrote about the long trip in a most positive way: "Our journey was as pleasant as could be expected in a country of this sort.... The boys stood it manfully and indeed improved on it, and my Dame, taking advantage of frequent opportunities for a nap...defied the crowding, squeezing, and scrambling."

Among the postings that were too far or inconvenient to include Mary and the children were his assignments in the Southwest in the 1840s, as relations with Mexico became more and more rocky. Thus Mary was left behind with their children at Arlington as Robert was sent to Texas.

When the Mexican War then broke out, Robert E. Lee was in the refiner's fire...and proved to be a fast learner. He took back with him valuable lessons in strategy from Winfield Scott's ambitious and triumphant Mexico City campaign, and these he would attempt to use on the battlefields in Virginia fifteen years later. In the meantime, for his bravery and meritorious conduct during the war, he endeared himself to Scott, not only Lee's commander in the field, but now a longtime friend and mentor.

With the war in Mexico successfully prosecuted and put behind him, the returning soldier from Virginia, now *Colonel* Lee, arrived in Washington anxious to go the last short distance across the river to his family. Not finding a waiting carriage sent from Arlington, he prevailed upon the army for a horse and was quickly on his way. As he galloped up the hill toward Arlington, no one recognized the returning hero except the old family dog, Spec, a terrier Lee had found years before and adopted. It was only minutes, though, before an excited gaggle of greeters—both Mary and the children—crowded the entrance hall to embrace the long-absent father. Lee, who had been away for twenty-one months, hugged all the children and then, realizing he had not seen his namesake Rob, by now four and a half years old, looked about in puzzlement. "Where is my little boy," he asked. He then spied a youngster and swept him up in his arms, only to be told, "I'm not Rob. I'm Armistead Lippitt" (a playmate of little Robert's).

With little Rob of course soon trotted forward, the Lee family now would be moving to Baltimore, where the army's engineers had long recommended new harbor defenses for the port. Old Fort McHenry, famous for inspiring Francis Scott Key's "Star-Spangled Banner" during the War of 1812, was judged to be inadequate as a defense for the city. Thus, the colonel and family were off once again to a new posting…and perhaps just as well, since, to tell the truth, Robert and his father-in-law had maintained a somewhat strained relationship from the beginning. Also, when the family spent long periods at Arlington, Mary seemed to revert to her old role of an indulged only child.

To tell a truth again, bearing seven children in fourteen years had taken a toll on Mary's health. Fortunately, though, all seven lived to adulthood, certainly *not* typical of the times. That record was all the more surprising since Mary herself did not enjoy robust health. She in fact was often sickly, had fevers, and once even contracted mumps—probably along with the children. The birth of her second child seemed to go well until she developed an infection that persisted for more than two months. A cure seemed to elude the doctors, who wrung their hands and drew blood. Finally she wrote to Robert and begged him to come home. His reply was less than understanding, as Emory Thomas pointed out in his essay "The Lee Marriage," for *Intimate Strategies of the Civil War.* "But why do you urge my immediate return, & tempt one in the strongest manner, to endeavor to get excused from the performance of a duty, imposed on me by my Profession for the pure gratification of my private feelings?"

When he did return a few months later, however, he realized the severity of her condition and became very solicitous of her well-being. Still, her often shaky health was a frustration for Lee, who himself enjoyed excellent health until the last few years of his life. The ironic added fact is that Lee had cared for his invalid mother in her final years, and now he would find himself taking care of a wife crippled by arthritis.

That was one similarity the two women shared. In addition, both were quite religious, and both loved Robert. But that's where the likenesses ended. Lee's mother, Anne Carter Lee, a woman who had made the best of adverse circumstances alone, lived to see her children in successful careers and marriages. Mary Custis Lee, on the other hand, was, in the words of historian Thomas, "a pampered child of wealth and privilege who never outgrew the assumption that others—parents, husband, servants—would see to her needs and comfort."

But more than health was a sometime source of contention between Mary and Robert. They were so different in so many ways. He was a stickler for promptness—she was habitually late and forgetful of her engagements. He was cadet-neat—she was, to put it mildly, inactive in household management. When at West Point he had gained distinction as the "Marble Model" and was especially handsome in his gray cadet uniform with its white bullet buttons. His natural good looks and genteel manners always generated admiring looks from women and the respectful glances of men. Mary, by contrast, was careless in her personal appearance and untidy generally. "Despite these shortcomings and later a nervous whimsicality that sometimes puzzled him," wrote biographer Freeman, "she held the love of Robert Lee through life."

Her upbringing as a pampered only child may account for her lazy ways, but expecting—and indeed accepting—caretaker attentions from husband Robert as she became pitifully crippled is understandable. Whatever their differences, rarely has a woman been more a part of her husband's life. As for Lee, all the evidence is that his first thoughts were always for Mary.

What could have been the mutual attraction for these two Virginia aristocrats, other than that very connection itself? Some have suggested he was charmed by her wealth...and indeed, several other Lee men had married up. Robert, for that matter, would become executor of the vast Custis estate, even if he himself inherited little from his father-in-law. Further, his wife and children inherited lands that, if carefully managed, could produce great wealth. Quite responsibly, he took leave from the army to manage the somewhat neglected Custis properties, including Arlington, and spent two years virtually as a farmer.

If Lee cared little for the wealth now surrounding him, it also has been suggested, perhaps he was smitten by the privilege of joining a historic family by marrying the great-granddaughter of Martha Washington.

Less calculatingly, perhaps it was a simple case of love. Perhaps, too, as Freeman suggested, Mary and Robert were attracted to each other "because of his simplicity and her fineness of spirit." As a religious woman, Mary was a strong influence in her husband's spiritual growth. Yet her keen interest in public affairs often led to her voicing a fiery opinion vastly different from her husband's. He, on the other hand, "because of his sense of justice or his reserved manner would say little." At the same time, Mary's willingness to listen and her quick smile won her many friends. With her husband absent for long periods on his distant assignments, she found companionship with many friends. Entertaining her women friends—often sewing while they did their gossiping—Mary typically would steer the conversation to events of the day.

When the Civil War broke onto the scene, it hardly needs saying, everything for so many people changed...drastically! For Mary and Robert E. Lee, however, the changes, the losses—in both the personal and the historic sense—were so great, so irretrievable, most of us today can hardly imagine the pain. They of course lost their majestic Arlington, overlooking the very city named for Mary's stepforebear. And though they were spared the heartbreak of losing a son on the battlefield, daughter Anne died of typhoid in 1863. In addition, they were not spared the anxiety of having three sons—Custis, William Henry Fitzhugh "Rooney" and Robert Jr. "Rob"—in the army; one of them, Rooney, was not only wounded but captured on his bed by federal raiders. (Rooney's wife, Charlotte, died during his captivity.) Imagine also the burdensome thoughts of command responsibilities, of the thousands of men lost in battle, of a hopeless war finally lost, of the good friends killed or maimed, that Robert E. Lee, commander of the battered Army of Northern Virginia, must have carried to his grave! ("I did only what my duty demanded," he wrote after the war. "I could have taken no other course without dishonor. And if it all were to be done over again, I should act in precisely the same manner.")

Lee himself had been opposed to secession. He had held a deep devotion to the Union, and he certainly had served it at risk of life and limb. All the Lees had been patriots imbued with the ideals of the Revolution. But when Virginia left the Union, Lee's deeper loyalty was to his state...which at first did not join the Confederacy. Deep in his heart, he had hoped that Virginia would not secede. He believed that secession meant ruination for the nation and would "be the beginning of sorrows."

And how true. On a personal level, Lee was grieved to separate from his brother officers and had no desire to fight against a Union his forefathers had helped to form, against the flag that he himself had served. On a fateful night in April 1861, however, he went upstairs at Arlington to write his letter of resignation from the army, together with a personal letter to the same Gen. Winfield Scott under whom he had served during the Mexican War, now seemingly so long before in the past. Later, he came downstairs and told his wife very calmly, "Well, Mary, the question is settled. Here is my letter of resignation and a letter I have written General Scott." She understood and was relieved that the agonizing decision had been made. He then wrote his sister, Laura Marshall, to explain his decision. Her husband was a Union sympathizer, as was she, and her son Louis was already a captain in the Union army.

On April 22, 1861, Robert E. Lee left Arlington for Richmond to take his place in the annals of history. He would never again enter the halls of that magnificent mansion.

Months later, with heavy heart, Mary wrote to a friend, "My husband has wept tears of blood over this terrible war, but as a man of honor and a Virginian, he must follow the destiny of his state." As she could have added, she also, like her husband, had prayed that the war would not come, but when it did, she too would stand behind their Virginia.

Mary quickly started her own war effort by inviting friends to come to Arlington for knitting bees. This was a tremendous contribution, since the Confederate army was not always able to supply its men with needed clothes. (Socks were a favorite item…in fact, Lee late in the war would write to Mary that he had just received a "bag of socks" from her, adding, "I sent them at once to the Stonewall brigade." In the same letter of April 12, 1864, he commented that Jeb Stuart "says socks are the hardest thing to count in the world." As a company officer in charge of clothing some time before, Stuart "always made mistakes in that article." Jeb Stuart, incidentally, died of a fatal combat wound exactly a month later, on May 12, 1864.)

Meanwhile, Mary's beloved Arlington House itself soon appeared in jeopardy as federal troops occupied the Virginia side of the Potomac. The grand old mansion's ideal vantage point high above the river, overlooking the capital city, made it a danger to Washington and a prime goal for the Union troops. Long aware that her historic home was under the threat of federal seizure, Mary didn't make preparations to leave until a young cousin, William Orton Williams, still a Union officer himself, one day came to warn her. (Orton joined the Confederacy soon after and later in the war was executed as a Southern spy.)

Rightly or wrongly, Mary was convinced that Winfield Scott had sent the cousin as a courtesy to an old friend and comrade-in-arms. Either way, the warning was convincing. And so, with a heavy heart, she quickly packed a few family valuables and sent them on to friends to be kept until the war was over. She then rode away from the childhood home her father had built long ago, the place where she had given birth to her children, the home and safe haven where she and Robert had lived for so long. Now, all that was left behind. Arlington, occupied by the Federals the very next morning, soon would be a Union graveyard.

Mary first sought refuge with her sister-in-law and family at Ravensworth, but since they were Union sympathizers, this proved to be an embarrassment for all concerned. Mary felt constrained to move on…thus began her wandering days. From one healing springs to another, from one friend's or relative's home to another, she and her daughters sought safety and solace in many places as the war escalated in horrifying earnest.

Fast-forward again, this time to Christmas 1861, as Mary tried to gather her family at White House, the family plantation on the Pamunkey River where she was staying (for the moment). In her book, *The Lee Girls*, Mary P. Coulling reconstructed the first Lee family wartime Christmas. Young son Rob, for instance, wrote that he would travel from Charlottesville, where he was attending the University of Virginia, but that he had been "studying so many languages that I can hardly write English properly." Teenage daughter Mildred remained at school in Winchester, studying so hard, she apparently feared, that her hair was falling out. Daughter Agnes urged her to cut her hair, just as she herself had done. "It waves & twists itself up: some say it is very becoming," Agnes wrote. "It is quite fashionable now."

On Christmas Day itself, General Lee, based for now in South Carolina, sent a holiday letter to the partially assembled family and a separate letter to daughter Mary Custis, who was staying in Richmond with family friends. But daughters Annie and Agnes, son Custis, Rooney's wife Charlotte and their son, "Little Rob," all gathered together for the holidays.

How different it must have seemed, as Coulling suggested, with its "chilling rains and frequent…melting…snows," from the many cheerful vacations they all had spent at Arlington.

The Lee family perhaps typifies the struggles that so many families faced during the terrible upheaval of the war. So many were displaced, to live with friends or families from time to time. So many husbands and wives were separated for so long. So many men were killed, wounded, taken prisoner, or simply missing. For their part, despite the long separations and the loss of their home, Mary and Robert kept in touch by letter and were never apart spiritually.

In 1862, the White House plantation was lost to federal seizure—its riverside grounds in fact had become a major supply depot for George B. McClellan's Peninsula campaign—and Mary Lee was forced to move on again. Caught behind federal lines for a time, she was permitted to cross to the Confederate side and make her way to Richmond, where she established a temporary home away from home and once more could be with her husband after months of separation. In the three years of war still left, he would come and go while rising to his exalted and legendary status as the great commander of the Army of Northern Virginia, beating back McClellan's from the Peninsula; twice invading the North, with Gettysburg as his "high water mark"; fighting the hard battles of Second Manassas, Antietam, Fredericksburg, Chancellorsville, the Wilderness, Spotsylvania, and Cold Harbor with varying degrees of success; enduring the siege of Petersburg and always defending Richmond to the bitter end.

Then, in the first weeks after that bitter end at Appomattox Court House, the Lees found themselves facing immediate questions: Where to go? What to do? Where to settle? Nor were they alone—many Southern families were in the same situation. Except that Robert E. Lee, the war hero, was now a demigod in the eyes of most Southerners, who even now, with the war over, continued looking to him as a leader.

"Our returned soldiers…must all set to work," Lee wrote to his aide-de-camp, Col. Walter Taylor, as Coulling noted, "and if they cannot do what they prefer, do what they can. Virginia wants all their aid, all their support, and the presence of all her sons to sustain and recuperate her." Though these thoughts were addressed to the men, surely he also expected the women to follow suit. In his hopes for reconciliation of the whole nation, however, Lee underestimated the "fierce resentment noncombatants felt toward the Yankees," Coulling also noted. After all, women had managed the farms, kept the account books, taken clerical jobs, nursed the sick and wounded, been subject to house arrest by the enemy, and endured frightening days under fire and occupation, all without the support of the menfolk, all somehow the fault of the enemy, too. Although Lee's surviving daughters Agnes, Mary Custis, and Mildred had not experienced all of these hardships, they had a sense of "hopelessness about the future." And they resented the fact that their father failed to recognize their "lingering bitterness and their new self-reliance."

Meanwhile, with their mother now crippled by her arthritis and their father Robert now dangerously worn down by the war, all in the family wondered where destiny would take them. Offers of all descriptions came pouring in for Lee—promises of fine homes, monetary gifts, and chances for positions of power and prestige. While Lee would have none of that, he did consider buying a piece of land on the Pamunkey, where Rooney and Rob were trying to restore the family's burned-out estates. But pessimistic reports from his sons discouraged the plan. Instead and for the time being, the Lees took up the offer of Mrs. Elizabeth Cocke to rest as long as they liked at Derwent, her cottage in Powhatan County just fifty miles west of Richmond and close by the James River.

After her parents' move there, daughter Mary Custis, who had chosen to stay in Staunton, chanced to meet Col. Bolivar Christian, a trustee of Lexington's struggling, war-damaged Washington College. As noted by Coulling, he overheard the outspoken Lee daughter complain that "the people of the South are offering my father everything but work; and work is the only thing he will accept at their hands."

The colonel quickly formed an idea, took it to the next meeting of the school's trustees, and as the saying goes, the rest is history.

The little town of Lexington in the Shenandoah Valley made national news the day of Robert E. Lee's inauguration as president of Washington College. It was a simple oath-taking ceremony, and the reporter from the *New York Herald* sent to cover the story was the same who had been sent to cover the story of Lee's surrender.

Mary and Robert thus began the final chapter of their life together…a short chapter, to be sure. They took up residence in the college president's house, so isolated from the world and even eastern Virginia that it could be reached only by a single winding road or by canal from Lynchburg. But both made the best of their new situation—the quiet backwater community of Lexington in many ways was the right place at the right time for them to be in the aftermath of the terrible war. Wrote daughter Mildred some years afterward, "Coming here as we did when all was over—homeless, poor, exiled as we were—we found kindness in every heart and home, and my mother valued everyone according to his real merit and was soon beloved by the whole community as much as my Father."

As time passed, Mary naturally worried about her husband's gradual decline in health, but still she was unprepared for the events of September 29, 1870, a cold, dreary, rainy day. Going out that evening to attend a vestry meeting at the

Grace Episcopal Church, he was gone a long time. Upon his return, he stood at the foot of the dining-room table "but did not utter a word & sank back in his chair," Mary wrote to a cousin.

For days after that, he seldom spoke and slept a great deal. Mary wasn't normally the superstitious type, but she knew the old wives' tale that a portrait fallen from the wall "portended a death," wrote MacDonald in her biography of Mary. And one day after Robert E. Lee fell ill, his portrait fell from a wall in their home. "If I were superstitious," she told a caller, "I would feel disturbed."

Soon after "came the day when the doctors told Mrs. Lee that there was no hope." Through that night, she kept a vigil by his side, leaning close to hear "the words he was so faintly whispering." At the very end, though, he spoke loud and clear for all in the room to hear as he said, so fittingly, "Strike the tent." With that, on October 12, 1870, just five years and seven months after his surrender to Ulysses S. Grant at Appomattox Court House, Robert E. Lee, age sixty-three, died.

Mary Anna Randolph Custis Lee, greatly crippled by arthritis and rheumatic fever, clung on to life for another three years before she too succumbed in the same house on the campus of Washington College (in our day, of course, Washington and _Lee_ University). In the interim, son Custis had succeeded his late father as president of the small school; an illness had taken daughter Agnes, who once upon a distant time had been considered the intended of young William Orton Williams, the ill-fated young man who came to warn that the Federals were about to seize Arlington.

As for Arlington itself, her husband Robert never returned to the now so-storied national cemetery of today, but Mary Lee did, just once, just months before her death. In the years since the war and all its devastation, wrote biographer MacDonald, the War Department "had done everything possible to restore it [Arlington] to its natural beauty and former grandeur of forested hills and sloping lawns." Thus "the terraces, which had been battered down by the constant tramping of man and horse and utterly denuded of turf, had been built up and re-sodded. Drives had been restored, and emerald lawns again stretched away in velvety beauty from the mansion."

But no matter. To Mary Lee, it was "so changed," she wrote, "it seemed but as a dream of the past—I could not have realized that it was Arlington but for the few old oaks they had spared & the trees planted on the lawn by the Genl & myself which are raising their tall branches to the Heaven which seems to smile on the desecration around them." After that brief visit in June 1873, she had no wish, she told her surviving family, ever to see Arlington again.

UNION
Julia Dent Grant

FROM THE VERY BEGINNING, THIS pampered Southern belle was reinforced in the idea that she should and could have her way. Arriving into a family of four boys, she was adored by her indulgent father. If he wanted her to do something, he would say, "Will little daughter like to do this?" If Little Daughter said no, then Little Daughter did not do it.

Even so, she always insisted that she was not spoiled, and she certainly did extend many little kindnesses of her own to the family's menservants, whom she called Uncle so-and-so, as did many Southerners, who also referred to their slaves as their servants. She in fact recalled her "uncles" Charles, Bob, Willis, William, and Jim, "who invariably came to me when they wanted a little tobacco, whiskey, or money." As a little girl, she quickly ran to answer their requests and "thrust my hand into Papa's pocket up to my elbow until my hand caught a half dollar or a quarter." When asked what she was doing, she would tell him the truth—for instance, one of the "uncles was going home that night and wanted to buy his wife some sugar or flour." And Julia's father just smiled and said something like, "You little rascal."

This "little rascal" came from good stock. Her father's people came to America in 1643 from England. The three Dent brothers then settled in Maryland. One of them, Grandfather George Dent, married Susanna Marbury, and they lived in Cumberland, Maryland, but he died before Julia was born. Her mother gave her a delightful verbal picture of dapper Grandpa Dent. "He wore knee breeches, a chapeau, a queue tied with black ribbon, buckles on his shoes, ruffles on his shirtfront and he was a very handsome and distinguished man."

Her mother, Ellen Bray Wrenshall—herself born in England—came with her family to America when she was very young. Grandpa Wrenshall was a merchant who owned ships and exported ginseng to China, where it was very popular. A Methodist of the Wesleyan school, he considered dancing and enjoyment of any kind a sin, according to Julia, who chose not to follow in his "strict and uncompromising" ways.

Julia's mother and Maryland-born father, Frederick Dent, after two years of marriage, became pioneers of a sort, starting west to upper Louisiana (St. Louis, Missouri) from Pittsburgh on a flotilla of three rafts made of huge logs fastened together with chains. "Nearly all Pittsburgh assembled on the river bank to wish pretty Ellen Wrenshall and her brave young husband Godspeed," Julia herself wrote in *The Personal Memoirs of Julia Dent Grant (Mrs. Ulysses S. Grant)*.

After eight years in St. Louis, her father, by then a successful merchant, bought a thousand acres of land ten miles south on the Gravois Creek, in St. Louis County, and built a mansion, which he named White Haven after the home of his English forefathers. Eventually, Mr. Dent gave up his business practice and became a country gentleman. He had earned the honorary title of colonel, not from military service, but because of his gregarious personality, social status, and wealth. He had no compulsion about owning slaves but treated them kindly. His wife, Ellen, a quiet, elegant lady, preferred the interaction of city life, but their country estate became a social center under her fine management.

School days were happy times for Julia. Her winning ways, her charm and natural cheerfulness overcame any lack of beauty and her crossed eyes. At a young age she and her older brothers attended a school nearby. Most of the children walked together, but little Miss Julia was often carried pack-saddle style by her two older brothers, who clasped their hands together for a make-shift sedan. Other times Old Kitty, her mammy, carried her in her arms, or she chose to ride her mother's pony.

At the tender age of ten, she was sent to boarding school in St. Louis. She studied just about what she liked, she confessed in her memoirs. After her first year, the teachers attempted to discipline her, but to no avail. "I, feeling that they had been a little, or very, unreasonable, did just as I pleased, declining to recite again in English grammar and absolutely refusing to look at the multiplication table," she cheerfully admitted in her memoirs.

She found it much more valuable to spend her time reading. In the long run, perhaps, her choice of books such as *Ivanhoe*, *The Bandit's Bride*, or *Elizabeth of Siberia* may have been better preparation for her own exciting times ahead.

One Sunday afternoon, she and her classmates were stretched out on the grass, reading their Sunday-school books—all but Miss Julia, who had her nose in something with a more worldly title—*The Dashing Lieutenant*. One of the girls, bored with her reading, suggested that they all name the occupation of choice of their future husbands, "when we get them, as we all expect to some day." Doctor, lawyer, judge, farmer, and banker came the obvious answers. Then came Julia's turn. "I declared emphatically a soldier, a gallant, brave, dashing soldier," she wrote in her memoir, "and I got him, did I not?"

Exasperated with her own behavior, meanwhile, Julia did finally apply herself to her studies in philosophy, mythology, and history, leaving school in good standing the very month her brother Fred graduated from West Point in the class of 1843. After a pleasant summer with the family at the plantation, she then went to St. Louis for the winter social season. Spring brought Miss Julia back home to White Haven, just five miles from the Jefferson Barracks, then the largest military post in the United States, and ten miles from St. Louis, and thus ideally situated for the younger set to fill the halls with laughter and frivolity. Indeed, young army officers frequently came calling on Julia and her sisters, Nellie and Emma, as well as their older brothers. The popular Julia had been back on this springtime visit only three days when a Lieutenant Grant from the barracks came to pay his weekly visit at the gracious estate. He had been invited by Frederick Dent, his roommate from West Point days, to come as often as he could. Julia and the handsome lieutenant met, and his weekly visits became daily visits.

"Such delightful rides we all used to take!" Julia wrote in middle age as she reminisced about those years of innocence. The vigor of youth as well as the graceful horsemanship of the lovely Julia as she rode her chestnut brown Arabian alongside her handsome young army officer on those carefree spring days forever captured his heart. "Such rides!" Julia continued, "in the early spring, the tender young foliage scarcely throwing a shadow." In this poetic vein she continued, "Well, I cannot tell of those winged months. He was always by my side, walking or riding."

It was on one such ride—as she was returning, in fact, from attendance as a bridesmaid at a friend's wedding in St. Louis—that her "gallant, brave dashing soldier" declared his love for her and said that life without her would be "insupportable." She liked the idea of being engaged but not the thought of marriage—after all, she was only eighteen. And anyway, he soon would be leaving for a new assignment and couldn't take her with him, leaving him no choice but to be patient and accept the idea of engagement for now. All of which was just as well, since a war now interfered with any plans they might have made.

Before leaving for his assignment in Louisiana, Capt. Ulysses S. Grant found the opportunity to speak with her father about his love for Julia. The country gentleman, who had given his daughter every advantage for a happy life and a good marriage, did not think the life of an army officer would suit her, though he had no objection to the man himself. More pointedly, there hung in the air between the two men the unspoken concern for Grant's lack of wealth. The young captain was prepared for such fatherly doubts and offered to give up the army, should Julia become unhappy in that life.

As events turned out, destiny would take a very firm, even harsh, hand in the couple's affairs—four years of army assignments for Grant and the Mexican War would keep the lovers apart. Their anxiously awaited letters kept their love alive until at last the dashing soldier returned from the war and claimed his bride. They were married on August 22, 1848, in a Methodist service at the family's tow house in St. Louis. A cousin gave Julia "a magnificent, rich, soft, white, watered silk" gown, touched off by a white tulle veil trimmed with a wide fringe. A friend brought a bouquet of white cape jasmines, which she cradled in her arms after pinning a few extra blossoms to her veil, which "floated around my head and enveloped me in its fleecy folds…and could not have been improved." On that date, by the way, who could have foretold that two of the groomsmen (Cadmus M. Wilcox and Bernard Pratte III) would serve the Confederacy as generals and surrender to Julia's new husband at Appomattox just a few years later?

It would be a long time before such comforts and elegance would enfold the young bride again, but Julia met the wandering from one army post to another cheerfully, as long as she could be with her "Ulys," as she called him.

Their wandering began with a dreary cold winter in Sackets Harbor, New York, but in the spring of 1849, the Grants moved to Detroit, a much more desirable post. Here Julia found the social activities more in keeping with her expectations, although she soon returned to St. Louis to give birth on May 30, 1850, to Frederick Dent Grant, named for his maternal grandfather. At this time Grant again was assigned to Sackets Harbor, but this time he found a house for his growing family.

Ulysses's next assignment would send him to the Pacific Coast in 1852. The thought of being separated by a vast continent made Julia determined to go with her Ulys. But such a journey would entail a dangerous trek across the jungle-infested Isthmus of Panama—Ulysses would not think of allowing his wife and baby to take such a risk. And, besides, she was pregnant. Thus Julia went to stay with the Grant relatives in the Buckeye State of Ohio, and here she gave birth to a second son, Ulysses S. Grant Jr., on July 22, 1852. The baby was quickly nicknamed—what else—Buckeye, later shortened to Buck, a sobriquet he carried through life. Meanwhile, many in the party that Grant led across the narrow Panamanian neck from one port to the next, on the Pacific side, came down with cholera and died.

Once at his new posting, Fort Vancouver above San Francisco, the new father tried to supplement his income so he could send for his wife and two sons. Unfortunately, all his investments and even his attempts at part-time farming went sour—the lonely army officer despaired of seeing his wife and children anytime soon. Julia returned to St. Louis in hopes of receiving word to come and join him, but she waited in vain, since Ulysses now was reassigned to the even more isolated Fort Humboldt, California. Here, as he suffered from malaria and migraines, he began to wonder if army life were his destiny after all. In 1854 he resigned his commission and returned to his little family after two years of separation.

Strangely enough, although a West Point graduate, Grant had always wanted to be a farmer. Now, at last, he began plans to farm the land Julia's father had given her near White Haven. He built a log house with his own hands on a property appropriately named Hardscrabble. In his first year as a farmer, however, his crops did not yield the numbers that he had calculated on paper…and they never did. For once, Julia's positive outlook failed her. She hated Hardscrabble, and she became very doubtful that farming would ever support the growing family. And growing it was, at that. Two more babies were born at Hardscrabble. On July 4, 1855, daughter Nellie arrived, named Ellen for her grandmother, even though Grant wanted to name her after his wife. And on February 6, 1858, along came a third son, Jesse Jr.

As a farmer's wife, Julia was not much better than her husband. Writing in her memoirs years later, she expounded somewhat wryly on her chicken-feeding skills, but churning butter was something else. One day she took up the dasher—the up-and-down type—on an old-fashioned butter churn. A young servant girl sent to a nearby spring to get some water to cool the butter cautioned that before she could return, Julia would be exhausted by the churning. In less than ten minutes the girl returned with sparkling clear water, and sure enough Julia told her to hurry and relieve her. Julia's cookbook had warned that if you stop moving the dasher too soon, the butter would be spoiled. The young servant rushed to her side and opened the churn. "Miss Julia," she exclaimed. "Only see, surely! surely! the fairies have been here and helped you." The churn was full of golden butter.

With that, Julia decided to rest on her laurels, saying this was her "first and last attempt at such work."

In a short time, the nation's financial panic of 1857 and the death of Julia's mother in the same year ended the couple's attempt at farming and cleared the way for them to return to the comfort of White Haven.

Unhappily, too, Grant's failed attempt at farming only mirrored the failures he would suffer in other ventures, such as real-estate sales or clerking in St. Louis. In their respective memoirs of later years, neither Julia nor Ulysses dwelt upon these seven years of hardship, during which Julia had to prove her skills in economizing and managing the tight family budget. Still, reality made it clear that her husband had to find some better way to support his family. On a typical evening, Julia later wrote, the children could be "happily playing in the garden under a pink cloud of peach and apple blossom, all unconscious of the anxiety that filled the hearts of their parents."

Finally, Grant went to visit his father, Jesse Grant, who suggested that Ulys and Julia and family move to Galena, Illinois, where the family leather business was thriving. In fact, this very frugal elder Grant was in a better position financially to advise his son than the high-living Colonel Dent, who ran his Missouri estate as if it were a resort. Accordingly, the Grants took passage on a steamer out of St. Louis in the spring of 1860. A journey of four days brought them to "a charming, bustling town nestled in the ore-laden hills of northern Illinois," wrote the ever-sunny Julia. Grant settled his family in a rented house and went to work as a clerk in his brothers' leather goods store.

Here, for the moment, was economic salvation of a sort, but surely no great happiness for the former soldier who had hated the family tanning business, especially as a young boy. Even then, his greatest love had been horses—and horsemanship was the only area in which the young Grant had shone while at West Point.

Meanwhile, none of these events occurred in a vacuum; they in fact had come about as the nation teetered toward war over slavery, states' rights, secession, and other divisive issues. As the Grants hardly could avoid noticing, Galena was throbbing with patriotism that winter. Thus, when the men of the area formed a militia company, former U.S. Army captain Grant felt it his duty to join and give them the benefit of his West Point training.

With the newspapers full of discussion for and against secession, Julia, like so many others, was torn in her own heart. As she remembered those terrible but exciting times, "I was very much disturbed in my political sentiments, feeling that the states had a right to go out of the Union if they wished to," she wrote years later, "and yet thought it the duty of the national government to prevent a dismemberment of the Union, even if coercion should be necessary."

Unlike her husband, Julia was very much a Southerner in her emotional makeup, having been born in a Southern-tinged Border State and raised in the "mint-julep and magnolias" sentiments of the plantation society, with slaves to wait on her and answer her every whim.

One of her clearest and dearest childhood memories was of sitting on the piazza and hearing the family slave "Dear Old Bob" loudly praying and singing "down in the meadow by the big walnut tree nearly half a mile off."

As part of the atmosphere in which she grew up, many of her servants tended to be superstitious and even to believe in fairies. Thus the young Julia developed her own superstitious ways and a belief in dreams. Her memoirs contain vivid accounts of her childhood dreams as well as psychic revelations. Once, when her bedroom was redecorated, she invited a friend to spend the night in her new bed. The friend was delighted and reminded her of the custom of naming bedposts after special people. As the young girls went to sleep, they both believed that any dreams they had the first night in the new bed would "surely come true." Upon awakening, Julia told her friend she had dreamed that Captain Grant would be coming to visit the following Monday and would be dressed in civilian clothes. This was most unlikely, since he was off at an army post and was not expected at all. But, true to the dream, when Julia's friend left on Monday, who should be standing at the gate in civilian clothes but Grant himself!

She was convinced of the truth that dreams foretold events. Dreams would appear often in her memoirs. One of the most striking came up during the unsettling days of the spring of 1861. Ulysses, as an officer in the Illinois volunteers, had gone to Kentucky to meet with George B. McClellan, a fellow West Pointer who had graduated three years behind Grant. Before leaving, Ulys had asked Julia to be sure to open any official mail and forward it if it seemed important. He had only been gone a few days when Julia had a dream that a strange package arrived, and when she opened it, out fell a ring wrapped in tissue paper. In the dream and in real life, a ring her mother had meant for her had been claimed by her sister Nellie at her mother's death. And now, in the dream, as she unwrapped the ring, an array of stars flashed on the paper.

Julia then wrote to her sister Emma about the dream, expecting Emma to pass the word to Nellie that the ring should be forthcoming. The next day a letter came with the legend "Official Business" stamped on the envelope. Julia opened the letter and saw a sheet of vellum covered with tissue paper, just like the ring in her dream. As she drew back the tissue, she exposed the seal of the state of Illinois, which is spangled with stars. When she read the contents of the official letter, she saw that it was the commission of U. S. Grant as colonel of the Twenty-First Illinois Volunteer Infantry.

It was then that Julia tied her "ring dream" to a startling prophecy her mother had made several years before, in the summer of 1857. After dinner one evening, the gentlemen, including Julia's father, brother, and husband, left the ladies to enjoy a smoke on the piazza. Mrs. Dent had been listening to the men discussing politics and events of the day. Now, wearing the very ring that would later appear in Julia's dream, she pointed toward the men outdoors and said: "My daughters, listen to me. I want to make a prophecy this Sunday afternoon. Remember what I say." Singling out Julia's husband, she added: "That little man will fill the highest place in this government. His light is now hid under a bushel, but circumstances will occur, and at no distant day, when his worth and wisdom will be shown and appreciated. He is a philosopher. He is a great statesman. You will all live to see it, but I will not."

Julia of course would never forget her mother's unexpected prophecy, which came out of the blue just when her son-in-law Ulys had gone through seven years of failed ventures. If it seemed odd that Mrs. Dent should have such a glorious vision of him at that particular time and place in his life, the fact is, she had always been his ally, even when her husband had doubts about the young captain.

Julia, for her part, might have wished at times for a life of greater comfort and financial stability, but she never lost faith in her Ulys. And she believed in psychic revelations and dreams as harbingers of real events.

By the summer of 1861, with "secession fever" now erupted into angry war and both sides digging in their boot heels, Grant had been promoted to brigadier general of volunteers, but his immediate concern was where his family would live. In truth they had no real place to call home, and all options were found lacking. They had not established strong roots in Galena, and a move to his parents' new home in Kentucky was not attractive to Julia, who remembered their frugal ways. On the other hand, her own family home in Missouri offered too many Southern sympathizers, such as her father and brother John, while brother Fred, who had been Grant's roommate at West Point, would be fighting for the Union.

Many other old friends from the military academy would now be Grant's enemies. By the same token, as with so many families across the land, in Julia's family also it was to be brother against brother. In her case, however, it was clear for all to see that her love for Grant transcended both her politics and her ties with a Southern family and old friends. At the same time, her innate tenderness, kindness, and forgiving ways would overshadow any of the future hatreds that plagued so many in the aftermath of the bloody war.

After Grant had fought his first real battle—at Belmont, Missouri—Julia and the children would join him at his headquarters at Cairo, Illinois, a "Northern" town that actually lies farther south than the Confederate capital of Richmond, Virginia, as pointed out by John Y. Simon in his essay "A Marriage Tested by War," in the book *Intimate Strategies of the Civil War: Military Commanders and Their Wives*.

Grant, commanding the District of Southeast Missouri, now launched southward in a campaign to open the Tennessee and Cumberland rivers. "When Confederate General Simon B. Buckner accepted Grant's terms of 'immediate and unconditional surrender' [of fifteen thousand Confederate troops] at Fort Donelson on February 16, 1862," noted Simon, "Grant suddenly became famous." Julia, elated at the news, must have felt that her mother's prophecy was coming to fruition.

In that part of her memoir concerning this period, she tells the story of a strange dream she had a few days before she and the children were to leave for Cairo. In it, she saw her husband's head and shoulders coming toward her, as if on horseback. He was looking at her so "earnestly" and "reproachfully" that she rose up and called out his name. A friend in the next room came running to see what was the matter, and upon hearing what she dreamed, reassured her and sent her on her way to meet Grant.

Before the train to Cairo had even stopped, there he was, waving from the platform. She couldn't wait to tell him about the dream, it had been so vivid. When he then asked what day and time this happened, he was obviously taken aback. "That is singular," he said. "Just about that time I was on horseback and in great peril."

After gaining fame for his victories at Forts Henry and Donelson in Tennessee, Grant was criticized for what was perceived as a slow reaction to events the first day at Shiloh, the bloodiest battle of the war thus far. He held firm on the second day, however, with the help of reinforcements, and in fact drove the Confederates from the field, still incurring heavy casualties. Unfortunately, some Northern newspapers attacked Grant's alleged lack of preparedness and rumored drinking. Julia was heartsick over such talk, while Grant himself briefly doubted his abilities as a leader and considered resignation. He had a firm and admiring ally in Washington, though—Abraham Lincoln. And the fortunes of war were on the ascendancy for both Grant and the Union.

Before Grant next plunged into the long campaign to seize Vicksburg, sometimes called the "Gibraltar of the South," Julia was able to join him at Memphis for a time in the summer of 1862. Since she probably visited her husband more often than most officers' wives throughout the war, some critics and gossips whispered that her presence was needed strictly to keep him sober, ignoring the possibility that the two simply may have wanted to be together. And Grant, as a rising star in the Union firmament, had the rank to make such arrangements possible.

Later in 1862, the frequently traveled Julia flirted with capture. It happened when Confederate Gen. Earl Van Dorn raided the Union supply base at Holly Springs, Mississippi, on December 20, 1862. Julia had left just before the raid and barely escaped falling into Confederate hands. Truly, she was a bit nonchalant in her attitude toward the war's dangers. After that escapade, she returned to St. Louis for a time, then rejoined her general when Union gunboats and transports ran the Vicksburg batteries in April 1863 as prelude to the siege of the great Confederate bastion. She wrote later of how exciting was the nighttime spectacle. She next returned to St. Louis, since her general-husband was so busy with the all-important task of subduing Vicksburg, but their thirteen-year-old son Fred had sneaked ashore and joined his father, to remain with him throughout the skillful campaign that ended with the capture of Vicksburg on July 4, 1863.

"The country simply went wild over the success of the General," she wrote in her memoir. Actually, the Union, headed by a relieved President Lincoln, also went wild—perhaps even more so—over the Union victory at Gettysburg in the three-day battle that ended July 3. The two defeats for the South, one in the East and the other in the West, spelled doom for the fortunes of the Confederacy, even if the war would now drag on for almost two more years. Young Fred, up to his neck in the victorious Vicksburg campaign with his famous father, was swept up in the war mania. He brought back war trophies consisting of "grapeshots, two empty cigar boxes, and a pipe or two." These treasures he shared with the younger children, which quickly made him a hero in their eyes. "Jess, who was only four, was, of course, given…a small cannon-ball," wrote the loving mother in her memoir, "and while rolling it tenderly on the windowsill, it fell on his poor little foot, causing him to give a loud cry of pain." Fred was quick to tell him that brave soldiers never cry, and with that the "dear little fellow grasped his wounded foot in both hands and sank quivering and pale on the floor, but no sob escaped him." Thereafter he was a hero too—"Fred called him a little Spartan."

Once again the wandering army wife joined her husband. This time she and her general lived in grand Southern style on the first floor of a mansion in occupied Vicksburg. Apparently the owners were allowed to live on the second floor, and relations between the two families were cordial. As always, Julia's gracious manner won her many friends, while her "tender heart," noted Simon, often moved her to intervene in special hardship cases that came before Grant. She left at the end of summer to arrange for her children's schooling, but she rejoined Grant when she learned he had been injured in New Orleans after his horse stepped on a rolling stone and fell on him. She nursed him back to health just in time for him to take command of the campaign to relieve Gen. William S. Rosecrans's trapped army at Chattanooga. Here again, Grant was the victor and hero of the day.

By now, not only the general but his wife was gaining in prominence. Julia's every action was scrutinized, and more and more people were approaching her in hopes of gaining the general's ear. Whenever she was "home" visiting in St. Louis, though, it was just the opposite—here, her every move was watched with suspicion, since it was well known that the Dent family was Southern in sympathy. Both she and Mary Todd Lincoln were suspected of disloyalty to the Union because of their family ties to plantations and slave ownership. As time moved on, however, Julia's sincere personality, sunny spirit, and obvious adoration of the Union's favorite hero won over most doubters.

An invitation by President Lincoln in March 1864 to Grant caused quite a stir. It was for the ceremony held at the White House to honor Grant's promotion to the rarified rank of lieutenant general and his assignment as general-in-chief, commanding all the armies of the United States. It was the first time the two leaders had met.

But Julia, stricken with eye trouble, could not attend, so she sent Fred to accompany his father. Thus, to her undying chagrin, she missed the reception—and seeing her Ulys stand on a sofa so everyone in the crowded room would have a chance to see the war hero. The next day, at another ceremony that included members of the cabinet and other dignitaries, Lincoln made a brief speech investing Grant with his new responsibilities, and Grant in turn made a brief speech. When the president then extended an invitation to a state dinner, Grant declined. The war hero decided that he had had enough of "this show business."

While Julia was making her way to Washington later, Gen. William Tecumseh Sherman joined her. Since this would be her first visit to the capital, she was anxious about what was proper etiquette in the city. Knowing that Sherman had often been there, she asked him what she must do when she arrived. He seemed annoyed as he repeated the question, Julia recalled in her memoir. "What shall you do in Washington?" he said. "Why, return all of your calls, every one of them, and promptly too, and you will be all right."

She never did return all her calls, perhaps because she had too many from those who wanted to meet the wife of the war hero, but she said that she did succeeded "in arranging a tolerably fair list, so that in a few weeks I might have done so."

Then came an exciting invitation from President and Mrs. Lincoln to General and Mrs. Grant to attend a reception at the White House. Julia was determined to go this time, even if her husband had already left for the Virginia war front. She felt she would have "a sufficient escort in Admiral David G. Farragut," she wrote, "who was just then being tremendously lionized by society" as well as two of her husband's staff officers who had not yet joined Grant in the field.

She entered the Red Room at the White House on the arm of the admiral. When they reached the president in the reception line, he immediately recognized the admiral, who then introduced Julia. Both President and Mrs. Lincoln graciously welcomed Mrs. Grant, who relished the attention she was sharing with her escort and other prominent wartime leaders. And who knows? Perhaps Grant's starry-eyed wife was already thinking of the postwar years…after all, with the Lincolns gone back to Illinois, lightning could strike and could make her husband president.

Just then, it seems, she was asked if her husband would capture Richmond. With hardly a moment's hesitation, she demurely replied, "Mr. Grant always was a very obstinate man."

Julia's exciting visit in Washington was followed by a stop in New York City as a guest of old friends, Col. William S. Hillyer and his wife, Anna. Now that she had acquired the status of a newsworthy person, many distinguished persons came calling. And she was kept abreast of events to the south by none other than the Secretary of War Edwin M. Stanton, who "kindly sent me all telegraphic reports from the seat of war."

She stayed in New York longer than intended, knowing that the children were in good hands back home with friends and family. Among her many activities in New York, she attended the Sanitary Commission Fair, a fund-raiser for the organization's charitable work and nursing care in military hospitals. For a one-dollar donation, fairgoers could vote for their favorite general. The general with the most votes would receive "a magnificent jewel-hilted sword." The two leading contenders were George B. McClellan and Grant, but Julia's escort, Colonel Hillyer, was surprised to see that Julia voted for McClellan. Why, he wondered aloud. And she replied, "Of course, I wish my husband to get the sword, but, Colonel, it would not be in good taste for me to vote for my husband, would it?"

She added in her memoir that the only time in her life she had voted before was in a school election for May queen. "I am sure the etiquette on such occasions should be that the rival queens vote for each other," she wrote. The newspapers were full of praise for this gallant little act, but when the news stories about her gracious gesture reached her husband, he reacted negatively—not because she had voted for McClellan, but because it created such a stir in the press. Julia, on the other hand, having acquired celebrity status, was totally enjoying the spotlight. And yes, her general did win the sword, which he proudly kept among his memorabilia until the time of his death. Still, he never was happy about all the news it had generated.

When Julia returned at last to St. Louis, she found the children well, happy, and full of delightful details about their own Sanitary Commission Fair. Little Nellie was proud of her part in raising money while representing the nursery rhyme's old woman who lived in the shoe. "Nellie was delighted with her metamorphosis, seated as she was in a mammoth black pasteboard shoe filled with beautiful dolls of all sizes," Julia wrote. "Nellie wore over her pretty curls a ruffled cap and a pair of huge spectacles across her pretty, rosy, dimpled face." She proudly boasted that she sold dolls and photos of herself and brought in half a dollar for each.

With the war slowed but still dragging on, Julia and the children would spend the summer of 1864 with the general at City Point—Hopewell, Virginia, today—while neighboring Petersburg came under the longest siege ever endured by an American city. When summer ended, Julia put the three older children in a school she had found in Quaker-dominated Burlington, New Jersey, and returned with young Jesse to her general at City Point. Here, she was "snugly nestled away in my husband's Log cabin Head quarters." Her reference was to the rustic little cabin that had been built by quartermaster Rufus Ingalls "for the General so I could be with him." The little domicile, later moved to Fairmount Park in Philadelphia for public display, stood near a grand manor house that the general declined to commandeer. Here, Julia said, she enjoyed having "such long talks with my husband, when all have retired."

Whenever Julia visited City Point (she did come and go at different times), Grant would cruise down the James River to meet her and any traveling companions at Fort Monroe overlooking Hampton Roads and take the party upriver by boat, arriving at City Point early the next day. One morning, as Julia was stepping out of her stateroom, "an excited young woman approached me carrying a rosy baby in her arms." Weeping and distraught, the young woman blurted out that it was all her own fault that her equally young soldier-husband had finally responded to her pleas to return home and see their baby. Captured and returned to his unit, he was to be shot as a deserter that very day.

The woman declared she *must* see General Grant and explain that her husband was not really a deserter. With hardly any more ado, Julia agreed to intercede, but when she awoke her sleeping general with the pitiful story, he, unsurprisingly, refused to see the woman. After all, there were procedures for such situations.

In response, Julia simply threw open the door and let the woman plead her own case. Apparently at least partially convinced, Grant then wrote out a pardon and sent the happy young wife on her way. When Julia went in to thank her husband for his kindness, he somewhat ruefully replied, "I'm sure I did wrong. I've no doubt I have pardoned a bounty jumper who ought to have been hanged."

Thus ended a happy, albeit small episode of the war well known at least to Julia Grant, wife of general-in-chief Ulysses S. Grant, if not to many others. Meanwhile, another little-known episode of the war that would have surprised most people at the time came when a group of Confederate emissaries appeared at Grant's headquarters at City Point in late January 1865 to request a meeting with Lincoln in Washington. In reply, Lincoln sent a message that no negotiations were possible unless the emissaries were prepared to discuss a "common country." Furthermore, Lincoln instructed Grant—who had cordially welcomed, wined, and dined the commissioners—to allow "nothing which is transpiring, [to] change, hinder or delay your Military movements, or plans."

The commissioners had been pleasantly impressed with Grant's friendliness, and especially by the cordiality of Julia Grant. She, however, had an ulterior motive in mind—she hoped the Confederates would release her brother John, who had felt free to travel about in the South but was now being held prisoner despite his Rebel sympathies. Until now, Julia's husband refused to exchange his civilian brother-in-law for any Union soldiers. The visiting commissioners, exploring other avenues toward negotiations, remembered Julia Grant's distant kinship to Gen. James Longstreet and proposed a meeting between his wife, Louise, and Julia, who were old friends from St. Louis. The idea was that a social visit—a tea party if you will—could start a conversation between officers of both sides that might bring Robert E. Lee and Grant to suspend hostilities and come together for peace negotiations. "How enchanting, how thrilling!" Julia exclaimed when she heard of the scheme.

"Do say I may go," she entreated her general. But he replied that the whole proposal was "simply absurd." And Lincoln meanwhile sent word that Grant was to have no conference with Lee, but rather "press to the utmost your military advantage." According to historian Simon, it was thought that Julia's presence at the City Point headquarters might have strengthened Lincoln's determination to limit Grant's peacemaking authority.

The Grants, at the behest of Lincoln's eldest son, Robert Todd Lincoln, had invited the president and Mrs. Lincoln to visit the City Point headquarters.

The Lincolns complied, and soon the president's boat, the *River Queen*, was anchored in the James River near Grant's dispatch boat, where Julia had taken up quarters. While Mary Todd Lincoln's bad temper and public displays of jealousy during the visit were a strain all around, Julia felt only admiration for the president. "The president had stood by my hero when dark clouds were in his sky, and I felt grateful," she wrote.

After Richmond and Petersburg fell in early April, the Lincolns and their party prepared for the return to Washington. None knew it, but the crucial surrender at Appomattox Court House was just days away. Even so, Richmond finally was in Union hands, and now a farewell celebration would be held aboard the *River Queen* on the evening of his departure. Oddly, Julia had not received an invitation. Hurt that she had been overlooked, she was not going to sit around pouting. Not this Julia. She quickly sent for the captain of the dispatch boat, requested a brass band and told him she wished a sail downriver that evening. The result was a cruise she would relish for years to come. She interpreted the turnout of sailors aboard the navy ships they passed as a personal salute to her, and just as she passed the president's vessel, she had the band play…not a patriotic tune, as the band master expected, but a popular piece titled, "Now You'll Remember Me."

Mary Lincoln did remember Julia later in Washington, after Lee surrendered to Grant on April 9, 1865. With the war thus grinding to a halt, the lights of victory in the city brightened everybody's hearts. Mrs. Lincoln invited the Grants to attend the theater with her and the president. The invitation was declined because, as Julia wrote in her memoir, "I dispatched a note to General Grant entreating him to go home [to New Jersey] that evening…I do not know what possessed me to take such a freak, but go home I felt I must."

They did travel home by train late that fateful April 14, 1865, the very night Abraham Lincoln was fatally shot at Ford's Theatre.

★★★

Additional note: With the end of the Civil War, the Grants were only beginning their path to fame and glory. In a few years Julia would be the first lady of the land and her hero husband would be president. After his two terms, Julia shed tears upon leaving the White House but was assuaged by a trip around the world. Their two-year tour brought the little Southern girl from Missouri into the company of kings, emperors, pashas, princes, emirs, and a few fellow presidents and their respective ladies.

Ulysses, fighting for his life with throat cancer, managed to finish his personal memoir shortly before his death in 1885. A tremendous literary success, it would provide financial security for Julia as she began her final years—and work on her own life story. She perhaps began intending it as a tribute to her beloved Ulysses, but in the end, it became her very personal and typically cheerful reflection of her life before and after her Ulys came into it. How to describe or define that story? Except, as essayist John Y. Simon expressed it so perfectly, it had been a love story that began at White Haven and endured until 1902, when they would again lie together in Grant's Tomb in New York City.

CONFEDERATE
Mary Anna Morrison Jackson

MARY ANNA MORRISON JACKSON, WHO once said that she would never marry a Democrat, a widower, or a soldier, had just murmured "I do" to all three. As a result, she would spend the rest of her life nurturing the legacy of her bigger-than-life hero, Thomas Jonathan "Stonewall" Jackson.

Anna Morrison, granddaughter of Gen. Joseph Graham of Revolutionary fame, daughter to Robert Hall Morrison and Mary Graham, came into this world on July 21, 1831, as one of six daughters and four sons born to an illustrious family that would include an uncle (her mother's brother), William A. Graham, destined to become governor of North Carolina, a U.S. senator, and secretary of the navy under Millard Fillmore. Her own father, moreover, achieved success all his own after graduating third in his class at the University of North Carolina that included future president James Knox Polk. Anna's father then continued his studies at Princeton Seminary and was ordained to the Presbyterian ministry. After serving many churches in the Charlotte-Fayetteville area of North Carolina, he was at the center of the effort to establish Davidson College in North Carolina. He raised the first funds and oversaw the ground-breaking and building of the Presbyterian school, which he later served as its first president. He maintained his close association with Davidson as a member of its board of trustees for another quarter of a century.

Anna studied at Salem Academy in Winston-Salem but did not graduate, perhaps because a Southern belle of her day was expected to marry one of the young men of her social set, settle down, and raise children. Whatever the reason, she hadn't finished her studies when she and her closest sister, Eugenia, were allowed to travel to Lexington, Virginia, in 1853 to visit a married sister, Isabella Morrison Hill, whose husband, Daniel Harvey Hill, was a professor of mathematics at Washington College. The two single sisters were delighted to get away from the home life of a parsonage and entertain the prospect of meeting interesting young men in socially active Lexington.

Still, neither one could have guessed what was in store for Anna.

As they certainly knew, their brother-in-law, the future Confederate general known as D. H. Hill, not only was a mathematics professor, he also was a West Point graduate who had served in the Mexican War. That's where he had met fellow West Pointer Thomas J. Jackson. They became good friends—such good friends, Hill became a confidant to the serious young war veteran when Jackson was hired to teach natural and experimental philosophy at the Virginia Military Institute (VMI), which was right next door to Washington College. Two other close friends and prominent citizens, John Preston and John Blair Lyle—he later opened a bookstore in Lexington that would become a sort of clubhouse for professional men from both schools—also welcomed Major Jackson.

Jackson arrived in 1851 to a community of only 1,105 whites and 638 blacks, a backwater town that would grow only by 400 in the next decade. But social activities, VMI duties, and other new vistas filled his hours. He had made arrangements to board at the Lexington Hotel, and from the window of his second-floor room, he wrote to his sister, Laura, "I have a lovely view of the mountain scenery." He also reported that his health had improved and that he was "very much pleased with my situation."

Even more pleasing would be the arrival of the two sisters visiting the Harvey Hills two years later, at which time, who should come frequently calling but the tall, shy Virginia gentleman and hero of the Mexican War now turned professor: Major Jackson himself. Anna was immediately attracted, according to Sarah E. Gardner in her essay "A Sweet Solace to My Lonely Heart" for *Intimate Strategies of the Civil War: Military Commanders and Their Wives.*

The young Southern belle from North Carolina later recalled that "he was more soldierly-looking than anything else, his erect bearing and military dress being quite striking." Anna found his "dark blue frock-coat with shoulder straps, double breasted, and buttoned up to the chin with brass buttons, and faultless white linen pantaloons" all quite becoming. According to Gardner, too, Anna would hold that picture of him in her heart for the rest of her life.

Before Anna could hold the man himself in her arms, however, other events would transpire. The sisters had arrived at the beginning of the spring social season, and Major Jackson, offering to escort the visitors wherever they wished to go, suggested that they simply think of him as a brother. Aware of the local gossip, the visiting sisters teased Jackson about his rumored engagement to a local Presbyterian minister's daughter, Elinor "Ellie" Junkin. "Jackson blushed, smiled and admitted nothing," noted James I. Robertson Jr. in his biography, *Stonewall Jackson: The Man, The Soldier, The Legend.*

For the six weeks that the North Carolina belles were guests at the Hill home, Jackson was an everyday visitor. But all the time, he actually was making wedding plans. After obtaining a marriage license, he once more called on the Morrison sisters and sat quietly listening as they sang duets. Finally he made his intentions clear—Ellie Junkin was the girl he loved.

The visiting sisters returned to Cottage Home—a misnomer since it was a substantial mansion of grand proportions about twenty miles north of Charlotte—while up in Virginia on August 7, 1853, Thomas and Ellie were married in a quiet ceremony at the home of the bride. The following year, on October 22, 1854, Ellie gave birth to a stillborn son. An hour later, complications from childbirth caused severe hemorrhaging and she died.

To assuage the loss of "my Ellie," the grieving Jackson spent the following summer abroad. The ocean voyage home gave him time to reminisce on all he had seen and done in Europe. Refreshed, Jackson now saw "the hand of God in every phase of his trip." According to biographer Robertson, the returning traveler told an aunt, "It appeared that Providence had opened the way for my long-contemplated visit [to Europe] and I am much gratified at having gone."

Perhaps providence, but certainly Jackson himself now had a hand in a trip he would make the following year at Christmastime. He was determined to find happiness again with a wife, and having been orphaned as a young boy, he longed for family life. Now he again went calling on the Morrison sisters, but this time he did not want to be thought of as a brother. Perish that thought, as events turned out.

The Morrisons of course knew about Ellie's death, but none in the family quite expected the romantic intentions soon made clear by the "tall man with brass buttons on his cap [and] wearing very large boots," as the maid described the man at the front door. The "intended," it soon became evident as well, was Anna, seven years younger than the caller from Virginia.

Surprised or not, Anna's parents were favorably disposed toward Major Jackson. Her clergyman father was impressed by Jackson's pious expressions of faith, and according to Robertson, the mother's heart "went out to this man who exuded a combination of shyness and courtesy." Anna herself had only fond memories of the friendship Jackson had shown her and her sister that spring seemingly so long ago in Lexington. In sum, when he now asked for her hand in marriage, both she and her parents accepted. And so, at Christmastime 1856, the major from Virginia and the belle from North Carolina became betrothed.

So began the love story of Anna and Thomas, and it only was a beginning, since their time together would be short. But their story is one that continues to enchant romantics even today. "In my daily walks I think much of you," Thomas wrote to his betrothed that spring, when both still were going about their separate lives while making preparations for their wedding. He continued, "And as my mind dwells on you, I love to give it a devotional turn, by thinking of you as a gift from our Heavenly Father." So much and so often did Jackson combine his thoughts of romance with his expressions of piety in his letters, Robertson observed, "It is abundantly clear…that he viewed the forthcoming marriage as that between three beings: himself, Anna, and God."

To the modern ear, terms of endearment mixed with religious overtones may seem a bit melodramatic. But in the Victorian era, to those of deep faith, it was more the usual than the exception. The letters of Jackson to his wife, which she cherished, would form loving evidence of both the pious and tender side of her hero that she sought to show the world after his death.

In the meantime, they became man and wife in a small ceremony at the bride's home on July 16, 1857. As Robertson points out, it was a hot day and an uncommonly busy day that began with the commencement ceremonies at Davidson College (during which Jackson fell asleep), followed by a sixteen-mile trip by carriage "through thick dust and heat" to the Morrisons' Cottage Home. Here, late in the afternoon, Jackson and a friend struggled with a stiff "stand-up" collar that turned so limp it had to be abandoned for another stiff collar. To make that one work, they had to cut buttonholes in it. But he finally was ready to take his vows in his VMI professor's uniform.

Anna, for her part, had to wait until practically the last minute to receive her trousseau, including her wedding gown, all shipped from New York and arriving only two hours before the scheduled wedding ceremony. Adding to the strain, notes Robertson, "Some technicality then arose over the marriage license. One of the groomsmen had to gallop to the county seat at Lincolnton to unravel that snag." In the end, though, they were united as man and wife.

And as Robertson observed, Anna thus had pledged herself to a Democrat, a widower, and a soldier after once saying she never would marry any one of those three sorts of men.

Ironically enough, during the war to come, she would crave news of her husband's life and exploits as a soldier, but usually in vain. If Jackson was reticent in peacetime, it turns out, he was even more so in wartime. As Henry M. Fields wrote in the introduction to Anna Jackson's posthumous biography of her husband, *Memoirs of Stonewall Jackson by His Widow*, "of the war itself she has but little to tell us; for he did not confide his plans even to her." No matter how she pleaded for news of the front lines, his letters were answered in generalities and related more to day-to-day matters—and his love for her, of course—but little, if anything, of his feats in battle.

One wonders what drove Anna to glorify her husband for the rest of her life. Perhaps, as a woman from a historically distinguished family, Anna may have felt the need to stake out an exalted place in history for herself, albeit through her husband. Perhaps, too, like so many other women of the Civil War era, she simply wished to dedicate her life to the memory of her fallen hero. This was especially true of the women of the Confederacy, a region where so many town squares even today boast monuments to their fallen warriors.

Through their long wartime separations, husband and wife maintained a steady stream of letters, but still she craved more than mere glimpses of his life as a military leader. Once, in a news account of a battle in which Jackson and his brigade took part, the *Lexington Gazette* did not give a glowing report about her husband. Instead, the paper merely said, "General Jackson, too, was riding along the front, urging our men to their duty—his whole appearance was that of a man determined to conquer or die." Anna thought this account not complete enough. In a letter, she complained to her husband of what she considered an omission of his brave deeds in the battle. His reply was stinging: "And so you think the papers ought to say more about your husband! My brigade is not a brigade of newspaper correspondents." As is well known today, of course, Jackson stood out during the first two years of the war as one of the most reliable and brilliant of all the Confederate generals.

Meanwhile, lonely at home in Lexington, and finding it ever more difficult to manage the house, her husband's vegetable gardens, and her own flowers, Anna decided to close their beloved home and return to her family in North Carolina for the duration of the war. For that matter, Lexington wasn't the happiest place to be just then, since it would remind her of the traumatic outcome to her only pregnancy thus far. It happened in 1858, and it was doubly sad because everything at first seemed to be going so well for the newly married couple and their first child—a girl, Mary Graham Jackson, born on April 30. But only at first, since it was soon clear that the infant suffered from the liver disorder commonly called yellow jaundice. She died on May 25, and both parents grieved. Then, just a week later, came more harrowing news—Anna's sister Eugenia had died of typhoid in North Carolina.

To help assuage his wife's grief, Jackson took her on a trip north that included, as Robertson noted, elements of "pleasure, business and health." They first stopped at Fort Monroe in eastern Virginia, where Jackson the soldier assiduously inspected "every nook and cranny," then traveled by steamer to Cape May, New Jersey, where they both could enjoy the sun and ocean bathing, and finally they spent a few days in New York City, where they did some sightseeing and shopped for goods that were cheaper here than in isolated Lexington.

Their visit to New York, in fact, was quite a major shopping expedition intended to outfit a future home that would replace their boardinghouse quarters. As summarized by Robertson, they shipped back to Lexington "three stoves, a tub, a piano, nineteen boxes of roofing tin, thirteen boxes of furniture, plus other goods that filled a barrel, a keg, a bale, and four boxes." As for the health aspect of the trip, Jackson saw a specialist for his recurring ear-nose-and-throat problems who surgically "pared off" a part of his swollen right tonsil.

That fall, Jackson's health problems hadn't really improved, but Anna and her husband at last found the house that would be their real home. The brick town house on Washington Street was "old, large, and badly in need of repairs," but for three thousand dollars it was all theirs. They moved into the two-story dwelling in January 1859, together with Jackson's teenage namesake nephew, Thomas Jackson Arnold. Here, as teacher, homemaker, and husband, Jackson followed a precise and rigid daily schedule of prayer, work, and study. To the outside world he presented a stone face, but in the sanctity of his own home, alone with Anna, he was totally different. In an unpublished letter cited by Robertson, she wrote:

No man could be more demonstrative, & he was almost invariably playful & cheerful & and as confiding as possible. He commenced educating me (if I may so speak) to be demonstrative as soon as we were married, thought it added quality to happiness, & we rarely ever met alone without caresses & endearing epithets. I almost always met him on his return from the Institute, & his face would beam with happiness, & he would spend a few moments in petting me, as he called it, & then go to his duties.

Joining the Jackson household—in addition to young Arnold—were six slaves, two of whom had beseeched the VMI professor to purchase them rather than trust their fate to other owners. One of those was a man named Albert, who by mutual agreement was hired out for wages in order to buy his freedom. The second was a woman named Amy, who, about to be sold at public auction, had begged Jackson to buy her. He did and then placed her with a Christian family. As soon as the Jacksons had acquired the house on Washington Street, he brought Amy into his own family as a servant and cook. Anna once said she was "a real treasure to me in my new experience as a housekeeper."

The remaining slaves in the Jackson household included a mother (Hetty) and two teenage sons (Cyrus and George) who were—be prepared for a shock—a "wedding gift" from Anna's father. One more black member of the household, appearing in 1859 or 1860 "as a welcome home gift" to Anna, was a four-year-old orphan who had "some degree of learning disability." Jackson apparently was determined to teach her "a child's catechism," in Anna's words.

Clearly Jackson was a decent, well-intentioned, and God-fearing human being. Likewise for his wife and his clergyman father-in-law, but…slaves as "gifts"? What was the good, decent Christian's justification? Few biographers have known their subjects as well as Robertson, and he speculated on Jackson's feelings on the subject: "Jackson neither apologized for nor spoke in favor of the practice of slavery. He probably opposed the institution. Yet in his mind the Creator had sanctioned slavery, and man had no moral right to challenge its existence. The good Christian slaveholder was one who treated his servants fairly and humanely at all times."

While the nation's sectional rivalry was nearing a boiling point in 1859 and 1860, the Jacksons tended to personal business—their new home, his teaching duties, their churchgoing…and their respective illnesses. Hers at first was facial neuralgia, although by the spring of 1860, she had trouble walking. His ranged from throat inflammations to kidney pain to various forms of dyspepsia, and he was partially deaf. Their ailments in fact made them a well-traveled couple quite familiar with the Northeast, since one or both sought treatment in New York, Vermont, and Massachusetts in addition to the traditional spas in Virginia. Jackson was a great believer in hydropathic therapy, apparently with good, if coincidental, reason. When they visited the popular Round Hill Water Cure establishment in Northampton, Massachusetts, in the summer of

1860, Jackson soon was cured of, in his words, a "bilious attack attended with high fever," and Robertson reports that Anna, no longer lame, suddenly was "walking five miles a day."

Their therapy travels also resulted in their first separations as a married couple. First, Anna spent time in New York by herself, undergoing treatment of her facial neuralgia, which, oddly, also had afflicted Jackson's first wife. Now, in the fall of 1860, she would remain behind in Northampton for a few weeks of added treatment while he returned to his teaching duties at VMI. By this time on the nation's historical clock, the abolitionist John Brown's seizure of the federal armory at Harpers Ferry had come and gone, the Democratic Party had split into three warring factions in disastrous preparation for the 1860 presidential race, and the upstart Republicans had picked an upstart midwesterner, Abraham Lincoln, to carry their presidential banner.

In the meantime, both the VMI faculty and its precisely drilled cadets, along with other state military units, had played a standby role in the execution of John Brown at Charlestown, strictly as a precaution against intervention by outside parties. But no such trouble manifested itself. Major Jackson, conducting himself admirably, had been in charge of the small VMI artillery unit taking part in the grim affair. All these national developments had people astir, North and South. The political tension was palpable. In Virginia, still long before secession, notes Robertson, "state officials already were acting as if war was imminent. The General Assembly appropriated $500,000 for the manufacture and purchase of weapons." In addition, VMI superintendent Francis H. Smith was appointed to a three-man commission for the public defense.

Amid the growing furor, Jackson followed current events but kept his own counsel. As Robertson related: "Everyone voiced an opinion, and many did so often—with the exception of Jackson. He listened and remained silent. Firm allegiance to the Union was still one of his basic tenets. At the same time, however, Jackson was a states' rights adherent who did not think that the federal government had the authority to hold a state in the Union by force. 'He never was a secessionist,' Mrs. Jackson asserted, 'and (he) maintained that it was better for the South to fight for her rights *in the Union than out of it.*'" He did "quietly" endorse Vice President John C. Breckinridge of Kentucky, the so-called Southern Democrat in the race for president.

With the election of Lincoln, however, Jackson took a more activist role, joining a local group that held a town meeting to consider the state of affairs and to determine "the safest course for us to pursue in the event of a dissolution of the Federal government." When not much happened and the group's sessions became "more inflammatory," he dropped out.

His view, as expressed to a visiting Presbyterian minister (Jackson was a deacon in his church), was not to worry; dissolution could only come "by God's permission." But he also confided to his pastor that he feared war as "the sum of all evils." He wondered if prayer by all the peoples of the land might not yet avert war.

In early 1861, the Confederacy already a fact and Virginia about to hold a secession convention, Jackson wrote his pro-Union sister, Laura, that he was "gratified to see a strong Union feeling in my portion of the state." He would, himself, "vote for the Union candidates for the convention." Still, if the so-called Free States of the North and West would insist upon depriving "us" of constitutionally guaranteed rights, he then would be "in favor of secession."

At a debate on South Carolina's secession held in little Washington College, next to the VMI campus, Jackson was asked to state his views. He merely stood and said he would not make a speech on the subject and sat down. But then, after the surrender of Fort Sumter, came a day of competing demonstrations in downtown Lexington by the cadets, in favor of secession, and pro-Union advocates among the local citizenry. Tempers were hot, and when a rumor later spread that some mountain men had killed some cadets, virtually the whole cadet corps rushed from the campus armed with muskets and bayonets to confront the pro-Union townspeople. They paid not a whit of attention to their officers' commands to desist, until Major Jackson, often called "Tom Fool" for all his peculiarities, appeared from nowhere, strode in front of them and, "eyes blazing," stared them down with no words uttered, until they turned and returned to their campus.

Next, as capstone for an immediate assembly called by Superintendent Smith to scold his young charges for their rash and insubordinate conduct, "Tom Fool" Jackson was asked to speak last. "What the cadets saw that night," Robertson reported, "was a ramrod straight, inflexible soldier standing before them. Jackson remained erect and silent for several moments. What the cadets then heard was an authoritarian voice of a quality never before perceived in the major. 'Military men make short speeches,' he stated in measured terms, 'and as for myself I am no hand at speaking anyhow. The time for war has not yet come, but it will come and that soon, and when it does come, my advice is to draw the sword and throw away the scabbard.'" While that didn't really address the issues at hand, the reaction of the cadets of course was an uproar of approval.

In fact, even for the usually noncommittal Jackson, the die was cast. When

Lincoln issued his call the next week for seventy-five thousand volunteers, including three regiments from Virginia, "to make war against the South," there was room for no further equivocation on anybody's part. And Jackson's loyalty would be to his state rather than to the Union, for which he had fought in the Mexican War. "He loved the Union as only one who had fought under its flag could love it," said Anna later. "He would have died to have saved it in its purity and its just relations. But he believed the constitutional rights of the States had been invaded, and he never had a doubt as to where his allegiance was due. His sword belonged to his State."

God and faith, too, were factors. "An all-wise Providence had placed a malediction on the land," observed Robertson. "That curse must be washed away by the bloodshed of war."

Right away, Jackson was caught in one of those unhappy familial splits so often brought about by the Civil War. His original father-in-law, George Junkin, the late Ellie's father—also a Presbyterian minister and president of Washington College—was a vehement Unionist. With Virginia seceding, his own faculty turning against him, and the college students raising a flag of rebellion, he resigned and returned home to Pennsylvania, leaving close family members behind. Secession, he declared, was "the essence of all immorality." Jackson's sister, Laura, for that matter would remain in western Virginia, herself a Unionist in spirit.

But Jackson had an even more emotional issue to deal with. Ordered to lead the VMI cadets to Richmond to train the eager military recruits and militiamen flocking to Virginia's capital to serve in the now widely expected war, he would be leaving Anna and their new home in Lexington for an uncertain future. In fact, he never would see their brick town house again. He would be seeing Anna from time to time, and of course their letters would pass between them as they had during their previous separations.

In Richmond, having delivered the cadets, Jackson—not all that well known yet—was left to his own devices. Then he was accorded the same major's rank he had held for years and given an uninteresting engineering assignment. But a friend put in a word to Governor John Letcher, who happened to be from Lexington and of course knew Jackson well enough to give him a commission as colonel in the Virginia volunteer forces. That was on April 26, and the very next day, with Jackson's commission already confirmed by the appropriate state bodies, Letcher informed the VMI professor he would be placed in command of the Harpers Ferry garrison.

Here, Jackson would labor for a month imposing order in the chaos of another center for militia and as-yet-untrained recruits, but this one was a highly vulnerable outpost at the juncture of the Shenandoah and Potomac Rivers, close by the Baltimore and Ohio Railroad and the Chesapeake and Ohio Canal, each a major east-west Union conduit of goods. Just across the Potomac was the Southern-leaning state of Maryland, its goodwill and possible commitment ardently desired by the Confederacy.

After a month, during which Virginia joined the Confederacy, Colonel Jackson was relieved as the outpost's commander by Brig. Gen. Joseph E. Johnston. Still wearing his blue VMI uniform jacket, Jackson would stay on as the officer in charge of all Virginia troops at Harpers Ferry.

Not long after the change in command, Johnston obtained permission to abandon Harpers Ferry because it was so vulnerable to Union attack—he ordered Jackson to see to the destruction or removal of all militarily useful facilities and materials at Harpers Ferry as the Confederates then pulled back toward Winchester to establish a better defensive position. Ironically, barely more than a year later, Jackson would be called upon to seize the same arsenal town, manned by a Union garrison of twelve thousand troops, while on his way to support Lee at Sharpsburg.

In the meantime, however, the legend of the stoic, nonwavering "Stonewall" was to be born in a major battle and Confederate victory in the countryside by Bull Run. The famous sobriquet was bestowed by fellow West Pointer Barnard E. Bee just before he himself was mortally wounded in the same desperate struggle in which the steadfastness of Jackson's brigade played a key role.

For a modest, God-fearing man who would not read a letter from his own wife on a Sunday, the Sabbath, this great personal triumph for Jackson on July 21, 1861, had to be doubly or even triply emotional, because it was fought, Robertson pointed out, on a Sunday that also was Anna's thirtieth birthday.

In August 1861, the war quiet again, rumors were flying that there might be an extended lull in the fighting. That gave Anna good reason to implore her husband to visit her, since he wouldn't allow her to visit him at camp. Adamant, while at the same time writing back to her tenderly, reported Robertson, Jackson answered, "My darling, I can't be absent from my command" and then explained why he could not do so. He used an endearing Spanish expression he learned during his time in Mexico, "*esposito*," meaning little wife. "[Since] my soldiers are not permitted to go and see their wives and families," he wrote, "I ought not to see my *esposito*, as it might make the troops feel that they were badly treated."

But the stoic leader yearned to see and be with his *esposito*. From Fairfax

Court House, he wrote: "This morning I had a kind of longing to see our lot—not our house, for I did not want to enter its desolate chambers, as it would be too sad not to find my little sunshine there." In another letter, his loneliness for her showed through again as he signed off: "I know not one day what will take place the next, but I do know that I am your doting *esposo*."

When the rumored period of inactivity did prove to be the case for a while, Anna's *esposo* saw an opportunity for her to travel safely to him. By September 8, all their plans were in readiness, and Anna, escorted by Capt. J. Harvey White, who was on leave to visit a sick brother, started what would be a long and eventful journey. One can only imagine Anna's excitement as she boarded the northbound train in Richmond. She wired her *esposo* to meet her at Manassas Junction. As fate would have it, he did not receive the telegram until too late to make the connection. A very downhearted Anna searched the platform in vain for her general. Fortunately still under Captain White's protection, Anna reboarded the crowded train and continued on to Fairfax. Here she spent the night in a cramped railcar because there were no rooms available in the overcrowded town. As Robertson described the dramatic scene of the couple's reunion: "Sunday morning, September 9, found a lonely, hungry, and tired Anna sitting in the passenger car. Suddenly, a team pulling a military wagon came galloping up beside the tracks. Out bounded Jackson. The couple had not seen one another in five months. They exchanged embraces and conversation all the way to the brigade encampment."

Jackson was able to rent a room for Anna at a nearby home. Her room was small, but she was happy to take her meals with his staff outdoors beneath the trees. The loving couple spent ten delightful days together, with Anna's general—now a major general—squiring her around, showing her sites of interest. Among them, none too cheerful, to be sure, was the same Bull Run battleground where her handsome soldier first had gained fame—and the Stonewall sobriquet that would ring down through the ages.

In the winter of 1861, Anna was elated by the news that she again could travel to be with her general for the holidays, this time in Winchester. She hurriedly packed and was off, without even waiting for the military aide her husband had promised to send her as an escort for the journey. Instead, she traveled with friends to Richmond, and from there she was accompanied by an elderly clergyman she described as "kind-hearted but absent-minded." Again she experienced mishaps along the way. The final stagecoach ride brought Anna to Winchester late at night, and when she disembarked in front of the Taylor Hotel, no one was there to greet her. In addition, her trunk had been lost along the way.

Glancing around to see if she could spy her husband, she did not see him. She started up the steps of the hotel. Then, as Robertson describes: "A heavily bearded soldier stepped away from a group of people on the sidewalk and slowly walked up behind her. Powerful arms swung Anna around; kisses rained on her face. It was Jackson." Hoping she would arrive on the midnight coach, the gallant soldier had been rewarded!

Over the next few days, Anna was received at Jackson's headquarters as a welcome morale boost for his men. So pronounced was the lovely Anna's effect that it was as if their own wives—or in some cases, mothers—had come to visit. She also was graciously accepted in Winchester society, and Jackson even attended occasional social functions with his wife.

Christmas Day was gray and cold, but with normal military duties suspended for the day, celebrations brightened the atmosphere. Jackson and his staff were invited to dinner at the Hunter Holmes McGuire home a few blocks from headquarters, and conviviality permeated the family-like gathering. John Preston, Jackson's old friend from Lexington, kept Anna entertained in conversation. The dining table was groaning with the abundance of food, and everyone enjoyed the feast, except the ever-frugal Jackson, who dined on corn bread and buttermilk.

Soon after Anna's arrival, Jackson began his Romney campaign. Before he left, he made arrangements with the reverend and Mrs. James R. Graham for his wife to stay in their home during his absence, an arrangement that gave Anna a comfortable home in the midst of war. When Jackson returned, he was so delighted, Anna later related, he exclaimed, "Oh! this is the very essence of comfort!" At the Reverend Graham's invitation, Jackson moved in with her for the time being.

Anna was ecstatic when her husband returned from the campaign but was unhappy with the rumors that followed him back from Romney. His men had openly complained of the cold and their hunger, saying the general pressed ever onward despite their fatigue. Once again, the label "Tom Fool Jackson" was heard.

Anna would counter this impression in her later writings by suggesting that the general's men trusted him thoroughly. Giving as an example a conversation between an officer and a woman in Winchester who asked him what he thought of Jackson, the officer said, "I have the *most explicit confidence in him*, madam. At first I did not know what to think of his bold and aggressive mode of warfare; but since I [now] know the man, and have witnessed his ability and his patriotic devotion, *I would follow him anywhere*."

Whether or not this conversation was actually overheard by Anna that winter in Winchester, the story reflects her admiration of Jackson…and the version of his persona she wanted the world to understand. In the second edition of her biography of her husband she added a series of laudatory quotes from Jackson's men in reference to her dashing general.

Meanwhile, after their happy Christmastime sojourn together in Winchester, Anna returned to Cottage Home in North Carolina. She would not see her husband again for thirteen months.

The letters between them still flowed as the war dragged on and on. But now Anna was very occupied with the coming of a baby! Although Victorian women did not often discuss the fact that they were in a motherly way, she did write about the coming blessed event. And on November 28, a quick note from Anna's sister Harriet Irwin announced that Anna had given birth to a baby girl. A few days later, noted Robertson, another letter arrived at headquarters written in the same handwriting:

> My own dear Father,
>
> As my mother's letter has been cut short by my arrival, I think it but justice that I should continue it. I know that you are rejoiced to hear of my coming, and I hope that God has sent me to radiate your pathway through life. I am a very tiny little thing. I weigh only eight and a half pounds, and Aunt Harriet says I am the express image of my darling papa, and so does our kind friend, Mrs. Obsorne, and this greatly delights my mother.

The reticent general was elated by the news that mother and child were fine, and though he was most anxious to see his loved ones, he still would not leave his post. It is interesting to note that members of his staff did not hear of the birth of his daughter until a month or more later.

According to Robertson, Jackson had initially hoped for a son because, as he told Anna, "men have a larger sphere of usefulness than women." But with the arrival of his daughter, the general, who truly loved children, was thankful that wife and child had come through childbirth safely, and he changed his preference to that of a girl.

Surely, too, he must have felt doubly blessed when remembering the loss of his first wife and child in childbirth and the death of his and Anna's first child. He quickly wrote Anna upon receiving the happy news, "Oh! How thankful I am to our kind Heavenly Father for having spared my precious wife and given us a little daughter!"

It would be another five long winter months before the family-loving man would see his wife and baby girl. For one thing, the infant Julia came down with a case of chicken pox that put off one planned visit. And for another, there was the war. By mid-April 1863, however, Jackson could wait no longer, especially since other generals' wives (Mrs. James Longstreet and Mrs. Ambrose Powell Hill among them) came to spend time with their husbands. Do not hesitate if not already on the way, Jackson wrote at one point, because he and his troops might be moving on very shortly. The next thing he knew, his old Lexington friend, John Letcher, sent word that Anna and the baby had stopped overnight at the governor's mansion in Richmond. Could he join them there?

But no, he had to stay at the front…even so, she and little Julia could still see him. Send them by train to Guiney Station (just south of Fredericksburg), he wired back.

As a result, Anna and Julia soon appeared by northbound train—at last the little family was united for nine delightful spring days together. Nine days, but they would have to last a lifetime.

The next time Anna would see her beloved husband would be on his deathbed.

A full two years before the grueling war would end, the Confederacy lost one of its most outstanding heroes. It happened in the gathering dusk of May 2, 1863, during the battle of Chancellorsville, not due to enemy fire, but due to mistaken shots fired by his own men. As a result, Stonewall Jackson had his wounded left arm amputated two inches below the shoulder. Then, initially pleased with his apparent progress, the doctors transferred him to a safer haven south of the battle zone. Here—at Guiney Station, ironically—he developed pneumonia. Here, too, Anna came to his side one last time.

Years later she would give her agonizing account of his death: "My own heart almost stood still under the weight of horror and apprehension which then oppressed me," she wrote. "His fearful wounds, his mutilated arm, the scratches upon his face, and above all the pneumonia, which flushed his cheeks, oppressing his breathing, and benumbing his senses, wrung my soul with such grief and anguish as it had never before experienced."

After the death of Stonewall Jackson on May 10, 1863, Mary Anna Morrison Jackson, age thirty-one, became another widow of the Civil War, and her five-month-old baby, Julia, another of its fatherless children. But Anna Jackson would not be satisfied to become a mere statistic. The death of Stonewall Jackson simply strengthened her need to see her husband's military feats celebrated. In addition to maintaining his grave in Lexington, Anna devoted her time and energy, as noted by Sarah Gardner, "to ensuring a place for her husband's memorial at the Confederate Museum in Richmond, Virginia." Often called the "Widow of the Confederacy," Anna would become one of the most popular women in the country. Fifty-two years his widow, she never remarried. Little Julia, their only child, often known as "Daughter of Stonewall," unfortunately would die in her twenties of typhoid fever.

After Jackson's death, Anna returned to her family home in North Carolina, where she spent much of her time glorifying her general and assuring his place among the greats of military history. In so doing she assured her place by his side. Several biographies of Jackson were written after the war, including some she authorized. But she was not satisfied with these and other tomes, all written from a military point of view, and so, in 1891, she published her own memoir-biography, *The Life and Letters of General Thomas J. Jackson*. Following her own death at age eighty-three in Charlotte in 1915—due also to pneumonia—she was buried beside her husband in Lexington.

UNION
Ellen Ewing Sherman

THEY GREW UP TOGETHER, BUT not as childhood sweethearts. Rather, they first were neighborhood playmates, then they became brother and sister under the same roof. Finally, as young adults, they became husband and wife.

Their unusual saga began in 1829, when the boy's father, Justice Charles Sherman, an eminent jurist seemingly secure in position and reputation in his sinecure as a member of Ohio's supreme court, suddenly died.

The unexpected loss left behind a widow with a home heavy in debt and eleven children. That was when, after a brief period of grief, Ellen's father, Thomas Ewing, one of the most respected attorneys in the state, stepped forward to help the family of his lost friend and neighbor by offering to take in and raise one of the late judge's fatherless boys. "I want one of them," he told Elizabeth Sherman. "Give me the brightest of the lot, and I will make a man of him."

By the same account, the bereaved mother, who lived just a half block from the Ewing family's brick mansion at the summit of a hill in New Lancaster, Ohio, quickly decided on her redheaded tyke "Cump" as the "smartest" of the lot.

Thomas Ewing then led the nine-year-old Tecumseh Sherman by the hand up the hill, where five-year-old Ellen was watching with great interest.

From that moment on, the Ewing family absorbed the young redhead into their home as if he had always been a part of their growing brood—three of their own, with yet another expected in two months. In fact, after losing a son, George, earlier, the Ewings would wind up as parents of Philemon, Ellen, Hugh Boyle, Thomas Jr., Charles, and Maria Theresa, born in 1837, while just down the same hill, Elizabeth Sherman had borne Mary Elizabeth, James, Amelia, Julia, Tecumseh, Lampson, John, Susan, Hoyt, and Fanny. (The Shermans' eldest, Charles Taylor, had been born in Connecticut before the family moved to Ohio.) In short, by the time Judge Sherman died in 1829, the two bustling families already were well started as one big conglomerate of children.

In a way, Cump, as he was known, always had been a part of his "new" family, since he almost always played with Philemon, the Ewing boy nearest him in age, with little sister Ellen tagging along. It all seemed so right to move up "The Hill," that Cump just seemed to be swapping beds while continuing to pop in and out of his mother's two-story frame house down the street for long visits and an occasional meal with her and his siblings. It was a tribute to his father the judge that friends and relatives readily came to take over others of the many children in his family, thus lightening the load of the widowed mother. It also eased Cump's changed status as more and more of his siblings joined other families. His brother John, meanwhile, remained his lifelong friend, and they stayed in frequent contact.

Thomas Ewing's attitude toward his new ward was one of kindness, and both he and his wife were scrupulously fair. Ewing intended to raise the boy as one of his own, but he did not expect the youngster to give up his father's name. Soon after joining his new family, however, Cump *gained* a name and changed religious affiliation. His foster mother, Maria Boyle Ewing, a devout Catholic, insisted that he be baptized into the Roman Catholic faith, but first she went down the hill to ask the Widow Sherman if her son could be baptized by the Catholic priest. When she agreed, the priest from the monastery at nearby Somerset, who visited once a month and stayed for a week to give the Ewing children instruction, was prevailed upon to baptize the new member of the family.

When he asked the name of the newcomer in the Ewing flock, the priest was somewhat taken aback by the reference to a pagan Indian chief and insisted the boy should have a saint's name as well. Since that day was the Feast of Saint William, June 25, William it was. From then on, Cump would sign his name as William Tecumseh Sherman, or simply as W. T. For the time being, too, he would attend Mass with his newly acquired family.

While the issue of religion later would be a bone of contention between Cump and Ellen, religious practice was no cause of friction in the Ewing household, since Ewing, born a Presbyterian, attended Mass with his wife and children. Apparently his attitude was, if he could not accept all the dogma of the church, so be it; let the family find happiness in it. As Cump explained years later, according to Lloyd Lewis in his biography, *Sherman: Fighting Prophet*, Thomas Ewing thought it "made little difference whether the religion was Methodist, Presbyterian, Baptist, or Catholic, provided the acts were half as good as their profession." Maria Ewing, on the other hand, was so staunch in her faith "that though she loved her children better than herself, she would have seen them die with less pang than to depart from the faith."

Meanwhile, if young Cump indeed had been baptized anew, it was not his foster mother's Roman Catholicism that would capture his later attention, but rather his foster father's political "religion" of federalism. Intellectual life in New Lancaster centered on The Hill, as the Ewing home was called, where well-educated, politically minded men gave the children listening at the door plenty of good grammar and raging national policy disputes to hear about. Much of this talk centered upon the latest battles in Congress over slavery.

While most of these men were freethinkers, with a bit of Jeffersonian skepticism thrown in, "The pioneers of the Northwest were amazing talkers," observed Lloyd Lewis. "Men rose to fame and influence on their abilities as conversationalists." Despite the young town's prosperity, its fine private school, built in 1820 with Thomas Ewing and Philemon Beecher footing most of the bill, big-city newspapers were few and new books scarce, putting a high value on storytellers and weavers of folktales. "That lawyer or politician who could pour the most humor, philosophy, and poetry into his speech or informal conversations was the idol of his community," noted Lewis as well—a reference that brings to mind a lanky boy across the woods in Illinois who would rise to fame in large part due to his power of speech.

Between the ages of six and sixteen, Cump would be one of the eager youngsters listening to a good many brilliant conversations in the Ewing household and thus gaining quite an ability in this area himself. Shy in his youth, by middle age he would be considered a brilliant conversationalist, and by many observers, "the best in America," added biographer Lewis.

Meanwhile, Cump and Ellen lived a comfortable family life together as brother and sister. In the private school they attended, both were good students, he helping her when she needed tutoring, especially in math. "She enjoyed the attention and began looking up to him, as she later said, as her 'protector,'" John F. Marszalek wrote in his essay "General and Mrs. William T. Sherman, a Contentious Union" for *Intimate Strategies of the Civil War: Military Commanders and their Wives*.

In the year Cump and Ellen became brother and sister, 1829, times were good in the prosperous town of New Lancaster, which was situated on the Hocking River in southeastern Ohio. The Ewings had amassed quite a fortune and were among the leading citizens. The Shermans, because of an early debt that Charles Sherman once was determined to pay off, would find it difficult to find any financial prosperity for themselves, yet they, too, were among the town's most respected citizens.

The fast-growing community had been founded in 1800, and by 1829 it had a population of about a thousand persons. The town boasted a courthouse, a bank, a jail, two newspapers (one English and one German), and perhaps two hundred homes, many made of brick, some of half timbers, while log houses were all but gone. Mechanics, merchants, and even lawyers such as Sherman and Ewing contributed to the prosperity, along with gunsmiths, silversmiths, and spinning-wheel makers, who also repaired their products.

The strong friendship between Cump's father and Ellen's father began years before, in 1815, when the young Ewing, aspiring to become a lawyer, met the brilliant and dignified Charles Sherman, reputed to be the ablest lawyer in southeastern Ohio. Sherman had gained the lifelong friendship of men of distinction from across the state. He was a rising legal star of twenty-six at the time he took Tom Ewing, one year his junior, under his wing. From that point on, both households were destined to prosper and live well. By working at a grimy saltworks, Ewing had made enough money to pay for an education and then to study law. Hearing from his new friend that the best opportunity for his future as a lawyer would be at New Lancaster at the upper end of the Hocking Valley, Tom Ewing could only agree. Here immigrants from Pennsylvania and Virginia had been streaming into town over Zane's road. The first wagoners, hailing from Lancaster, Pennsylvania, had named the new town for the one they had left behind. A progressive and cultured town, New Lancaster had been receiving mail delivery once a week for sixteen years.

For the next ten years, Ewing would become successful both as a lawyer and as owner of the very same saltworks where he had once worked. He was strong in body and mind, and everyone knew of his early struggles to gain an education among the salt kettles of Kanawha. This gained him the sobriquet

"The Salt-Boiler." But his reputation as a lawyer really began when his great friend and mentor, Charles Sherman, invited him to help prosecute a case that involved a prominent Methodist. Ewing presented his plea in a crowded courtroom, winning not only his case and the respect of the powerful Methodist community, but also the hearts and minds of the town.

Into this small but secure little world, the two great friends sired their growing families. And it indeed was an idyllic place for the children to roam and play. There were ponds for ice-skating in winter and fishing or swimming in summer. There were woods for adventurous wandering or hunting. Their respective homes were well run by devoted mothers and loving fathers. Unfortunately, tragedy shows no favors, and in the prime of life, the renowned Justice Sherman, while making an obligatory court circuit around the state, caught a fever and died before his wife could reach his bedside.

The loss of course would linger in William Tecumseh Sherman's mind, but the care shown his mother by the community made the drastic transition in his life easier. Cump, with the love and support of his new family, enjoyed a happy childhood with Ellen and the many Ewing siblings as they all grew into their teen years. Cump apparently adjusted to his extended-family situation so easily, he would always hold his foster father—later his father-in-law—in highest esteem. Still, as he matured, he was a little bewildered by his more profound understanding of things that once had seemed so matter of fact. He was not quite certain whether he was a Sherman or a Ewing. And this left him with a sense of insecurity.

Ellen, by contrast, was quite sure of who she was. As her mother's daughter, she was a devout Catholic, and her love and admiration for her father was, while extreme, endearing. By the time her redheaded "brother" had grown to thirteen, not so incidentally, her father was in Washington, D.C., as one of Ohio's representatives in the Senate. And both mother and father were busy planning a future for her older brothers, Cump and Phil.

The good senator realized the value of a good education, and at his disposal were appointments to the U.S. Military Academy at West Point, New York, now midway through its third decade of service and not yet universally popular in the Midwest and the West, but still, for many a young man, a good starting place for a career. Rather than bestow the appointment on Phil, the opportunity to attend West Point went to Cump, and off he went in 1836 as a lad of sixteen.

As reputed, the daily physical and study regimen here was tough, rigorous, and nearly all-consuming. Like a monastery or convent, the academy was a world unto itself…and religion was a part of it. The way events turned out, however, the Episcopal worship services taking place here on Sundays had no more effect on Cump than had his Catholic upbringing in Lancaster. "As soon as he left New Lancaster for West Point," wrote biographer Lewis, "the practice of any particular creed fell from him almost unnoticed and was never picked up again."

Little Ellen in the meantime was attending a Catholic school in Somerset, Ohio. She was also becoming Cump's most ardent letter writer, reporting on happenings at her school and especially activities in the old neighborhood. Suddenly, as the letters went back and forth, their age difference no longer seemed to matter. He wrote and told her about his life as a cadet and invited her to one of the dances there. When that didn't work out, more time passed— they did not see each other again until he finished his second academic year.

When that day finally came, and Cump stepped off the stagecoach, Ellen Ewing, almost fourteen, saw that her returning playmate had come back to her as a man. Later in life, according to biographer Lewis, she would tell their children "about that moment—how strong and straight he was, how clear-eyed and bright, how light of heart and how proud of his uniform."

Lewis posed the question: Was this "the first twinge of love"?

In any case, within a short time, Cump was not the only family member studying in the East. Ellen for a time attended Monsieur and Madame Picot's school in Philadelphia, where all the "first families" sent their young ladies to be educated. The Catholic zeal of Mrs. Ewing, perhaps encouraged by Ellen herself, then persuaded her father to enroll her in the Catholic Academy of the Visitation in Georgetown, next door to Washington, D.C. For that matter, the devoted daughter Ellen may simply have wanted to be that much closer to her senator-father.

When summer came, she was again in New Lancaster with the family. As always, her letters were Cump's best Lancaster news source, but he often was lax in replying. His missives were filled with excuses as to why he hadn't written sooner, but he wrote often enough to make it an increasingly personal correspondence.

As the years flew by, young Cump suddenly was starting his fourth and final year at the military academy. As a veteran cadet looking over the green plebes appearing for registration, Sherman soon noticed that among them was a young Ohio youth who insisted that his name was Hiram Ulysses Grant. But the registrars with military precision decided that his name had been submitted by his congressional sponsor as Ulysses S. Grant, and so it would be. Giving up on the point, the newcomer soon accepted the fact he would be called Sam—sometimes even "Uncle Sam." Two decades later, destiny would have them fighting a desperate war together and becoming lifelong friends. For now, though, "from the irksome detail of West Point etiquette the two Ohio boys, Grant and Sherman, found escape in varying ways," wrote biographer Lewis "Grant in riding wild horses and Sherman in gregarious nocturnal pranks."

When Cump graduated sixth in the Class of 1840, he felt he had disappointed Ellen's father—and would continue to. As he wrote Ellen, "I fear I have a difficult part to act for the next three years, because I am almost confident that your father's wishes and intentions will clash with my inclinations." What was even more on his mind was Ellen's own wish for him to resign his commission and come home to New Lancaster.

Mercifully, Sherman that summer after graduation saw little of his foster father, who was off stumping the state with Tom Corwin, the Whig candidate for governor. In the meantime, Ellen had returned to New Lancaster from Washington for the summer, just as newly commissioned second lieutenant Sherman came home on furlough. She held a formal party in his honor, and of course, he made a big hit in his U.S. Army uniform, but he would ever be remembered in Lancaster for shooing a stray bat out the door in an incident the partygoers laughingly called "Sherman's first battle."

The sweet summer came to an end as Ellen returned to Washington to complete her studies and Sherman set off for Fort Pierce, Florida, to fight in the Seminole War. He later would be happy to leave swampy Florida for assignments that took him to Fort Morgan at Mobile and then Fort Moultrie in Charleston Harbor. During this period, Ellen returned to New Lancaster and continued to write, keeping him abreast of family activities. More and more, her letters also asked about his religious practices. He bluntly answered that he practiced no religion. Meanwhile, it also was clear that he had no intention of leaving the army.

It was on another of his furloughs to New Lancaster, in 1843, that the two who had once been congenial young siblings, then grown to maturity apart, truly fell in love. In those days of yore, apparently, absence did make the heart grow fonder. Among their many letters saved for posterity, there is no declaration of their first passionate discovery, no sudden burst of romantic poetry between them. But the understanding that crept in was that they would someday be married. Ellen, for her part, had never considered anyone else, while Cump, whatever else he felt, could hardly consider going from ward to son-in-law of the respected and wealthy Thomas Ewing as an undesirable change in status.

Marriage for the now-loving pen pals still was far in the future. For now, the first lieutenant became increasingly enthralled as he found himself assigned to all of the most desirable army posts in Alabama, Georgia, South Carolina, Louisiana, and Mississippi. Indeed, he was having a love affair with the South. He visited Mobile several times and wrote Ellen that the bright buttons on his uniforms were a passport at all times "to the houses of the best." According to biographer Lewis, the happy Cump continued in his flowery way, saying that "it would take a volume to name the ladies, their beauties and accomplishments." On and on he went, with descriptions of rose-covered fences, moss-draped oak trees, and the soft enticement of the patrician South. He freely moved about in the notoriously exclusive Charleston society, which happened to be rife with states' righters and fire-eaters for the Southern cause. Cump himself did not enter the frequent arguments and was often prevailed upon to cool tempers around him. At a Fourth of July celebration, Sherman once prevented a duel between fellow officer Braxton Bragg and a journalist named Stewart, a rabid Secessionist. Bragg, though a Southerner, resented the loose talk of the journalist aimed at Bragg's native state of North Carolina. Both he and Sherman were pro-Union, as were any number of other Southerners in and out of army circles when talk of secession came up.

Delighted with the snow-free South and thoroughly enjoying his army assignments, Cump wrote to Ellen that he knew her father wanted him to prepare for the practice of some other profession and to leave the army. For now, he could not do so because it would mean dependence on others while he established his career. Remembering his father's financial difficulties and his mother's subsequent dependency on others, this he could not do. As he once explained in a letter to Ellen: "I am endeavoring so to qualify myself that should you not like to encounter the vicissitudes that I am liable to, I may be enabled to begin life anew in a totally new sphere."

Any marriage plan now had to be pushed further into the future when the Mexican War loomed on the horizon—Cump was well aware if he were to advance in the army, he would have to get into that war. Instead, he was sent to California. Advancement in his chosen field was one thing, but to leave Ellen behind was another. As essayist Marszalek noted, Cump's farewell letter said he was saddened by "the thought of the trouble my wayward life has already given you," and then asked, "You will think of me will you not?"

For the next four long years, Cump was despaired of advancing his army career, not only because he did not get into the Mexican War, as so many of his fellow West Pointers did, but because he was stuck out west in what he considered dead-end postings. Both he and Ellen were lonely during this period and suffering from health problems. He had attacks of asthma; she was suffering from repeated boils and gynecological problems. At one point, her health had so deteriorated that she wrote he ought to find someone better suited to become his wife. His answer certainly was unequivocal, "My love for you has never abated, never wavered in the least and upon it you may constantly rely." But Marszalek, citing that firm statement, suggested that the relationship between the two was less of romance than it was of mutual dependence.

In fact, the four years apart had not deterred Cump in his resolve to marry the girl who had always been a part of his life. And, at last, came the end of his isolation from civilization. He was sent to New York to deliver dispatches to Gen. Winfield Scott. Then invited to stay for dinner, Sherman was entertained by Scott's stories of the Mexican War, but according to British military historian B. H. Liddell Hart's biography, *Sherman: Soldier Realist American*, this only depressed the returning soldier, who thought the now-concluded Mexican War had been "the last and only chance in my day and that my career as a soldier was at an end."

From New York, Sherman traveled to Washington to make a quick stop at the War Department to deliver more dispatches before surprising Ellen, who was living with her family there. Thomas Ewing by this time had become an important and famous man as secretary of the new Home Department—soon renamed the Department of the Interior—in President Zachary Taylor's cabinet.

These were still leisurely times in the capital, with old-fashioned Southern hospitality still very much in sway. All the galas Ellen attended did not turn her heart from the man who had always been a part of her life. In addition to being her "protector," he now was a widely traveled and adventuresome man—with, added Hart, "a halo of romance well calculated to reinforce the ties of common upbringing in counteracting the paler attractions of the city-bred youths she met at dances."

Wedding plans were quickly arranged with, of course, parental approval, but Ellen's friends lamented that she was throwing herself away on a penniless lieutenant. But no matter. Ellen had tied her destiny to the man—the only man—of her dreams. The wedding date was set for May Day 1850, romantically enough. As preparations continued, the happy couple roamed the capital, seeing all the sights. Often Sherman sat with his father-in-law-to-be for long sessions in the Senate gallery, listening to speeches. Here they saw the three intellectual giants—Daniel Webster, Henry Clay, and John C. Calhoun—making their appearances on the floor of the Senate. Of these three old men, all born when the Revolution was roaring, demigods in the eyes of their followers, two were willing to sacrifice everything to save the sacred Union, but one of them, South Carolina's Calhoun, was more and more convinced that the only hope for his beloved South was in separation from the North.

The capital was all abloom as the wedding day arrived. Held at the home of the bride, their wedding was the social event of the season, with President and Mrs. Taylor, cabinet members and their wives, and many others of the city's great men swelling the ranks of the three hundred guests. Ellen carried a silver bouquet holder given to her by Henry Clay, who arrived late and handed her a huge bouquet. Cump wore his full dress uniform, as did the large number of his army friends. In all, it was an elegant and festive affair, but behind all the gaiety there remained their differences—she wanting to be near her family, he wanting to stay in the army, she attending Mass almost every day, he practicing no religion. The president of Georgetown University, also a priest, performed the ceremony, even though it did not take place in a church. "The popping of champagne corks exemplified the festive nature of the event and camouflaged any discomfort over religion," commented Marszalek. The bride and groom left for a honeymoon in Niagara Falls and then returned to their hometown of New Lancaster for a brief time together.

Newly wed or not, they soon parted company again—he to fresh assignment in St. Louis and she to remain in New Lancaster awaiting the birth of their first daughter. Born January 28, 1851, she was named Maria, after Ellen's mother, but quickly became Minnie for short. The next year, all three lived in St. Louis, but Ellen longed to be near her parents. In 1852, Ellen would return to New Lancaster to spend the summer. She was happy to be back home, but Cump now suffered from asthma and depression. He felt that her family stood between them, but he could not in good conscience complain about his father-in-law, to whom he owed so much. So he tended to focus his complaining on the town of New Lancaster itself.

In October 1852 Cump was reassigned to New Orleans, and once again he went alone. Ellen stayed home with her parents—just in time to give birth to a second daughter, born on November 17. She was named for Cump's recently deceased mother, Mary Elizabeth. The two girls and Ellen then arrived in New Orleans for Christmas. Now more than ever, Ellen was pressuring her husband to leave the army and take up a profession in New Lancaster. An army buddy settled that argument when he offered Cump a job as managing agent of a California branch of a bank of St. Louis. Cump accepted and resigned his commission.

San Francisco, when he returned after an absence of three years, was booming, thanks to the gold rush begun in 1849. Yerba Buena, its name when he left it, was now prosperous and filled with large brick and granite buildings, along with many new wharfs for the oceangoing vessels that kept the port bustling. It had become a magnet for entrepreneurs, merchants, and tradesmen from all over the world—and, of course, many a gambler and lady of the night. "This is a great country for rich people but death to a poor one," he wrote to Ellen before she joined him in the exciting West. Back in the East, the aging Thomas Ewing naturally preferred to keep the family nearby, especially since he was enjoying his granddaughters. In deference to his feelings, Minnie would remain with the grandparents while the infant Lizzie, still less than a year old, would accompany her parents to San Francisco.

Once again it didn't take long for Ellen to get homesick. She wrote her father that she thought the climate was bad for Cump's health, but this was countered by Cump's fierce argument that he could make money in California. For that matter, he mentioned Cuba as a possibility as well. All that aside, in June 1856, baby William Ewing Sherman was born, and soon after Cump wrote to Ewing that, in truth, the fog in San Francisco was affecting his bronchial tubes. By now, according to Lewis, Cump had "given up hope that Ellen would become reconciled [to staying in San Francisco]," and therefore he decided "to let her and all the family go home in the spring for a long while."

In November, when Cump heard that brother John had been elected to Congress on an antislavery platform, he wrote him a bit of warning: "Having lived in the South I think I know practically more of slavery than you do.... Slavery being a fact is chargeable on the past; it cannot, by our system, be abolished except by force and consequent breaking up of our present government." He predicted there would be significant strife over the slavery issue.

In the meantime, Sherman obviously was discouraged by the course his life was taking. To Ellen, still back home in New Lancaster, he wrote: "I am doomed to be a vagabond, and shall no longer struggle against my fate.... I look upon myself as a dead cock in the pit, not worthy of further notice, and will take my chances as they come." And for a time, failure heaped upon failure dogged the young "vagabond's" life.

After the closing of the California bank branch (and its St. Louis home office), he returned to New Lancaster and tried both real estate and, in Leavenworth,

Kansas, the practice of law with two of his brothers, only to meet with failure in each arena. Then, through his father-in-law's connections, came an offer from Cincinnati financiers to be their representative at a bank in London. At the same time, through his own inquiries, came opportunity to become superintendent at a new state military college in Louisiana (the Louisiana State Seminary of Learning and Military Academy, then at Pineville but now the Louisiana State University at Baton Rouge). Given that choice, Sherman decided the gracious South likely would be forgiving of his commercial failures, while the London bank venture was no more secure than banking in general. Thus, to his mind, the Louisiana offer was a much better guarantee of future security for him and his growing family.

And yet, this was 1859, a year with inflamed feelings on both sides widening the dichotomy between North and South even as the West Point graduate left his wife and children at New Lancaster to establish a new home for them in Louisiana. In October, abolitionist John Brown seized the government arsenal at Harpers Ferry, Virginia, as part of a plan to arm the slaves and march them to freedom. He was captured and executed, but in the South, demands were heard for military science courses at state universities—Alabama and Mississippi already had such courses in their curricula. Fire-eaters in the South were refusing to send their young men to such "abolitionist" colleges as Harvard, Yale, and Princeton.

As the fires smoldered on both sides of the slavery issue, Sherman set off to the South to begin a new career, but one in which he already was knowledgeable—supervising and teaching a curriculum of military science. There were, at the same time, differences with Ellen over the choice he had made. She had wished him to go to London while she stayed in New Lancaster with the children. In the meantime, obviously a factor in her thinking, a new baby had been born to them. "Number Five," as he described the latest arrival to his brother John, was Eleanor Mary, born September 5, 1859. If Ellen needed a reason not to leave her beloved family in her hometown, this was it.

Ellen, in fact, was determined never to go to Louisiana. And now, the pressure put forth by Ellen and her father for Cump to resign from the military school and return to New Lancaster was all the more unwelcome because, for the first time in his adult career, he was enjoying personal success. Still, he resigned from the military school on March 1, 1860, with the lament, noted Marszalek, "I have made desperate efforts to escape but I see it as inevitable and so I might as well surrender." As the South was to learn in a few years, however, surrender was not his style, and by the end of March he was back to withdraw his resignation. Naturally, he still was hoping he could persuade Ellen to join him in his new life.

On the national scene, meanwhile, feelings continued to run high as many a Northern church rushed to give the recently executed John Brown a martyr's halo. Ellen Sherman herself was among those who saw the slavery question as a religious issue. In the South, where her husband now was staking out a new career, Southerners were outraged at the thought of painting John Brown in the sackcloth of martyrdom and began wondering where newcomer Sherman stood on the question of slavery.

As noted by Lewis, a letter from Sherman to Tom Ewing Jr. made Cump's position clear. He was willing, he said, to help Louisiana "in defending herself against her enemies so long as she remains a state in the general confederacy," but should she or any other state act against the Union, "I am out." Then, the straw that broke this camel's back came even before the firing on Fort Sumter at Charleston. One day in January 1861 Superintendent Sherman was asked to accept receipt for some of the arms seized from the federal arsenal at Baton Rouge a few days beforehand. Immediately tendering his resignation to the governor, Sherman now made his feelings doubly clear: "On no earthly account will I do any act or think any thought hostile…to the…United States."

Despite his love of the South and so much about the South, his side would be the Union side. But there still was no war, and he wore no uniform as yet. Instead, he spent some weeks running a streetcar company in St. Louis until winning reappointment in the U.S. Army on May 14—after the surrender of Fort Sumter—as colonel of the Thirteenth Infantry Regiment.

While Sherman now found himself awaiting action in a real war, Ellen awaited yet another imminent birthing. She would have another girl, Rachael Ewing Sherman, born July 5, 1861.

If Cump's life now had changed in a dramatic fashion that soon would make him a famous and even a historic figure in the outer world, Ellen remained tied to her father's home and her mother's religion. She and Cump had both aged since they had been married eleven years before. They had produced six children, meaning that on average Ellen had had a child about every twenty-one months, a pace that clearly took a toll on her health. She continued to suffer from boils, weight gain, and chronic anxiety. As Marszalek surmised, "The stresses of being disappointed in her husband's profession and religious life, and her own poor health and numerous pregnancies drained the youth from her." Ellen retreated more and more from social activities until she became a recluse.

Cump, on the other hand, maintained his slim figure and reddish brown hair, though he continued to have asthma attacks and bouts of depression. As he aged, he became wrinkled and more eccentric, sometimes to the point of being accused of insanity. Ellen continued to hope that Cump would come back to New Lancaster, manage one of her father's enterprises, and one day become a practicing Catholic. But destiny has a way of disrupting even the most sincere wishes or carefully laid plans.

The marriage of Cump and Ellen, troublesome to start with, certainly was not a typically Victorian, strong man–dependent woman relationship, but they were both open and honest with each other, and their letters often seemed to echo the thoughts of two people having a good argument. Like many couples then and now, they both had expected more and wanted more from their marriage. All the familiarity of their shared childhood may somehow have created unrealistic expectations, as opposed to reducing the novelty of living together. Whatever the emotional and psychological ingredients of their marriage, through it all, Marszalek noted, they remained true to each other. In short, they "accepted their frequently exasperating love…and never thought of life with any other partner."

The Civil War of course brought more separation and more stress to the two. And now, in the first days of the war, aside from personal feelings, Cump had real concerns about the Union's ability to come through the war victorious and still intact. When he observed President Lincoln on several occasions in his capacity as inspector general under the army's commanding general, Winfield Scott, he was astounded by the army's lack of preparedness and by Lincoln's seemingly nonchalant attitude toward the conflict (which of course did not really seem to pose that great a threat until the battle of First Manassas was fought just outside Washington).

When he wrote Ellen of his concern for the military, especially around Washington, she offered to come to Georgetown and bring the children to cheer him up. But no, this suggestion was countermanded by his saying that his wife's presence would set a bad example for his civilian volunteers, whom he hoped to turn into reliable soldiers. Still, he must have thought it a loving gesture on her part even to think of leaving New Lancaster and traveling all that way just to cheer him up. In any case, soon given the chance to serve in Kentucky (after the Union debacle at First Manassas), Sherman was glad to leave what he considered the weak military position of the capital.

Ellen traveled to Cincinnati with the children to spend a week together while he was on his way to Kentucky. Afterward, his depression deepened when he arrived in Louisville to find the Union military situation as bad or worse than conditions he had seen in Washington. Looking totally unkempt, he paced the floor of his hotel room and sent an unending stream of reports to Washington predicting pessimistic outcomes for the Union forces. Secretary of War Simon Cameron, passing through on an inspection tour, was alarmed at what he heard about Sherman's erratic behavior and rumors to the effect that local officials had begun to question his sanity. Also hearing odd reports, Ellen wanted to come to his side and calm him. She asked her brother Phil, who had remained close to Cump throughout the years since childhood, to escort her and to help try to soothe the troubled Cump. They remained a week, seemingly without good result. By now, whispers about Sherman's sanity were being heard loudly. Assistant Secretary of War Thomas W. Scott was convinced that "Sherman's gone in the head, he's loony."

When Sherman's behavior did not improve, an old friend from California days, Henry W. Halleck, became so concerned that he ordered him back to headquarters, where Ellen was awaiting him, to Cump's great surprise. She took him home to New Lancaster for a rest that she and his friends hoped would restore him to health, both physical and mental. During this time, the December 11, 1861, issue of the *Cincinnati Commercial* carried an article that publicly declared him to be insane.

Now Ellen, her father, and the entire family rallied to refute this terrible article. They contacted newspapers around the country and demanded retractions. Ellen wrote the president and then visited him in Washington. While Lincoln took no action on Sherman's behalf just then, Ellen found him disarming; she would always be convinced that he was fair toward her husband.

The fact that Cump once again was being aided—if not saved—by his wife and her father did not please him, but he apparently could do nothing to help himself. Finally, he was sent back to Halleck, who gave him the less-stressful job of forwarding troops to the Union's rising star of the West, Ulysses S. Grant. The two West Pointers, once prankster buddies as cadets, would now develop a working relationship and close friendship that was to sustain them for the rest of the war. After a faltering start, they together were on the victorious side at Shiloh in April 1862, a development that went far to restore Cump's reputation. He then continued to succeed in his war efforts while gaining control of his emotions. He not only began to have confidence in himself but in the Union's war effort as well.

During this time, Ellen maintained her support and love. Once in their childhood, Ellen had called Cump her protector, but now—at least for the moment—their roles were reversed. And though Cump was beginning to develop a sense of his own worth, he still craved the approval of his father-in-law…and he was getting that as well.

In another role reversal, throughout Sherman's string of military successes, beginning with Shiloh and extending to the victory he shared with Grant at Vicksburg in July 1863, Ellen pleaded to visit him rather than quietly remain at home in New Lancaster. At last, with Vicksburg safely in the Union's control, he did send for Ellen and the children. As a result, four of the oldest children—twelve-year-old Minnie, eleven-year-old Lizzie, nine-year-old Willy, and six-year-old Tommy—all arrived in August to spend six weeks with their father the general.

This visit apparently was a joy for all concerned. The young boys slept in a Ewing uncle's tent (three of Cump's Ewing brothers were also Union generals), while the rest of the family shared two tents rigged up to form a house of sorts. Young Willy clearly enjoyed army life, especially when the men of the Thirteenth Infantry made him an honorary sergeant and included him in ceremonial activities. Everyone seemed to enjoy having the Sherman children around, which pleased the proud parents. They socialized with the Grants and counted the whole experience a happy time.

Soon receiving orders to relieve William S. Rosecrans at Chattanooga, Sherman planned to take the family down the Mississippi with him as far as Memphis. As their riverboat prepared to leave, however, Willy complained that he was feeling ill. Ellen called for a physician, who diagnosed dysentery and malaria. After that, nothing the doctor could do seemed to help, and soon after arriving in Memphis, Ellen sent for a Catholic priest. When she began to cry, the dying youngster bravely held her face in his hands and died peacefully.

Of all times, the grieving family now had to separate once more, with the grieving Sherman going back to the war and Ellen, also devastated, returning to New Lancaster. The next time the family could gather again was Christmas 1863, spent in New Lancaster, still a most gloomy time for them all.

Willy had always been his father's favorite, and the loss of his son left an ache that Sherman would never resolve. It was an equally difficult time for Ellen, since she, too, had to grieve alone. Both would find the loss almost unbearable.

But back in New Lancaster, the following June, Ellen gave birth to another boy, Charles Celestine Sherman. And the war now carried Cump from success to success as he won the Atlanta campaign and executed his March to the Sea, for which he was to become a household name—and an object of hatred in the

South for generations to come. Ellen now made major changes in her life. She decided to leave her father's house and move to South Bend, Indiana, to be near Notre Dame for the boys and neighboring St. Mary's for the girls.

Ellen at last could be proud of her husband's successes, and though she missed him, she had become used to the long separations and was making a life on her own. As one outlet, she kept busy planning and then participating in a Sanitary Commission fair held in Chicago. But once again tragedy struck the family when little Charles died a few weeks before Christmas 1864. This time Ellen had to bear the grief alone, because Cump could not be reached until the last of December, so cut off was he in the South. Seeing a pattern in his successes and their losses of Willy and Charles, she cautioned Cump that their deaths were "a lesson to us of the vanity of human glory." Along similar lines, he wrote that his glory and honors, if worth anything, "will accrue to you and the children."

While Sherman at last had earned the plaudits of so many, certainly in the North and among his military peers, what meant the most to him was that he had shown his father-in-law that he could stand on his own. As Marszalek notes, Sherman could write to Thomas Ewing: "Of course I feel just pride in the satisfaction you express and would rather please and gratify you than all the world beside."

Sherman left the war a national hero, with his marriage still intact. For the first time since their marriage, he and Ellen could have time together. As they now traveled the country, Cump enjoyed the glory afforded him along the way and was grateful for the honors and gifts he received. New Lancaster itself remembered its native son with a $100,000 fund-raising drive for the family. In 1866, he succeeded both Winfield Scott and Ulysses S. Grant as a lieutenant general, and in 1869, as Grant became president, Cump, now a full general, was named general-in-chief of the army. He had no financial worries as he owned homes in St. Louis and Washington, gifts from a grateful public. In the meantime, Ellen had borne him a final child in January 1867: Philemon Tecumseh Sherman…quickly nicknamed "Cumpy."

When Sherman retired from the army in 1884 at the age of sixty-three, he and Ellen moved to New York to be close to their grown-up children. He turned aside entreaties to run for president, and they lived in the exclusive Fifth Avenue Hotel. As Ellen aged and her health grew worse, Cump bought her a house at 75 West Seventy-First Street. They had been in the new house but a few months when Ellen, now a recluse, spent most of her time in bed. Cump hired a nurse for her, even though he thought her illnesses were not serious. Not long after, according to Lewis, Cump was sitting in his office when the nurse came and told him to hurry, his wife was dying. He rushed up the steps calling out, "Wait for me, Ellen. No one ever loved you as I love you." But he was too late for her to reply.

In his grief, he believed that her Catholicism had been her lifelong mainstay, and he was content to say, according to Liddell Hart, "No mortal was ever better prepared to put on immortality."

Less than three years later, on February 14, 1891, Valentine's Day, Union hero William Tecumseh Sherman, seventy-one, followed her in death. He was buried next to Ellen in St. Louis. And there, noted Marszalek, Ellen lies under a large cross of granite and Sherman beneath sculpted military flags, also of granite. In sum, "In death, as in life, they remain together, side by side, but their debate, it seems, goes on."

Bibliography

Bill, Alfred Hoyt. *The Beleaguered City, Richmond, 1861–1865*. New York: Knopf, 1946.

Bleser, Carol K., and J. Gordon Lesley, eds. *Intimate Strategies of the Civil War: Military Commanders and Their Wives*. New York: Oxford University Press, 2001.

Commager, Henry Steele. *The Blue and the Gray: The Story of the Civil War as Told by the Participants*. New York: Bobbs-Merrill Company, 1950.

Coulling, Mary P. *The Lee Girls*. Winston-Salem: John F. Blair, 1987.

Davis, Burke. *The Long Surrender*. New York: Random House, 1985.

D'Este, Carlo. *Patton: A Genius for War*. New York, HarperCollins, 1995.

Donald, David Herbert. *Lincoln*. New York: Simon & Schuster, 1995.

Eggenberger, David. *An Encyclopedia of Battles: Accounts of over 1,560 Battles from 1479 B.C. to the Present*. 1867. Reprint, New York: Dover, 1985.

Freeman, Douglas Southall. *Lee: An Abridgement in One Volume, by Richard Harwell, of the Four-Volume R. E. Lee*. New York: Scribner, 1961.

Hart, B. H. Liddell. *Sherman: Soldier, Realist, American*. New York: Da Capo, 1993.

Hutton, Paul Andrew, ed. *Soldiers West, Biographies from the Military Frontier*. Lincoln: University of Nebraska Press, 1987.

Kelly, C. Brian, with Ingrid Smyer. *Best Little Ironies, Oddities, and Mysteries of the Civil War*. Nashville, TN: Cumberland House, 2000.

———. *Best Little Stories from the Civil War*. Nashville, TN: Cumberland House, 1997.

———. *Best Little Stories from the White House*. 2nd ed. Nashville, TN: Cumberland House, 2005.

Lee, Robert E. Jr., ed. and comp. *Recollections and Letters of General Robert E. Lee*. 1904. Reprint, Old Saybrook, CT: Konecky and Konecky, n.d.

Leech, Margaret. *Reveille in Washington, 1861–1865*. New York: Harper & Brothers, 1941.

Lewis, Lloyd. *Sherman, Fighting Prophet*. New York: Harcourt, Brace and Company, 1932.

Long, E. B., with Barbara Long. *The Civil War Day by Day: An Almanac, 1861–1865*. New York: Doubleday, 1971.

MacDonald, Rose Mortimer Ellzey. *Mrs. Robert E. Lee*. Boston: Ginn, 1939.

McElroy, Joseph. *Jefferson Davis: The Unreal and the Real*. New York: HarperCollins, 1937.

McHenry, Robert, ed. *Webster's American Military Biographies*. 1978. Reprint, New York: Dover, 1984.

Mitchell, Mary H. *Hollywood Cemetery: The History of a Southern Shrine*. Richmond: Virginia State Library, 1985.

Neely, Mark E. Jr. *The Abraham Lincoln Encyclopedia*. New York: McGraw-Hill, 1982.

Robertson, James I. Jr. *Stonewall Jackson: The Man, The Soldier, The Legend*. New York: Macmillan, 1997.

Simpson, Brooks D., and Jean V. Berlin, eds. *Sherman's Civil War: Selected Correspondence of William T. Sherman, 1860–1865*. Chapel Hill: University of North Carolina Press, 1999.

Thomas, Emory M. *Robert E. Lee: A Biography*. New York: Norton, 1995.

Townsend, Edward D. *Anecdotes of the Civil War in the United States*. New York: Appleton, 1884.

Schlesinger, Arthur M. Jr., gen. ed. *The Almanac of American History*. Greenwich, CT: Bison Books, 1983.

Warner, Ezra J. *Generals in Blue: Lives of the Union Commanders*. Baton Rouge: Louisiana State University Press, 1964.

———. *Generals in Gray: Lives of the Confederate Commanders*. Baton Rouge: Louisiana State University Press, 1959.

Welsh, Jack D. *Medical Histories of Confederate Generals*. Kent, OH: Kent State University Press, 1995.

Index